W9-BCF-343

Africa:
The Geography of a
Changing Continent

J.M. Pritchard

Africana Publishing Corporation
New York

Published
in the United States of America 1971
by Africana Publishing Corporation
101 Fifth Avenue
New York, N.Y. 10003

Library of Congress Catalog Card No. 71-145838
ISBN 0-8419-0071-X

Printed in Hong Kong by
Dai Nippon Printing Co., (International) Ltd.

ABOUT THIS BOOK

This book has been primarily written for those students who are beginning to study the geography of Africa at an advanced level. It attempts to present a clear and up-to-date picture of the geography of a continent which has been the focus of attention over the last score of years for an ever increasing number of research workers. There is a tremendous volume of material now available of a geographic or economic nature, but much of it is not always readily available to the student and much of it is of a very high academic standard unsuited to his needs.

I have attempted to bridge this gap by presenting geographic material in a way which breaks away from the more formal approach. Instead of the more usual method of description on a political and regional basis the book selects those aspects of Africa's geography which are most important and, especially in the economic sections, which reflect modern trends and conditions. The method is thus, after preliminary discussion where necessary, to sample in depth rather than give broad general pictures.

By virtue of its very technique the book does not claim to cover every aspect of a rapidly developing continent but as wide a selection of sample studies as possible has been chosen, although greater attention has been given to regions lying south of the Sahara in view of examination tendencies.

At the end of each chapter, where appropriate, the work for the student is divided into several sections—general questions based partly on the text and partly to guide research work; a selection of topics which have been designed for group discussion, followed by suggestions for practical work in the field, and statistical exercises. In the economic sections the opportunity is given for practice in transforming up-to-date statistics into pictorial graphs and charts. In addition, a selected reading list of textbooks to aid further studies has been included. Magazine articles are also a very valuable source of information for the geography student. Often written by experts on the spot and well illustrated, they can present a very clear picture of local geographic conditions; accordingly I have included a list of articles from leading magazines.

Great reliance has been placed on statistics and tables, especially in the economic sections, and every effort has been made to obtain the latest facts available. I have attempted to draw the maps and diagrams as clearly as possible, omitting those which the student can find readily in any atlas and concentrating on illustrating specific themes in the text.

In conclusion, it is hoped that this new approach to the study of the geography of Africa will prove refreshing and stimulating to both teacher and student.

J.M.P.
December, 1968

ACKNOWLEDGEMENTS

The author wishes to thank very sincerely the following people and organisations for their considerable help in preparing the material for this book:

S. D. Asimeng of the Ghana High Commission; D. G. Mackenzie of East Africa Industries; the Information Division of Unilever Limited; the Chief Inspector of Mines, Mines Division of the Ministry of Lands, Mines and Labour, Sierra Leone; W. D. Anderson of Esso Standard Libya Inc.; the Town Clerk, Lagos City Council, Lagos, Nigeria; the Nigerian Federal Ministry of Information, Lagos, Nigeria; E. Hainsworth, Director of the Tea Research Institute of East Africa, Kericho, Kenya; E. D. Gleason of the Anglo-American Corporation (Central Africa) Limited, Kitwe, Zambia; W. W. Nelson of the Transvaal and Orange Free State Chamber of Mines, Johannesburg, South Africa; J. H. Bevier of the Firestone Plantations Company, Harbel, Liberia; R. Lukman of the Ministry of Mines and Power, Lagos, Nigeria; E. Hawi of the United Arab Republic Embassy; W. Stuart of the Coast Province Cotton Committee, Malindi, Kenya; the Public Relations Office of the Department of Information, Dar es Salaam, Tanzania; E. Mungai, Settlement Officer, Kikuyu Estates, Kenya; T. Agar, Limuru, Kenya; D. G. Hunt, Mwea Irrigation Scheme, Kerugoya, Kenya; E. Potts, Morogoro Sisal Estate, Tanzania; the Press and Information Office of the Federal Government of West Germany; I. Izat, Sassa Coffee Estate, Kenya; Y. F. O. Masakhalia, Ministry of Economic Planning and Development, Nairobi, Kenya; the Chief Research Officer, High Level Sisal Research Centre, Thika, Kenya; G. S. Dugdale, Librarian, the Royal Geographical Society; Miss G. D. Callard, Associate Editor's Secretary, The Geographical Magazine; the Hon. Secretary, the Geographical Association.

We are grateful to the following for permission to reproduce copyright material:

Barrie & Rockliffe Limited and Coward-McCann Inc. for abridged extracts from *Sahara* by George Gerster; author and the London weekly journal *East Africa and Rhodesia* for extracts from 'Farming in the Rhodesias' by Rt. Hon. Lord Hastings; The Proprietors of *The Geographical Magazine, London* for an extract from 'The Bamenda Highlands' by Michael Thomas from issue dated August 1966; The Ministry of Agriculture for an abridged account from *Rhodesia Agricultural Journal*.

CONTENTS

CHAPTER ONE

THE PHYSICAL BACKGROUND

A: The Land

The Origins of Africa

The Theory of Continental Drift—the movement of the lighter continents on the heavier, softer rocks of the earth's crust—is popularly associated with the name of A. Wegener who expounded his ideas in 1912 and 1924 but the concept had been stated earlier in 1910 by F. B. Taylor and in 1911 by H. B. Baker.

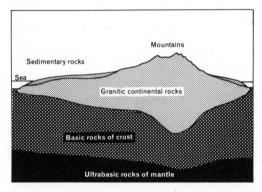

FIG. 1: Relationship of continental landmass to basic rocks

It was suggested that Africa had been part of one huge continent, Gondwanaland, and attention was drawn to the similar rock structures along the coasts of western Africa and eastern South America and the jig-saw fit of the southern continents. Again it was found that there was an almost identical geological sequence of strata in the Karoo of South Africa, the Deccan Plateau of India and the plateaux of South America and Antarctica; several small folded ranges in Argentina and the Falkland Islands are similar in structure and age to the folded Cape Ranges of South Africa; glacial striations on rock surfaces in South Africa suggested to the geologists that ice movement was not from the Antarctic region but from some large landmass which once existed to the north-east in what is now the Indian Ocean (Fig. 1:**26B**, page 16). The Permo-Carboniferous

formations in South Africa and Australia show striking similarities which suggest they were formed under identical climatic conditions, possibly as one continuous belt. Recent research into the remnant magnetic properties of rocks in relation to the earth's

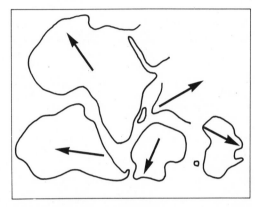

FIG. 2: The break-up of Gondwanaland

polar axis seems to support the theory and to suggest that by the end of the Mesozoic Period Africa had become almost stationary (about 70 million years ago).

The acceptance of the Continental Drift Theory would explain several features of Africa's structure and relief: the folded Atlas ranges would have originated when sedimentary rocks were squeezed between northward drifting Africa and rigid Eurasia (Fig. 1:**18**, page 11); the warping and faulting of Africa's plateau surface might have been caused by the sundering of Gondwanaland's several parts from the keystone of Africa; the numerous basin-like depressions of Africa's surface may have been internal drainage basins for the original rivers of Gondwanaland.

Size, Shape and Position

Compared with other continents Africa possesses at once similarities and contrasts. Its huge area of 11,700,000 square miles (nearly twenty per cent of

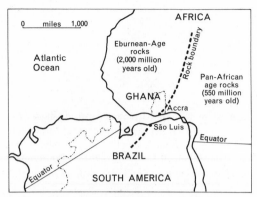

FIG. 3: Recent evidence of the Drift of the Continents: The above map is based on recent work by geophysicist Sir Edward Bullard of Cambridge University and American geologist Prof. Patrick M. Hurley. Radioactive dating of Africa's rocks reveals that the continent is divided into two distinct geological regions—the eastern Pan-African region some 550 million years old and the western Eburnean region 2,000 million years old. A computer study of the shorelines of the two continents by Bullard revealed that the rocks would match perfectly down to a depth of 500 fathoms if the continents were joined. Further work by Hurley and others shows that the boundary between the two geological regions in Africa is continued in north-east Brazil exactly where it was predicted.

Another modern geological technique, that of studying the changing patterns of the earth's magnetic field, indicates that the ocean floor between Africa and South America is widening at the rate of two centimetres a year and this rate exactly accounts for the present distance apart of the two continents if drift began 200 million years ago—the estimated time at which the continents are believed to have begun drifting apart.

Although this would seem conclusive proof, there are still many geophysicists who are sceptical of Continental Drift. Prof. V. V. Beloussov, Professor of Dynamic Geology at Moscow University, believes that the crust and upper mantle of the earth are indivisible and that one cannot move without the other; lateral movement could not occur in the upper crust since it has simply nowhere to go. Beloussov also states that if continents had drifted this action would have concentrated radioactivity into localised areas but in fact this is not the case and the heat flow through the ocean floors is at least as high as in the continents. The fact that sedimentary beds in the oceans are horizontal and undeformed would also seem to Beloussov to be incompatible with the Theory of Continental Drift

the earth's land surface) is remarkably compact with none of the penetrations of ocean common to Europe, North America or Asia. Thus, although Africa is the second largest continent after Asia (17 million square miles), three times the size of Europe (4 million square miles), and bigger than North America (8 million square miles), it has a much shorter coastline. Africa has similar plateau surfaces to those of Australia, South America and India but no vast mountain barrier to create sudden climatic and vegetational contrasts.

Africa's position is unique for it fairly straddles the equator stretching 2,500 miles to north and south; 77 per cent of its area lies within the tropics and over 25 per cent is covered by the great wastes of the Sahara.

Africa is huge, sprawling over 72 degrees of latitude from 37°51′N (just west of Cape Blanc) in Tunisia to Cape Aghulas at latitude 34°51′S, a distance of 5,000 miles or equal to a journey between New York and Hawaii, London and Tibet, or Tokyo and Brisbane. The greatest length east-west, approximately 4,500 miles, lies between Ras Hafun (51°50′E) and Cape Verde (17°32′W). The continent is virtually an island connected to the Sinai Peninsula by a narrow isthmus sliced by the Suez Canal and separated from Spain by the nine-mile wide Straits of Gibraltar. The Straits of Bab el Mandeb separate Africa from Arabia by only 20 miles of water.

Africa's position has clearly affected its historical and political development. Its huge bulk jutting out into the southern oceans presented a troublesome obstacle to be rounded as swiftly as possible by sailing vessels plying to and from the East. As an appendage to politically minded Europe of the late nineteenth century it was laid open to nearly eighty years of colonial rule, a period of experiment unparalleled in any other continent. Africa's position in relation to the industrial regions of Europe and North America created for the continent a rôle of

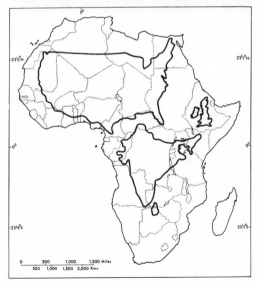

FIG. 4: The size of Africa

raw materials supplier, a period from which it is now beginning to emerge.

The Relief and Structure of Africa

Africa consists of a series of plateaux, higher in the east but gradually sinking towards the west, the general altitude relieved by great shallow basins and their river systems, by the deep incision of the Rift Valley, and by the often magnificent volcanoes, fault blocks and inselbergs.

The basis of this simple relief is a stable block of ancient crystalline rocks of Precambrian origin, rocks which sometimes rise to the surface in parts of the continent but are often masked by later sedimentaries and volcanic outpourings. This rigid block has withstood the tremendous forces which elsewhere have formed the Alps of Europe and the Himalayas of India and fold ranges of this age are confined to the edges of the block in the Atlas region. But the plateau crust has not entirely escaped the effects of earth movements for vast warpings have formed huge shallow basins and great vertical movements have cracked the surface into giant fault lines.

The Plateaux

Although the volcanoes and rift valleys are spectacular the most lasting impression of Africa's relief is one of monotonous level plateau surfaces varying between 2,000 and 8,500 feet (in the Maluti mountains in Lesotho), surfaces often so flat that they are called plains. They result from long periods of erosion. In order to adjust itself to the redistribution of these eroded sediments from higher to lower altitudes, the continent has risen slowly over thousands of years, a process termed isostatic readjustment. The rise was greatest in the east and south of Africa where the Drakensberg and Maluti mountains average between 5,000 and 7,000 feet rising to over 10,760 feet in the Mont aux Sources. The uplift did not take place all at once but in stages, each stage separated by long periods when the forces of erosion had more time to smooth down the surfaces. The most important of these erosion levels are often separated by steep, low escarpments, the lowest of which usually form an abrupt drop to the narrow coastal plains; at this junction point rivers usually form rapids and waterfalls.

Remnants of old land surfaces sometimes jut up from these plateau surfaces; these are inselbergs

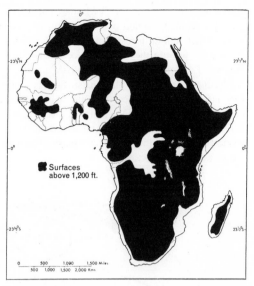

FIG. 5: Approximately one-third of Africa can be termed low-lying. Certain of the structural basins (Fig. 7) lie at considerable altitudes

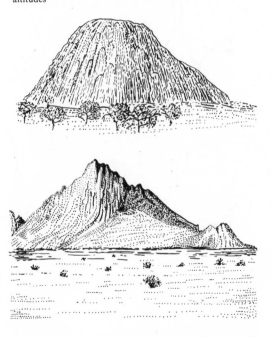

FIG. 6: Examples of inselbergs: Upper: A granitic inselberg in southern Nigeria. Height about 600 feet. Lower: The Great Spitzkop which rises over 2,000 feet above the Namib plain in South-West Africa. Usually of granitic rocks, inselbergs form abrupt mountainous islands above the level surface. They are resistant mountain or hill cores which will be removed gradually by exfoliation on their surfaces and the erosion process of the flat plains at their bases (the pediplain)

3

(island mountains, monadnocks, kopjes, bornhardts are other names), the 'left overs' from former landscapes which remain as resistant mounds. Usually of hard, solid granite they are well seen in northern Nigeria, Tanzania, Kenya and South Africa.

The distribution of the plateaux surfaces is seen in Fig. 1:**6**. Practically all eastern and central Africa lies over 3,000 feet while the plateau surface falls to 1,000 feet and less in the Sahara and West Africa where the general altitude is increased by overlying sedimentaries and rock wastes.

The Basins and Divides

A striking feature of Africa's relief is the number of broad, shallow, plate-like basins separated by plateaux, fault blocks and mountain ranges. These basins have been the deposition areas for the rock waste eroded from the plateau surface and, unable to support the weight, they have gradually subsided leaving between them mountainous divides. The most prominent basins are the Congo (covering over 1·6 million square miles; equal to slightly over half the area of Australia), Chad, El Djouf, Sudan and

FIG. 7: The relief of Africa— structural basins and their divides

4

Kalahari, and smaller ones, e.g. L. Victoria-Kyoga. Generally between 1,000 and 3,000 feet, these basins were formed by massive forces (probably originating in the semi-molten rocks below the earth's crust) which have downwarped parts of the plateau. These shallow basins were then invaded by the sea or rivers, the weight of lacustrine and marine deposits causing further depression. Some basins may once have extended beyond the present coasts as the drainage systems indicate, particularly in southern Africa. Here, the Orange flows westwards following the general gradient of the land, but the Limpopo and the Zambesi flow to the east. It is possible to explain these flow directions by accepting that Africa was once a vast area of internal drainage with no coasts (the keystone of Gondwanaland) and the rivers poured their sediments and waters into depressions to form gigantic lakes. When Gondwanaland foundered the lakes drained away and the original rivers found outlets to the sea

I **Major River Systems**

1. Niger
2. Congo
3. Nile
4. Zambesi
5. Orange

II **Regional Drainage Systems**

6. North-western
7. Western
8. West Equatorial
9. South-Western
10. Southern
11. South-Eastern
12. Eastern

III **Basins of Internal Drainage**

13. Chad
14. Okavango
15. Tanzania
16. Rudolf

IV **Regions with Intermittent or No Drainage**

17. Sahara
18. North-eastern

FIG. 8: Africa—the pattern of drainage

across the basins or, like the Chad basin, persisted as regions of internal drainage. The effect of local back-tilting of areas of the plateau surface is seen in many parts of Uganda where the reduction of gradients has caused rivers to form irregular marshy lakes such as Lake Kyoga and profoundly altered the flow patterns of many rivers (Fig. 1:**9**).

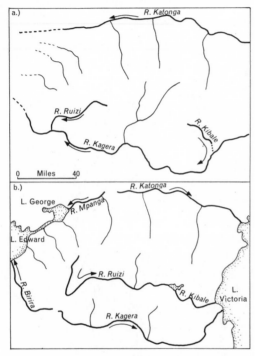

FIG. 9: Uganda—reversal of drainage patterns due to back tilting of plateau surface. (*Simplified after J. C. Doornkamp and P. H. Temple*)

Bordering the basins are sharp divides which in the case of the Ruwenzoris rise to nearly 17,000 feet. These dividing rims may consist of higher parts of the plateau, e.g. the Jos and Futa Djalon regions and other crystalline and volcanic massifs such as the Ahaggar and Tibesti plateaux (Fig. 1:**21** and 1:**23**). Volcanic cones and the tilt of fault blocks often add to their heights. Other important divides are the Drakensberg and Maluti Mountains between the Kalahari and the east coast plain, the Ennedi, Dar Fur and Bongos between the Chad, Sudan and Congo basins and the Bihé between the Congo and the Kalahari.

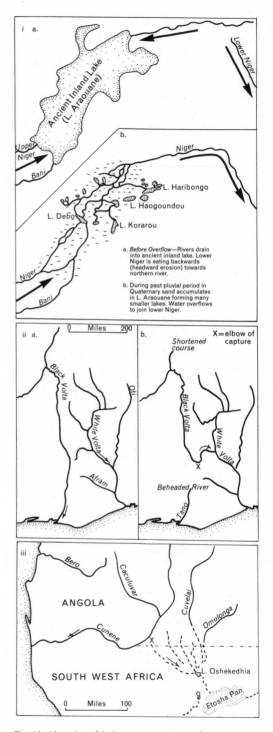

FIG. 10: Alteration of drainage patterns by overflow and capture

6

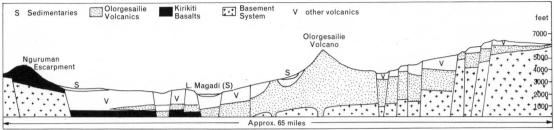

| S Sedimentaries | Olorgesailie Volcanics | Kirikiti Basalts | Basement System | V other volcanics | feet |

FIG. 11: The Great Rift Valley. The above diagram is a cross-section of the valley at Latitude 1°45′S. (*Simplified from Report No.* 42, *Geol. Survey of Kenya*, 1958.) Right: Extent of Rift Valley in eastern Africa

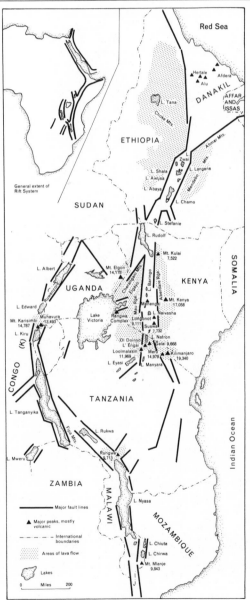

The Great Rift Valley

The great Rift Valley is probably the most spectacular of all Africa's surface features. Approximately 4,500 miles long with 3,500 miles within Africa, it begins near Beira and extends northwards to Lake Malawi. Here it divides into a western arm through Lakes Tanganyika, Kivu, Edward and Albert, fading out gradually about 150 miles north of Lake Albert, and an eastern arm marked by low (500–1,000 feet) escarpments in Tanzania. The latter is clearly marked in Kenya by several small lakes occupying fault basins and depressions—Lakes Magadi, Naivasha, Elementaita, Nakuru, Hannington, Baringo and Rudolf. Here the valley sides fall steeply from the plateau surface at about 7,000 feet to 5,000 feet on the valley floor with the Mau and Aberdare fault blocks towering to over 10,000 feet above sea level.

In Ethiopia several small lakes mark the valley's course—Stefanie, Chama, Abaya, Langana and Zwai. The valley follows the Awash river course then spreads over a wide area in the Danakil region; here it divides into the Gulf of Aden and the Red Sea, the latter 1,250 miles long and 215 miles broad and forking at its north-western end into the Gulf of Suez and the Gulf of Aqaba, the latter leading northwards into the Jordan Valley.

The Rift Valley thus forms a long scar on the surface of Africa equal in length to one fifth of the earth's longitudinal circumference. Its floor width varies from 20 to 60 miles with valley sides often rising two or three thousand feet above the graben floor, the heights often accentuated by the upthrown and tilted horst blocks flanking the valley—Mitumba Mountains, the Aberdares, the Cheranganis, the Mau Ranges. The height of the floor also

7

varies considerably from 2,140 feet below sea level in Tanzania and 300 feet below sea level in Lake Malawi to 5,000 feet above sea level in the Lake Kivu region.

Such a tremendous feature could only have been formed by colossal forces causing pressure and tensions within the plateau crust of Africa. Several theories have evolved none of which has yet been fully proved or accepted. There are two major theories, however:

a that forces of tension have caused a lengthening of the upwarped crust by means of tension of normal faults;

b that forces of compression have caused the shortening of the arced crust by means of thrust or reversed faults, older rocks being forced to override younger rocks on both flanks of the valley.

The tension theory suggests that the African plateaux in the Rift region were first upwarped and that the central part of this upwarped arch—'the keystone'—dropped. Step-faulting occurred on both sides of the valley (Fig. 1:**12a**). Many of the fault slopes in Kenya and Tanzania, especially those in offshoot rifts such as the Rukwa depression, have been shown to be normal or tensional faults and most geologists believe the eastern arm of the valley was formed by tensional faults.

Upwarping of the crust is also postulated in the compression theory, but in this case the crest of the arch is thrust downwards by the weight of the flanking blocks pushing over it in reversed faults (Fig. 1:**12b**). Certain sections of the Western Rift in the Ruwenzori region and along the eastern shores of L. Albert show evidence of reversed faulting.

In both theories it will be seen that step-faulting can occur, and this often masks the true nature of the major faults in many areas. Certainly there is evidence for both theories, compressionists stating that it would take considerable horizontal pressure to raise the valley floors to the heights they attain in the L. Kivu, Ruwenzori and Kenya regions while tensionists cite the great depths of the floor in Malawi and Tanzania as evidence of tremendous forces of tension.

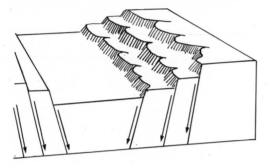

a Tension theory, normal faulting

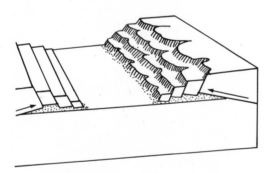

b Compression theory, thrust faulting

Fig. 12: Theories regarding the formation of the Rift Valley

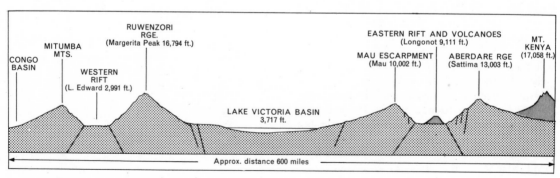

Fig. 13: Diagrammatic cross-section from the eastern Congo to western Kenya

But whatever forces formed the Rift Valley these same forces are still at work, since the region is still affected by earth tremors and shock waves on a minor scale which testify to the instability of this part of Africa.

Volcanic Activity

The colossal pressures responsible for the Rift Valley were also the initial cause of the volcanic activity associated with the Rift region and on the adjacent plateaux. Deep caps of lava and numerous magnificent volcanoes were formed—Kilimanjaro, Africa's highest peak (19,340 feet), Mt Kenya (17,058 feet), Mt Elgon (14,178 feet), the eroded plug of Tororo rock, Uganda, Mt Meru (14,979 feet), Jaeger Summit (10,565 feet) and Loolmalasin

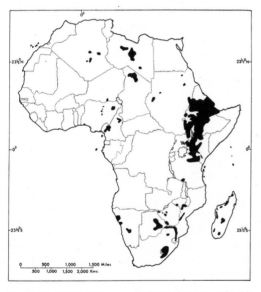

FIG. 14: The extent of cretaceous, tertiary and quaternary lavas in Africa

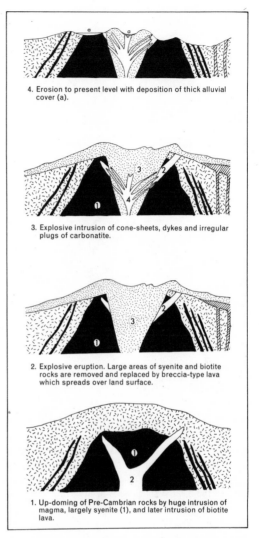

4. Erosion to present level with deposition of thick alluvial cover (a).

3. Explosive intrusion of cone-sheets, dykes and irregular plugs of carbonatite.

2. Explosive eruption. Large areas of syenite and biotite rocks are removed and replaced by breccia-type lava which spreads over land surface.

1. Up-doming of Pre-Cambrian rocks by huge intrusion of magma, largely syenite (1), and later intrusion of biotite lava.

FIG. 15: Kenya—the evolution of the Rangwa complex and the Kisingiri volcano, Nyanza, Western Kenya. (*After G. J. H. McCall*)

(11,969 feet); these are all associated with the eastern arm of the Rift. In the west lie the Mufumbiros where the extinct volcano Muhavura (13,493 feet) marks the borders between Uganda, the Congo and Rwanda. More localised faulting in East Africa caused many minor volcanoes to form such as those of the Gwasi area south of the Kavirondo Gulf in Kenya (Fig. 1:**15**). Volcanoes such as Longonot (9,111 feet) on the floor of the Rift Valley 35 miles north-west of Nairobi show evidence

of comparatively recent activity; Longonot is an explosive type which has developed a huge crater. Steam jets and hot springs are common in this region.

In West Africa evidence of volcanic activity is associated with the Jos and Aïr plateaux, the Cameroon and Bamenda Highlands and the islands of Fernando Po, São Thomé, Principe and Annobon. Just south of Kumasi is the volcanic caldera some 6 miles in diameter, now filled with water,

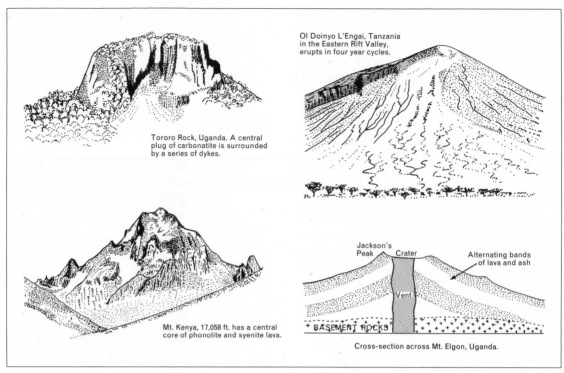

Tororo Rock, Uganda. A central plug of carbonatite is surrounded by a series of dykes.

Ol Doinyo L'Engai, Tanzania in the Eastern Rift Valley, erupts in four year cycles.

Mt. Kenya, 17,058 ft. has a central core of phonolite and syenite lava.

Jackson's Peak   Crater   Alternating bands of lava and ash

Vent

BASEMENT ROCKS

Cross-section across Mt. Elgon, Uganda.

FIG. 16: East Africa—some volcanic forms

called Lake Bosumtwi[1], while near Dakar there are extensive lava flows. Further north in the Sahara the Ahaggar and Tibesti Plateaux form weird regions of sculptured volcanic pillars and plugs (page 14).

Southern Africa was also subject to igneous activity. In the Transvaal masses of lava intruded into

[1] There is a belief, however, that L. Bosumtwi's crater may be due to a meteor striking the earth at this point.

overlying rocks, piercing the surface and spreading over the plateau for some 300 miles, their great weight causing the downward sinking of the underlying rocks; in some places these lava cappings are nearly 6 miles thick. Many of the volcanic necks and pipes have been plugged by solidified lava and contain numerous diamonds as well as other minerals— tin, chromite and platinum.

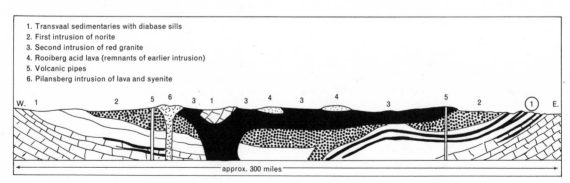

1. Transvaal sedimentaries with diabase sills
2. First intrusion of norite
3. Second intrusion of red granite
4. Rooiberg acid lava (remnants of earlier intrusion)
5. Volcanic pipes
6. Pilansberg intrusion of lava and syenite

W.   1   2   5 6   3 1   3   3   4   3   5   2   1   E.

approx. 300 miles

FIG. 17: South Africa—diagrammatic section across the bushveld volcanic complex. (*After A. L. du Toit*)

Folded Mountains

The folded mountain ranges of the Atlas and Cape regions at the northern and southern extremities of Africa form entirely different landscapes from those already discussed. Structurally the *Atlas Mountains* of the Maghreb are similar to the great alpine system of southern and central Europe and were formed at about the same geological period. They consist of folded layers of sedimentary rocks, mainly limestone, formed in some vast sea which lay between Africa and Europe, while some deeper crystalline rocks have also been thrust upwards testifying to the power of the folding processes. Several steep-sided distinct ranges have been eroded into rugged and wild landscapes quite unlike anything else in Africa.

The coastal ranges rise in the western Rif to over 7,000 feet and continue westwards into the Tell region in a separate more broken range between 3,000 and 6,000 feet, highest in the Great and Little Kablye Mountains; they end as high cliffs at Cape Blanc in eastern Tunisia.

A central chain is formed by the High and Sahara Atlas. The High Atlas (13,000 feet) extends from Agadir on the Moroccan coast north-eastwards for some 500 miles. High peaks of basic crystalline rock —Jebel Toubkal (13,761 feet), Irhil M'Goun (13,356 feet) and Volcan du Siroua (10,846 feet)— illustrate the tremendous nature of the folding. In the lower north-east the crystalline ranges sink below lime-

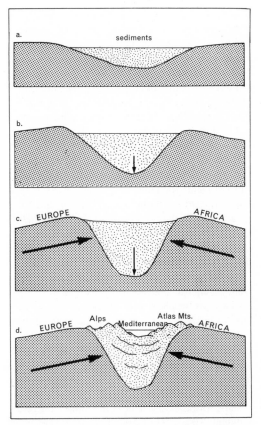

FIG. 18: The folded mountains of North Africa—one theory regarding their origin

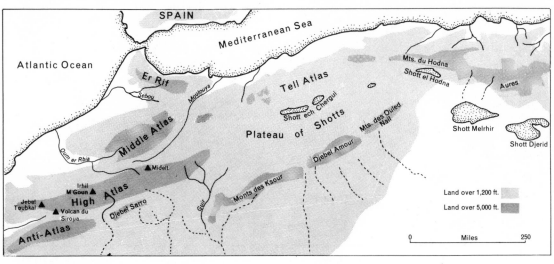

FIG. 19: The Atlas Region

11

stone rocks. To the east of the High Atlas and parallel to it lies the Saharan Atlas, a series of sandstone and limestone ridges and plateaux—the Monts des Ksour, the Djebel Amour and the Monts des Ouled Naïl which continue into the Aures Mountains. In Tunisia the Aures (4,000–6,000 feet) turn north-eastwards towards the Tell Atlas and end at Cape Bon. The Middle Atlas is shorter than the other ranges but is still a formidable barrier rising to 10,958 feet above the River Moulouya.

Between the Tellian and High Atlas lies the Plateau of Shotts (a shott is a shallow salty lake) which stretches for about 500 miles from east to west but is pinched out in the east by the Tell and Atlas ranges. The Plateau stands at about 3,000 to 4,000 feet, is very monotonous and is lowest in the east. Its many lakes dwindle with the dry season but are fed by small rivers during the winter rains.

To the west lies the Moroccan Meseta or table land, an ancient plateau which formed a resistant boss against which parts of the ranges were folded. Subject to tremendous pressures the plateau mass wilted and subsided, especially in the south.

In the extreme south of Africa lie the *folded mountains* of the Cape region. These were formed at a much earlier period than the Atlas ranges and were possibly connected with the Sierra Ranges near Buenos Aires, Argentina and the mountains of the Falkland Islands. The Cape ranges have been worn down and then uplifted to form a complex system.

The Oliphants and Cedarberg Mts trend NNW then give way to the east-west trending Langeberg and Groote Swarteberg ranges. A series of ranges then continues for 200 miles to the eastern coast, averaging between 4,500 and 7,000 feet in altitude—the Kougaberge, the Groot-Swartbergreeks, the Kammanassiesberge, the Outeniquaberge and the Groot-Winterhoekberge. The ranges are separated by flat, fertile valleys in the west which become increasingly drier towards the east.

An interesting feature is the way in which rivers such as the Traka, Groot, Dwyka and Gourits cut across the ranges through narrow gaps instead of continuing along the general eastward trend of the major valleys. This is an example of superimposed drainage where a drainage pattern formed on a previous flat plateau landscape of sedimentary rocks. As the softer sedimentaries were worn down the set pattern of the rivers remained unchanged and was etched into the emerging folded ranges.

Desert Landscapes

So far we have been concerned with the effects of structure on the surface features of Africa. But landscapes change with time and the steady work of erosive forces. Nowhere is this more evident than in the Sahara which extends 3,000 miles from the Atlantic shores to the Red Sea coast with a maximum width of 1,200 miles and covers one quarter of

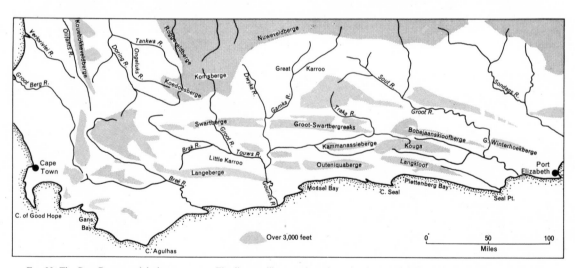

FIG. 20: The Cape Ranges and drainage patterns. The diagram illustrates how the major rivers such as the Gourits and Groot cut sharply through the west-east trending ranges

Africa's surface. Such a desert could blanket the whole of Europe between the Mediterranean and the Baltic shores from Ireland to the Urals. Within its confines there is a considerable diversity of landscape.

These landscapes are the result of powerful erosive forces. The changes between the hot furnace of the day and the freezing conditions at night expand and contract rock surfaces and break off thin flakes (exfoliation); these flakes are further broken down and their minerals with their different rates of expansion are prised loose. The desert sands are the result.

Winds sculpture the exposed rocks. Sand particles are rubbed smooth by jostling one against the other, during storms particles are flung at rocks and, since sand (as opposed to dust) never rises more than a few feet from the ground, it is the bases of the rocks that become undercut. Wind and its agents, sand grains, reduce the surfaces of the deserts by removing all loose particles (deflation), smooth and polish bare rock surfaces (abrasion), and wear down the eroded particles one against the other (attrition).

Rain, despite its scarcity, is also an effective erosive agent. Sudden freak rainstorms are very destructive since there is little vegetation to protect the desert surface; wadis become raging torrents for a few brief minutes and huge amounts of loose sand and stones are moved. The chemical effect on rock cements, as in sandstone, rots away or crumbles the surface layers.

Desert landscapes may thus vary with the dominant erosive agent and the particular rock of a region (sedimentary, volcanic or basement). *Hamada* is a flat, rocky desert which has been swept clear of sand particles and any dust by the action of the wind. The

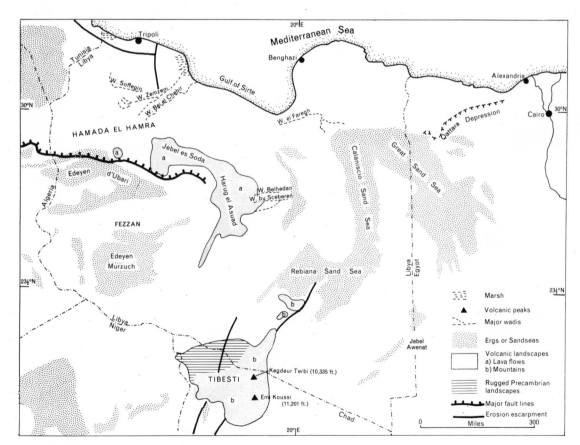

FIG. 21: Libya—showing distribution of desert landscapes

13

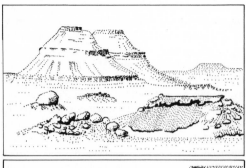

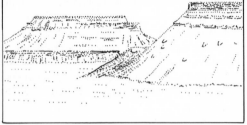

FIG. 22: Libya—desert landforms near Zelten oilfield. In both cases the flat, table-like surface of the mesas (lower) and buttes (upper), and the resistant rock strata forming distinct ridges on the slopes. The uniformity of the altitude of the hard limestone beds indicate that they once covered larger areas. The softer sandstone is retreating at a much greater rate under desert erosion

Resistant rocky massifs form a different class of desert landscape. In the Fezzan of Libya the scenery is wild and rugged and fades south-eastwards into the Acacus, an area of steep limestone cliffs falling steeply towards the west and criss-crossed and gashed by narrow gorges. Here Jebel Awenat is a vast crystalline mountainous massif cut by a series of steep valleys of alpine nature and rising from a table-land 5,500 feet high. To the south, granite rocks form an uneven surface 2,000 feet above the desert levels; here enormous blocks have been cut by deep fissures and tortuous defiles, the broken rocks lying in irregular heaps called *gargaf*. There is no doubt that many of these features could not have resulted from the present scant rainfalls of these desert areas, but that they are more the relic features produced by running water during past pluvial periods.

More volcanic and crystalline massifs are seen in the Aïr, Tibesti and Hoggar (or Ahaggar) plateaux. These massifs, subject to thousands of years of desert erosion, have been transformed into a weird lunar landscape of towering pinnacles, volcanic plugs and cones:

> In the Hoggar the crystalline base, which elsewhere is thousands or even tens of thousands of feet down, comes to the surface. The Hoggar Massif is a shallow almost circular vault of granite and gneiss. It is only at the crown of the vault, which the Tuareg call Atakor, that the Hoggar looks like a mountain range. Originally this too was a high plateau, 6,500 feet above sea level, then volcanic action turned it into a forest of stone. Enormous deposits of lava cover the granite, at some points from seven to ten different layers as much as six or seven hundred feet thick. Towering up from the lava to a height of ten thousand feet are great needles and turrets of rock and rock walls that have been worn and weather-beaten into fantastic shapes. In the Assekrem area alone there are at least three hundred of these weird formations, most of them of phonolite, a volcanic rock which has broken up into long prisms.[1]

[1] Abridged from Georg Gerster's, *Sahara*, Chapter Eight, page 133, published by Barrie and Rockcliffe, London, 1960.

FIG. 23: Landforms in the Hoggar. Note the contrast with Fig. 22. Here, resistant volcanic plugs stand above the more gentle slopes of rock waste

Hamada or el-Hamra or Red Desert, lying between Tripolitania and the Fezzan (Fig. 1:**21**) is such a pebble strewn desert extending for nearly 200 miles. It rises gradually to the 4,000 foot peak of Jebel-Es-Soda, the Black Mountain, where dark basalt lavas form an extensive cover.

Ergs or sand seas (Libyan—*Ramla*, Tuareg—*Edeyenor Idehan*) are found over much of eastern Libya and in the Murzuk and Ubari regions of the Fezzan where, just south of the Hamla region, lies a vast area of shifting sand dunes and jagged rocks. The colours vary from the dazzling white of limestone through the red and grey of argil deposits of the black of basalt lava sands. But ergs are seen at their best in the western Sahara where they occupy about 15 per cent of the surface area. The sand seas have different landscapes; some consist of rank after rank of barchan dunes (Fig. 1:**24**), huge

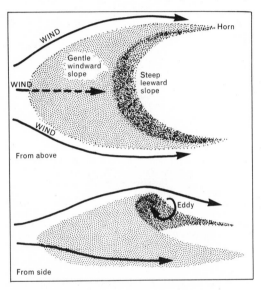

Fig. 24: A barchan dune

crescent-shaped hills of sand trending north-east to south-west in response to the prevailing winds. The dunes travel slowly across the landscape by the removal of sand from rear to front until they become 'fossilised', that is, too ponderous at their centres, and remain fixed, a stage usually reached when the barchan is about 1,250 feet wide and 115 feet high.

In other ergs the seif dune may dominate the scene. Seif dunes occur in large groups or in ridges up to fifty miles long and 300 feet high. They are elongated in the direction of the winds and are found in regions where winds are apt to change course giving rise to a fairly strong secondary wind. Thus a barchan may form first during strong north-easterly winds but has one of its horns elongated by a change to a more easterly wind.

In the Sahara there are no perennial water courses but the large number of *wadis* testify to the erosive effect of water produced by infrequent storms. The Wadi Zemzem in Libya is about 100 miles long and flows, when filled, into the Tauorga marshes. It has a straight course and, like its tributaries to the south, carries their combined waters in times of flood to the Gulf of Sirte, after crossing wide stretches of desert and steppe. The Wadi Bey el Kebir and the Wadi Tamet el Mgenes are its two most important tributaries. The more impressive wadis with steep, rocky walls have been proved to be the result of powerful water action when the climate of the region was wetter.

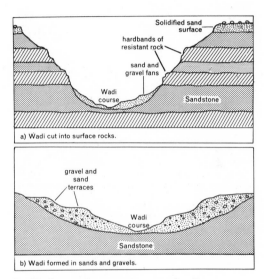

Fig. 25: Cross-sections across two types of wadi

The Coasts of Africa

Africa's coastline has no deep gulfs, penetrating estuaries, or extensive deep fiords such as those found in Europe or North America. The old sailing ships found few good harbours which offered natural protection; instead there were river mouths blocked by sand bars, hazardous coral reefs, shallow lagoons and beyond, the desert, rain forest or mountain ranges. The map (Fig. 1:.**27**) shows the major types of coastline along Africa's shores; of these the most prominent are:

Sand Bar and Lagoon Coasts—these stretch 1,200 miles along the West African coast from Cape St Ann to a point just east of Lagos. The shallow waters just off-shore break the rotational motion of

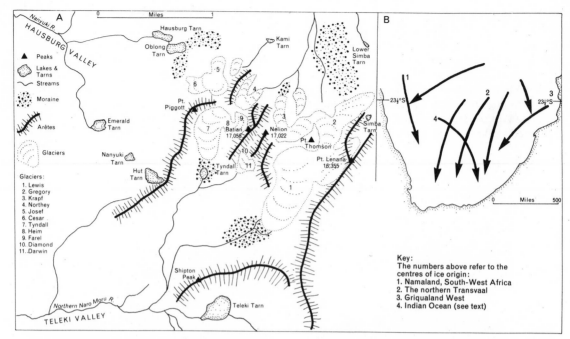

Key:
The numbers above refer to the
centres of ice origin:
1. Namaland, South-West Africa
2. The northern Transvaal
3. Griqualand West
4. Indian Ocean (see text)

FIG. 26: Glaciated Regions in Africa. Existing glaciers in Africa are limited to the higher parts of the Ruwenzori Range and to Mt Kenya (*Diagram A*), a volcanic peak now greatly eroded. Mt Kenya once probably reached to over 20,000 feet and the original plug, made of resistant nepheline syenite, is now exposed and forms several jagged peaks the highest of which are Batian and Nelion. Pt Piggott and Lenana are also remnants of the old plug. Glaciated valleys extend down to 10,000 feet but the twelve remaining glaciers are retreating fairly rapidly and none is below about 15,000 feet today. The greatest ice erosion probably occurred at about the same time as the Great Ice Age of Europe.

Diagram B shows the main direction of the Dwyka Ice sheets over southern Africa. This glaciation occurred towards the end of the Palaeozoic and left behind it large areas of tills which have since compacted into tillites; some of these tillites have been found as far north as the Congo Basin. The main movement of the ice sheets is from north-east to south-west and this is also put forward as evidence of the theory of continental drift which suggests that when the southern continents were joined together they were covered by a single vast ice sheet

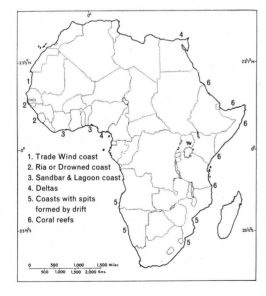

1. Trade Wind coast
2. Ria or Drowned coast
3. Sandbar & Lagoon coast
4. Deltas
5. Coasts with spits
   formed by drift
6. Coral reefs

FIG. 27: Africa—types of coastline. At 1 the prevailing trade winds have caused sand to drift southwards, filling the bays and smoothing the coastline.

approaching waves which deposit long lines of sand a short distance from the coast to form bars backed by shallow lagoons. While these lagoons form a natural inland waterway for light craft they are too shallow for ocean-going vessels which have to anchor in the deeper open sea. Entrance channels to ports have to be constantly dredged and artificial harbours have been built at Sekondi-Takoradi, Abidjan and Lagos (see page 119). Behind the off-shore bars the lagoons may be split into a complicated network of sandy islands and water channels. The water drains away through narrow gaps in the outer bars which are often made very shallow by a submerged bar.

Many of the lagoons are being gradually filled with river silt and will eventually become marshy

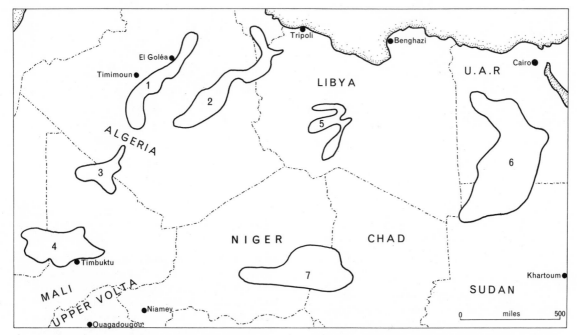

FIG. 28: The underground water reservoirs of the Sahara. The Sahara is the world's largest desert, covering nearly 3·1 million square miles. This vast, barren region could support a considerable higher population than at present if its subterranean water supplies were used more fully. Geologists have only recently realised the full extent of these underground aquifers, much of the information coming to light with extensive explorations for oil. As the map shows, the Sahara's underground water supplies are mainly contained in seven large basins. These basins and their estimated storage capacities in millions of cubic metres are: 1 Great Western Erg (1,500,000); 2 Great Eastern Erg (1,700,000); 3 Tanezrouft (400,000); 4 Niger (1,800,000); 5 Fezzan (400,000); 6 Western Egyptian Desert (6,000,000); 7 Chad (3,500,000).

Most of the water in these aquifers was laid down in past millenniums during pluvial periods when the Sahara experienced far more rain than it does today. They are constantly being recharged by rainwater falling along the wetter fringes of the desert and soaking along porous beds.

Some of the problems which will have to be solved before these water resources can be fully used are *a* the improvement of the present wasteful systems of irrigation practised by many oasis arabs; *b* the prevention of salt concentration in the soil due to the high rates of evaporation; *c* the maintenance of the balance between water use and re-charging rates, and *d* the solving of political difficulties which may develop since most of the basins lie across international boundaries

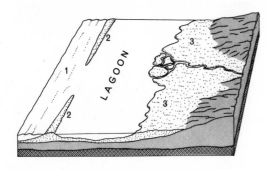

1. Rotary motion of waves is broken in shallow water.

2. Sand particles accumulate to form bar.

3. Silt brought down by rivers accumulates in lagoon.

FIG. 29: Block diagram illustrating a sandbar and lagoon coast

strips. Occasionally the line of sandspits and bars is broken by prominent rocky headlands chosen as sites for early trading posts and forts. These then are coasts of aggradation—they are being continuously added to and built up with sediments.

Ria Coasts extend in a 630-mile long strip from Dakar to Sherbro Island including the coasts of Sierra Leone, Guinea and Portuguese Guinea. Lowland and river valleys have been submerged by a rise in sea-level to produce a jig-saw pattern of deep inlets and small islands. The Sierra Leone estuary is a superb example of a ria with mountains on the south rising sheer out of the sea to nearly 3,000 feet, one of the finest natural inlets to be found on the West African coast.

17

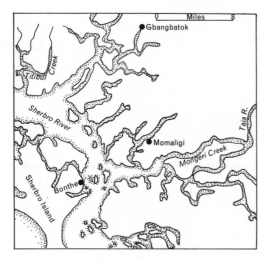

FIG. 30: Sierra Leone—ria coastline

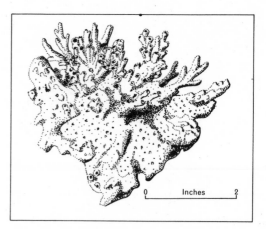

FIG. 31: A piece of coral

Coral Reef and Lagoon Coasts occur along the shores of the Red Sea, Somalia, Kenya, Tanzania and Mozambique. Here natural conditions are ideal for the growth of polyps, the minute sea creatures which live in colonies, forming their hard skeletons from calcium carbonate extracted from the sea water. It is the skeleton which remains after the polyps' death to pile up and form off-shore reefs and extensive lagoon floors. Polyps will only live, however, in shallow, clear, warm (68°F [20°C]) water and thus do not flourish along the cooler Atlantic shores of Africa. The reefs, lying between a half to one mile out to sea according to water depth, enclose calm stretches of shallow water in the lagoons which are fringed on the landward side by dazzling white beaches of eroded coral grains. Large islands of coral, formed when the land was more submerged than at present, lie off-shore, their bases undercut by

wave action; inland, raised beaches of coral are common. Where muddy streams enter the sea the polyps cannot exist and there are breaks in the reef. Such coasts provide few good harbours except where there has been local sinking of the land as at Mombasa's Kilindini Harbour (the Place of the Deep Waters).

Other Coastal Features

One of the contributory factors to the smoothness of Africa's coastline is the lack of river *estuaries*. Only the River Gambia has an estuary of a length comparable with those found in Europe or North America; it extends some 95 miles upstream to Elephant Island and was formed by an increase of sea level. It is approximately $7\frac{1}{2}$ miles wide near the sea but narrows to between $1\frac{1}{2}$ and 2 miles wide further upstream and is lined with level banks of silt called the *banto faros*.

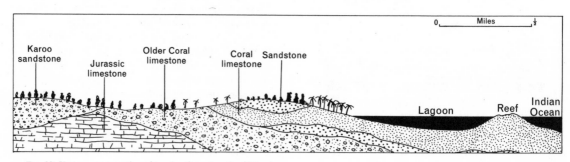

FIG. 32: Kenya—cross-section of coral reef coast north of Mombasa

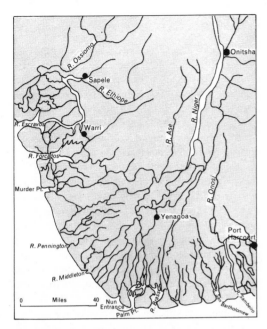

FIG. 33: Nigeria—the Niger delta

apex is about 115 miles. The numerous distributaries are banked by levees and in the case of the two main arms these levees have been built out into the Mediterranean at the Masabb Rashid (Rosetta Mouth) and the Masabb Dumyat (Damietta Mouth). Light currents along the coast have formed long sandspits enclosing large lagoons— the Bahra Maryut, the Bahra el Idku, the Bahra el Burullus (37 miles long by 9 miles wide) and the Bahra el Manzala (30 miles long by 11 miles wide). Surrounding these lagoons are broad areas of marsh too salty to reclaim.

Longshore drift is found along various stretches of the African coast where there are strong currents and wind. Sand accumulation in bays and the development of sandpits are the result. Bathurst stands on a hooked sandspit which ends at Banyan Point and is backed by low, swampy St Mary's Island. Sand

But *deltas* are the usual natural feature of Africa's river mouths and the Niger and the Nile form outstanding examples. The Niger delta is a cuspate or arcuate type, its curved shores extending 300 miles from near the Benin River to Opobo, fifty miles west of the Cross River outlet. The Niger outlet marks the extreme point of the arc at the Nun entrance west of Palm Point. Numerous other rivers, some distributaries, others separate from the Niger, form a broad fan. Called the 'Oil Rivers' due to the large quantities of palm oil produced in this region many are navigable by ocean-going vessels for short distances while others, particularly those on the west coast, have had their entrances blocked by drifting sands caused by long-shore drift. Entrances to ports such as Sapele and Warri along the Escravos and Forcados rivers must be kept dredged and protected from drift by breakwaters. Transport overland in the delta is made difficult by the wide areas of mangrove swamps and population densities are comparatively low.

The Nile delta, on the other hand, is densely populated over about 70 per cent of its area and, while being smaller than the Niger delta, is nevertheless a magnificent example. Its coastal arc is some 150 miles long and its greatest extent inland at the delta

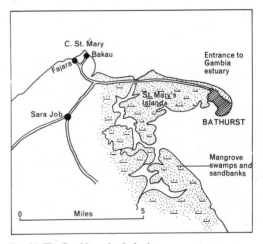

FIG. 34: The Gambia—a hooked spit

eroded from sandstone rocks and silt from the interior brought by the Gambia River have collected at a point where the river current slackens in deeper water and meets drift caused by south-west winds. At Walvis Bay in South-West Africa the northward drift of sediments carried by the Benguela Current has formed a nine-mile long spit backed by salt marshes and a shallow lagoon. The opposite effect is seen on the east coast in Mozambique where the Inhaca Peninsula acts as a gathering arm for drifting silt brought down into

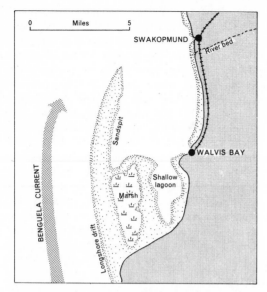

FIG. 35: South-West Africa—sandspit formation near Swakopmund

Delagoa Bay by the southward flowing Mozambique Current; added to this are the sediments of the Tembe and Esperito Santo rivers. Constant dredging of Lourenço Marques harbour is necessary.

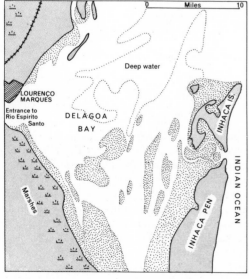

FIG. 36: Mozambique—silt accumulation in Delagoa Bay

B : The Climate

With over three quarters of its surface within the tropics Africa does not experience the great temperature contrasts of Europe, Asia and North America. While in those continents much of the climate can be explained by the effect of air masses of greatly differing temperatures, the explanation of Africa's climate is more of a problem. The isolation of vast regions and the large expanses of desert and rain forest have made the collection of reliable data difficult. However, many of Africa's climatic characteristics can be explained by the movement of air masses which differ from one another in their amount of moisture and their relative stability rather than in their temperatures. These air masses come into contact along a broad ill-defined convergence zone which moves across the continent in response to temperature and wind changes—the Inter Tropical Convergence Zone or ITCZ—to which many meteorologists have given the characteristics of a frontal zone similar to those of Europe and North America. The conditions which give rise to the movement of air masses and produce this frontal zone may be described as follows:

Climatic Conditions—the Southern Hemisphere's Summer

Temperatures

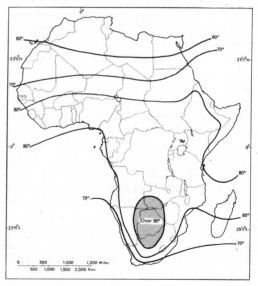

FIG. 37: January—actual surface temperatures

By January the sun produces intense heating in Botswana, Zambia and Rhodesia, and most of the southern half of Africa has temperatures between 70 and 80°F [22 and 27°C][1] with extremes of 90°F [32°C] and over in Bushmanland. In contrast, the northern part of the continent is relatively cool with mean temperatures of 50°F [10°C] in the Atlas region and 60°F [15·5°C] in the northern Sahara.

Pressures

The intensity of insolation over southern Africa from November to April causes low pressure conditions in this region, while relatively high pressures develop over the cooler south Atlantic and Indian

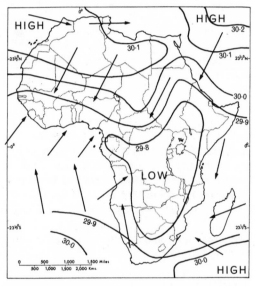

FIG. 38: Pressure and winds—general conditions from November to April

oceans. Over cooler north Africa high pressure develops, separated from that of continental Europe by a low pressure system over the relatively warm surface of the Mediterranean Sea.

Winds

Winds from the northern high pressure zone penetrate southwards through the interior of the continent towards the low pressure zone of the south. Relatively high pressure over the south Atlantic and

[1] Figures in square brackets are centigrade temperatures, rounded to the nearest half-figure throughout. In later chapters metric measurements also appear in square brackets after measurements in feet and inches.

the south-westerly monsoons oppose their progress in the west. Along the eastern coast the North-East Trades and Asiatic monsoonal winds also penetrate southwards to converge with easterly trade winds and Atlantic south-westerlies onto the low pressure system of the south.

The ITCZ

This follows the West African coast, bends southwards through the Cameroons and Congo, then eastwards through Botswana and the Mozambique coast.

Air Masses

Virtually the whole of the Sahara, West Africa and the northern Congo are influenced by dry, stable air. The eastern half of Africa receives similar dry air from Arabia borne by the north-east trades. Towards the south-east this air mass has picked up

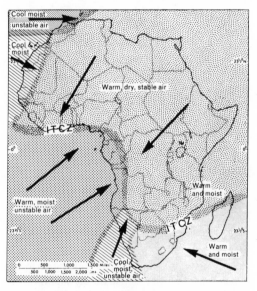

FIG. 39: January—diagrammatic representation of airmass movement and position of airmass fronts

moisture over the Indian Ocean and becomes warm and moist. Easterly trade winds bring similar air to Madagascar, the Natal coast and the eastern veld. Warm, moist, generally unstable air affects most of the western coast south of the Equator. In the Maghreb region of the north-west cool, moist, unstable air masses are brought by westerly air streams.

21

Climatic Conditions—the Northern Hemisphere's Summer

Temperatures

Over the broad land mass of northern Africa the sun, now overhead between the equator and the Tropic of Cancer, creates temperatures rising to over 100°F [38°C] in the shade in the Sahara. The

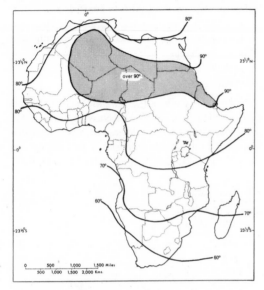

FIG. 40: July—actual surface temperatures

whole of western and central Africa has mean actual-temperatures between 60 and 80°F [15·5 and 26·5°C] while the south is quite cool with actual temperatures below 60°F [15·5°C].

Pressures

A broad zone of low pressure exists throughout the Sahara and into Arabia broken only by occasional small zones of high pressure on the cool Ethiopian Highlands. A high pressure concentration lies over South Africa south of Capricorn. Low pressure systems move eastwards sometimes affecting the southern tip of the Cape.

Winds

The south-east Trade winds of the South Atlantic move across the equator and are drawn in across the coast of West Africa by the low pressure zone of

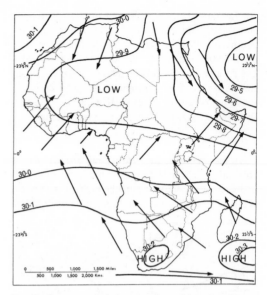

FIG. 41: Pressure and winds—general conditions from May to October

the Sahara to become powerful south-west monsoonal winds heavily laden with moisture. The north-east trades retreat to become a weak zone of winds affecting Africa north of Cancer. Most of eastern and central Africa is affected by easterly Trade winds from the Indian Ocean while variable winds, associated with the anti-clockwise movement around the South African high and with the low pressure systems off the southern coast, affect Africa south of Capricorn.

The ITCZ

This lies between the weak north-east winds and the strong south-west monsoonal region. It extends in an almost straight line east-west from the coast of Mauritania to the Red Sea shores of the Sudan.

Air Masses

While Africa north of the ITCZ is under the influence of warm, dry air masses, warm, moist air brought by the south-west monsoons pours over the whole of West Africa, penetrating as far as the Ethiopian Highlands to the east and bringing warm, moist, unstable conditions very favourable to turbulent convectional thunderstorms and heavy rainfall. Warm, moist air also approaches from the south-east moving in over the Mozambique and

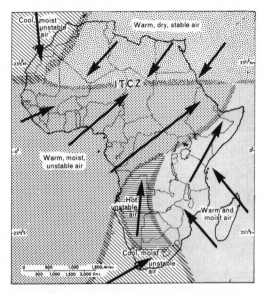

FIG. 42: July—diagrammatic representation of airmass movement and position of airmass fronts

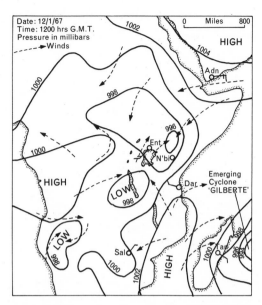

FIG. 43: Meteorological conditions over central and southern Africa in January 1967. A belt of low pressure extends throughout central and east Africa from the Angolan coast in the south-west to the Kenya Highlands in the north-east. Relatively high pressure zones are centred over the Congo Basin, the southern Arabian peninsula and over the Mozambique Channel. The birth of the tropical cyclone 'Gilberte' at about 12°S to the east of Malagasy seems to be hastening the collapse of the south-easterly high-pressure belt. The northern part of the region shown experienced generally dry weather but rain fell over much of Tanzania, northern Angola and the western coast of Malagasy. Dry, stable air masses over Kenya and Somalia prevented any large-scale convective rainfall but later in the week a relatively cold air mass, the remnants of an extra-tropical cold front from the Mediterranean, caused cloud and scattered thunderstorms in the lake region of western Uganda. (*See also page 39 for exercises on meteorological maps of Africa*)

East African coasts. The southern tip of Africa is affected by cool, moist, unstable air brought by depressions.

The conditions described above are the two extremes when the sun is at its extremities in the northern and southern hemispheres. Throughout the year as the sun and its heat move over the continent between the tropics, the pressure belts respond and the wind systems weaken or increase in strength bringing with them associated air masses. This idealised picture is thus never stable but constantly changing. Fig. 1:**43** shows actual climatic conditions for one day in January 1967.[1]

The Effects of the ITCZ

The effects of the ITCZ may only be felt temporarily in any one region as it moves in response to waxing and waning air masses. But its effects may not be clearly seen due to other climatic influences; in East Africa it is not known how much the weather is affected by the ITCZ for variations in altitude, the effects of large water expanses in the lakes, and convectional air currents mask its influence. It is clearly seen in West Africa, however, where its passage

[1] For diagrams showing other daily conditions see exercise maps Figs 1:**75**, 1:**76** and 1:**77**, page 40.

over the land is marked by a line of squalls and turbulent, changeable weather (Fig. 1:**44** and 1:**45**). From March onwards the warm, moist air brought by the south-west monsoonal wind sweeps in from the Gulf of Guinea. Like a broad wedge the air mass slices in under the drier, hotter air lying over the continent and forces it to rise. The stronger monsoons make gradual headway against the weakening Harmattan and their convergence zone, the ITCZ, moves slowly northwards. The weather, which up to April or May consisted of dry, dusty days which parch the soil and make nose and eyes smart, begins to change as the south-west winds increase their influence. The once cloudless skies are now fluffed with small white cumulus clouds, temperatures are a little lower and a warm moistness

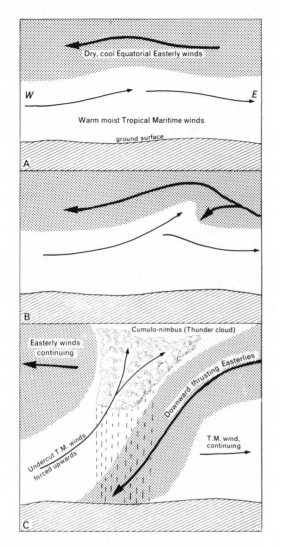

replaces the harsh dryness. Winds veer from north-east to south-west and blustery weather brings rain showers; these conditions gradually give way to skies heavy with black cumulo-nimbus accompanied by lightning, thunder and heavy rain. As the ITCZ pushes northwards the steady rains of the rainy season proper begin, to last until September or October according to location (Fig. 1:45).

Rainfall Belts

In Africa rainfall is thus associated with the passage of the ITCZ, the convectional nature of hot tropical air, and the movement of moist air masses over higher ground (orographical or relief rain). As these influences pass over Africa the associated rainbelt moves with them. From May to October the whole of southern Africa is receiving some rain (Fig. 1:46); the north coast receives rain from the Atlantic while the rest of north Africa comes under the influence of the hot, dry Saharan air mass which extends itself into West Africa by the Harmattan. The Harmattan rarely reaches the West African coast, which receives some rain from the weak south-westerly monsoon. Rainfall in the southern part of the continent is brought by the south-east trades from the Indian Ocean and from westerly air streams from the South Atlantic, both of which meet at the ITCZ and produce frontal rainfall. Intense heating produces many convectional rain storms. In the deserts of South-West Africa little rain falls. This is due to the lack of

FIG. 44 (left): West Africa—causes of turbulence along the squall line

FIG. 45 (below): Nigeria—weather zones associated with the movement of the ITCZ

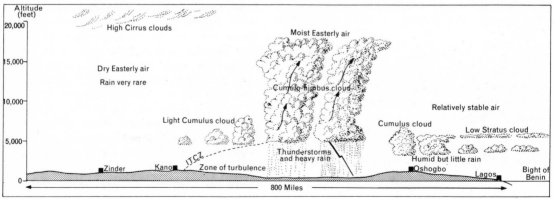

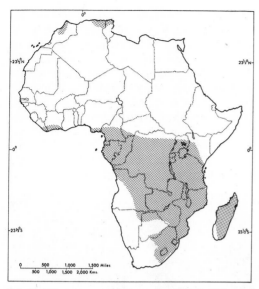

FIG. 46: Africa—areas receiving more than 20 inches [508mm] of rain between 1 November and 30 April

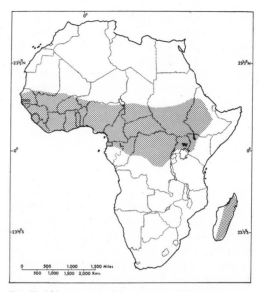

FIG. 47: Africa—areas receiving more than 20 inches [508mm] of rain between 1 May and 31 October

any major relief feature which would trigger off relief rain and to the presence of cool, stable air over an ocean cooled by the Benguela Current. Moreover, the southern Atlantic air streams meet no opposing air mass to cause frontal rain in this region.

Gradually the rain belts and air masses move northwards following the apparent movement of the sun and the northward moving pressure belts. Between November and April a huge belt of rainfall extends from the equator northwards to 15° north latitude and from the coasts of Sierra Leone to the western borders of Somalia (Fig. 1:**47**). Strong south-westerly air streams blow directly on-shore bringing heavy rainfall in regions of sharp relief— the Colony Mts (Freetown receives 37 inches [940mm] in July), the Futa Djalon, the Jos Plateau and the Cameroon (Debundja has 59·1 inches [1501mm] in July) and Bamenda Highlands. The Ethiopian Highlands experience heavy rain brought by easterly trade winds. Except for the rain brought by the westerly air currents in the south-west Cape region the rest of Africa receives less than 1 inch of rainfall in July in most areas.

The effect of the movement of rainfall zones across Africa is to produce differing patterns of rainfall throughout the year in different parts of the continent. Flanking the equator are regions which receive rainfall all the year round since they lie where the extreme southern and northern parts of the seasonal rainbelts overlap. To the north-east and south of this core region lie areas which receive rainfall when the rain belt passes over them, the season varying from three to six months according to position, and a long period of drought when the rainbelt is in the opposite hemisphere. In the Mediterranean coastal fringe rain occurs when the westerly air streams migrate south from Europe, while a three- to four-month drought period is experienced when the region comes under the influence of the dry Saharan air mass. A similar climate with the seasons occurring at opposite times of the year (winter from May to July and summer drought from November to January) occurs in the south-west Cape region when westerly air streams migrate north or south.

Factors Affecting Climatic Characteristics

While Africa's climatic regions fall into a relatively simple pattern, variations in climatic types are caused by several natural influences:

Altitude

Altitude results in the limitation of true Equatorial Climate to the Congo Basin. East Africa and

Ethiopia do not experience the enervating moistness and stuffiness of the Congo while Ethiopia also escapes the great blanket of heat which lies over the Sahara in the northern summer months. Altitudes of between 5,000 and 9,000 feet reduce temperatures by between 15 and 25°F [8·3 and 13·8°C] giving pleasant annual averages around 65 and 75°F [18 and 24°C]. Such climates are of a more tropical nature than those normally associated with equatorial regions.

Relief

Relief can create very great local differences in climate. We have seen the effects in West Africa. In East Africa the Kilimanjaro region of Tanzania is very well watered on its south-eastern side (up to 60 inches [1524mm] annually) while a few miles to the north-east in the Nyika rain totals fall as low as 10 inches [254mm] a year. Relief rain is experienced all along the eastward-facing slopes of the Drakensberg Mts (Pietermaritzburg's annual total is 36 inches [914mm]) while to the west the High Veld becomes progressively drier.

Configuration

Configuration of coastlines may have an effect on rainfall amount received. On the Kenya coast rain-

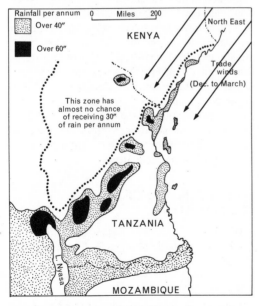

FIG. 48: East Africa—the effect of altitude and coast alignment on annual rainfall totals

fall is not high for an equatorial region (Mombasa 47·5 inches [1206·5mm]) and totals decrease northwards (Lamu 36·6 inches [929mm]). This may be partly attributed to the north-east alignment of the coast, for the north-east trades flow parallel to it for several months instead of blowing directly inland. A similar occurrence is found in Ghana east of Cape Three Points where rainfall totals fall well below 30 inches [762mm] in a region which should experience between 70 and 80 inches [1778 and 2032mm]. This is partly due to the sharp bend of the coast from a north-westerly alignment (at right

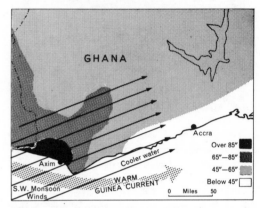

FIG. 49: Ghana—the effect of ocean currents and coast alignment on annual rainfall totals

angles to the south-westerly monsoon) to a north-easterly one (parallel to the monsoon) and to an upwelling of cold waters near the coast. Thus Axim receives over 80 inches [2032mm] a year while Accra gets only 29 inches [737mm].

Ocean Currents

Ocean currents also affect climate. The cool Benguela Current flowing northwards along the coast of South-West Africa produces a considerable drop in temperatures for stations along the coast (compare Walvis Bay's annual average temperature of 62°F [17°C] with that of Windhoek's 66°F [19°C]) and also cools air masses passing over it so that when they cross the heated land surface they release little or no moisture; this accounts for the narrow strip of pure desert—the Namib—along this coast. The cool Canaries current flowing southward along the Moroccan coast often produces cool, cloudy days and frequent fogs. Casablanca has a July average of 71°F [22°C] which is 8°F

[4·4°C] lower than Tripoli on the same latitude.

In contrast temperatures are raised slightly on the Mozambique and Natal coasts by the southward flowing warm Mozambique Current. Thus Durban's July temperature of 64·3°F [18°C] is 7·8°F [4·3°C] higher than Swakopmund's 56·5°F [13·5°C], while Durban has a January temperature of 76·3°F [25°C] and Swakopmund 62·6°F [17°C]. The warm Mozambique current has a direct economic effect since it allows sugar cane to be grown at a much lower latitude than normal (30° south—see page 101).

C: Natural Regions—their Climate, Vegetation and Economic Use

The correlation between climate and vegetation is easily seen in Africa where, despite rapid removal of plant life by animal and man, extensive vegetation zones exist. The climate and its associated vegetation affects the patterns of life which man can choose to lead and has a direct bearing on the economic development of a region. Climatic and vegetation regions will be considered as natural regions and their economic use briefly discussed.

Equatorial Regions

Climate

Equatorial climates are limited to areas within 10° of the equator. They are characterised by high daily temperatures of around 80°F [26·5°C], a small annual range of from 3 to 5°F [1·7 to 2·8°C] and a small diurnal range of 10 to 15°F [5·6 to 8·3°C]. Rainfall is heavy throughout the year, often exceeding 80 inches [2032mm]. While no month is really dry there may be two rainfall maxima with the passage of the 'thermal equator' and much rain is largely convectional often falling in continual sheets for hours. Days and nights are of approximately the same length, the sun rising between 6 and 6.30 a.m. and setting between 6 and 6.30 p.m.

Morning weather is often quite sunny and clear but the heat builds up during the day until by about 2 p.m. cumulus clouds develop, growing into towering cumulo-nimbus which give heavy rainfall

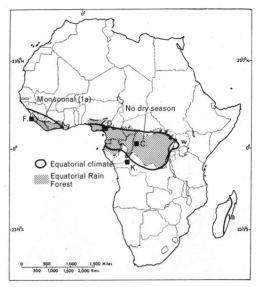

FIG. 50: Africa—the equatorial regions

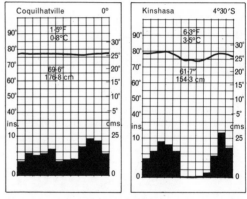

FIG. 51: Two types of equatorial climate from the Congo Basin. Coquilhatville is almost exactly on the Equator, while Kinshasa lies nearly 5°S and displays a short dry season

accompanied by thunder and lightning. As temperatures cool during the evening the clouds thin or disappear and nights may be moonlit and starry.

Some of the rain may be due to frontal conditions. Warm, moist unstable air from the South Atlantic meets more stable drier air from the north-east. There is also the possibility that air streams from the Indian Ocean may penetrate far enough to bring rain to the eastern Congo.

Along the West African coast the Monsoonal

27

Equatorial Climate (see area marked 1a on Fig. 1:**50**) differs from that of the Congo by having a definite, though short, dry period. Much of the rain is orographical and totals are high, usually between 100 and 170 inches [2540 and 4318mm] a

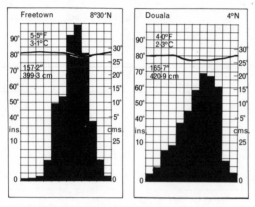

FIG. 52: Equatorial climate—the effects of relief

year; Debundja in the Cameroons is the extreme with an annual average rainfall of 374 inches [9497mm] with nearly 60 inches [1524mm] falling in July and only 7½ inches [190·5mm] in January.

Vegetation

The hot, rainy, humid conditions give rise to dense tropical rain forests which stretch in a broken 600-mile wide zone for 1,400 miles from the eastern Congo boundary to the Gabon and Cameroon coasts; they are continued along the West African coast in a strip 150 to 200 miles wide in places from the Niger Delta to the Sierra Leone coast and in narrow ribbons along the lower reaches of tropical rivers. Tropical rain forest covers 880,000 square miles (8 per cent of Africa's surface).

The rain forest consists of a wide variety of trees, the tallest reaching up to 130 feet, their smooth, straight trunks crowned with feathery leaves and branches. Younger and smaller species form a secondary 'canopy' between 60 and 70 feet. Between the trees straggle parasitic lianas while the floor is thickly covered with herbs, ground creepers and low bushes. Many trees develop buttressed trunks and, near river banks, stilt roots. Trees overhang rivers to form tunnels or galleries (gallerial forest). There are no 'pure stands' of trees as in temperate coniferous forests; balsa, rubber, mahogany, sapele and ebony grow close together, a hundred varieties often being found in one square mile. The rate of plant growth is very rapid and secondary growth soon springs up in cleared patches.

Economic Uses of the Environment

The tropical rain forests contain many useful plants and trees. Durable and expensive woods are selected and floated down to saw mills (see page 176), large plantations grow oil palm, rubber, cacao, citrus fruits, bananas and coffee. A wide variety of vegetables and fruits is also grown for subsistence—bananas, pineapples, mangoes, rice, yams, sweet

FIG. 53: Equatorial rain forest

potatoes, sugar cane, ginger, groundnuts, tobacco and cotton.[1] Oil for cooking, for lamp fuel, for soap and for sale to plantations is provided by the oil palm; the kola nut is grown as a stimulant; the raffia palm supplies fibre for baskets, nets ropes and mats. The wild life of the forests is hunted by small isolated groups of people with bows and arrows, snares, nets, pits and traps, and yields a wide range of meats. At one time large areas of these forests remained virtually untouched by man but they are now being extensively cleared for cultivation and for the extraction of minerals.

Tropical Regions

Climate

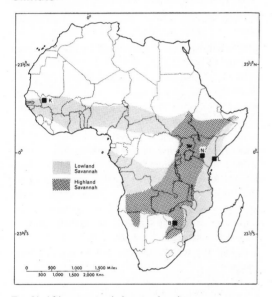

FIG. 54: Africa—two tropical savannah regions

Tropical climates and their associated savannah vegetation lie in a broad zone fringing the Equatorial Region forming a transition zone towards the true desert. Hot season temperatures are higher, cool season lower, and diurnal (25 to 30°F) [13·8 to 16·6°C] and annual ranges (up to 15°F) [8·3°C] are greater. They differ most in the annual distribution and amount of rainfall varying from 80 inches [2032mm] on equatorial margins to 15 inches [381mm] towards semi-deserts. The characteristic wet and dry seasons are caused by the north-south

[1] The last three crops can be grown on the drier fringes of the region (see p. 67).

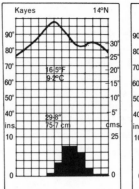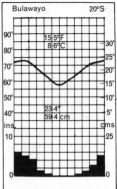

FIG. 55: Africa—two examples of tropical climate

shifts of the rain belts over Africa. In West Africa a dry season dominated by the Harmattan (November-March) is followed by a generally cooler, rainy period brought by the south-west monsoons.[1] In East Africa double rainfall maxima occur (March–April, September–October) brought by the north-east and south-east trade winds. Tropical climates thus display both dry, semi-desert conditions and rainy periods of almost equatorial intensity.

Modification due to altitude occurs on highland regions throughout East and Central Africa and in West Africa. Temperatures are lowered by 15 to 20°F [8·3 to 11·1°C] to annual averages of between 65 and 70°F [18 and 21°C] although annual

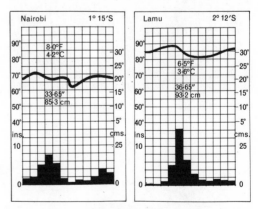

FIG. 56: Two examples of modified tropical climate. Nairobi's temperatures are reduced by approximately 15°F [9·4°C] since it stands at 5,495 feet and its double rainfall maxima is caused by the North-East and South-East Trades; Lamu has an exaggerated 'Long Rains' due to on-shore South-East Trades (see Fig. 1:42)

[1] Nearer the equator the hottest months occur in March or April and September or October as the sun apparently crosses the equator.

and diurnal ranges remain the same. Nights can be decidedly chilly and in certain months of the year, e.g. in June and July in the Kenya Highlands, comparatively cold weather occurs with layers of grey cloud and early morning mists. Variations in rainfall may occur within small areas due to the rain shadow effect of high mountains. Thus Nanyuki, Nyeri and Meru all lie within a thirty mile radius of Mt Kenya but Nanyuki (28·1 inches) [713·7mm] and Nyeri (29·9 inches) [759·5mm] lie in the rain shadow while Meru (52·3 inches) [1328mm] stands on exposed eastern slopes.

Vegetation

Savannah is the usual vegetation of tropical climates but there is a great difference between that of the equatorial fringes and that of the semi-desert margins. Three types of savannah are illustrated. Considerable areas of savannah are 'derived' from

FIG. 58: Thorn bush savannah. Typical of drier (20 ins/50·8 cms) regions

denser natural vegetation thinned by bush fires and clearing by man.

In the cooler, wetter climates of tropical highlands dense forests of very tall trees (cedar, podo, camphor, yellowwood) with yellowish-white trunks and feathery crowns of branches and leaves are the natural vegetation. The trees rise to 150 feet and the undergrowth is dense with creepers, bushes, shrubs, sedges, flowering plants, giant ferns and lianas. Dense leaf canopies restrict light penetration and the trees grow very close together. Fewer species grow in these altitudes but tree growth is very rapid, some camphor trees adding six feet a year in their younger stages. These forests lie between 7,000 and 8,000 feet and give way to bamboo and grasslands at higher levels.

Economic Uses of the Environment

The savannah lands were once the roving grounds of vast herds of wild animals but today such herds are

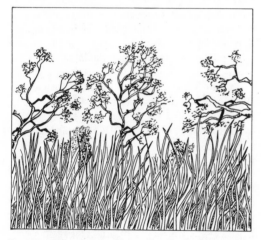

FIG. 57: High grass—low tree savannah. Typical of wetter savannah regions in Uganda

FIG. 59: Acacia savannah. Often associated with special soil conditions, particularly back clay plains in southern Kenya and Tanzania

relatively few, due to the ravages of poachers and hunters. To see game in its natural state one must go to the big game parks and reserves (Ngorongoro Crater in Tanzania, Tsavo Park in Kenya, Kruger National Park, South Africa).

The wetter zones provide numerous useful trees (oil palm, shea butter tree, kola nut tree) and where intensive farming is possible the drier bush is cleared and burnt to plant crops during the rains. In some areas small plantations of coffee, sisal, rubber and cotton have been established.

The acacia savannah provides extensive grazing land for nomadic tribes (page 81) but the longer drought season limits the range of crops to grains (millet, sorghum, maize) and groundnuts, beans and sweet potatoes. Cash crops, e.g. tobacco and cotton, can be grown with irrigation. The better watered areas are suitable for low-density cattle rearing. In the desert grass areas serious overgrazing may occur; here some poor grains may be grown and cattle are often moved to wetter uplands in the dry season.

The montane forest zones once extended down to about 5,000 feet but they have been greatly cleared for cultivation by both Europeans (in East Africa) and Africans. These tsetse free areas provide some of the finest grazing and agricultural land in Africa, highly suitable for dairy and beef cattle, sheep and plantation crops. African settlement is dense and crops are grown for subsistence and cash. In the East African highlands cultivation is extended above 8,000 feet and even some exotic forest areas are being cleared.

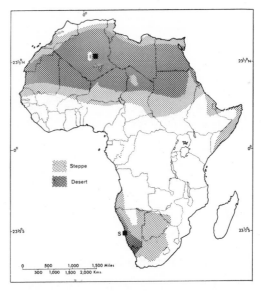

FIG. 60: Africa—the steppe and desert regions

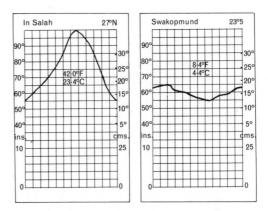

FIG. 61: Two examples of desert climate

Steppe and Desert Regions

Climate

These are regions of low rainfall and high evaporation. Semi-desert regions receive between 15 and 20 inches [381 and 508mm] of rain a year but the air is usually very dry and sultry. True deserts display climatic extremes 136°F [58°C] in the shade in the Sahara summer falling to 40°F [4°C] at night. Mean annual temperatures vary between 50 and 95°F [10 and 35°C]; skies are cloudless and burning hot days give way to clear, sparkling cold nights when rapid radiation often produces frost. The irregular rainfall is usually below 10 inches [254mm] a year and evaporation rates are so high that rain may never reach the ground.

Vegetation

In semi-desert regions cacti, bunch grass, small woody plants and patches of dry, short grass occur with an outburst of flowering plants during brief rain storms. Flowers derived from wind-borne seeds may appear briefly in true desert areas.

31

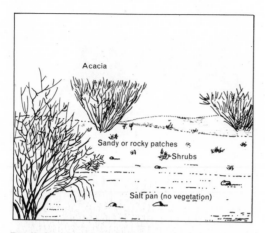

FIG. 62: Semi-desert vegetation

Economic Uses of the Environment

The semi-deserts may be used briefly by herders in a particular rainy season. In the deserts cultivation is non-existent except at oases. The Sahara, however, is the centre of intense economic interest in view of the many mineral reserves it contains (see Chapter Eight).

Mediterranean Regions
Climate

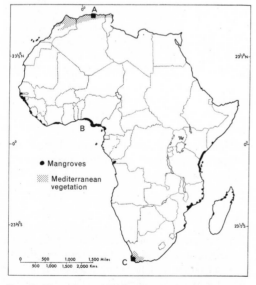

FIG. 63: The regions of Mediterranean vegetation and mangroves—both are a response to a limited climatic environment

The Mediterranean climate displays part desert and part cool temperate influences. Hot, dry summers about three months long give way to the light showers and cooler temperatures of autumn, winter and spring. Great variation is caused by altitude; in the Atlas ranges 60 inches [155·5mm] of rain may fall annually with snow in winter while coastal zones receive less than 20 inches [508mm] in dry years. Summers are hot (75°F [24°C] August) and sunny but winters are cool (55°F [13°C] January) with many clouds, damp air and rain. In the Plateau of Shotts the altitude creates cold winters with frost, bitter winds and snow storms; the summers are desert-like with cool nights and hot days with clear, cloudless skies.

In the southern Cape the hottest, cloudless period is in January and February with temperatures in the 70°Fs [22–26°C]; these drop to 55°F [13°C] during

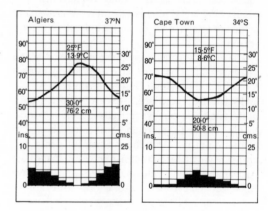

FIG. 64: Two examples of Mediterranean climate

the cool season (June–August) when skies are overcast and blustery rainstorms are brought by westerly air streams.

Vegetation

This varies with altitude, rainfall amount and the length of the dry season. The higher Atlas are clothed with open forests of medium-sized cork oak, cedar, ordinary oak, Spanish Chestnut, pine and fir trees with short grass slopes. In the lower valleys and hills small trees and bushes (brambles, myrtle, clematis, wild rose) often form impenetrable thickets and this type of vegetation is referred to as Maquis.

Economic Uses of the Environment

The Atlas forests produce cork and timber and esparto grass. Here cereals and potatoes are grown and sheep, goats and cattle grazed. The lowlands produce wheat, citrus fruit, olives, grapes and vegetables as well as supporting livestock. Parts of these regions have long been settled by European farmers (see Chapter Five).

The High Veld Grasslands

Climate

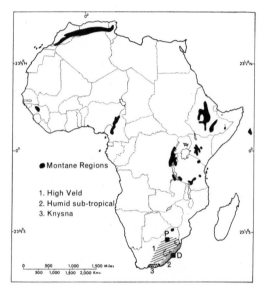

FIG. 65: Africa—the high veld, humid sub-tropical, and Knysna and montane regions

This is a temperate interior or continental climate with low temperatures (for Africa) ranging between 50 and 65°F [10 and 18°C] with a frost risk during cool season nights (late May to mid-August). Rainfall ranges from about 30 inches [762mm] in the east to 16 inches [400mm] further west with a fairly dry period during the cool months. The moisture is rought by westerly air streams from the Indian Ocean.

Vegetation

Trees are rare at the low rainfall levels and the southern Transvaal and Orange Free States are pure grassland areas with an unbroken grass cover about three feet high which withers to a drab brown in the dry season. Trees may grow along river valleys, in the wetter east, or in high water table areas. Similar grassland is found on the Kenya, Tanzania and West African plateau surfaces.

Economic Uses of the Environment

This is good grazing land and can support large herds of cattle, sheep and goats with good management but the dry season is always a problem. The main crops include maize, potatoes, citrus fruits and deciduous fruits grown with irrigation.

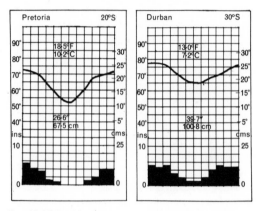

FIG. 66: High veld and humid sub-tropical climatic types

The Humid Sub-tropical Region

Climate

This region is limited by the sudden rise of the plateau to the west. It extends along the Mozambique, Natal and eastern Cape Province coastal strips. Here the rainfall is between 35 and 45 inches [889 and 1143mm] with most falling during the summer (November–April). Temperatures decrease towards the interior and frost is a great risk in cooler months. Heavy relief and convectional rain occurs through-.out the region.

Vegetation

A narrow strip of palm trees grows along the warm, moist coast while inland much of the former acacia and savannah bushland has been cleared for settlement and cultivation. On the cooler, wetter slopes to the west temperate rain forest appears.

Economic Uses of the Environment

The warm, moist coastal belt is ideal for sugar cane growth. Citrus fruits, bananas, some rice, pineapples and some cotton under irrigation are grown, with dairying and market gardening near the bigger centres. Cattle are reared in Zululand. Inland, wattle tree plantations and small farms concentrating on dairying, and the growing of maize, citrus fruits, potatoes, cotton and tung oil are important.

Warm Temperate Coastal Region (Knysna Region)

This is a small region extending for about 200 miles from west to east between Mossel and Algoa (near Pt Elizabeth) bays. It is a transition zone between the Mediterranean zone of the south-west and the humid subtropical zone of the eastern coast. It receives rainfall all the year round, in winter from the cyclonic storms of the westerly wind belt and in summer from easterly winds. Port Elizabeth receives 22·7 inches [577mm] annually and C. St Francis 26·8 inches [681mm], although in some areas the annual rainfall may exceed 50 inches [1270mm].

This climate gives rise to a dense temperate evergreen forest with some tall trees rising up to 150 feet (but with an average canopy height of 30 to 70 feet). The trees include yellowwoods, stinkwood, black ironwood, Cape Beech and white ironwood although there are many other varieties. The undergrowth is often very dense with much fern growth. Much of the forest has been cleared but that which remains is state protected.

Alpine Regions

On the highlands of Ethiopia, Kenya, western Uganda, Rwanda-Urundi and Malawi, above 8,000 to 8,500 feet the bamboo forests give way to alpine meadows of tussocky grasses, lichens and mosses which in turn fade into windswept rocky slopes and ice fields. Even on the higher slopes weird plants such as giant lobelia and groundsel exist. These areas are too cold and inaccessible to be economically useful. The effect of altitude on vegetation is seen in Fig. 1 :**67**.

Coastal Vegetation

Along salty or brackish water courses—coastal creeks, lake shores and river mouths—in tropical Africa one usually encounters mangrove swamps. They occur in the Niger delta, along most of the West African coast and from Somalia to Natal. These forests grow along the water line between high and low water marks where there is rich, silty soil. The trees may reach 75 feet but are usually between 25 and 40 feet. They form dense bushy stands with tangles of stilt-like roots exposed at low tide. The East African mangroves are similar to those found over most of the Far East. Freshwater mangroves are found around lake shores.

The mangrove does have some economic uses. Its leaves serve as fodder for camels, the light wood is used in carpentry or for fish net supports, the bark has a high tannin content and the wood makes excellent fuel. In East Africa there is a considerable trade with Arabia which uses the rot-resisting poles (boriti) for house construction.

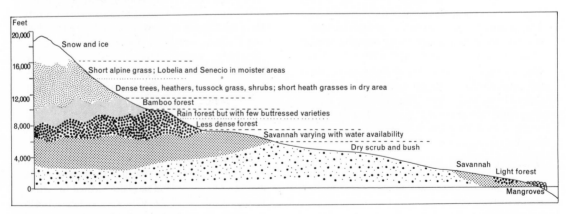

FIG. 67: The effect of altitude on vegetation

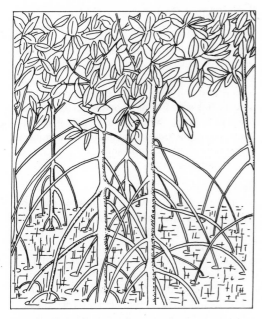

FIG. 68: Mangroves

D: The Soils of Africa

Soil Formation

Soils are the result of the interaction of the factors so far discussed—rocks, climate and vegetation. Soil is a tangible element which can be seen, felt, modified, improved and also ruined by bad farming methods. Soil is the material in which all plant life grows; it is the loose substance which rests on the upper part of the rock surface and is formed by bacteria and other agents breaking down organic substances and mingling them with minute minerals derived from the underlying rocks. Soil thus contains minerals, humus (decayed vegetative matter) and, in its pores, water and air. Without soil all life would cease to exist.

Climate, living organisms, the parent rock, the relief, and time all play an important part in soil formation.

Climate

Weak carbonic acids in rain water, the alternate wetting and drying in tropical regions, expansion and contraction caused by heating and cooling in deserts, and deflation by winds gradually break down rocks to minute particles. The heavier the rainfall the higher the temperatures, the greater the degree of weathering of parent rock and the deeper the soil formation. Once formed, however, the soil may be leached of its surface minerals by heavy downpours. But in Africa the deepest soils are not often formed in the regions of heaviest rainfall and highest temperatures for these areas usually have lateritic soils so hard that they prevent deep soil formation.

Living Organisms

Man and domesticated animals alter the soil by adding fertiliser, overgrazing the land and cultivating certain crops. Vegetation protects soil from the rain's leaching effects, extracts carbon, oxygen or nitrogen from the atmosphere and passes it through the soil, and the plant enriches the soil when it decays. Rock may be shattered by root growth and acids exhuded by roots. Bacteria and small organisms are very active in hot, wet tropical climates, decomposing dead vegetation and releasing nutriments. Termites churn up the surface soils changing the local soil type and the resultant vegetation.

The Parent Rock

African soils are formed from volcanic, granitic or sedimentary rocks with smaller zones of aeolian,

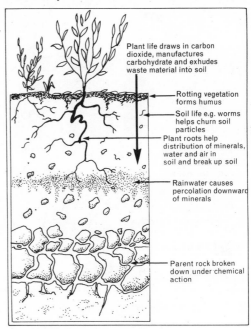

Plant life draws in carbon dioxide, manufactures carbohydrate and exhudes waste material into soil

Rotting vegetation forms humus

Soil life e.g. worms helps churn soil particles

Plant roots help distribution of minerals, water and air in soil and break up soil

Rainwater causes percolation downward of minerals

Parent rock broken down under chemical action

FIG. 69: Elements of soil formation

lacustrine or alluvial sediments. Volcanic soils are often clayey with a low quartz content; sandstone and granitic soils are high in quartz and looser in structure. This looseness assists the downward leaching processes of rain water.

Relief

In steep, mountainous areas soils are thin because of powerful erosion and thinner vegetation cover at high altitudes. In flat or undulating country soils have more time to develop and erosion is less; it is here that more mature soil profiles are found.

Time

Soil passes through periods of youth when it is thin and not properly formed, maturity when it is deep and fertile, and senility when the soil has been leached or mined of its minerals by bad farming. Deep soils retain more water and help plants and man to survive longer periods of drought.

The distribution of the major soil types of Africa is seen on the map (Fig. 1:**70**).

Four Major Soil Types of Africa
Laterite and Latosolic Soils[1]

Chiefly in equatorial and savannah regions. Heavily leached of salts and silica; upper layer contains much aluminium and iron oxides, has reddish colour. Soft soil when first exposed but sets brick-hard in hot sun. Forms above water table where constant alternate wetting and drying penetrates. Aluminium minerals may dominate surface minerals to form bauxite. A poor soil, acid and lacking mineral nutrients.

Red Loams

Another tropical soil. Well developed on rolling or dissected land with rainfalls exceeding 40 inches [1016mm] and high temperatures. Parent rock—granite, schist or sandstone. Mainly found in wetter savannah regions and not too heavily leached. Long dry seasons check effectiveness of bacteria but there is often good humus development. Colour—dark red to brown. These soils are fairly fertile; they are deficient in alumina but fairly rich in ferrous oxides and silica.

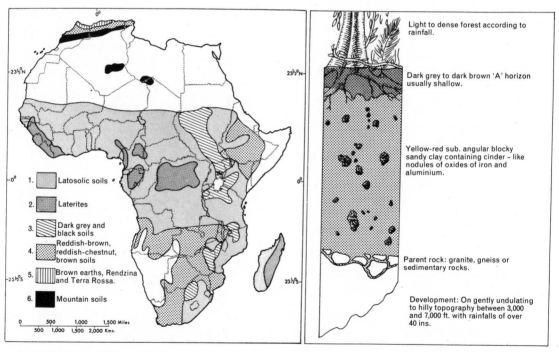

FIG. 70: Africa—simplified map of soil types

FIG. 71: A latosolic soil: sandy clay loam

[1]Laterite is harder than latosols, often forming a rock-like layer composed mainly of iron (Fe) and aluminium (Al). Some authorities describe laterisation as ferralisation.

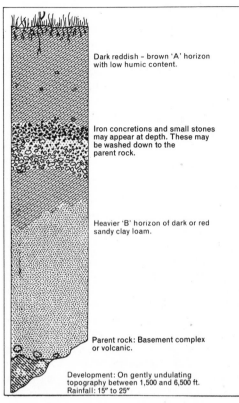

Dark reddish – brown 'A' horizon with low humic content.

Iron concretions and small stones may appear at depth. These may be washed down to the parent rock.

Heavier 'B' horizon of dark or red sandy clay loam.

Parent rock: Basement complex or volcanic.

Development: On gently undulating topography between 1,500 and 6,500 ft. Rainfall: 15″ to 25″

FIG. 72: A dark red soil

Dark Grey and Black Soils

Usually developed on flat level plains and associated with dark-coloured igneous rocks. Colour—dark grey to black. Heavy textured with high lime content in upper layers with varying proportions of phosphorous and nitrogen. Physically bad for cultivation—dried and cracked during dry seasons, sticky and heavy in rains; the best crops are pineapples and rice. Occur in areas with between 20 and 30 inches [508 and 762mm] of rain. Sometimes called *Black Cotton* but are not as rich as the chernozems of America and Russia.

Desert Soils

Shallow profiles due to absence of leaching by rainfall. Thin, stony or sandy. Colour: yellowish grey to reddish brown with no humus. High lime content. Many of these soils are aeolian in origin and thus bear little relation to the rock over which they rest. Some are very alkaline where water has evaporated

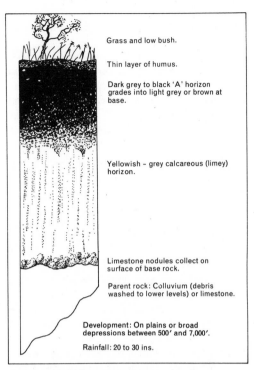

Grass and low bush.

Thin layer of humus.

Dark grey to black 'A' horizon grades into light grey or brown at base.

Yellowish – grey calcareous (limey) horizon.

Limestone nodules collect on surface of base rock.

Parent rock: Colluvium (debris washed to lower levels) or limestone.

Development: On plains or broad depressions between 500′ and 7,000′.

Rainfall: 20 to 30 ins.

FIG. 73: A black soil (black cotton)

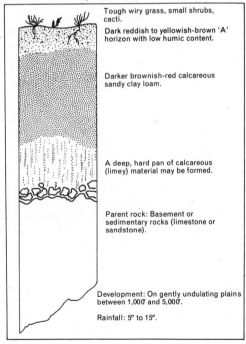

Tough wiry grass, small shrubs, cacti.

Dark reddish to yellowish-brown 'A' horizon with low humic content.

Darker brownish-red calcareous sandy clay loam.

A deep, hard pan of calcareous (limey) material may be formed.

Parent rock: Basement or sedimentary rocks (limestone or sandstone).

Development: On gently undulating plains between 1,000′ and 5,000′.

Rainfall: 5″ to 15″.

FIG. 74: A red desert soil

in pans leaving behind thick accumulations of minerals. They are of little use for cultivation unless irrigated.

Other soil types occur in smaller areas in Africa. The *Brown Earths* are dark brown in colour, loamy to sandy, are generally leached of potash and nitrogen and are only moderately fertile. The *Rendzinas* are dark brown to grey, loamy and associated with limestone regions and thus have a high lime content.

The Erosion of the Soil

The soils of Africa are not particularly rich and if food production is to be maintained this rather poor asset must be carefully protected against the action of natural forces—winds, rain and gulleying—and of man and his animals.

The Removal of Forest Cover

This action leaves the soil unprotected. In Liberia 700,000 acres of forest are burnt each year for crop clearings while in Ghana 700 square miles are cleared each year and already two-thirds of the forests have been cleared. Imagine the effect of a sudden tropical downpour on such unprotected surfaces. A one-inch fall in one square mile would release 60,000 tons of water on the soil or 100 tons per acre in a hour. Such heavy torrents occur in semi-desert areas on rare occasions and here, where there is little protective vegetation, the whole top soil may be washed away along gulleys, dongas and wadis. In the semi-desert regions of Kenya and northern Tanzania the unusual heavy November rains of 1961 created havoc with soils. The heavy falls were often fifteen times greater than the normal averages.

Overgrazing

Overgrazing by domesticated animals on the fringes of semi-desert areas helps soil erosion. In the Masai region of southern Kenya where cattle need as much as five acres each to live comfortably, only about 2·5 acres are available for each head of Masai stock and the herds of goats and sheep. The grass is first nibbled to the roots and the exposed dusty top soil is removed by wind. In Swaziland there are nearly 600,000 cattle (450,000 owned by the Swazi), nearly a quarter of a million goats and 50,000 sheep living on a land area which can only support about 450,000 cattle alone; soil erosion in this small country is an ever-present menace.

Over-cultivation

Over-cultivation will exhaust soils. In Senegambia moderately good soils have been turned into semi-desert wastes by over-cropping with groundnuts and millet; in view of declining soil fertility the Ibo-speaking farmer of southern Nigeria must reduce the number of years of fallow and give up crops which take too great a toll of soil minerals; in Eastern Nigeria small gulleys, initiated by the removal of a patch of forest for cultivation, have developed into huge scars over 500 feet deep now impossible to check. The constant growing of the same crop year after year removes the vital minerals which cannot be replaced, due to the high cost of imported artificial fertiliser. In West Africa groundnuts extract much of the phosphorus and nitrogen from the soil. Some 40,000 tons of phosphate are lost from Nigeria's northern soils by her exports of over 700,000 tons of groundnuts each year. The soils of Lesotho (Basutoland), already naturally poor due to unreliable rainfall, steep slopes and sparse vegetation cover, are being gradually destroyed by overgrazing and unchecked gulleying. In nearby Swaziland sixty-foot deep gulleys have been eroded by heavy rainstorms. Danger areas in South Africa lie in the summer rainfall zone of Natal on the eastern slopes and in the Karoo, where surface vegetation is often killed by drought leaving the surface soil unprotected against sudden thunder showers; gulleying and sheet erosion result.

Soil Conservation

Soil erosion can be checked by several methods; among the most important are afforestation, controlled grazing, irrigation, soil stabilisation, contour ploughing, planned crop rotation, herd reduction and the reduction of pastoral farming areas in semi-arid regions.

Forests planted in highland regions prevent rapid run-off, increase the amount of moisture in the atmosphere and provide a source of national wealth. Trees grow quickly in tropical regions; tall cypresses and pines grown in the *Kenya* and *Tanzania* highlands can be felled after 35 years but would take 100 years to mature in Scandinavia. Pines yield 250 cubic feet per annum compared with 50 feet in Europe. In Kenya 15,000 acres of exotic pine are planted each year and there are now over a quarter of a million acres of plantations producing £400,000 worth of soft woods annually. In *Swaziland* plantations of pine (180,000 acres) and eucalyptus (15,000 acres) in the Pigg's Peak and Mankaiana Districts provide soil protection and £2·3 million worth of wood products a year.

In timber-rich *Nigeria* (139,000 acres of forest) careful conservation is necessary, selected trees being immediately replaced with new saplings, while in *Ghana* the forest reserves of 5,600 square miles are only just sufficient to retain rainfall and prevent rapid runoff. At one time dense forests covered most of *Sierra Leone* while today only 4·5 per cent of this land is forested and forest management was introduced as early as 1911; now trees are replaced as soon as they are cut, essential on the steep slopes of this country.

In *Lesotho* (formerly Basutoland) a soil conservation programme has been in operation since 1936. Even so, soil erosion and expanding cultivation have reduced the available arable land to only 12·5 per cent of the country's area. Graded terraces, dams, water disposal spillways, and contour buffer grass strips in mountain areas are all in use. Half a million acres have been terraced, nearly 700,000 acres given buffer strips, 670 dams constructed and nearly 3 million trees planted, while livestock is controlled in communal grazing areas.

In desert areas wind breaks of palm trees surround oases to prevent soil removal and desert encroachment. Hardy shrubs are planted to bind the soil and in *Libya* surface spraying of the dunes with oil has successfully stabilised the sands.

Even so much more could be done. Many Governments have inaugurated agricultural schools and financed travelling experts to teach lessons of soil conservation to African farmers, for it is the farmer himself who is, in the end, responsible for the use or mis-use of the soil of Africa.

Questions

1 With the aid of a sketch-map, analyse the main structural divisions of Africa.
2 What is meant by the Theory of Continental Drift? What are the various proofs cited for this theory? Answer these questions with specific reference to the continent of Africa.
3 Outline the major relief features of one of the following regions of Africa, and indicate briefly their effects on the climate of the area you have chosen:
   East Africa, West Africa, North Africa or Africa south of the Zambesi.

4 Show, by means of annotated sketch-maps and diagrams only, the physical features of *three* of the following:
   (i) a lagoon coastline; (ii) a ria coastline; (iii) a coral reef coastline; (iv) a coast with sandspit development; (v) a delta coastline. All your examples should be in Africa.
5 With the aid of sketch-maps and diagrams describe the extent of the Rift Valley of Africa and discuss the theories regarding its origin.
6 With special reference to Africa, describe the land forms most commonly associated with volcanic activity.
7 Write an essay entitled 'Desert Landscapes in Africa'.
8 Comment on the character and distribution of forest in Africa.
9 Draw a large clear sketch-map to show the divisions of Africa into major climatic regions, and justify your divisions.
10 On a blank map of Africa draw the main regions of vegetation, give a brief description of the vegetation of each region and relate these to the climatic conditions.
11 What is meant by the soil profile? To what extent may variations in the soil profile be related to differences in climatic regime? Specific reference should be made to climate and soil zones in Africa.
12 Discuss the main factors, both natural and human, which lead to erosion of soil in Africa. With reference to specific work being carried on in the continent show in what ways soil erosion is being combated.
13 Figs. 1:**75**, 1:**76** and 1:**77** show climatic developments over Africa on three separate days in 1966. For each, write a description of the climatic conditions similar to that for Fig. 1:**43**, page 23.

Discussion Topics

The following is a list of topics which would provide the basis for group discussion, essays or additional notes:

1 The structure of the southern continents and their apparent relationship to one another.
2 Local weather conditions and their relationship to general climatic controls and influences affecting the climate of the country or region as a whole.
3 Which is most important in soil development—parent rock, climate or vegetation?

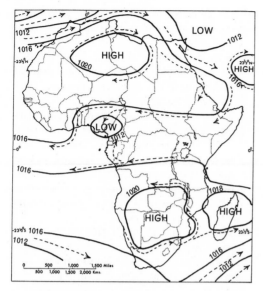

FIG. 75: Climatic exercise. Map 1

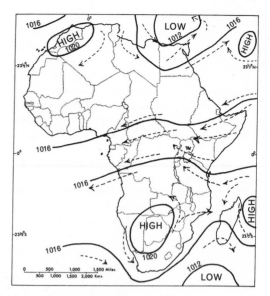

FIG. 76: Climatic exercise. Map 2

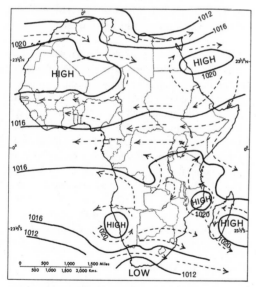

FIG. 77: Climatic exercise. Map 3

Practical Work

Examining bodies are tending more and more to attach importance to questions which demand evidence of a student's fieldwork and first-hand knowl-

edge of a subject. Typical questions on physical geography might be:

1 Discuss the soil type and vegetation of two contrasted areas with which you are familiar *in the field.*

2 Describe a soil survey which *you have personally carried out.* A large clear map is essential.

3 Describe the physical features, climate and vegetation cover and soils of any area *with which you are familiar.* Sketch-maps and diagrams are essential.

The following topics are suggested as vacation work which the student might find useful and profitable:

1 The study of local relief features—hills, rivers and coastlines. If possible the student should obtain the local geological publications for the area for an explanation of the landforms.

2 The study of local climatic factors and the collection of climatic data. This entails the use of simple meteorological instruments.

3 The digging of a section through the soil to give a soil profile. This might be done in several areas of the student's home district where the soil varies noticeably. Relate the soil profile to rainfall amount, vegetation cover and parent rock. Areas of soil erosion and conservation methods could be located and described.

CHAPTER TWO

A BRIEF HISTORICAL GEOGRAPHY OF AFRICA

The attraction of history for the geographer is that it enables him to visualise the life of man in relation to his environment at past stages of his evolution, and gives important clues to the present pattern of settlement and economic development. In this chapter we shall be concerned with the geographical aspects of man's record on the African continent— the migrations of peoples from the earliest times, their adaptation to their environments, the economic growth of powerful states, the development of trade and the growth of urban centres. Such investigation depends on the written evidence of early travellers and, because of the paucity of written records beyond the tenth century A.D., on the evidence produced by archaeologists working in Africa.

Early Man in Africa

It is becoming more and more certain that it was in Africa that man began to develop as a separate being, distinct from the animal primates by his ability to walk erect and to fashion simple tools for his own use. Discoveries on Rusinga Island in Lake Victoria by Dr Leakey have suggested that a creature called Proconsul Man dwelt there more than 25 million years ago, and that some two million years ago Zinjanthropus was fashioning crude stone tools in the Olduvai Gorge region of Tanzania. In southern Africa another tool fashioner named Australopithecus is known to have existed and there is evidence from Morocco of a more advanced being called Pithecanthropus.

A great deal of material has been discovered in East Africa where pre-historians believe that Homo Sapiens first appeared. Here, beginning about half a million years ago, archaeologists have distinguished four distinct pluvial or rainy periods roughly coinciding with the Ice Age periods of Europe; it was in the last of these, some 12,000 to 14,000 years ago, that we know that Homo Sapiens was well established in Africa as a hunter and gatherer who knew the use of fire and dwelt largely in caves. In the denser forests to the west early man was using grub-

bing sticks to gather roots, and perhaps a few simple tools to cultivate plants.

At this point in time we begin to get the emergence of different racial types among Homo Sapiens—an ancestral type of Bushman who occupied parts of the Sahara, the plateaux of the north-east, and who lived over much of southern Africa; a distinct negroid type beginning to move outwards from the forested regions; the forefathers of the Pygmy peoples whose origin may have been part negroid and part Bushman since he bore similarities to both racial stocks; and a Caucasian group which some anthropologists have termed Hamitic and who may have migrated from regions outside Africa to the north-east.[1]

The economy of these different racial groups was at first based on hunting and fishing, the latter occupation particularly among the negroid peoples who seem to have been the only ones with a resemblance to a settled way of life. But about 7,000 years ago a new phase of life was begun involving the cultivation of plants and the domestication of wild animals. In lower Egypt the change was relatively sudden and based on the fertile inundations of the Nile, but elsewhere the change was a gradual one, hunting and fishing among the negroid peoples being combined with the cultivation of a few small patches. By 4,000 B.C. a relatively densely settled area had begun to emerge in the lower Nile valley with its peoples depending on the cultivation of wheat, barley, flax and vegetables on the higher land away from the marshes and on the tending of herds of sheep, goats, pigs and cattle. There is evidence here of activities such as pottery making and linen weaving.

In the lighter woodlands of the savannah regions in central and west Africa, negroid groups were beginning to cultivate poorer cereals such as millet and rice; and at Nok in the Jos Plateau region stone tools, pottery and iron and jewelry working were

---

[1] There is still a great deal of argument regarding the classification and names of these early peoples; the word 'Hamitic' for example is used to describe both race and language.

known at least by 1,000 B.C. Basing evidence on modern language distribution, archaeologists have suggested the gradual movement outwards of Bantu-speaking peoples from a source region believed to be near the Cameroon Mts onto the surrounding plateaux, absorbing all but the remotest of the negroid and bushman stocks. These Bantu-speakers practised dry pastoralism and cultivation in wetter areas.

Ancient African Kingdoms

There is some evidence to suggest that there was a movement of negroid peoples towards *Egypt* and one school of thought believes that these migrants had some influence on the development of culture and civilisation in ancient Egypt. Certainly by 4,000 B.C. the beginnings of an organised kingdom first appeared on the African continent in the lower Nile, and this was to have a profound effect on the development of later African kingdoms. For several thousands of years the dynastic kingdom of Egypt was the centre of culture, trade, religion and political power, its ships sailing round the north-eastern coast of Africa in the quest for gold, ivory and slaves, its expeditions penetrating deeply along the Nile valley.

The influence of Egypt spread southwards along the corridor of the Nile valley to its vassal states of *Nubia* and *Kush*. The latter's power grew especially from the third century B.C. when its capital moved southwards from Napata to Meroë. Here it lay at the centre of trading routes for ivory, ebony, gold, slaves and ostrich feathers along the Nile valley and the Sudan regions to the west, and here there were large deposits of iron ore and the wood fuel to develop the iron industry. Cloth weaving and irrigation were well-known arts.

But by the middle of the first century A.D. Kush began to decline and gave way to the growth of another kingdom—*Axum (Aksum)* noted for its huge ivory market, its splendid stone buildings and monuments, its pottery manufacture, and its trade in gold, silver, camels and slaves. By the middle of the fourth century A.D., Axum's armies caused the final breakup of Kush to the north, and some historians believe that many Kushites fled to the west where they influenced the development of the great Sudanic kingdoms.

Before we discuss the Sudanic kingdoms let us consider developments in northern Africa. *Carthage*, founded by the Phoenicians and therefore non-African in origin, developed an oriental culture and acquired a semitic language which owed much to the Egyptians. Its power lay in its merchant fleets which sailed to northern Europe, the Middle East and present-day Turkey and Greece, and to the shores of West Africa, carrying cargoes of dyed cloths, skins, hides, ostrich feathers, precious metals and stones, copper and bronze.

Eventually the Phoenicians were absorbed by the *Berbers*—the inhabitants of the Maghreb or Western Lands. The name Berber is of Latin origin but the original language of the Berbers has affinities with that of the present-day Tuaregs of the Sahara. The Berbers were hunters, cultivators and nomadic pastoralists. Very few pure Berbers can be found today, due to centuries of inter-marriage with the Arabs, but many people of Berber origin still live in the higher mountainous regions of the Maghreb and in the Sahara.

Egypt and the Berber lands succumbed to the might of the *Romans*, who built towns and strategic routeways, ports and aqueducts, bridges and archways throughout the northern coastlands of Africa. Christianity followed them but the whole was later swamped by the *Arabic invasions* from the east, first of Egypt in the seventh century A.D. and then the whole of North Africa in the eighth. The influence of these peoples was thus superimposed on the earlier cultures and within Africa itself an Arabic culture developed, more associated with the mixture of peoples in North Africa and with Spanish influence than a pure product of the east. Even today there remain fundamental differences between the Arabs of the Maghreb and those of Egypt.

Between approximately the fifth century and the sixteenth century several organised kingdoms waxed and waned in the Sudanic regions of West Africa. These kingdoms were often quite large, sometimes containing over a million people of different origins and speaking different tongues, but generally ruled by one strong group who controlled the central core of the empire and held sway by military superiority over a vast outlying area of subjugated peoples; their external boundaries were often ill-defined.

Ancient Ghana, whose last capital was centred on Kumbi Saleh, was the first powerful state to make its appearance in West Africa. There is much evidence to show that this kingdom's cultural and political

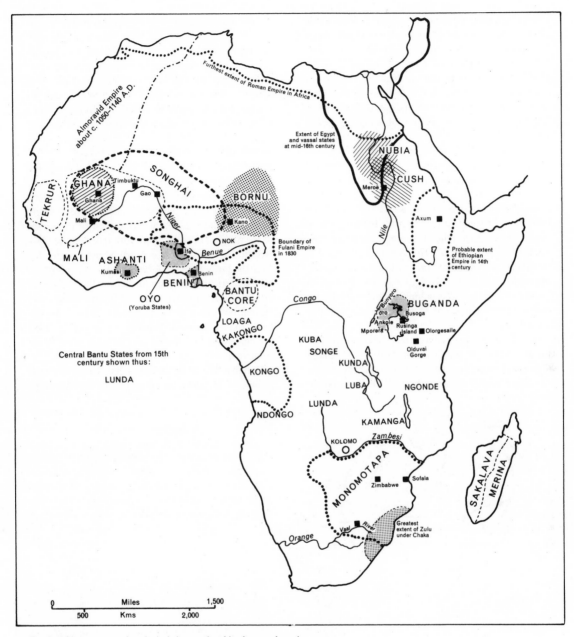

Fig. 1: Africa—some archaeological sites, ancient kingdoms and empires

history extended back to the fourth or fifth century A.D., although the first written record occurs in the work of an eighth-century Arab author. At first Ghana developed as a loose confederacy of states lying between the Senegal and the upper Niger, its ill-defined boundaries expanding and contracting in response to its changing fortunes. Certainly by the eighth century, and probably before, Ghana had become an important commercial centre, peopled by traders and sedentary cultivators. Through trade

43

Ghana acquired tremendous wealth, which made possible the formation of large well-equipped armies to further extend its empire. For hundreds of years its stable government was based on the profits of the trade with nations to the north in gold, precious stones, kola and slaves and with those to the south in salt, and also in other commodities such as copper and iron. A system of taxation operated for goods leaving and entering the country, and Ghana's commercial interests spread as far as Morocco.

The contacts with North Africa helped the spread of Islam throughout Ghana in the tenth century, until, weakened by internal struggles over the division of spoils and revenues, and hard hit by the disruption of trade with the north, the capital city eventually fell to the invading Muslims (the Almoravid Berbers) in 1076. A series of droughts weakened the resistance of the fast-decaying empire, and it had virtually ceased to exist by the twelfth century. There was to be a long period of confusion before the foundation of Mali brought more stable conditions.

The decline of the Ghana empire was accompanied by the increase in power of the *Mali* (or *Manding*) *kingdom*, whose first ruler came from the small state of Kangaba, near the head waters of the River Niger.

By the mid-thirteenth century Mali's power was at its zenith; its capital lay at Niani on the left bank of the Niger which had been the capital of Kangaba. Under Mansa Musa, Sundiata's even more illustrious successor, the Mali empire grew to enclose Jenne, Timbuktu and Gao, and its power and influence was widespread. Trading caravans came from as far as the Maghreb, Ethiopia, Libya and Egypt, and Timbuktu and Jenne became great centres of Muslim scholarship. But those who followed Mansa Musa were unable to harness the power of the empire he had built, and control the rivalries among the member states that had been absorbed into it. In the fifteenth century Mali began to decline and eventually succumbed to the power of the *Songhai* or *Gao empire* with its capital at Gao. By the early sixteenth century Songhai extended over the former area of Ghana and into parts of the Hausa territories of present-day northern Nigeria. Organised armies, extensive trade and progressive agriculture brought great stability to Gao. By the time that Columbus reached America in 1492 Songhai was established as the dominant West African power.

Songhai flourished for about 200 years, before the Moroccan invaders, equipped for the first time on a

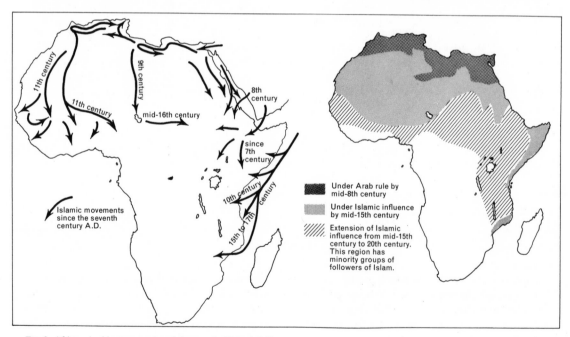

FIG. 2: Africa—Arabic movements and the spread of Islamic influence

44

large scale with firearms, and aided by internal dissensions, swept through Timbuktu and Gao at the end of the sixteenth century, although guerrilla resistance continued throughout the former empire, contributing to the disruption of organised government for many years. There is also little doubt that the encroachment of the slave traders in the south about this time also played a part in Songhai's downfall and the subsequent confusion. By the end of the sixteenth century the last of the great mediaeval empires in the savannah zone had disappeared, to be replaced by a number of minor states of the Hausa and Kanuri (from Bornu), the Mossi and Bambara, which had already been significant before the fall of Songhai, and many of which later came under the control of the Fulani.

From the tenth century onwards centres of strong government developed in the dense forest zone of West Africa. Here the forces of Islam feared to penetrate an environment unsuited to methods of warfare which had evolved in the open savannah. They had come to rely on the superiority of cavalry over infantry, but in the forested areas, not only was the movement of horsemen restricted, but it was difficult to obtain fodder for the horses, who quickly fell prey to the sleeping sickness carried by the tsetse fly. This was an important factor in limiting the extent of the various Sudanic empires and the areas controlled by invaders, as examination of an atlas will readily confirm. In the forests, kingdoms based on urban organisation in large heavily defended cities and towns developed—*Oyo* which flourished from the tenth century onwards and reached the height of its powers in the seventeenth and early eighteenth centuries, and *Benin*, which reached its zenith in the sixteenth and seventeenth centuries and whose king was reputed to be able to raise an army of at least 100,000 men. The economy of Benin rested on its exports of cloth, beads and various luxuries, as well as the trade in slaves, although this of course did not develop until the sixteenth century.

Another great independent kingdom which developed during the late eighteenth and early nineteenth centuries was *Ashanti* with its capital of Kumasi. Its power was based on its huge trade in gold, slaves and kola and its well-organised army. The collapse of Ashanti in the nineteenth century was due partly to the inherent weaknesses of the provincial system of administration, which had never fully incorporated vassal states into the empire and given them a sense

of allegiance to it. More important still was the intervention of the British, which resulted in the destruction of the empire's military strength.

South of the equator our information regarding the ancient African kingdoms is so far less full. The *Kongo Kingdom* was the most important of several states in the Congo Basin and was well known to the Portuguese. The date of the Kongo's foundation is not certain, possibly some time in the thirteenth century, but it is known that the state was well-organised and sent ambassadors to Europe. It possessed a small well-trained army, a system of taxation collection and several industries—iron and copper smelting, palm oil extraction, boat building, pottery making and weaving. The fostering of the slave trade, intrigues and internal wars among its peoples by the Portuguese greatly contributed to the decline of the Kingdom of Kongo.

In the present-day area of Rhodesia it is known that another great nation existed, probably centred on Zimbabwe and its people the ancestors of the Mashona. The nation was a confederacy of small 'states'—the *Makalanga Empire*, or the empire of Monomotapa as the Portuguese named it on their maps. In the early sixteenth century the empire entered into trade with the Portuguese (who took over trading interests from the Arabs) through Swahili 'middlemen' who brought gold, ivory and slaves down to the port of Sofala in exchange for cotton textiles and beads. This trade was, however, interrupted by the constant clashes between Bantu tribes in the interior. At its greatest extent the Makalanga Kingdom is believed to have extended from the coast as far inland as the Okavango Basin and as far south as the Orange and Vaal Rivers.

In this southern lobe of Africa, records are obscured by the waves of *Bantu* invasions which swept southwards from the central regions of Africa. These movements began about the beginning of the Christian era and, by about the eleventh century, loosely organised tribal confederations were developing, their economy based largely on pastoral farming. By the end of the seventeenth century the pastoral Bantu were firmly settled on the high veld and the loose tribal associations had been welded into small but powerful nations. But under the incursions of the European, the Zulu and the Matabele, the nations of the veld Bantu began to disintegrate. From the ensuing chaos at least one national identity was preserved—that of the Basuto peoples whose leader Moshesh gathered his followers together in the Basuto Highlands and accepted British protection for the small state, now called Lesotho, before his death in 1870.

Other great kingdoms of the interior include the well-organised *Kingdom of Buganda*, discovered by the early explorers as the seat of power in Uganda and surrounded by several smaller states—Toro, Bunyoro, Ankole and Busoga—which had experienced similar power in previous years.

Some Great Cities of the Past

Before we discuss the external influences on Africa's more recent history we should, as geographers, take note of some of the great urban centres which flourished in Africa. *Meroë*, for example, the capital of Kush, was a flourishing city some two thousand years ago. It grew in importance as a political centre when the capital was moved from Napata, and it was a noted iron mining and smelting centre. Meroë also lay close to the caravan routes along the Atbara corridor, from the north to Ethiopia and to the ports along the Indian Ocean. Meroë's iron products were exchanged for silks and bronzes from China, for cotton goods from India, and for the products of Arabia. By the first century B.C. Meroë was a city with thick-walled palaces and pyramids decorated with mural paintings.

In the ancient Sudanese kingdoms in West Africa the towns and cities grew as trading centres, and centres of administration and defence. *Audaghost*, now long vanished, lay at the southern terminal of trans-Saharan caravan routes. When discovered by the Arabs it was a very large city with large fine public buildings, several markets and surrounded by date palm groves. In 1076 the Almoravids took *Kumbi Saleh*, the capital of Ghana. From their reports it appears that Kumbi consisted of two towns some distance apart but connected by housing which had spread between them. One citadel was the royal seat of the king enclosed by a defensive wall, while the other was the commercial sector containing the Muslim market and warehouses. The city covered approximately one square mile and had a population of about 30,000—a very large city for those days. It was an entrepôt for the salt and copper from the north and the gold from the headwaters of the Senegal. Glass, Mediterranean pottery, agricultural tools, iron spears, nails, knives and lances

found at the site indicate the nature of trade. Taxes were levied on all goods leaving and entering the city walls.

Although *Timbuktu* never became the centre of an important state or empire because it was too vulnerable to the attacks of Saharan raiders, it had become by the twelfth century a trading centre of great importance, and it lasted much longer than other cities founded at approximately the same time in the west. Salt, gold, copper and slaves were again the basis of commerce and the city had many court buildings and numerous commercial warehouses. Silk cloth, refined weapons, horses and camels were brought here from the Mediterranean and deserts to the north, and kola nuts from the forest zones of the south. By the fifteenth century it was also renowned as a centre of learning and scholarship. Today the city that was once one of the key points of the ancient Mali empire is part of the modern Republic of Mali.

Kano was another great trading centre at the terminus of trans-Saharan routes. It has been well described as it was in the mid-nineteenth century, that is, before the coming of the colonisers, by Heinrich Barth, the German explorer. He estimated the population to be about 30,000 in 1855 and noted that the wall enclosed a very large area, probably to give protection to people from without in times of trouble. Between January and April, the busiest time of the year, the population swelled to 60,000. The cotton and cloth woven and dyed in Kano was carried by camel to Timbuktu (Barth estimated this trade as 300 camel loads annually), to Ghat, Ghadames and Tuat. Shoes, leather sandals and twisted leather straps made in Kano were exported across the Sahara to North Africa, while tanned hides and dyed sheepskins were sent to Tripoli. The kola nut was imported from the south in large quantities—five hundred ass-loads a year—and natron (sodium carbonate) and salt were important commodities which provided employment for many people.

Descriptions of the forest cities to the south are few. *Benin*, according to one description, was the largest city in the southern regions of Nigeria in the late seventeenth century. The palace quarter was separated from the main town but the whole was enclosed by a ten foot high wall of stakes with several gates. The city is said to have had a perimeter of eight leagues (about 23 miles). There were thirty main streets with many intersecting streets, the buildings being one-storied structures of wood. Benin was centrally situated for the administration of the Benin state and was close enough to the distributaries of the Niger to control much of the trade with European merchants through its outport at Gotton. Cotton cloth manufactured in the city, together with coral, slaves, jasper stones, leopard skins and pepper were exchanged for velvet, brass bracelets, beads, mirrors, iron bars, printed cloths, crystal beads and citrus fruits.

Much conjecture surrounds the origins of *Zimbabwe*, the mediaeval city of Monomotapa, but the evidence sifted so far seems to suggest that this was a great Bantu capital which was first developed in the eleventh century A.D. (although iron working people had probably lived there since the seventh century), and which later became the greatest of a string of settlements from central to southern Africa. It may have been the centre of a vast mineral empire of gold, copper, tin and iron workings which spread in their thousands from present-day Katanga to Botswana and Natal. Its trade dealt in these minerals and also in slaves, salt, cloth, ivory and other luxury goods from China and India, and articles of trade brought by the Portuguese to the port of Sofala.

These are but a few of the great urban developments of Old Africa which flourished in the distant past. Many other examples are to be found throughout northern Africa and along the eastern coasts.

Obstacles to Foreign Penetration

The existence of such well-organised kingdoms in Africa did much to prevent penetration of the interior by European and Arab traders and travellers. Although the coasts were well charted by the early eighteenth century, much of the interior was practically unknown to outsiders. It is not hard to find reasons for this lack of knowledge. The coasts were bordered by harsh deserts, swamps and dense forests and there was little to attract the fleeting voyager who stopped only to take on water and fresh fruit or to make minor repairs. Moreover, the coastline had few deep inlets to allow vessels to penetrate deeply inland without risk of attack. There were few harbours and many hazardous sand-bars, coral reefs and off-shore winds. The major rivers were often impassable for large vessels, due to falls and rapids.

It is often stated that the penetration of the interior was also hindered by tropical diseases and the lack of organised routes. But Europeans were at this time successfully settling in similar environments in the Caribbean, in South America and in parts of Asia. Again, Africa at the time of first colonisation was much more thickly populated than was say, North America or Brazil, and the continent was crossed by many well-tried routes.

But the main obstacle to inland penetration was provided by the people of Africa themselves. The coastal Africans were usually hostile, associating the explorer with the slave trader. Wherever slave trading flourished, as along the coasts of East Africa, the trader (usually an Arab) discouraged any settlement which might reduce his influence. Certainly in West Africa it was the unshakable determination of the well-organised and powerful African states to brook no interference in their internal affairs which prevented inland penetration by foreigners for so long.

Early Traders

It is well known that long before the Portuguese set foot on the African continent, organised trade was flourishing along the coasts. There were contacts with the Middle East, India, Indonesia and even mainland China soon after the dawn of the Christian era. In fact the first known reference to the slave trade appears in the *Periplus of the Erythrean Sea*, a Greek chronicle of the eastern seas, in 60 B.C., which states that slaves were the most important commercial article of the coasts of eastern Africa.

The *Arabs* themselves had begun settling along the East African coast as early as the first century A.D. and under them the slave trade flourished. Slave routes ran into the highlands and to the borders of the Congo and large slave markets were at various stages established at Bagamoyo, Kilwa, Mombasa, Malindi, Mogadishu and Mozambique. Again, their true power did not extend very far inland but lay in the small kingdoms and principalities along the coast, each with its fortified town. Industry was encouraged—the minting of coins, weaving, pottery making, wood and ivory carving, and leather working; trade grew in gold, slaves, skins, rhinoceros horn, ivory and ebony; and agriculture was fostered—sheep and cattle rearing and the cultivation of tropical fruits. But these activities were largely confined to the coasts.

The *Portuguese* were also content to set up their trading posts and forts along the coasts and nowhere did their control extend more than a few miles inland, except in Mashonaland where, in the seventeenth century, their traders safely traversed the lands of Monomotapa in their quest for gold and slaves. But north of Cape Delgado on the eastern coast the Portuguese had only a tenuous hold, and here their interests met with the opposition of the Arabs. Their most northerly stronghold of power lay at Fort Jesus, Mombasa, which succumbed to the forces of Oman in 1698.

European Travellers

The Portuguese, however, made a decided contribution to western Europe's knowledge of the geography of the African continent, particularly its coasts. They occupied Septa (now Ceuta) in 1413, discovered the Madeira Islands in 1418 and the Azores in 1432, and rounded Cape Bojador in 1435. In 1488 Bartholomew Dias sailed past the mouths of the Niger and landed at Mossel Bay, having reached the southernmost tip of Africa. Vasco da Gama, seeking a direct trade route from Europe to the Far East, landed at St Helena Bay in 1497 and sailed on to Mossel Bay. From there he skirted the eastern coasts, anchoring first in Mozambique Harbour and then at Mombasa in 1498, where he clashed with the Arabs. He visited Malindi and proceeded to Calicut on the south-west coast of India, which was his main objective.

The *Dutch*, too, were early travellers in Africa, their first settlement being made at the Cape by Jan van Riebeeck in 1652. More settlers arrived in 1684 and began to move outwards from the Cape. In 1685 an expedition under Simon van der Stel discovered the Copper Mts, but it was not until the Great Trek of 1835 that considerable exploration and settlement of the interior began.

The late eighteenth and the nineteenth centuries saw increasing European penetration into the interior of Africa. It is impossible here to give a detailed account of the journeys of individual travellers, but the main routes covered are shown on the map (Fig. 2:3).

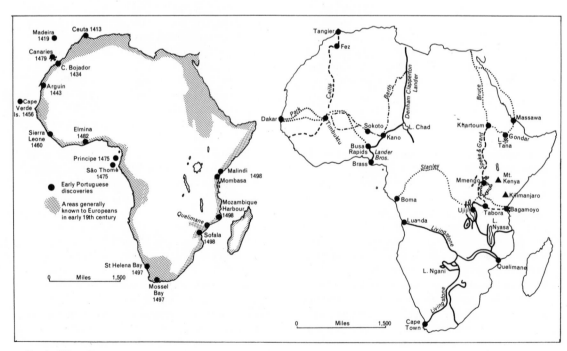

FIG. 3: Africa—European penetration

European Colonisation

These journeys heightened Europe's interest in the African continent and within the space of the next thirty years Africa came swifty under the political and economic control of the western European nations. The reasons for this rapid intervention at such a comparatively late date are numerous and intricate. Among the more important of them are:

1 *A desire for economic expansion.* Europe needed overseas resources and markets for her growing industries, and each country was spurred on by the interests of its rivals and the fear of being left out of a settlement.

2 *Political expansion* overseas and the extension of European culture were considered by some states, particularly France, to be essential to the full development of nationhood.

3 *The influence of missionaries* and reformers who realised that only government intervention could effectively suppress the slave trade, spread ideas of Christianity, and develop economic conditions for the benefit of both European settlers and Africans.

4 *The protection of nationals.* European governments considered they needed to 'protect' their nationals in Africa at mission stations and mineral workings, safeguard their trading interests and to protect vital communications.

5 *The greater knowledge of the geography* of Africa provided by the travellers, and the greater accessibility of the continent brought about by the opening of the Suez Canal in 1869 and the increased speed of the new ships.

By 1879 European politics were spreading into Africa. The interest of Belgium and Germany in acquiring territory in Africa caused a feverish scramble for land by Britain, France, Italy, Spain and Portugal. At the Berlin Conference of 1884 the spheres of interest of these countries were agreed on, but it was not until 1891 that they were finally settled and even then many clashes still occurred. Britain and France nearly went to war over the Sudan and Cecil Rhodes had many running flights with the Matabele and the Portuguese. Rhodes' ambition was to see Britain as the leading colonial power in a broad region from north to south Africa, and for this reason he took control of Bechuanaland to counter German moves in South-West Africa, and he attempted to gain control of the mineral wealth of the Boer Republic in the Transvaal, an

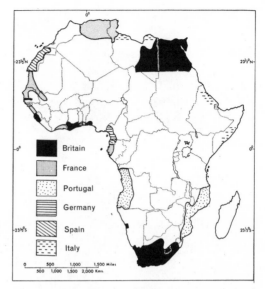

FIG. 4: European spheres of influence in Africa prior to the Berlin Conference of 1884

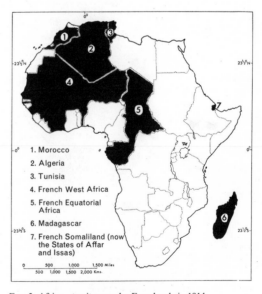

FIG. 5: Africa—territory under French rule in 1914

act which was eventually to lead to the outbreak of the Boer War in 1899. The occupation of Morocco by the French and of Libya by the Italians in 1911 ended the carving up of Africa between the European powers. Only Ethiopia and Liberia remained as independent nations.

49

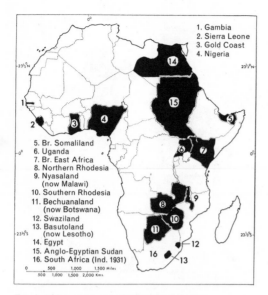

1. Gambia
2. Sierra Leone
3. Gold Coast
4. Nigeria

5. Br. Somaliland
6. Uganda
7. Br. East Africa
8. Northern Rhodesia
9. Nyasaland
   (now Malawi)
10. Southern Rhodesia
11. Bechuanaland
    (now Botswana)
12. Swaziland
13. Basutoland
    (now Lesotho)
14. Egypt
15. Anglo-Egyptian Sudan
16. South Africa (Ind. 1931)

FIG. 6: Africa—territory under British rule in 1914

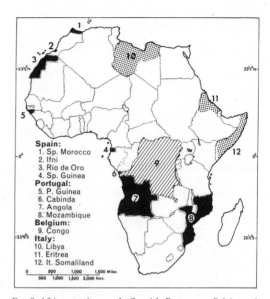

Spain:
1. Sp. Morocco
2. Ifni
3. Rio de Oro
4. Sp. Guinea
Portugal:
5. P. Guinea
6. Cabinda
7. Angola
8. Mozambique
Belgium:
9. Congo
Italy:
10. Libya
11. Eritrea
12. It. Somaliland

FIG. 8: Africa—territory under Spanish, Portuguese, Belgian and Italian rule in 1914

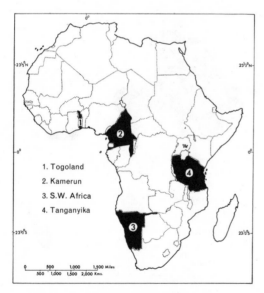

1. Togoland

2. Kamerun

3. S.W. Africa

4. Tanganyika

FIG. 7: Africa—territory under German rule in 1914

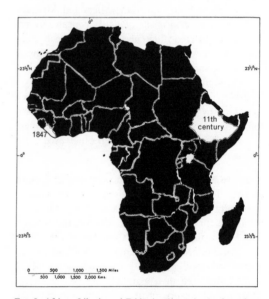

FIG. 9: Africa—Liberia and Ethiopia, the territories free of external political rule in 1914

The African colonies became symbols of European power in Africa. The Europeans soon came to the conclusion that, to maintain effective control, permanent administration based on a good communications network was essential. For this money was needed and to obtain revenue for deve-lopment they introduced new crops, stimulated European settlement, obtained the sale of mineral and land rights to individuals[1] and big companies,

[1] The 'selling' of land rights was often a direct contravention of the land tenure system known to Africans in many areas.

and improved communications. The railways became the key to effective administration, at least in easily accessible areas, and to the successful economic development and the ease of military operations in times of local resistance.

By 1914 the pattern of colonial government was already hardening. Policies differed, however, from one territory to another; the British favoured governing through chiefs while the French and Belgians largely replaced the traditional leaders with men of their own choosing. Portuguese, French and Italian possessions were considered as parts of the ruling country and in theory their inhabitants could claim to be citizens of Portugal, France or Italy, although in practice full citizenship rights were only granted to a selected few. In the British-ruled territories of East, Central and South Africa, settlement by Britons was encouraged, the settlers being expected to play an active part in the economic and political development of the country. This policy worked only in Rhodesia, where the European element built up tremendous power and dominated both the political and economic spheres of the country. In Kenya the European (mainly British) farming community, although much smaller in numbers than that in Rhodesia, also had an effective voice in the government, but its policies often clashed with those of the official colonial administration. Eventually this European minority was too small to have a significant effect upon official policy and the move to independence under African rule, but for two decades it posed a serious problem for the colonial government.

In contrast the European has come to dominate the economic and political life of South Africa where, since the seventeenth century, Europeans of Dutch and British ancestry have settled in large numbers. Since the end of the nineteenth century they have organised the African labour and natural resources of the region to found a powerful nation. The Afrikaners are a people who have forgotten much of their Dutch ancestry and do not regard themselves as having any ties with Europe.

The 1914–18 War produced several changes to the political map of Africa. Germany's ideas on running a colony were never allowed to develop, for by the Treaty of Versailles she was shorn of her African possessions by the victorious European powers, her rivals in Africa. Germany was thus the first major power to be forced out of Africa. South-West Africa became a mandated territory under South Africa, Togoland and the Cameroons were divided between the British and the French, and German East Africa was partitioned, Tanganyika and Rwanda Urundi becoming mandated territories under Britain and Belgium respectively.

Economic Trends

The inter-war period saw increasing activity by the European powers in the exploitation of Africa's resources, particularly her minerals. European farmers had evolved new methods, railways and roads were extended into remote areas to open them up for production and trade, and great investments were made in the extractive industries. The greatest economic development was in the south, where roads were planned to form a network to serve the mineral workings of the Rand, Katanga and Rhodesia. These mining areas became magnets for the emerging force of African industrial workers. But the pace of secondary industrial development in the colonies, as we shall see later, failed to keep up with that of the extractive industries. By the 1930s the African territories were still largely suppliers of raw materials or processed raw materials to the industrial nations of the world.

The Second World War (1939–45) resulted in the exclusion of Italy from Ethiopia (1941) and later her withdrawal from Libya (1951) and Eritrea, although she was allowed as a mandatory power in Somaliland for a further ten years. The war stimulated production in the mining, secondary industrial and agricultural spheres. The mining industries of the Congo and what is now Zambia were expanded, the latter country leaping to importance with its vast resources of copper. This boom extended itself into the post-war years, especially in southern Africa, and the trend has been to invest more capital into the development of secondary industries (see Chapter Nine). The trend in agriculture is to diversify and avoid too great a dependence on single crops such as coffee and cocoa which are frequently subject to the vicissitudes of the world market.

Recent Trends

The 1950s saw the development of several political trends in Africa. First, many of the former colonial territories have achieved their independence; secondly, the post-war years have seen the emergence of the Arab-speaking North African bloc; thirdly, there has been a deeper entrenchment of European power south of the Zambesi in Rhodesia, the Portuguese territories and South Africa, where any move to majority rule has been vigorously resisted.

The last fifteen years have seen the emergence of thirty new nations in Africa. It is as yet too early to predict whether these nations will continue in their present form. Africa is a continent which has been subject to outside pressures and influences since the earliest times of the Arab influx, and more so during this present century. Will these new nations succumb to new forms of exploitation or become spheres of interest and influence for external forces? These questions can only be answered by the geographers and historians of the future. Many African nations are rightly suspicious of any offers of aid from external sources and fear a more subtle form of exploitation, a fear which has led to a general policy of non-alignment.

This does not necessarily mean, however, that the nations of Europe should play a decreasing rôle in the economic development of Africa. On the contrary, the two continents have many incentives to encourage mutual co-operation in seeking solutions to their respective economic problems. Of all the world's continents they are the two which have had the greatest contact with one another down the ages, geographically they lie close to each other, while over seventy years of colonial rule have left their imprint on the laws, administration, culture and language of the new African states, and on the pattern of development of their social services. Moreover, 60 per cent of Africa's trade is with Europe.

Yet the closer association between these two continents should not be between individual nations, but should take place within the framework of regional organisations (see Chapter Eleven) so that no one country can dominate another. This aid on a regional basis has been advocated by the Council of Europe since 1957, but its inception presupposes closer co-operation between the nations of Europe themselves.

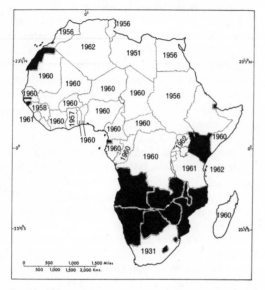

Fig. 10: Africa—territories free of external political rule in 1962

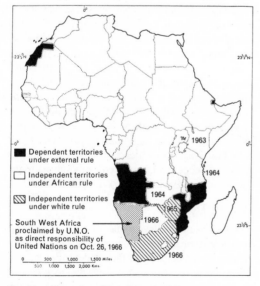

Fig. 11: Africa—the political picture in 1968

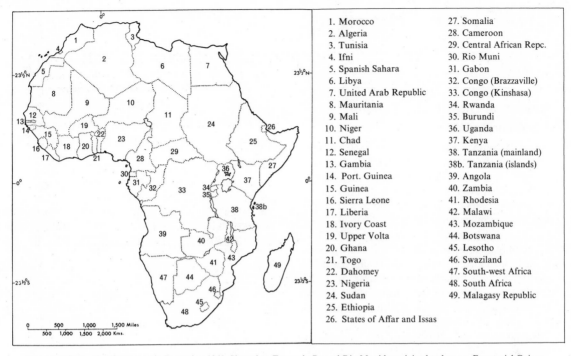

1. Morocco	27. Somalia
2. Algeria	28. Cameroon
3. Tunisia	29. Central African Repc.
4. Ifni	30. Rio Muni
5. Spanish Sahara	31. Gabon
6. Libya	32. Congo (Brazzaville)
7. United Arab Republic	33. Congo (Kinshasa)
8. Mauritania	34. Rwanda
9. Mali	35. Burundi
10. Niger	36. Uganda
11. Chad	37. Kenya
12. Senegal	38. Tanzania (mainland)
13. Gambia	38b. Tanzania (islands)
14. Port. Guinea	39. Angola
15. Guinea	40. Zambia
16. Sierra Leone	41. Rhodesia
17. Liberia	42. Malawi
18. Ivory Coast	43. Mozambique
19. Upper Volta	44. Botswana
20. Ghana	45. Lesotho
21. Togo	46. Swaziland
22. Dahomey	47. South-west Africa
23. Nigeria	48. South Africa
24. Sudan	49. Malagasy Republic
25. Ethiopia	
26. States of Affar and Issas	

FIG. 12: Africa—the 49 states as in December 1968. Since then Fernando Po and Rio Muni have joined to become Equatorial Guinea

CHAPTER THREE

POPULATION—ITS GROWTH, STRUCTURE AND DISTRIBUTION

Population Growth and Structure
Population Estimates

A United Nations estimate made in 1960 put the population of Africa at 254 million. With an estimated annual increase of 1·25 million the figures for 1968 stands at 264·0 million (nearly 10 per cent of the world's total population). Spread over Africa's area of 11·7 million square miles this gives an average density of just over 22·5 per square mile. This is certainly not dense when compared with the United Kingdom (577 per square mile) or, on a more continental scale, with the United States (55) and it is roughly equivalent to the density in the Soviet Union (26) and much greater than that of Australia (3·8).

But estimates of the population of Africa are extremely unreliable. Any enumeration of the population in Africa has always been regarded with suspicion as it usually preceded more efficient tax collection and in many remote areas the population was merely guessed at. Even the more recent censuses cannot be exactly accurate. In the Portuguese-ruled territories the main method is 'census by assembly' in which all the people of a certain district are told to assemble at a certain spot at a given time and they are there counted. Such a method was used in Uganda in the census of 1931 which was used as a basis for later estimates; the estimate for 1947 gave the figure of 4,063,000 but the 1948 census showed it to be 4,993,965—almost a million more. In Kenya a 1962 estimate judged the population to be approximately 6·8 million but the census of that year revealed it as 8·6 million, a tremendous difference in a country where people are relatively easily accessible. It was not until the early 1930s that British colonial territories received anything approaching adequate censuses, but since 1945 attempts have been made in practically every African country to produce reliable counts, essential to modern economic planning.

The Growth of the Population

Estimates of Africa's population must therefore be taken with reserve. It appears, however, that in 1650 (that is, before the immigration of Europeans and Asians) the population was about 100,000,000 but 200 years later in 1850 it had dropped to 95,000,000. Inter-tribal warfare, the slave trade, war against the colonisers and new infectious diseases account for this decline. By the turn of the century it had probably returned to the 100 million mark. Since then the rise has been steady (Fig. 3:1) to 140,000,000 in 1930, over 175,000,000 in 1940 and nearly 200,000,000 in 1950. This rapid rise is due to

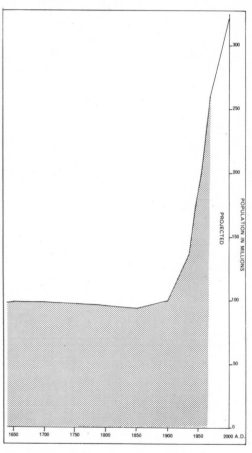

FIG. 1: The growth of Africa's population

better conditions of living, higher standards of hygiene and medical care, and improvements in diets and child welfare. While these things are welcome, the increasing population in many African countries is already beginning to create serious problems for the governments.

The Structure of the Population

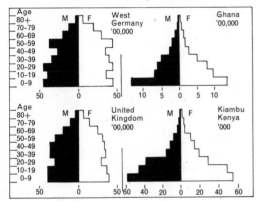

FIG. 2: Population structures from Europe and Africa

Fig. 3:**2** shows the population structure of two industrial countries of Western Europe, a developing country—Ghana, and a district in Kenya. These population structure diagrams illustrate very clearly the differences produced by economic conditions and historical factors.

In West Germany and the United Kingdom the structure diagram is fairly even all the way up until the age of 60 is reached and then there is a decided tapering off. In the United Kingdom the effect of the lower birth rates during the Second World War is clearly seen in the 20 to 29 age groups. In this type of structure it is clear that the working force (from say, 18 to 60) is in excess of or at least equal to those who are dependent.

Both Ghana and the Kiambu District of Kenya display population structures which are typical of the developing nations in Africa which are experiencing a rapid expansion of population growth due to increasing birth rates and improving medical facilities. Thus there is a very broad base to these diagrams where the numbers of children and young dependents far exceed those in any other age group. These dependents produce nothing because they are not working; moreover, they must be supported by the smaller working group.

Another factor must also be considered and that is the average expectancy of life in the developing nations (Fig. 3:**3**). The expectancy in the Congo (K),

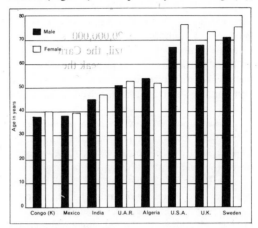

FIG. 3: Bar graph of life expectancy in selected countries

the U.A.R. and Algeria is seen to be about 20 years less than that of Sweden, the U.S.A. and the U.K. This means that the length of productivity of the average worker is shortened and that many within the dependent sector either have short or even no productive life.

The detrimental effect of this population imbalance to the economy of many developing countries is obvious. Enlightened African governments are tackling this problem from several angles—by encouraging the limitation of family size, by extending medical facilities to the older productive sections of the community and improving their working conditions generally, and by ensuring the health of junior age groups so that their active life is lengthened and they become an asset to the nation for a longer period in their adult years.

Population Migrations

We have seen in Chapter Two that the first large population migration to affect Africa was that of the *Arabs* or Semites who flooded northern Africa in the seventh and eighth centuries and penetrated into Spain between the eleventh and fourteenth centuries. They spread their religion and language throughout northern Africa and the Sahara, intermingling with the native Berber tribes of the Maghreb until the two became indistinguishable. People of Arabic blood in Africa number approximately 60 million.

At the beginning of the sixteenth century, however, Africa suffered great reductions in its native population due to the *slave trade*. The trade reached its peak in West Africa in the late eighteenth and early nineteenth centuries. It is estimated that from West Africa alone some 20,000,000 slaves were taken to plantations in Brazil, the Caribbean and southern North America. At its peak the great slave market in Zanzibar handled some 15,000 slaves each year for trans-shipment to the Middle East and India.

The beginnings of true *European settlement* in Africa were seen in the Dutch settlements of the Cape region from 1652 onwards and these were followed by the British settlers in the late eighteenth century. Between 1836 and 1846 the Boers migrated northwards to escape British rule (the Great Trek). Today, people of European descent in South Africa number 3·5 million, the largest single white group on the continent. Immigration into South Africa by Europeans reached 40,000 in 1965 and 48,000 in 1966.

Settlement in the Cape was paralleled by French movements into Algeria, especially after 1830. The French government encouraged emigration and by 1848 some 40,000 French had settled in Algeria. This figure had reached nearly two millions by the early 1950s. In Tunisia there were about 200,000 Europeans, mostly French at this period, and in Morocco 325,000.

Europeans spread to East and Central Africa at a later date, from about 1880 onwards, attracted by mineral discoveries and grants of good farming land. By 1960 nearly 300,000 had settled in Rhodesia and Zambia and nearly 100,000 in East Africa.

The last seventy years have also seen the steady influx of *Asians* from the Indian sub-continent, although this has been curtailed by law. There are some 350,000 Asians in East Africa and 525,000 in South Africa. The first Asian migrations to Africa began with the need for labour in the sugar plantations of Natal and skilled labour for the construction of railways in East Africa. Later influxes were due to the attraction of better standards of living and the commercial prospects in new markets.

Recent years have seen the *reversal of immigration trends*. With the granting of independence to African states many Europeans and Asians have returned to their former homelands. In Algeria the European population has dropped to under 170,000,

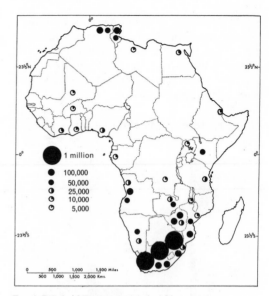

FIG. 4: People of European origin in Africa

in Kenya from nearly 66,000 in 1960 to 41,000 in 1968. This is due to the departure of farming communities who have been bought out in land resettlement schemes; in East Africa they are being replaced temporarily by officials, teachers, administrators, and businessmen. In many countries the old countries' representatives are being out numbered by whites from Russia, U.S.A., Israel, Germany, and eastern European countries as well as Chinese and Japanese businessmen and diplomats.

Considerable movement also takes place within Africa (Fig. 3:**5**). Many towns in Africa have large populations of African workers who are attracted by the good wages in industry (see pages 115 and 182). They try to save enough to buy land and then return to their original rural district. Eventually, however, many decide to stay in the towns. The Rand is a good example of this attraction to industry, for the mines and secondary industries attract Africans from Malawi, Rhodesia, Zambia, Botswana, Lesotho and Tanzania (page 182). In Kenya the main areas of attraction are the central highlands and the coast; in Nigeria the industrially developing coastal regions and, to a lesser extent, the Jos and Bauchi mining areas; in Zambia and Katanga, the Copper Belt; in Ghana the southern industrial towns and the cocoa belt; in Algeria there have been migrations from rural areas to France, and in Libya from oases to oilfields.

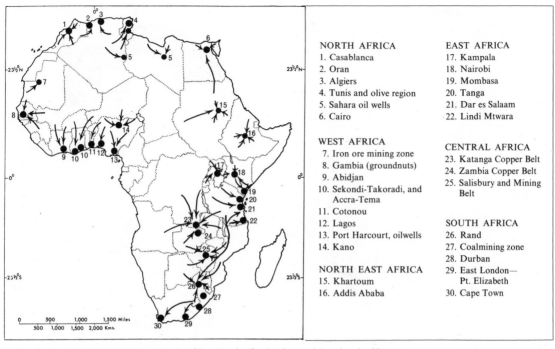

FIG. 5: Internal migration of population in Africa. (*Partly after Prothero and Dresch with additions*)

NORTH AFRICA	EAST AFRICA
1. Casablanca	17. Kampala
2. Oran	18. Nairobi
3. Algiers	19. Mombasa
4. Tunis and olive region	20. Tanga
5. Sahara oil wells	21. Dar es Salaam
6. Cairo	22. Lindi Mtwara

WEST AFRICA	CENTRAL AFRICA
7. Iron ore mining zone	23. Katanga Copper Belt
8. Gambia (groundnuts)	24. Zambia Copper Belt
9. Abidjan	25. Salisbury and Mining
10. Sekondi-Takoradi, and	Belt
Accra-Tema	
11. Cotonou	SOUTH AFRICA
12. Lagos	26. Rand
13. Port Harcourt, oilwells	27. Coalmining zone
14. Kano	28. Durban
	29. East London—
NORTH EAST AFRICA	Pt. Elizabeth
15. Khartoum	30. Cape Town
16. Addis Ababa	

Reasons Influencing the Distribution of Population

The distribution of population in Africa (Fig. 3:**6**) is the result of a combination of many factors—relief, climate, soils, vegetation, disease and human influences. Very often these factors do not act singly but combine with one another in influencing man's decision to live or not to live in a particular area. The reader will find more detailed reference to these factors throughout this book; it is therefore only necessary here to give an outline summary with references to the detailed studies which follow.

Physical Influences

a Relief has three main effects on population density and distribution. In extremely high regions —the Ruwenzoris, the upper slopes of high mountains such as Cameroon, Mt Kenya and Kilimanjaro, slopes are too steep, vegetation and soils almost non-existent and snow and ice prevent any permanent settlement by man; this requires little explanation. But remote areas of relatively high relief may, despite their paucity of natural resources, be chosen as refuges by man. Thus in West Africa remote areas of the Jos Plateau were chosen by the

Birom peoples to avoid the slave trader; the Fulani chose the remote higher plateaux of the Futa Djallon and Bamenda Highlands to avoid the tsetse fly; the Wanderobo still exist in the remoter, higher parts of the Aberdares in Kenya; the Lesotho peoples retreated into the Maluti Mountains to avoid the clashes of the Bantu on the plateaux of southern Africa. Such people have had to adapt their way of life to adverse physical conditions. Again, huge physical barriers such as the Atlas Mts and the Drakensberg Ranges influenced the direction of movement of people, channelling them along the coastal plains and hindering inland penetration. On the other hand, the vast expanses of level plateaux in interior Africa provided few obstacles to the early movements of racial groups (see Chapter Two).

b Climate is the biggest single influence on overall patterns of population in Africa. Temperatures have little to do with this, but rainfall amount and reliability exert a tremendous influence. Areas with generally less than 15 inches [381mm] per annum can support few crops unless the rain is concentrated in a short season, and even rainfalls of

57

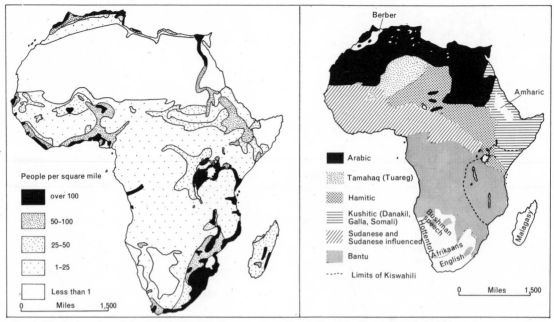

FIG. 6: Distribution of population in Africa (*simplified*)

FIG. 7: The major language groups in Africa

20 inches [508mm] or more are virtually useless if evaporation rates are high. The vast expanse of the Sahara, the Kalahari desert, the semi-desert regions of Somalia, the Nyika region of central and southern Kenya are naturally regions of low population density. However, people do obtain a meagre existence from these regions—the Bushmen, the Masai, the Turkana and the Bedouin—but their life is a precarious one and death rates are high during lean years. In these regions isolated pockets of dense population exist wherever water is plentiful—the oases of the deserts which are becoming overpopulated, the regions where rainfall is caused by increased elevation—the Hoggar in the Sahara, the Kilimanjaro region, the Marsabit region of Kenya, and the Futa Djalon plateau.

c Soils may affect settlement over a wide region or may exert purely local influences in small areas. Swamp soils, once drained, are rich and peaty and can support high densities of population, as along the coasts of Sierra Leone, the Gambia and Liberia. Lateric soils are difficult to work and deficient in minerals and cannot support dense populations. Low population in the 'Middle Belt' of West Africa and in the Congo is partly caused by lateric soils. In small areas man will try to settle the better soil areas

first and these are the most densely settled. Thus in the Kenya highlands the red volcanics were the first to be chosen by African and European alike, while the Black Cotton soils were neglected until population pressure enforced their gradual use.

d Vegetation, the result of climate and soils, can affect settlement in its own right. The dense rain forests of the Congo and West Africa hindered penetration and the development of communications and, as a result, settlements tended to keep on interfluves fairly close to the rivers. In the extreme southern parts of the Niger delta swamps have prevented settlement. The thorn scrub and tough grasses of the drier savannah lands are unattractive to most domesticated animals. Some vegetation zones, such as the miombo woodlands of Tanzania and dry bush areas, are the home of particular pests which exert a special control of man's settlement.

Human Influences

a Slave Trading is directly responsible for the pattern of settlement in some regions of Africa. The low density 'Middle Belt' of West Africa, lying approximately between latitudes $7\frac{1}{2}°$ and 10°N, is a poor area in soils and natural resources but it was

58

also a source region for slaves; it was assailed from both the coasts and from the northern interior.

b Ancient Political Kingdoms (Chapter Two), while no longer existing, can be said still to exert an influence over population distribution. Thus dense populations are found in southern Dahomey, Buganda, Benin and the areas of Yorubaland and Iboland. The areas between these old kingdoms were a kind of nomansland where tribal clashes were of frequent occurrence, and these tend to be regions of low population today.

c The Spread of Settlement by the Europeans and the development of resources by them has tended to alter the pattern of human settlement over the last century. In that period large population concentrations have appeared in the Rand, the Katanga-Zambia Copper Belt, and in the mining zones of West Africa (see Chapter Eight). In small remote areas one may suddenly find a concentration of people engaged in mining as at Kilembe in Western Uganda, the Mwadui diamond settlement in Tanzania, the Magadi Soda settlement in southern Kenya and the oilfields of the Sahara. Wherever communications have been improved or extended this has attracted settlement along their routes. Both ancient and new cities have become zones of population concentration and rapid growth (Chapter Six).

d Stability of Government in particular regions has attracted population settlement. Thus the Kano region is a zone of dense population because of stability of government brought throughout the centuries by first the Hausas, then the Fulani Emirs and later the British.

Africa's Population Problem

The major economic problem which faces Africa in the twentieth century is the question of the continent's ability to provide enough food to feed its rapidly increasing population. Because censuses have often been unreliable we cannot state with accuracy growth rate figures for the whole continent, but it is fairly certain that Africa's population is growing at a rate somewhere between 2 and 4 per cent per annum; the average annual population growth rate for the world is 1·9 per cent and in Britain and most of Europe it falls as low as 0·5 per cent. It is estimated that Africa's present population of almost 264 million will almost double to 517 million by the year 2000.

It is clear that most African countries will have to develop their economies, that is, improve their economic growth rate, by at least 3 per cent per annum merely to maintain the present standards of living of most of the population. Food supplies must therefore be increased at least at the same rate as the expanding population. But the supply of food must be increased much more than this if standards of diet and the amount of food available for each individual person are to be improved.

Many people point out the fact that there is still plenty of land left in Africa for cultivation and that only in a few areas such as Kikuyuland, Iboland and the Xhosa region is there considerable over-population. But these areas are usually the best in terms of soil and climate, and any future expansion in cultivation must make use of increasingly poor areas which in many cases are marginal for cultivation. At present the problems of feeding Africa's population are smoothed by loans, imports of foodstuffs and by the increasing productivity of the African farmer as he learns and develops better cultivation techniques. Most African governments give agriculture top priority when spending national funds.

But production of food is not enough. Money must be earned by producing goods which command high prices on world markets rather than by exporting raw materials. Britain, for example, is able to maintain a good standard of living for its population by the export of expensive manufactured articles in return for raw materials and food products. Thus industrialisation is one solution to Africa's population problem and many nations are vigorously engaged in attracting and establishing new industries. But the pace of industrial growth may be too slow to have a decisive effect; India, for example, suffers from under-industralisation and over-population. The Indian Government is in favour of birth-control and the limitation of family size, but in Africa there is no general feeling that birth control should be practised. As Fig. 3:1 shows, the next thirty years will be critical ones in Africa's population growth rate.

Questions

1 Describe and suggest reasons for the population distribution in *either* East Africa (Tanzania, Kenya and Uganda) *or* in Africa south of the Zambezi.

2 Show how the relief and climate of the Maghreb have affected the distribution of population.

3 What are the major factors influencing the distribution of population in the Republic of South Africa?

4 Relate the distribution of population to geographical conditions in any one country in West Africa.

5 With the aid of sketch-maps, outline the main population migrations to the African continent and within it.

6 Illustrate by means of a sketch-map the distribution of the European peoples in Africa. Attempt to explain this distribution on the grounds of climate, relief, commercial interest and history of settlement.

7 Trace the growth of European settlement in Africa and discuss present trends of European movement to and from the continent.

Discussion Topics

1 In what ways have climatic and other physical conditions and commercial interests attracted (or discouraged) European settlement in your country?

2 Discuss the importance of regular population enumerations (censuses) to economic planning in Africa.

3 You are to organise a census of your own country. You are asked to plan a census form on which you can ask ten questions. What questions would you ask and why?

Practical Work

Typical practical questions on the demographic geography of Africa might be:

1 In connection with any regional survey you have taken part in, (a) outline, by means of a sketch-map, the general distribution of the population; (b) suggest the reasons for this distribution.

2 Discuss and give reasons for the pattern of population in a region familiar to you.

3 Describe and explain the movements of population within your own country or in a district personally known to you.

The following topics are suggested as vacation work which the student may find interesting and profitable:

1 A visit to a local township to study the movement of population to and from the town. This can be done by noting the number of vehicles and pedestrians entering the town on various routes. This could be done on several different occasions to obtain an average, and maps drawn to illustrate the volume of flow.

2 A visit to a local factory might reveal information regarding the movement of people to and from the factory on a daily basis. If possible the manager should be approached regarding the origins of his employees. Usually factories keep records of an employee's tribal group and place of birth, and maps using the dot method could be plotted to show where the people have come from.

3 The study of local survey maps on a scale of 1:125,000 and less will indicate population patterns and trends of settlement. Simplified dot maps and shading maps could be prepared from the information shown on the survey map.

Statistical Exercises

1 On a base map of southern Africa showing political divisions, construct a population density map based on the following statistics. Limit yourself to five different shadings in black and white:

TERRITORY	LAND AREA (SQ. MLS)	TOTAL POPULATION
Swaziland	6,700	290,000
Lesotho	12,000	745,000
Botswana	275,000	542,700
South West Africa	318,000	555,000
REPUBLIC OF SOUTH AFRICA:		
i Cape Province	278,000	5,328,000
ii Natal	34,000	2,933,000
iii O.F.S.	50,000	1,374,000
iv Transvaal	110,000	6,225,000

Note: Figures for South Africa are for 1960 prior to the formation of the political unit of the Transkei which has an area of 16,500 square miles and a population of 3,044,000.

2 By means of divided proportional circles (pie graphs) drawn on a political base map of southern Africa, illustrate the following statistics (1960):

TERRITORY	POPULATION ACCORDING TO RACE (IN THOUSANDS)				
	AFRICANS	EUROPEANS	COLOUREDS	ASIANS	TOTAL
Rhodesia	3,610	221	11	7	3,849
Zambia	2,430	75	2	8	2,515
Cape Province	2,977	997	1,314	20	5,328
Natal	2,156	340	43	394	2,933
O.F.S.	1,073	275	26	—	1,374
Transvaal	4,602	1,455	105	63	6,225
S.W. Africa	428	73	24	—	525

3 The following statistics give the total populations of two districts in Kenya by sex and age groups (1962 census). Using graph paper as a base, for each set of figures draw a neat age-sex graph.

AGE GROUP	NYERI DISTRICT				CENTRAL NYANZA			
	MALES	% OF TOTAL	FEMALES	% OF TOTAL	MALES	% OF TOTAL	FEMALES	% OF TOTAL
00–04	22,726	18·96	22,207	16·82	53,874	16·71	54,989	15·90
05–09	17,771	14·9	18,707	14·16	50,827	16·69	50,865	14·50
10–14	19,927	16·75	17,744	13·45	45,082	14·81	37,678	10·89
15–19	12,414	10·40	12,686	9·56	29,723	9·78	28,010	8·11
20–24	6,174	5·14	9,764	7·41	17,268	5·70	32,005	9·26
25–29	6,417	5·35	9,927	7·53	17,196	5·68	34,414	9·96
30–34	4,928	4·10	7,860	5·92	13,833	4·58	26,722	7·71
35–39	4,823	4·01	7,328	5·55	14,177	4·69	20,650	5·98
40–44	4,431	3·70	5,553	4·21	12,535	4·20	15,740	4·56
45–49	4,450	3·70	4,646	3·52	12,202	4·04	13,546	3·93
50–54	3,542	2·94	4,176	3·18	9,687	3·24	9,911	2·87
55–59	2,199	1·92	2,023	1·54	8,009	2·68	6,555	1·91
60–64	2,975	2·50	3,436	2·62	7,742	2·58	6,265	1·82
65–69	2,021	1·70	1,776	1·38	4,593	1·56	3,280	0·96
70–74	1,659	1·40	1,537	1·18	3,133	1·08	2,373	0·70
75–79	1,289	1·06	845	0·64	1,824	0·68	1,069	0·32
80–84	910	0·76	942	0·72	1,667	0·60	948	0·29
85+	991	0·81	916	0·63	1,974	0·70	1,103	0·33
TOTAL	119,674	100·0	132,071	100·0	305,346	100·0	346,112	100·0

CHAPTER FOUR

AGRICULTURE—MAN AND THE LAND (1)

The greater part of Africa's population, probably seven out of every ten adults, lives directly off the land either by cultivating the soil or by grazing animals, while some very small groups still live by collecting wild fruits and nuts and by hunting. Most of the remainder depend indirectly on the land since their occupations involve the processing of primary products, e.g. palm oil extraction, fruit and vegetable canning, the spinning and weaving of cotton, the processing of tea and coffee. Over the last seventy years the European immigrant farmer in eastern, central and southern Africa and in the Maghreb has emphasised the rôle which agriculture plays in Africa's economy by introducing new techniques, modern machinery, and scientific methods to check disease and soil decline. Irrigation and road and rail development have opened up vast new areas to agricultural production, while the industrial demands of Europe and North America have encouraged the spread of plantations throughout tropical Africa.

The Pattern of Land Use

Today Africa displays practically every type of agricultural system, from the shifting agriculture of remote people to the carefully evolved crop rotations of the Ibo farmer, from the experimental state farms in Ghana to the dairy farms and vineyards of Englishman and Afrikaner, and from the small Busoga shamba to the huge Unilever plantation. The map (Fig. 4:1) shows how the land is used and illustrates the close relationship to the climatic and vegetational zones of the continent. Hunting and gathering and the cultivation of oil palms, cacao, yams, rubber, bananas and cassava are largely associated with regions of equatorial climate and the rain forests. Tropical agriculture—the growing of grains needing a dry season and crops such as tobacco—is found in those regions of tropical climate with a long dry season, a long wet season and plenty of sunshine. Where rains fall below 25 inches [635mm] a year cattle ranching becomes more important. In the better favoured parts of Africa—the

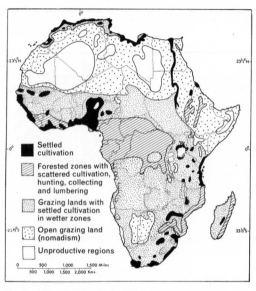

FIG. 1: Africa—land use (*simplified*)

highlands of East Africa, Rhodesia and Malawi, the fertile lowlands of Natal and the irrigated Nile valley—commercial crops of cotton, coffee, tea, sugar cane and fruit are grown, sometimes on large plantations. The northern strip of Mediterranean cultivation (vines, citrus, olives) is separated from the tropics by the vast stretch of the Sahara, where cultivation is limited to the meagre fringes of the oases.

Influences on Crop Distribution and Man's Use of the Land[1]

While temperatures in Africa provide few problems for plant growth, *rainfall amount and reliability* are of great significance. Some plants are severely limited by rainfall amounts which are more than adequate for others. The oil palm needs annual rainfalls above 60 inches [1524mm] and temperatures above 68°F [20°C]; its culture is thus limited to

[1] See Appendix 2 for notes on the needs of Africa's main cash and subsistence crops.

regions flanking the equator. Sisal, however, can tolerate a wide range of rainfall (18 to 50 inches [457 to 1270mm] a year) and variable soil conditions. But its great need is sunshine and, while it is grown widely in East Africa, it is of little commercial importance in the more cloudy climates of West Africa. Cassava, a basic subsistence crop, is tolerant of wide rainfall variations, variable soils, and can grow in temperatures varying from 50 to 70°F [10 to 22°C]; it is found throughout the tropics and has become a staple food from Mozambique to Gambia. But maize is more limited since, although it grows under a wide range of temperature, 50 to 90°F [10 to 32°C], and rainfall, 10 to 200 inches [254 to 5080mm], it requires a better soil and does best in humus-rich, well-drained loams. It is not important in the Congo Basin but is popular in the better soils of the Kenya highlands, Uganda, South Africa, southern Ghana and Nigeria.

Besides the natural limit of rainfall and soil fertility there are the *economic limits* imposed by man himself. A farmer will not cultivate a crop which, after production and transport costs have been taken into account, returns insufficient profit to justify the work and capital he invests. Rhodesian farmers grow tobacco because it brings large profits and commands a high price on world markets; it can withstand the relatively high costs of transport from land-locked Rhodesia to the outlets of Beira and Lourenço Marques and it has helped to finance a mixed farming economy (cattle, maize, tobacco).

Pests and diseases are other hazards to farming in Africa. The tsetse brings sleeping sickness to man and the disease trypanosomiasis to cattle and, because of its presence, large stretches of land have been neglected and abandoned which might have been farmed successfully. The fly likes bushland and the only permanent solution is to clear the bush and encourage soil ploughing. In some parts the fly attacks cattle but not man, so in these areas it is possible to grow crops but it means excluding meat from an often starchy diet.[1] The fly prevents large areas of Africa from being cultivated and so increases the population of tsetse-free zones.

The locust is another scourge mainly affecting north-eastern Africa (Fig. 4:3). A swarm of locusts

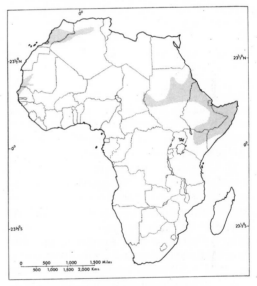

FIG. 3: Africa—area affected by migratory locusts

may contain as many as 75,000 million insects and weigh approximately 30,000 tons. Since a locust eats its own weight in green food daily, such a swarm destroys 30,000 tons of vegetation each day. In the late 1930s a plague of locusts devastated many countries of West and East Africa. At that time no properly organised method of control existed and

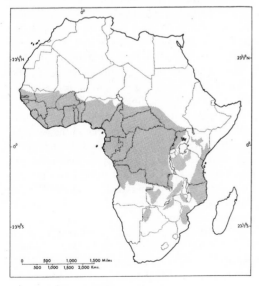

FIG. 2: Africa—area affected by tsetse fly

[1] To increase the protein content of diets, governments are giving great attention to increasing fish catches, see page 88 and Table 11.

63

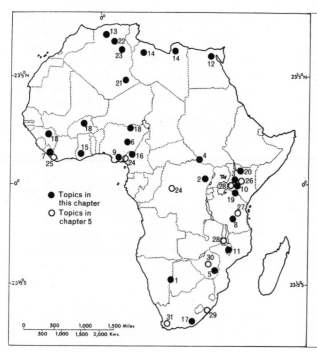

FIG. 4: Location of major topics discussed

fire, beating and poison were of little use. Modern methods which are keeping the locusts in check in East Africa include the spraying of swarms with insecticide from landrovers and aircraft.

Another insect which saps man's energies and sometimes causes death is the mosquito which transmits malaria[1] and yellow fever; the river fly spreads River Blindness; ticks carry fevers including leprosy; worms bring bilharzia and hookworm. Many of these diseases are being successfully combated by national and international organisations such as the W.H.O. (World Health Organisation) and United Nations health teams, but in many areas they are still a great problem affecting not only man's health but his ability to make full use of the land.

Sample Studies—African Land Use

Let us now examine some of the methods of land-use in Africa. The samples which follow are chosen from as wide and varied a field as possible and, in most

[1] Malaria is still Africa's gravest health problem. In any average rural community it is estimated that two-thirds of the people will have the infection in their blood at any one time.

cases, are representative of the methods employed over wide regions. In general, although all the samples are based on those existing in Africa today, they have been described in the order in which they probably evolved throughout history (see Chapter Two). Thus man was first a hunter and gatherer and this way of life still exists today (the Bushman and the Pygmy) although very few people now practise it. This is followed by the next stage of evolution —shifting cultivation—as still practised by the Azande and the Chipinga, and it is again emphasised that this occupies only small groups of African people. Gradually a more settled form of cultivation developed, as now seen in the Miombo woodlands (bush fallowing), which became more and more complicated as populations grew and which is seen in its most advanced form in many areas, especially in Uganda and in southern Nigeria. Variations of this system are seen in the Kikuyu areas of Kenya and the importance of the cash crop, e.g. in Ghana, is stressed. The adaptation of European methods of cultivation in African systems (particularly in North Africa) is next described. We then turn to the less favoured parts of the continent where cultivation is virtually impossible without irrigation and where man follows a nomadic existence. Finally, a summary of the main trends affecting African cultivation today is included, together with a discussion of some economic problems and their solutions.

Hunters and Collectors—The Bushmen, the Pygmies, the Wanderobo

In the remote unfavourable areas of Africa indigenous people such as *the Bushmen* lead lives which have changed little for centuries. The Bushman's way of life, however, is ideally suited to the harsh conditions of the Kalahari Desert, the waterless 'thirstland' which receives only about 10 inches (about 250mm) of rain a year; only occasionally do dried up lake beds and clay pans retain some surface water. During the brief rains in September and October and between January and April the grass grows tall amid the thorny scrub, but generally it is burned brown by heat and bush fires.

Here live the Bushmen, a small people (5 feet to 5 feet 6 inches) with dry, yellowish skins and tightly whorled 'peppercorn' hair. Their ancestors once roamed much of southern Africa and the fringes of the Sahara, but when the white man arrived in the

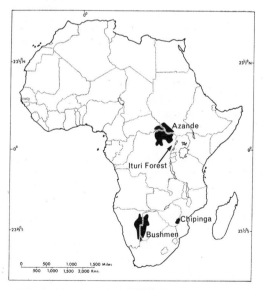

FIG. 5: Location of Bushmen (hunters), Azande and Chipinga (shifting cultivators)

Cape their numbers had been reduced to 10,000 and they were forced to retreat to remoter parts. They are now found in the Kalahari region of western Botswana and eastern South-West Africa.

Despite its dry harshness the Kalahari supports a surprising variety of game and edible plants—wild orange, wild fig, berries, nuts, roots, bulbs and tubers which flourish during the rains. The Bushman's diet also includes frogs, snakes, lizards, ants, scorpions, locusts, bees and their honey. But hunting provides the main food and during the dry season snares are set for the smaller game—anteaters, ostriches and guinea fowl. Duikers are hunted with clubs and poisoned arrows, especially during the dry season when they congregate round water holes. Little is wasted—blood, bones and marrow are eaten; the skins used to make quivers, pouches and blankets; the sinews for thread and bow strings; the bones for whistles, pipes and knives, and the horns for spoons. Flint stones are fashioned into tools and wood is carved into throwing sticks, fire drills and spear shafts. Hunting is men's work while the women collect berries and roots. Long sticks, bent inwards and tied and thatched with grass provide temporary shelters. This hut is left behind when the group moves on and new camps are built some distance from the water pans for fear of disturbing the game. Water is stored in empty ostrich eggs plugged with clay, and on the trek a sucking tube is used to draw water from the sub-soil.

By his skill as a hunter, his trained ability to recognise water sources and his clever use of natural materials, the Bushman is able to use the meagre resources of the Kalahari. He is a nomad like *the Pygmies* of the Ituri Forest in the eastern Congo Basin who also move around in search of game. Their environment, however, is not as harsh as the Bushman's and they are able to hunt, gather fruits and nuts and berries more easily and to trade with cultivating peoples. Unlike the Bushmen the Pygmies have contacts and their life is freely chosen.

Hunting and collecting must have been very widespread throughout ancient Africa when dense forests covered a wider area. *The Wanderobo*, now found only in remote spots of the Kenya Highlands, once hunted in the dense forests which formerly clothed the lower slopes of the Aberdares. Their way of life, still carried on on a small scale today, is typical of the forest hunter and collector.

65

The Wanderobo once inhabited most of the land between the present site of Nairobi and the Chania River, now called the Kiambu District. To the north the Kikuyu practised shifting cultivation while the Wanderobo were skilled forest hunters and nomads, building temporary huts in the forest depths and keeping to their family groups. They trapped game in pits and collected wild honey, suspending this in skins over pits until needed for beer-making. They traded honey, skins and shields for Masai cattle, Kikuyu goats and sheep and Kamba arrow poison, while the Kikuyu occasionally hired them to set snares around their cultivated patches. But hunting was their chief occupation, each family having a strip of forest covering about 200 acres and bounded by streams and ridge tops. Richer families had two such hunting grounds. Gradually, the Wanderobo were either absorbed by the Kikuyu or their land was bought from them (see page 73).

African Cultivation Methods[1]

Early man in Africa lived much as the Bushman in dry regions or as the Pygmies and Wanderobo in the forests do today. But gradually rudimentary systems of cultivation developed, becoming more complicated and efficient as populations increased. The various stages of this agricultural evolution can still be seen in many parts of Africa today.

Shifting Cultivation

The most basic agricultural system still in use in remote parts of Africa—the northern Congo, the miombo woodlands of Tanzania, parts of Malawi, Zambia, Liberia and Uganda—is termed shifting cultivation. In its original form shifting cultivation can only operate where the population is sparse. It is characterised by the following features:

a The cultivator burns down about an acre of forest and sows seeds in the intermixed ash and soil;

b he uses only elementary tools—pangas (machetes), hoes, digging sticks, rough axes;

c little attention is given to the crops until they sprout and ripen;

d when crop yields decline, usually after three years, the patch is abandoned and a fresh area

[1] Other accounts of African cultivation, particularly modern schemes, are discussed in conjunction with the power and irrigation projects in Chapter Seven, page 140. Other references to African agriculture are to be found by consulting the index.

cleared. The cultivator may return to the original patch after many years but usually he seldom returns.

This system uses much land but there are certain advantages. The constant moves ensure fresh sites and less risk of disease; the organisation of the work allows time for fishing and hunting; soil erosion is not serious since only small patches are exposed and these support many crops so that little bare earth is seen, and any soil washed away is trapped at the forest edge or in the dense tangle of crop roots.

But there is a very considerable waste of valuable timber which may have taken over a hundred years to grow and is destroyed in a few days. Green manure is ruined and the soil profile profoundly altered by the destruction of bacteria and humus.

The methods used in shifting agriculture vary with the people, their customs, and the variety of their crops. Two variations are seen in the following accounts of the Azande and Chipinga methods.

Shifting Cultivation by the Azande

The Azande live to the north of the great bend of the Congo River and west of the Nile's headwaters. Their territory of rain forest and open woodland extends 250 miles east to west and 200 miles from north to south, where the boundaries of the Sudan, Congo and Central African Republics meet. The region has an equatorial climate with a short dry season (November to January) brought by north-easterly winds. There is a wide range of soils and vegetation—dense galerial forest and elephant grass border the rivers, springs and swamps. Deciduous woodland grows on valley slopes; on higher, level land lies more open savannah, greatly ravaged by fire, and towards the south-west lie the dense forests of the Congo. Black soils are common near marshy hollows, with better dark brown and reddish loams in wooded areas.

Here the Azande practise shifting cultivation. They keep few animals, except hunting dogs and chickens, because of the tsetse. The men are mainly hunters, the women cultivators. The staple crop is finger millet (eleusine), easy to cultivate since it needs no guarding from wild animals and it can be stored for long periods. Maize is important especially in the southern moister soils, while other cereals include sorghum, bulrush millet and upland rice. The Azande also grow cowpeas, beans, bambarra nuts, groundnuts and sesame and collect wild

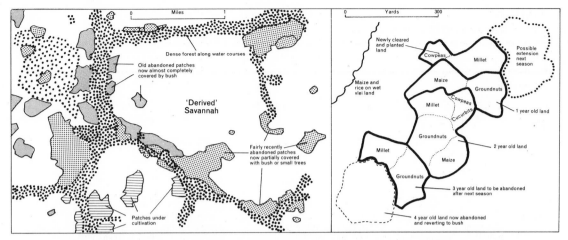

FIG. 6. Two examples of shifting agriculture. On the left, patches of shifting cultivation at various stages in the Benue Valley region of Nigeria near Makurdi (*based on an aerial photograph*). On the right, the Chipinga system

palm fruit. Root crops include cassava, sweet potatoes, yams, and cocoyams; fruits—pumpkins, calabashes, bananas, mangoes—and sugar cane, tobacco and chillies are grown. Hemp, cotton and bark are used to make cloth and rope.

Azande tools are elementary—the men possess spears, bows and arrows and throwing knives for hunting, and an iron digging stick for extracting edible roots. In the homestead, agricultural tools include digging sticks and knives for slashing the bush, house construction and for skinning animals.

Once a site has been chosen where there are few wild animals and a good water supply, the Azande fell the larger trees during the dry season and burn the leaves and twigs against the stumps. Huts for sleeping, cooking and storage are constructed of mud, wood and thatch. Then begins the year of activities shown in Table 1.

Crops are grown until there is a decline in yields, usually after three or four years although good harvests may continue for ten years in richer soil areas. The family then moves on to clear another patch.

Shifting Cultivation in the Chipinga District of Eastern Rhodesia

The following account, slightly abridged, illustrates the basic similarities and slight differences between Azande and Chipinga methods.

> While the ground is still workable in April or May, the trees are lopped and the branches piled round the bole. Trees bearing edible fruits are left for food and

others for ritual purposes. Only men use the axe, but the women help to pile the wood around the trunk. The land is (then) hoed by the women and the men because it is hard, new ground. The soil is left rough.

Some months later, when the wood is dry, the piles are burnt again and again the land is left alone. After rains have fallen, the seed is sown in December or January and covered by shallow hoeing, which helps to mix the ash with the soil.

A small portion of the land is planted to groundnuts and another to bambarra nuts. On sandveld soils the greater proportion will be groundnuts. On the larger part of the field a mixture of millet, finger millet, bulrush millet, cucurbits and cow peas is broadcast and hoed with the soil. Maize is also on the same land mixed with other crops, but small holes are made with the hoe and several maize seeds planted in each hole. The woman then scuffles soil over the hole with her feet.

One weeding is done in the first season after virgin land is broken up. The work of planting, weeding, reaping, threshing and the making of new land is carried out communally. . . .

A new field might be about two acres. Each year more virgin land is prepared and planted until, after four seasons, the

TABLE 1
The Azande Agricultural Year

MONTH	JAN.	FEB.	MARCH	APRIL	MAY	JUNE	JULY	AUG.	SEPT.	OCT.	NOV.	DEC.
Rainfall (*inches*)	0·0	0·0	1·5	3·0	7·5	9·1	7·6	7·8	5·0	4·5	3·5	0·2
(*mm*)	0·0	0·0	38·1	76·2	190·5	231·1	193·0	198·1	127·0	114·3	88·9	5·1
Temps. (°F)	77	79	78	78	78	78	77	76	74	73	74	75
(°C)	25	26·11	25·55	25·55	25·55	25·55	25	24·44	23·33	22·77	23·33	23·88

ACTIVITIES

a GENERAL:

Hunting. Repair of buildings. Termites caught for food.

Guarding of crops against wild animals and birds. Weeding of cultivated patches.

Second termite harvest. Repair of huts and tools.

Burning of bush for fresh cultivation. Hunting and fishing by men.

b PLANTING OF:

Early groundnuts, sweet potatoes, maize and sorghum.

Cassava, rice, yams, groundnuts, okra, maize, sesame, cotton. Finger millet, beans.

Sorghum.

c HARVESTING OF:

Old sweet potatoes and finger millet. Some cotton picked.

Mangoes. Sorghum.

Slack period. Harvesting of some unripe groundnuts.

Maize, finger millet, main groundnut harvest. Sweet potatoes, maize and vegetables. Cotton picking.

whole area is about four acres. Then a portion of the first prepared land is abandoned and a new piece added each year, so that land is cultivated for four years and then reverts to grass and bush. . . . In addition, vlei land is planted with maize and rice. The same patch is cultivated year after year and shifting tillage is not practised on this wet land.

The cultivator does not recognise any definite period of time for his grass and bush fallow. He judges that the land may be used again when the grass is tall and the bush is high. Alternatively, the whole kraal moves to a new area after four or five years, this being the more usual custom.[1]

[1] From a Southern Rhodesia Agricultural pamphlet. Similar methods of cultivation occur in Zambia where it is called 'slash and burn' agriculture, or the 'chitemene system'.

Efforts at Solution

Such methods are a serious threat to the natural vegetation and to soil fertility. Efforts are being made to convert the Azande to a cash crop system based on cotton but fluctuating prices, a lack of concerted effort between the Sudan, Congo and Central African governments and the remoteness of the area have hampered progress. An experimental station at Yambio, textile mills and strip farming have been introduced in Sudan's Equatoria Province but yields remain low and the region produces only 0·5 per cent of Sudan's cotton. Coffee and oil palms are also grown but the climate is rather marginal and yields are not high.

In Liberia shifting cultivation had assumed such proportions that 700,000 acres were being cleared every year for temporary rice plantations. Farmers burned the forest, scattered rice seeds, reaped a harvest for two or three years, then moved on. The yields—500 lb per acre or about half a pound per person per day. Liberia, faced with a rice shortage, imported 30,000 tons of rice in 1964. But the potential of the forest lands under organised cultivation is enormous; for example, there are 720,000 acres of freshwater swamps, ideal for rice growing, and each acre will yield up to 6,000 lb. a year—ten times that under shifting cultivation. The government is now actively encouraging swamp rice-growing; in 1961 there were 500 acres of swamp rice; in 1962, 10,000 acres; in 1963, 40,000 acres and in 1964, 50,000 acres. Over 5,000 farmers have been trained on twelve experimental schemes. The wasteful methods of shifting cultivation will be realised gradually once the Liberian farmer sees the tremendous yields of organised farming methods.

Bush Fallowing

In the description of shifting cultivation in Rhodesia it was suggested that the cultivator may return to an abandoned patch once the soil had recuperated. A fallow period is thus introduced which, strictly speaking, modifies the system to bush fallowing. Land is fallow when it is left to recover its fertility so that it can be used after a period of years for more crops. This is the essential difference from shifting cultivation where no long-term organised system of fields is recognised; the family unit occupied in bush fallowing is now fixed in one spot and uses several permanent fields. The length of the fallow period depends on population density, the ideal time being at least ten years, but this is rarely possible in densely peopled areas of Africa.

The Miombo Woodlands

In central and southern Tanzania many farmers use a simple fallowing system which is probably the first stage of transition from shifting cultivation to bush fallowing. Here lie the miombo woodlands, one of the largest uniform vegetation zones in Africa. The monsoonal climate with its alternating wet and dry seasons gives rise to flat-topped Brachystegia trees and grass.

A month before the rains the trees burst into leaf and in a few days the dry landscape is fresh and green. As the rains die out in May the countryside reverts to its hot, dry monotony and the trees shed their leaves. Man is forced to keep near streams to grow crops continuously and this encourages a fixed field system. The tsetse also hinders the spread of settlement, for clearings must be large enough to keep away the bush-loving fly and the settlements close to water supplies for domestic use and irrigation. A family clears seven or eight fields by chopping and burning, and sows these with maize, cassava and sweet potatoes. The cultivator may plant three crops of maize, two at the beginning and middle of the wet season and one under irrigation

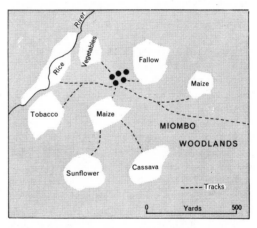

FIG. 7: Tanzania—bush fallowing in the miombo woodlands

TABLE 2
Climatic Statistics for Dodoma, Tanzania (alt. 3,675 feet)

MONTH	JAN.	FEB.	MARCH	APRIL	MAY	JUNE	JULY	AUG.	SEPT.	OCT.	NOV.	DEC.	YEAR
Temps. (°F) (°C)	75 23·88	75 23·88	74 23·33	73 22·77	71 21·66	69 20·55	67 19·44	69 20·55	71 21·66	74 23·33	76 24·44	76 24·44	73 22·77
Rainfall (inches) (mm)	6·1 154·9	4·3 109·2	5·7 144·8	1·7 43·2	0·2 5·1	0·0 0·0	0·0 0·0	0·0 0·0	0·1 2·5	0·2 5·1	1·2 30·5	3·8 96·5	23·. 591·8

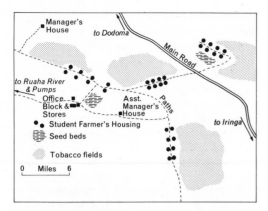

FIG. 8: The Kiwere Settlement Scheme in Tanzania. Situated 12 miles north of Iringa; altitude 4,000 feet; annual rainfall 35-45 inches [889-1143mm], maximum in December, minimum in November and April. May to September a very dry period. Temperature 75-85°F [24-29°C] during day to 65°F [18°C] at night. Irrigation water from nearby Little Ruaha River. Scheme first opened January 1963 with 30 student farmers, each pupil being given one acre in first year and three in second—two for tobacco and one for subsistence (maize and potatoes). In 1965 150 pupils taken on. The scheme now covers 7,000 acres. Tobacco is processed, graded and baled on the spot for shipment to Dar es Salaam

during the dry season. Rice and cash crops—tobacco, sunflowers and sesame—are grown by irrigation near the stream. One field is left fallow for four or five years and the others used in rotation.

The Tanzanian Government is taking steps to regulate this haphazard way of growing crops. This large area of territory with a population of only six per square mile has a tremendous potential. Although soils are rather gritty, sandy or clayey loams, they can be very productive with irrigation and scientific farming. Experimental plots are run near Iringa, Urambo, Nachingwea and other spots to teach African farmers how to grow cash crops, especially tobacco. The Kiwere Settlement Scheme twelve miles north of Iringa is one of these schemes (Fig. 4:**8**). By such schemes the government hopes to make a fuller use of the miombo woodlands, to extend areas suitable for settlement by bush clearance, and to provide important export crops.

The Coastal Lowlands of Nigeria[1]

The miombo woodlands are thinly peopled and bush fallowing there is still in its infancy. Gradually

[1] At the time of writing the Coastal Lowland region lies within the breakaway area of Biafra which was originally made up of the former East Central, South-Eastern and Rivers districts.

the fields will multiply and a more regulated system, separate from that of one's neighbour, will be adopted. This stage has been reached in the Coastal lowlands of South-eastern Nigeria. Here, centuries ago, man practised shifting cultivation, then limited bush fallowing followed as the population increased. Today, the Eastern Region covering 46,000 square miles supports nine million people (an average of 195 per square mile).

The Coastal lands of the Eastern Region are cut by numerous small streams, many of them tributaries of the main River Imo which bisects the region; these streams drain southwards from a low hilly region to flat lowlands and coastal swamps. The climate is hot—80°F [26·5°C] during the day dropping to 60°F [15·5°C] at night. Rainfall is heavy (120 inches [3048mm] in the south-east at Calabar to 91 inches [2311·5mm] inland at Aba) with a slackening off between November and March. Soils are generally well drained but heavily leached, are acid, contain few minerals and are soon exhausted.

Not, then, a very rich area to support the dense population and the land has been practically cleared of the natural forest. Here the Ibo-, Efik-, and Ibibio-speaking peoples are small-scale farmers growing

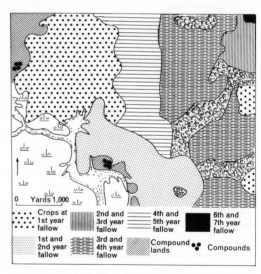

FIG. 9: Settlement and land use pattern north of Port Harcourt (Eastern Diobu), Nigeria. In this area the village compounds are well defined and there are no scattered dwellings. The large tracts of cultivated land belong to the village although individual farmers possess small cultivated plots near to their homes. The land is worked on an 8-year fallow system. (*After W. B. Morgan, Geographical Journal, September* 1955)

subsistence crops of yams, cassava, bananas, melons, okra, beans, cocoyams, calabashes, rice and vegetables. Most have small permanent vegetable plots near their homes but the main farm land is cultivated by a fallowing system. A family may have from 5 to 6 acres with 3 or 4 constantly bearing crops, and in some areas the fallow period has been reduced to three years. Palm groves, some natural, some planted, provide cooking oil and palm wine and this is the farmer's chief cash crop for, from the sale of palm oil, he receives on average about £45 per year.[1] Coconuts are a secondary cash crop nearer the coast.

The men do the harder work such as raking, hoeing, planting and constructing storage shelters and fences, while the women tend the small gardens and help with the harvests. The year's work is shown in Table 3.

All the cultivated land is used and the ground is completely covered by intercropping, for example, beans between maize. One field may yield a harvest

[1] The importance of the oil palm as a cash crop is also discussed on pages 136 and 150–53.

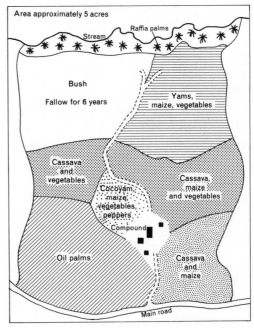

FIG. 10: Nigeria—typical farm layout in the coastal lowlands

TABLE 3
The Ibo Farmer's Agricultural Year[2]

MONTH	JAN.	FEB.	MARCH	APRIL	MAY	JUNE	JULY	AUG.	SEPT.	OCT.	NOV.	DEC.	YEAR
Temps. (°F) (°C)	79 26·11	81 27·22	81 27·22	80 26·66	79 26·11	79 26·11	78 25·55	77 25·0	77 25·0	79 26·11	79 26·11	79 26·11	79 26·11
Rainfall (inches) (mm)	2·1 53·3	2·7 68·6	6·4 162·6	7·9 200·7	11·9 302·3	15·7 398·8	16·9 429·3	16·2 411·5	16·3 414·0	12·8 325·1	7·5 190·5	2·1 53·3	118 2997·2

ACTIVITIES

a GENERAL:

    Bush clearing.   Weeding.   Clearing of bush.

            Preparation of yam hills.

b PLANTING OF:

            Yams, pumpkins, melons, maize, calabashes.   Beans, cassava, okra, cocoyams.
                                           Second maize crop.

c HARVESTING OF:

                                 Early yams.   Main yam crop.
                                 First maize.   Second maize crop.
                                 General harvesting of other crops.

[2] Climatic statistics for Calabar, altitude 40 feet.

71

FIG. 11: The intensive nature of African cultivation is well shown in these four examples from different parts of the continent.

Diagram A shows part of the Nile Delta region of Egypt, where irrigation canals form the framework of rectangular field patterns.

Diagram B shows the strip field pattern associated with villages elongated along road routes in the Eastern Region of Nigeria near Abakaliki.

Diagram C illustrates the field pattern in the Kipsigis peasant farming region near Kericho in western Kenya (the centre circle is a market and the black areas are planted tree wind-breaks).

Diagram D is an example of strip farming from Zezuro peasant farmer area near Salisbury, Rhodesia

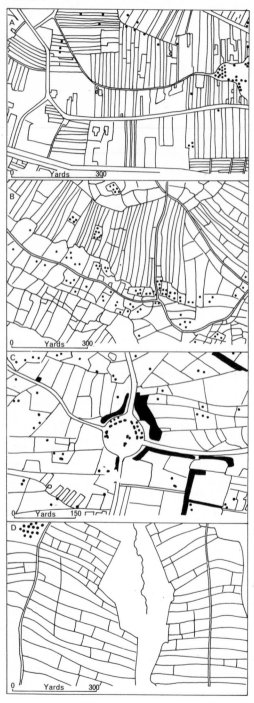

for one year using intensive methods while in the following year it will be sown with fewer crops, then it will fall fallow. Thus the Ibo are able to support the dense population by these intensive methods.

Farm Settlement Schemes are another cultivation method which the former Eastern (and Western) Nigerian Regional Governments were recently successfully applying. These are at Abak, Ohaji and Ulonna in the coastal region. Adapted from the kibbutz farming system of Israel the schemes involve the growing of cash crops (oil palm, cocoa, rubber and citrus fruits) together with subsistence crops for the farmers themselves on newly-cleared land. The schemes are a similar idea to those in the miombo woodlands of Tanzania and to the State Farms in Ghana, and are representative of the many agricultural experiments now being carried out in Africa. The Nigerian settlements vary from 3,000 to 12,000 acres in size. Each year between 100 and 120 student farmers are accepted until a maximum of 720 is reached on the bigger schemes. The students are housed in specially laid-out villages each with its own administration block, medical facilities, shops and schools. Each student is granted two acres of land for subsistence and, until his tree cash crops are producing, approximately 90 shillings a month. The farmers are supervised by expert agricultural officers who advise on seeds, fertilisation, cultivation and harvesting.

Land Fragmentation

The farmers of the coastal lowlands of South-Eastern Nigeria must supply increasing amounts of food for a growing population from a fixed area of land—the land must produce more. Another serious problem of many farming communities in Africa is land fragmentation—the division of land between members of the landowner's family until the plot size is so small that a severe limit is placed on its productivity. This stage had been reached in many parts

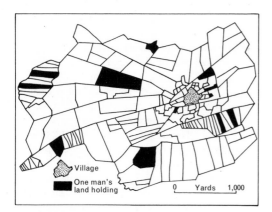

Village
One man's land holding

0   Yards   1,000

FIG. 12: The Maghreb—land fragmentation

of the Kikuyu lands in the Kenya Highlands until recently.

The Kikuyu number 1·6 million out of Kenya's population of 10 million and occupy a particularly fertile region on the lower slopes of the Aberdares between Nairobi and Mt Kenya. Here, between 5,000 and 6,000 feet, the soils are fertile, and the rainfall adequate and fairly reliable. See Table 4.

did not sell were surrounded by Kikuyu cultivated shambas and found that there was no game left. Thus the picture for fragmentation was set and to-day many Kikuyu own plots in the old Wanderobo zone (now Kiambu) and in the original Kikuyu zone (Murang'a District).

Other major causes of fragmentation are:

a Instalment Buying of Land: A Kikuyu farmer might buy one piece of land then save up to buy another some distance away.

b Kikuyu Family Customs: A man gave a plot of land to his wife; if he married again he gave another piece to the second wife; a new wife often gave land to other wives; a newly married son was given land by the mother.

c Tenant Lands: If a man had tenants and was short of land to give as gifts he would take small pieces from each tenant rather than take one tenant's whole holding.

This complicated system reduced the landscape to a patchwork of queerly shaped fragments where a man might own a dozen pieces scattered over a wide area. The disadvantages are obvious—time wasted between plots, higher fencing costs, inade-

TABLE 4
Climatic Statistics for Nyeri, Kenya Highlands (alt. 6,000 feet)

MONTH	JAN.	FEB.	MARCH	APRIL	MAY	JUNE	JULY	AUG.	SEPT.	OCT.	NOV.	DEC.	YEAR
Temps. (°F) (°C)	67 19·44	69 20·56	69 20·56	67 19·44	66 18·89	65 18·33	62 16·67	63 17·22	65 18·33	67 19·44	67 19·44	66 18·89	65·6 19·93
Rainfall (*inches*) (*mm*)	0·8 20·3	1·1 27·9	2·1 53·3	7·0 177·9	5·0 127·0	1·2 30·5	1·1 27·9	1·2 30·9	0·9 22·9	3·0 76·2	3·5 88·9	3·0 76·2	29·9 759·4

At the beginning of the nineteenth century most of this region was heavily forested; today it is a patchwork of fields, villages and small areas of forest and, before consolidation, it had fallen under the evils of fragmentation. This was a gradual process beginning with land purchases from the Wanderobo (page 65). The Kikuyu practised shifting cultivation north of the Chania River but between 1830 and 1890 the pressure of population forced them to buy land from the Wanderobo. Some Kikuyu families formed 'syndicates' to buy large sections of land and gradually the forests were cleared for cultivation. Wanderobo hunters who

quate protection against thieves and wild animals, soil decline because of the difficulties of carting manure, and the impossibility of using large-scale machinery on the small fields.

Land Consolidation

The answer to fragmentation, common to many parts of Africa, is land consolidation. This entails reorganisation of the land into single compact units so that the family has the same acreage, or land of equal productivity, as before. The new unit is based on the largest holding the man formerly possessed and, if he acquires better soil, he must take a slightly

73

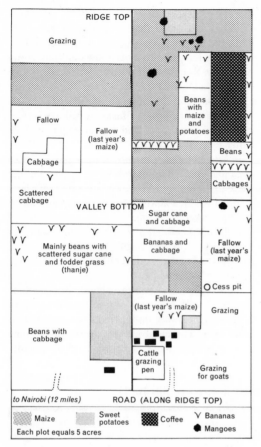

FIG. 13: Kenya—land consolidation. Intensive cultivation by the Kikuyu in the Fort Smith district 12 miles north-east of Nairobi

smaller land area. The new settlement is often based on the numerous ridges in Kikuyu areas with ridge and valley rivers forming boundaries. The slopes are terraced to check soil erosion and homesteads and villages set on top of the ridge (Fig. 4:**13**).

Land consolidation produced some striking increases in production in some parts of Africa, for example, in *Malawi*:

> There are now some thirty consolidation schemes in the Central and Southern Provinces. . . .[1] Striking improvements in crop production have resulted despite the fact that some individuals have a smaller area of land at their disposal. From

[1] Now defunct and replaced by schemes of planned large scale resettlement involving the Young Pioneer Movement.

samples taken before and after re-organisation it has been shown that where four acres once yielded 7·2 bags of maize and 120 pounds of beans to a value of £7, after re-organisation the same area of land yielded 7 bags of maize, 60 pounds of beans, 300 pounds of groundnuts, 200 pounds of pigeon peas, and 120 pounds of sweet potatoes to the value of £14. In addition to short term profits fertility is maintained by conservation measures, and the area available for grazing is increased by the withdrawal of marginal land from arable use.'[1]

Land Resettlement and the Growth of Co-operatives

But there are many Africans who possess no land to cultivate and yet have acquired considerable skill as farmers. Governments are trying to solve this problem by reorganising the land available and this involves a change of ownership and the sub-division of large estates. Resettlement programmes are found in most newly independent states such as Tanzania, Kenya, Algeria and in older states like Egypt (now the United Arab Republic), where much of the land was owned by a minority of rich landlords.

Egypt's land problem is a pressing one. Agriculture is the mainstay of the economy. Two-thirds of the country's 30 million people live directly off the land, seven out of ten industrial workers process agricultural products and practically all exports are agricultural. The land available for cultivation was about 6·25 million acres, owned in 1950 by a few thousand absentee landlords. About two-thirds of this land was rented to fellaheen in plots of two or three acres while the remainder consisted of large estates run by the land-owning class on whom the small farmer depended for fertiliser, seeds and credit.

To relieve this situation the government began a system of agrarian reform including the requisitioning of neglected land, limitation of estate size, compulsory sale of surplus land and government control of immaturely cultivated land or land whose ownership was in doubt. About 700,000 acres were thus made available for re-distribution to peasants.

[1] G. T. Rimmington—Malawi, A Geographical Study, O.U.P., page 177.

A co-operative scheme was set up to encourage farmers to give each other mutual aid. These co-operatives market the produce, make loans, and advise on seeds, fertilisers and crop rotation methods (a three year rotation is used at present).

The Maghreb region of Africa was once an area of considerable European settlement. In 1952 there were over one million Europeans in Algeria and some 26,000 of these were French farmers who worked one-third of Algeria's cultivated land. The majority of these farmers owned small farms between 20 and 25 acres although some were much larger. Most of the latter have now been sub-divided under Algerian agrarian reform measures. Few French farmers are left, for many returned to France with the granting of independence to Algeria. Their estates are now government-run or have been sub-divided among groups of peasant farmers. In Morocco for example, some 543,000 acres were nationalised in 1964 and divided among the peasant farmers. This reallocation of land is still proceeding and in 1966 some 15,000 acres of former French-owned estates were divided between 501 peasants in 13 large co-operatives. The methods used by the European farmers have been retained in these new settlement schemes.

Farms in the coastal Metidja near Algiers concentrate on fresh vegetables for the markets, and such farms are easy to work for the soil is rich and production per acre is ten times that of inland areas. Inland, however, farms are larger in order to be economically viable. The sample farming zone lies on the Saïda plateau where rainfalls are low enough to make dry farming methods necessary—the sowing of baraota seed, a soft wheat which comes to maturity quickly at the same time as the barley crop and avoids the scorching sirocco; the use of tougher strains of hard wheat imported from Tunisia; the growing of nitrogen-rich lentil crops on former fallow land, thus holding moisture in the soils; the rearing of the special Algerian breed of sheep which can withstand hot dry conditions; the careful selection and cross-breeding of cows to produce a tough, high yielding strain; the mixture of lucerne with clover which withstands the cold climate of January and February. The larger estates are worked on a co-operative basis and the yearly round of work is shown in Table 5.

TABLE 5
The Algerian Farmer's Agricultural Year on the Saïda Plateau

MONTH	JAN.	FEB.	MARCH	APRIL	MAY	JUNE	JULY	AUG.	SEPT.	OCT.	NOV.	DEC.	YEAR
Temps. (°F)	46	45	50	54	60	71	77	75	69	69	51	46	59·4
(°C)	7·77	7·22	10	13·33	15·55	21·66	25	23·88	20·55	20·55	10·55	7·77	15·22
Rainfall (inches)	3·2	2·3	2·0	1·2	1·2	0·7	0·6	0·4	1·6	2·3	3·2	3·3	22·0
(mm)	81·3	58·4	50·8	30·5	30·5	17·8	15·2	10·2	40·6	58·4	81·3	83·8	558·8

ACTIVITIES

a GENERAL

Cultivation and fertilisation of vineyards.	Ploughing of vineyards and fallow land.	Vine spraying. Harrowing and raking of vine soils.		Sorting of next year's seeds.	Preparation of ground for lentil crops, pruning vines.

b PLANTING OF:

Vine suckers. Wheat. Flowers, vegetables, potatoes.

Potatoes.

c HARVESTING OF:

Hay crop.
Wheat crop.
Lentils and potatoes.
Grape crop.

TABLE 6
Libya (Tripolitania): Climatic Statistics for Tripoli (alt. 56 feet)

MONTH	JAN.	FEB.	MARCH	APRIL	MAY	JUNE	JULY	AUG.	SEPT.	OCT.	NOV.	DEC.	YEAR
Temps. (°F)	54	56	60	65	69	74	79	80	78	74	65	58	68
(°C)	13·33	13·33	15·55	18·33	20·55	23·33	26·11	26·66	25·55	23·33	18·33	14·44	20
Rainfall (inches)	3·7	2·1	1·0	0·6	0·3	0·1	0·1	0·1	0·5	1·5	2·3	4·5	16·5
(mm)	94·0	53·3	25·4	15·2	7·6	2·5	2·5	2·5	12·7	38·1	58·4	114·3	419·1

An even more difficult environment in which Europeans applied agricultural techniques which have now been adopted by Libyans is found along *the Tripolitanian and Cyrenaican coasts*. Rainfall here is very low and unreliable and temperatures high from May to October. In this region crops may be ruined by the Ghibli, a hot dusty wind which springs up from the desert, especially in April and October.

During their occupation of Libya from 1911 to 1943 the Italians aimed to settle a third of a million farmers, but by 1939 only 110,000 Italians had settled and many of these left Libya after the war so that today there are only an estimated 1,500 Italians farming the land. Nevertheless many Libyan farmers have adopted the Italian techniques of farming and the Libyan Government is encouraging this. A typical farm (called a 'Demographic Farm' by the Italians) might be organised as shown in Table 7.

The co-operative idea is gaining ground in many parts of Africa where land reform is being carried out. Big estates are broken up and parcelled out to individual landowners who gradually repay government loans from their profits. Often the farmers find it profitable to band together to purchase seed, control water supplies and market their produce. A kind of small-scale collective farming develops but, unlike the farms of the Soviet Union, the individual owns the land and not the state.

The economic consequences of such schemes cannot be accurately assessed at present since many are still in their first stages. In many cases there has been an initial fall in production but this will taper off as the governments and farmers gain experience. One particular difficulty is the maintenance of cash crop production levels on the smaller farms and the limiting of the tendency to grow too many subsistence crops; this is necessary to maintain the level of cash crop exports.

TABLE 7
Libya (Tripolitania): A Demographic Farm

CROPS		ACREAGE	PERCENT TOTAL ACREAGE	COMMENTS
Field Crops— wheat, barley, groundnuts, vegetables, fodder		27	41·6	Grown in strict rotation—cereals, groundnuts, fodder
Tree Crops	olives	17	26·1	
	citrus	9	12·3	
	almonds	7	10·8	Main basis of farm economy, all under irrigation
	vines	4	6·1	
Buildings, vegetable plots		1	3·1	

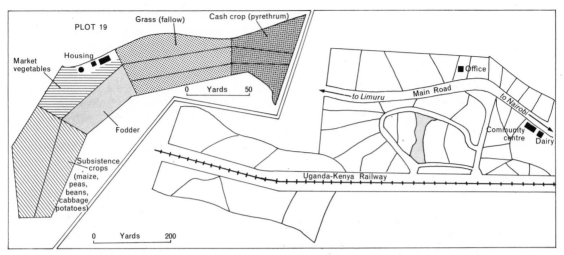

FIG. 14: Kenya—land resettlement, showing the Kikuyu use of former European-owned land. The Kikuyu Estates Co-operative (on the right) is made up of two ex-European farms of 624 acres. Altitude 6,900 feet; rainfall 30–40 inches [762–1016mm]; water by two bore-holes with reticulation to each plot, the 37 plots averaging 15 acres. Average purchase price £28 per acre. Soils are Kikuyu loam—a dark red to red loamy sand

Former land use: dairying, pyrethrum, wattle. Present land use: dairying, pyrethrum, vegetables, pigs, poultry, subsistence crops. Now supports about 620 people, previously about 50. Detail of one of the plots is shown on the left

TABLE 8
Ghana: Principal Exports, 1964 and 1966

ITEM	VALUE (IN ROUND FIGURES) £G		APPROX. PERCENTAGE OF TOTAL EXPORT VALUE	
	1964	1966	1964	1966
Cocoa Beans	68,117,000	51,528,000	60·9	52·0
Gold	10,308,000	8,527,000	9·3	8·7
Logs	8,077,000	5,442,000	7·2	5·5
Sawn Timber	6,665,000	4,988,000	5·6	5·0
Industrial Diamonds	6,120,000	5,421,000	5·5	5·5
Manganese Ore	4,336,000	6,075,000	3·9	6·1
Other Items[1]	5,475,000	10,053,000	5·9	10·1
Re-Exports	1,454,000	2,799,000	1·3	2·8
Total	111,756,000	98,833,000	99·6	99·7

[1] Includes cocoa butter and petroleum products.

The Danger of Crop Over-Concentration

While it is advisable for the African farmer to devote a high proportion of his land to cash crops for export, the dangers of over-concentration on certain cash crops are recognised by African governments. Already world over-production of coffee has resulted in many African farmers being forced to destroy coffee seedlings.

The danger of over-concentration on a particular cash crop was seen in *Ghana*. The importance of cocoa in Ghana's economy cannot be overstressed and, while other major economic activities are run by large companies, cocoa is almost entirely grown by African farmers on small plots. Nearly 65 per cent of Ghana's foreign revenue comes from the sale of cocoa beans and butter, as is shown in Table 8.

The export of beans began in 1891 with a shipment weighing only 80 lb., but in 1899 exports reached 324 tons. Rubber trees and oil palms were neglected and the government encouraged small-scale cocoa cultivation by refusing concessions to plantation companies. Cocoa cultivation spread to the empty landscape of the Akwapim area and by 1914 exports had risen to 50,000 tons. The speed of expansion and methods of the early cocoa farmers is described in the following quotation:

> From the early eighteen nineties the migrant cocoa farmers moved westward, on foot, towards the river (Densu), acquiring and planting as they went. In about 1896 the first real 'capitalist-farmers' acquired lands, most of them large ones, on the western bank and soon after 1900 the migration over the river became a mass movement. The women and children joined their menfolk as soon as they were established in the farming area, and in the first decade of the century the towns of the Akwapim ridge lost a great proportion of their population. To many farmers the investment of a large portion of the profits from one land in the acquisition of another land further west became a rapid, compulsive process and many of them soon became travelling managers supervising the work of relatives and paid labourers on their various farms. By about 1905 the most remarkable process of agricultural development ever achieved by unassisted African farmers was in full momentum; by 1911, largely owing to the efforts of these travelling farmers, Ghana became the largest cocoa producer in the world, although twenty years previously she had exported but 80 lb.[1]

In 1924 cocoa became the largest single export item, a position maintained to this day. Koforidua was the main area but cocoa planting spread along the communication routes around Kumasi. In 1931 just under a quarter of a million tons were exported; in 1936 over 310,000 tons (40 per cent world production); in 1964 381,506 tons were exported (35 per cent of world output). The main 1966–1967 crop, however, amounted to 363,399 tons, the lowest

[1] Polly Hill 'Three Types of Southern Ghanaian Cocoa Farmer', Chapter IX, African Agrarian systems, O.U.P.

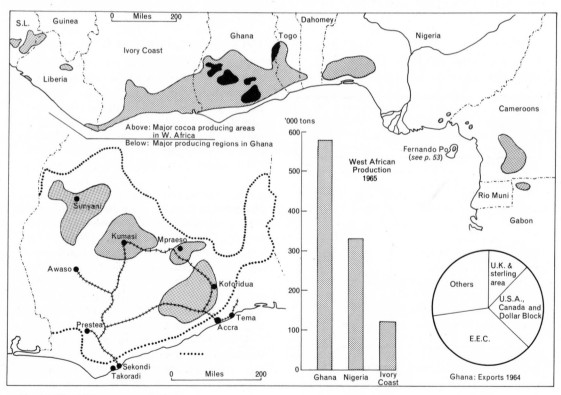

(see p. 53)

FIG. 15: West Africa—cocoa production

since 1959–60; of this the Soviet Union took 61,127 tons or slightly over 17·2 per cent, the United States took 60,075 tons, and the United Kingdom took 36,853 tons.

Cocoa farming has spread from the original south-eastern area inland to Kumasi and westwards to the Ivory Coast border. Rainfalls to the north are insufficient and in the south-west too heavy (70 inches [1778mm]). The optimum rainfall for cocoa lies between 50 and 60 inches [1270 and 1524mm] a year with a short dry season. The tree likes shade and protection from drying winds and too much moisture encourages fungus growth such as Black Pod, for cocoa is a particularly disease-prone plant. The best soils in the cocoa belt are derived from crystalline rocks such as granite.

Due to disease, the harvests of the original cocoa growing area have declined considerably, from 45 per cent of the total harvest in the 1930s to 15 per cent today. Swollen Shoot appeared in 1931 and by the late 1940s had invaded every cocoa area and reduced production by 60 per cent. No real check other than the cutting out of affected plants has yet been discovered.

Thus two dangers face cocoa growers—the spread of diseases and their (and the country's) dependence on one crop. Should world prices fall[1] Ghana's economy could be seriously affected. The Ghana Government is trying to diversify crop production[2] and introduce more industries, but farmers are reluctant to devote more land on their small two- to three-acre farms to less profitable crops.

Cocoa farmers do grow other crops—plantains, yams, cocoyams, maize, cassava, kola nuts and oil palms although cocoa cultivation is the chief occupation. To start a cocoa farm is relatively easy, the undergrowth being burned during dry January and February and seeds planted with other crops during the March rains. Until the plants produce after five years the farmer subsists on other crops. The trees begin to bear in their sixth year, produce their best harvests in the tenth, and begin to decline after the fifteenth year. The pods develop on the trunks between April and June and the plants must be weeded and brushed until harvesting in September, October and November. A second seed harvest is gathered in April and May.

[1] The highest price of cocoa recorded on the London market was £562 10s a ton in July 1954; in 1961 the price per ton had fallen by 73 per cent to £153 15s.

[2] See pages 87 and 84.

Once cut, the pods are split open, the beans extracted, piled into heaps, covered with leaves and allowed to ferment for six days. Then they are spread on mats to dry in the sun and are then sold to the cocoa co-operative.

Cocoa occupies a very important part in the life of the southern Ghanaian farmer and in the life of the country as a whole—some would say too important a part. But no matter what schemes of diversification or industrialisation the government may introduce, cocoa will dominate Ghana's economy for many years to come.

Other Problems Caused by Cash Cropping—The Bamenda Highlands

The cash crop has been an integral part of the farming system for many years in many parts of West Africa, particularly in the cocoa and oil palm regions. But in some parts of Africa, for example in East Africa, cash crop growing on a commercial scale by Africans was formerly restricted by colonial legislation and it is only relatively recently that cash crops such as coffee have been introduced into the African cultivation system. Often it has been necessary to clear new land to make room for these new crops and this has brought about problems of soil erosion, land tenure and often ill-feeling between African peoples with different economic interests. Some of these problems have been clearly described in the following passage relating to cultivation in the Bamenda Highlands of the Cameroon Republic:

> The basis of permanent settlement here, as in most areas of tropical Africa, is subsistence farming. In addition to maize, other New World crops that have become important here are cassava and, much more recently, the Irish potato, which grows well in the comparatively cool, rainy climate. Some of the most striking changes in the agricultural scene have followed upon the introduction of arabica coffee as a cash crop during the years following the Second World War. Promoted by the Agricultural Department, production has grown from a meagre fourteen tons in 1947 to well over 2,000 tons in recent years. Nearly all of this production has come from peasant farms. A single tea plantation at Ndu is another promising venture in commercial agriculture on the high lava plateau.

The coffee crop has had to be integrated with the peasant's subsistence agriculture in such a way that the farmer and his family can still rely to a high degree on their own farms for their food, while also raising their standard of living by marketing a cash crop. In many places this has been made possible by taking in new farming land on higher and steeper slopes of the farming valleys, risking both enmity with the Fulani, whose grazing land it had traditionally become, and soil erosion on very steep slopes, sometimes exceeding thirty-five degrees. The free-draining, humus-rich soils do not erode easily, and erosion has not yet become a problem on the lava slopes, but many of these changes are quite recent and their full effects are not yet seen. Meanwhile, relations with the Fulani have deteriorated and there exist delicate problems of land tenure and land use which must eventually be decided by legislation.

The coffee bushes are frequently grown on the best soils, forcing women to cultivate the food crops on the steeper and stonier slopes. The men, following advice of the Agricultural Department, employ simple contour ridging and mulching as conservation measures, but the women are either unwilling or unable to do this on the steep slopes, where it is vitally needed.[1]

Land Limitation

We have been concerned largely with man's efforts to increase the amount of land available for cultivation in order to keep abreast of population growth. In some parts of Africa the land has reached a point where the cultivable area available is unable to support the population and there is a continuous exodus to the towns. In some cases the land area has been reduced, causing a radical change in the life of the people.

The Xhosa of the south-eastern Cape Province of South Africa have had their way of life greatly altered by increases in their numbers and decreases in the land available. The climate of the Xhosa

[1] 'The Bamenda Highlands' by M. F. Thomas, Geographical Magazine, August 1966, pages 289–93.

reserves—temperatures between 60 and 70°F [15·5 and 21°C], annual rainfalls between 15 and 30 inches [381 and 762mm] with 60 per cent falling between October and March, the summer months— is suited to cattle ranching but is rather marginal for crops. The Xhosa once lived in scattered homesteads, tending their increasing herds in a rolling landscape of grassland and scattered trees. Cattle were only killed by disease or for ceremonies. The herds, tended by the men, moved from one pasture to another in a simple rotation. The woman cultivated small patches of millet and sorghum which were abandoned when the family followed the herds to fresh pastures. The Xhosa lived on milk and cereals and crops obtained by exchange for their dairy products.

Over the last hundred years the Xhosa have increased threefold and densities in the reserves have reached 150 per square mile. Xhosa grazing land has decreased due to the encroachment of cultivators and to the Xhosa's practice of growing more and more crops to sell in local markets. The people are now mainly cultivators of maize, wheat and potatoes. Some keep sheep, selling the wool, and there are still herds of cattle, but the pastures are inadequate to support large numbers and many die during droughts. Like the Masai of East Africa, the Xhosa tends to believe that numbers rather than quality are the best indication of a man's wealth. The Xhosa have never grown cash crops such as pineapples and citrus since the White farmer has already captured South African markets. Many men have left the land and today nearly half of the male Xhosa population work outside their reserves.

Measures are, however, being taken to provide alternative work for male Xhosa. The Xhosa people occupy part of the Transkei Bantustan, the largest of the African reserves in the Republic of South Africa. The Xhosa Development Corporation is becoming very active in promoting agricultural and industrial enterprises especially around Umtata. The Bantu peoples are gradually being trained in the fertilisation and irrigation of land, the planning and rotation of crops, and in modern grazing methods.

The Transkei has a cattle population of 1·5 million and the development of the meat processing industry could raise the national income of the Bantustan by some £2·25 million. The Transkei Meat Industry has recently opened a meat-packing factory near Umtata and there is a growing export of meat to the coastal towns of the Republic. Another venture is the expansion of the timber industry; it is planned to plant forest over 4 per cent of the Transkei. At present 4,500 Bantu are employed in forestry and this is expected to rise to 8,000.

Nomadic Pastoralism

The Xhosa are people who have turned from pastoralism to cultivation from sheer necessity. But large stretches of Africa support true nomadic herdsmen—the drier savannah of West Africa, the Nyika of East Africa, the Kalahari fringes of Botswana, the semi-deserts of Somalia—all are extensive grazing zones where man follows the shifting rainbelts with his herds.

The Fulani of West Africa

The Fulani number over seven million and are spread throughout the Sahel and Savannah zones of West Africa from Senegal to Lake Chad (Fig. 4:**16**). The savannah displays the long dry season brought by the parching north-easterly Harmattan from October to March and a wet season from April to September. Rainfalls average between 30 and 35 inches [762 and 889mm] a year. In the southern Sahel rainfall is lower, 20 to 30 inches [508 to 762mm], is less reliable and lasts for about four months only.

The climate in the savannah zone supports scattered doum palms, baobabs, shea butter trees and shrubs and, during the rains, short grass. In the Sahel the country is more open, trees are smaller and there are more thorn bushes; grass is tussocky and leathery but can still be grazed. The nomadic Fulani also make use of the higher plateaux such as the Futa Djalon and Bamenda Highlands where much of the former forests has been destroyed by fire and large stretches of secondary tsetse-free grasslands exist.

Like the early Xhosa the nomadic Fulani live almost wholly on the produce of their herds and obtain roots, grains and vegetables by barter from the peoples on whose land they graze. The Fulani move in family groups supported by about a dozen cattle in the savannah zone, while in the drier Sahel there are fewer cattle but more goats and sheep. The main problem of the Fulani is the dry season water shortage which causes the long migrations; the tsetse fly is less of a problem although most cattle are only partially immune.

The nomadic Fulani, like the Masai, practise transhumance. During the dry season the grass withers, pools and streams dwindle; the tsetse flies retreat slowly southwards, keeping close to the water courses, then later move north as the rains spread over the land in April and May. As the rains and flies approach the Fulani move steadily northwards with their herds or seek the tsetse-free uplands of

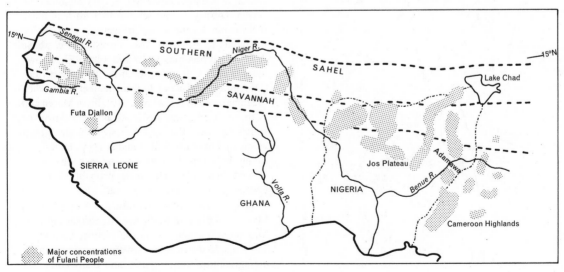

FIG. 16: West Africa—distribution of Fulani in relation to the Sahel and Savannah zones

Bamenda, Futa Djalon, Jos, Bauchi and the Cameroons. As the dry season returns the Fulani lead their cattle from the highlands and northern areas and move southwards.

The nomadic Fulani's way of life is thus dominated by the wet and dry seasons. During the dry season food is short, some cattle may be sold for food and roots and berries are collected. Wells must be dug and the cattle must be spread out in the search for water. During the rains the cattle thrive on the fresh grass and the Fulani's life is relatively easy.

The Masai of East Africa

The Masai are nomadic pastoralists but, unlike the Fulani, they have complete rights over much of their grazing land. They practise transhumance in a wedge of arid territory extending from Nairobi southwards into Tanzania between Kilimanjaro and Lake Manyara (Fig. 4:**17**).

Here again there are long wet and dry seasons with unreliable rains and long droughts. Average rainfalls are between 20 and 25 inches a year, mostly falling between November and April, and tempera-

tures are high, averaging 70°F [21°C] in the hot, dry seasons. The landscape affects sudden changes with the seasons; during droughts it is dry and dusty, small dust devils whirl across the plains and streams are dried-up sandy beds. The bark peels off the trees, bushes are coated with yellowish dust and the distant blue highlands shimmer in the heat. When the rains sweep across the land the rolling plains are covered anew with short grass, the winds bring a cool freshness, the streams fill with rushing water and murram roads are sticky with reddish-brown mud.

Here the Nilotic Masai graze their cattle. A tall, aristocratic people, many, but by no means all of them, have resisted modern influences and still live simply, scorning the use of modern tools and weapons. To them cattle, usually the hardy tsetse-resistant Zebu, are a symbol of wealth but at present Masailand is unable to support vast herds and overgrazing and resultant wind erosion are serious problems. The cattle die off in hundreds in prolonged droughts as in 1961 when piles of dusty cattle corpses littered the plains. The Masai keep donkeys for transport and, to save their precious herds, sheep and goats for meat. Their diet consists of blood taken from a harmless incision in the cow's throat, milk and meat and a few poor grains.

The Masai have a home area where they live in small enkangs (or kraals) and to which they return periodically. Movement from this home area is caused by the alternating wet and dry season of the Nyika. During the dry season the herdsmen move their cattle to the lower fringes of surrounding highlands such as the Mau Forest where, above 7,000 feet, it becomes cooler and wetter. This movement occurs with the onset of the two dry periods (December–February, July–September) but when the rains move over the lowland plains in March and again in October the herds are brought down the slopes to graze the fresh grass. Then the Masai women plant maize, millet and sweet potatoes, but tilling the soil is distasteful to the men who prefer to tend their herds. The Masai probably make the best use of a difficult environment.

Slowly, however, the traditional way of life of the Masai is beginning to change. In certain areas of Masailand, particularly in the Ngong, Loitokitok and Kajiado districts, the government is encouraging agricultural development and many co-operatives have been formed, cattle dips built, loans made

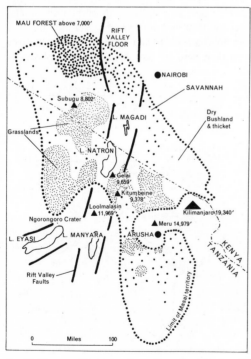

FIG. 17: Kenya and Tanzania—the territory of the Masai

to Masai farmers, and land demarcation carried out. In the Kajiado district some land has been consolidated, in the Ngong area some 800 acres of virgin soil have been formed into co-operative land for wheat growing and kenaf has been introduced to blend with and act as a substitute for sisal. Wheat growing and sheep rearing have been combined by Masai living in the Kericho and Nandi districts and Masai are being instructed in ranching and animal husbandry. There are plans for a new system of land tenure in Masailand which will protect the rights of the Masai in their homeland. These ventures represent the first stages of change in the Masai's traditional way of life but there are still many Masai who have not and will not change their nomadic existence for a more settled one.

The Turkana of Northern Kenya

An even more trying region is that of the Turkana of northern Kenya where rainfalls fall below 20 inches [5,080mm] a year (see Table 9). This is an inhospitable region of thornbush, dwarf shrubs and sparse grass growth. Depressions or pans sometimes retain a little water and here grasses flourish briefly.

The Tuareg of the Sahara

The rigorous conditions of environment impose upon the Masai and Turkana a set pattern of life, a pattern which is repeated in the Sahara, and the nomadic tribes must conform to those conditions in order to survive. The Tuareg, like the Fulani, Masai and Turkana, are a nomadic pastoral people who once ranged over the Sahara from the Niger River to Ouargla and Touggourt and as far west as Timbuktu but now, due to European and Arabic pressures, they are found chiefly in the Aïr, Tibesti and Hoggar plateaux and in northern Nigeria. There are approximately 160,000 Tuaregs of whom 12,000 live in the rugged Hoggar (see page 14).

The Hoggar rises to over 9,000 feet and derives a meagre rainfall from south-westerly and westerly air streams. Pastures consist of thin, permanent, wiry grass, scattered shrubs and thornbush concentrated mainly in hollows and along river beds, and the thicker grasses which flourish during brief showers. These are soon eaten by the cattle and the Tuareg are forced to move at least once a month between waterholes and pastures. They must be mobile, carry the minimum of baggage and travel in small family groups. Once a new site has been

TABLE 9
Rainfall Statistics for Lodwar, Kenya (Alt. 1,660 feet)

MONTH	JAN.	FEB.	MARCH	APRIL	MAY	JUNE	JULY	AUG.	SEPT.	OCT.	NOV.	DEC.	YEAR
Rainfall (inches)	0·2	0·3	0·6	1·6	0·9	0·3	0·4	0·3	0·2	0·3	0·3	0·3	5·7
(mm)	5·1	7·6	15·2	40·6	22·9	7·6	10·2	7·6	5·1	7·6	7·6	7·6	144·8

The camel is important here since it is able to eat the thornbush leaves and the leathery tufts of grass; it provides meat, milk and transport. Zebu cattle, goats and donkeys are also kept in this tsetse-free area and Persian black-faced lambs are reared. Some crops such as finger millet are planted where floods occur during occasional rainstorms. Like the Masai, the Turkana live in semi-permanent settlements of mud huts surrounded by thornbush thickets. Famine is a constant threat to the Turkana and each year famine relief measures are put into operation by the Kenya Government.

found the animals are set out to graze and scouts are sent to look for the next fresh pastures.

The Tuareg are also traders, setting out southwards in July, their camels loaded with dates and with salt from the desert pans; with herds of donkeys and with their special breed of white camels which are exchanged for 'morocco' leather, brass and silver ware, indigo dyed cloth, weapons, tools and pots and pans obtainable at centres such as Kano. The Tuareg return loaded with such goods in January and February. This trade once extended from the Atlas Mts to the countries of West Africa but today modern trucking companies have severely limited it. The Tuareg were once masters of all central Saharan trading routes, extracting tolls from merchants in exchange for protection, and plundering caravans. This activity has now ceased and many Tuareg have turned to the cultivation of small garden plots and palm groves often rented from more wealthy tribesmen.

Semi-nomadism

Many other nomadic tribes are also finding it increasingly difficult to maintain their traditional way of life. In the steppe lands of the Atlas fringes and inland from the coastal zone of Libya there are now very few pure nomads as formerly, and most are semi-nomads living in villages or encampments for long periods and cultivating poor cereals in wadi beds. Their traditional grazing grounds in the northern Atlas are now restricted or unavailable due to modern developments. In Tunisia the extension of olive plantations and cultivated land has led to the nomads in the south-east taking up regular wage-earning employment and migrating to take part in the olive, vine and wheat harvests of the coast regions.

In Libya *the Bedouin* are becoming more sedentary or semi-nomadic, living partly as traders, pastoralists and subsistence farmers.

> . . . the great majority of the tented Bedouins are essentially pastoralists—sheep, goat and cattle rearers—but also practise cultivation, mainly of barley but also some wheat. While more or less subsistence farmers, they do trade surplus stock, wool, skins, clarified butter, surplus barley, honey and wax for tea, sugar, rice and cloth, especially the jird, the woollen cloak of the country. The nomads and semi-nomads of Tripolitania live under similar conditions. . . . It is . . . in Cyrenaica that the proportions of nomads and semi-nomads is highest, reaching 44 per cent of the total population of all households and 45 per cent of the total population as against 20 per cent both as regards households and persons in Tripolitania and 8 per cent and 9 per cent respectively in the Fezzan.[1]

[1] Labour Survey of North Africa, published by the International Labour Office, Geneva, 1960, pages 76-81.

In *Egypt* the number of nomadic people has fallen considerably from 73,000 at the end of the nineteenth century to 45,000 today. They occupy the lands to the west of the Suez Canal and between Cyrenaica and the Nile delta, where they have settled in the narrow coastal strip growing barley, olives and figs, but a part of the population still follows the seasonal migration of their flocks. In the eastern areas near the Canal many nomads have taken to farming the areas which they graze, buying it from the local peasants and sharing the life of the village.

Sedentary People–The Souafa

In the Sahara proper the desert oases support a truly sedentary population now approaching one million who farm half a million cultivated acres. The stopping of feuds and tribal wars during colonial rule, the more hygienic and sanitary conditions, and the medical care and free food distributions in times of want have resulted in marked increases in population.

In the Souf area, a north-western extension of the Great Eastern Erg around El Oued, the Souafa people depend on underground water for their palms.

> The eternal glory of the Souf is its palm groves. Flying over the town is like flying over the moon. The Souafa have dug troughs in the dunes and ten, twenty even several hundred palm-trees grow in craters of widely differing sizes. Some of the craters are so deep that the crowns of the palm-trees are below ground-level. In almost all troughs there are draw-wells from which vegetables and tobacco plants are irrigated. They are not used to water palm-trees, for the Souafa have planted the trees so deep that the roots are in subsoil water. The healthy state of the palms shows that there is an underground river, for stagnant water would kill the trees.[1]

The Souf region is rapidly becoming overpopulated. At the end of the nineteenth century 160,000 trees supported 21,000 people; by the 1930s there were 65,000 people and about 400,000 palms, while today about 500,000 trees support 100,000 people. The water-table has dropped due to the

[1] George Gerster, *op. cit.*, page 75.

greater demands on the water supply and the Souafa must dig deeper craters for their palms.

But the Sahara is now being termed 'the Land of the Future' by the Arabs, for besides the great discoveries of minerals over the past ten years interest is being shown in the agricultural possibilities of the region for now there is money to invest. In 1955 there were only about half a million cultivated acres of land. The main products were dates from some ten million palm-trees, groundnuts, olives and small amounts of fruit and vegetables. The land supported about 1·5 million sheep and goats and 300,000 camels. Since then over 800 new boreholes and waterholes have been created and new plantations laid out, e.g. at Zelfana, where two million young eucalyptus trees to anchor the dunes have been planted and new fruit, cotton, vegetables and rice crops are being gathered.

Some General Aspects of African Cultivation

The foregoing accounts of the occupations of the African peoples illustrate the wide variety of cultivation methods and ways of earning a living. But we should not lose sight of some of the general trends and aspects of African agriculture. Some of these aspects are discussed below.

The Rôle of the Cash Crop in African Farming Economies

The cash crop has been an important part of the cultivation system of the African farmer throughout West Africa, in Egypt and Sudan since the turn of the century and it has become increasingly important in many other countries since the 1930s, largely because of the steady improvement in communications linking with markets. The African farmer has been particularly skilful in adapting the indigenous forest tree into his agrarian system; nowhere is this more evident than in Ghana (cocoa) and in Nigeria (the oil palm).

In *Nigeria* approximately 1 million acres are devoted to cocoa, mainly grown on small African farms especially in the Oyo and Ondo districts, and in a good season the annual crop brings £110 a ton to the farmer. In the north the groundnut is also predominantly a peasant crop and there are no large estates; the farmer receives about £30 a ton. But the oil palm is Nigeria's chief peasant cash crop and 94 per cent is grown on African-owned farms. The oil palm is indigenous to the southern part of

Nigeria, Eastern Nigeria supplying the vast bulk of the oil palm exports which suggests that it forms more of a staple foodstuff in Western Nigeria. The main core of the native palm oil producing regions lies in the scarplands and plains from Onitsha to Abakaliki. In the oil palm belt successful attempts

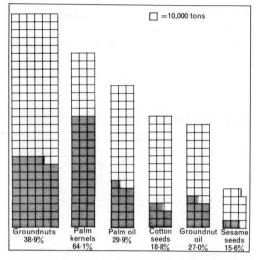

FIG. 18: Nigeria—share in world export of seed oil and oil seeds

have been made to improve on the older wasteful methods of oil extraction by introducing hand presses and centralised Pioneer oil mills by the government. In recent years several oil mills have been set up by private enterprise, while the regional governments are trying experiments to improve quality and production.

Another important cash crop of West Africa, particularly in the drier, sandier northern zones, is the groundnut. In *the Gambia* the farmers depend for the greater part of their income on groundnuts which are sown in June and July, and harvested in October and November. The crop is entirely raised by peasant farmers. The average annual output is about 80,000 tons, about one ton per farmer (for which he receives £27). Some of the crop is grown by the 'strange farmers' who come from Senegal, Mali and Portuguese Guinea during the planting season, plant their seeds, reap a harvest, sell it and return. Many of them now help Gambian farmers with their harvest and are paid for their labour and also cultivate a small patch of their own.

Other examples of important cash crops in the African farming economy include cotton in the

Sudan, Egypt, Nigeria and Uganda, rubber in Liberia, tobacco and oil seeds in Tanzania, and cereals and fruit in Algeria. In countries where the growing of cash crops was restricted by colonial legislation African farmers are now growing increasing amounts of export crops. In 1960 it was true to say that the European farmer of the *Kenya Highlands* grew nearly 80 per cent of that country's export crops (see Table 10).

But now the picture is changing radically as recent land reorganisation schemes are beginning to make progress. Consider, for example, the growing smallholder as in *Uganda*. Here nearly all cultivation is by Ugandan farmers who have over two million acres under cash crops (compared with about 86,000 acres of estate crops of coffee, sugar and tea). Cotton, tea, tobacco, sugar cane and coffee are produced mainly on small farms of between 3 and 4 acres. Actual cash incomes from these crops received by the Ugandan farmer have increased spectacularly—1950, £9·4 million; 1953, £16·2 million; 1960, £24·2 million. Coffee, cotton and tea earned Uganda £53·3 million in exports in 1966—79·5 per cent of all exports.

TABLE 10
Kenya: Production of Major Crops for Export, 1960[1]

CROP	% VALUE OF EXPORTS	OUTPUT IN TONS		% NON-AFRICAN OF TOTAL OUTPUT
		AFRICAN GROWN	NON-AFRICAN ALMOST WHOLLY EUROPEAN GROWN	
Coffee	29·0	4,600	18,800	80·3
Tea	4·4	100	13,500	99·2
Sisal	13·0	3,000	59,600	99·1
Pyrethrum	9·0	1,800	6,700	78·8
Wattle	2·0	19,000	31,000	62·0
Wheat	—	700	126,700	99·4

importance of African-grown tea to Kenya's economy. With the encouragement of the government some 2,623 new growers registered in the 1964/65 season, bringing the total of African small tea farmers to nearly 23,000. The average size of their tea holdings is 0·57 acres and over 4,772 new acres were planted to tea in the 1966/67 season. Today about 30 per cent of Kenya's 38,700 acres of tea consist of small African units. Again, the African farmers are producing increasing amounts of coffee. In 1963 there were approximately 79,000 acres of European-grown coffee and over 70,000 acres of African small holdings owned by 200,000 African farmers; they receive about £2·7 million annually for their crop. Unroasted coffee was worth £18·78 million to Kenya in exports in 1966—slightly over 30 per cent of all her exports.

Nowhere is production of an African country's cash crops so firmly in the hands of the African

Subsistence Crops

But the African farmer has often to support his family from the land and because of this subsistence crops play a large part in his cultivation system. Thus, while *Ugandan* farmers devote two million acres to cash crops they grow over six million acres of crops for domestic consumption and it is very rare for more than one-third of the shamba to be devoted to cash crops (Fig. 4:**19**). In *Malawi* cash crops do not form a large part of the cultivable system and the greater part of the farmer's land is used in growing subsistence foods although any surplus of maize (the staple), sorghums, millet, root crops, fruits, vegetables and pulses are sold in local markets to purchase necessities.

In the *Congo* (*Brazzaville*) some 60 per cent of the population is engaged in agriculture, mainly for home consumption, agricultural products representing only 20 per cent of exports (most exports are forestry products). About 75 per cent of all the crops grown are subsistence foods—oil palms, groundnuts, citrus fruits, tobacco, sugar cane, millets, and

[1] Source: Kenya; Statistical Abstracts, Economics and Statistical Division.

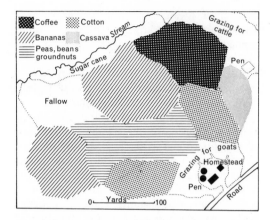

Fig. 19: Uganda—cash crop and subsistence cultivation on a Muganda shamba

rice. Small acreages of tobacco, cocoa and coffee are grown for sale.

In *Zambia* most of the people are engaged in the cultivation of subsistence crops and it is estimated that about 87 per cent of the total crop production is for home consumption only. Here the principal subsistence crops are maize, millets and cassava, and some livestock is reared for meat and milk. The main commodities marketed are maize, groundnuts, tobacco, cotton and cattle.

The Importance of Government Schemes and Development Programmes

Thus, in many of the remoter and less accessible parts of Africa the peasant farmer is still living at subsistence level. In many areas there is a great necessity to ensure adequate food supplies and raise standards of living to higher levels associated with modern agricultural production. Where regions are poorly served by communications and lie far from national markets the emphasis in agriculture must be laid on cash crops which can withstand long journeys and are of high value—tobacco for example.

The governments of African countries are making serious efforts to increase agricultural production through national schemes. We have already seen some of the measures taking place in Tanzania, the U.A.R., Kenya, Liberia and Algeria and more are described in Chapters Five and Seven. With the aid of international bodies such as the Food and Agricultural Organisation (the F.A.O.) agricultural ministries are investigating land use and mis-use,

problems of soil deficiency, farm planning, mechanised cultivation methods, livestock improvement, the proper use of fertilisers and so on.

In *Ghana* government-run State Farms were set up by the Nkrumah government to grow cash crops on a plantation basis. Nurseries have been established to produce the first seedlings for plantations of rubber, copra, coffee, pineapples and palm nuts (see page 148). In *Dahomey*, where the oil palm represents 75 per cent of exports by value, the government is planning several new oil palm plantations covering 39,600 acres, a project for which the European Economic Community has provided a large sum. Large ricefields are also being laid out in the Ouédé valley and efforts are being made to boost rice harvests and cut down on imports. The government is also encouraging processing industries which in turn stimulate the growing of cash crops, for example, at Cotonou, where a large textile complex is to be established so that the growing output of local cotton can be processed within the country.

In the *Gambia* farmers are taking advantage of government efforts to diversify the economy and reduce the reliance on groundnuts. The construction of access causeways into swamp and mangrove areas, tractor ploughing and discing, training programmes and demonstration plots have convinced the farmers of the value of rice cultivation. With the example of projects such as the Gambia Rice Farm at Sapu, between Georgetown and Kuntaur, and the rice station at Jenoi, a spectacular expansion of rice cultivation has taken place since the second world war. Rice is now the principal food crop in most parts of the Gambia and is being grown as a secondary cash crop.

Zambia's agricultural problems are being tackled by a series of peasant farming schemes. These provide capital for simple farm planning, land clearing, implements and oxen and enable subsistence cultivators to establish themselves as small-scale commercial farmers. More than 5,000 farmers cultivating some 105,000 acres are enrolled in such schemes. Livestock owners are encouraged by means of bonuses and subsidies to keep better stock and controlled grazing schemes are expanding. Experiments with drainage and irrigation are being carried out with the object of making use of over one million acres of undeveloped flood plain in Zambia.

The Agricultural Department in *Malawi* operates experimental stations in all parts of the country for research into maize breeding, potato and groundnut diseases, and variety growing of groundnuts, cotton and coffee. A programme of experimentation includes several small irrigation schemes, land reclamation in the Lower Shire Valley for sugar growing and the growing of crops of rice and cotton or other projects.

In addition, many governments in Africa are paying serious attention to increasing the amount of fish caught both in rivers and lakes and off their coasts. Uganda has led the way in the development of fish farms—large rectangular ponds specially stocked with Nile perch and tilapia—and has stocked many cattle watering points with additional supplies. There are now nearly 8,000 fish farms in the country and over 7,000 cattle watering points stocked with fish. It is estimated that these farms have a potential of over one million pounds of fish a year although at present they produce about 100,000 lb.

African countries caught a total of 2,810,000 tons of sea fish in 1963 (170,000 tons higher than in 1962). This amounted to 6 per cent of the world's total catch (see Table 11).

TABLE 11
Fish Catches of Selected African States, 1963

COUNTRY	FISH CATCH IN TONS 1962	1963	
Republic of S. Africa and S.W. Africa	1,061,000	1,147,000	
Angola	269,300	300,000	(est.)
Morocco	162,900	178,700	
Chad	80,000	80,000	(inland fishing)
Tanzania	60,200	74,000	
Uganda	64,500	60,200	(inland fishing)
Ghana	48,400	62,900	
Cameroun Republic	55,300	56,600	

The Growth of Co-operatives and their Importance to the African Farmer

The post-war years have seen the rapid development of co-operative societies in Africa. In *Uganda* the number of societies increased from 278 in 1950 to 1,709 in 1962 with a total membership of nearly 300,000 farmers, or nearly one-third of the farming population. In *Zambia* there were 10 societies in 1947 with 1,344 members; today there are over 230 with a membership of 36,000. *Malawi* now has 120 co-operatives; the *Gambia* 65. This growth has been the general trend in most African countries.

The work of the co-operative varies widely. Farmers' co-operatives market the produce, give advice on seed and fertiliser, grade and advertise produce, assist in financing agricultural experiments and provide training courses for farmers. Machinery can be hired more cheaply and used on a rotational basis through the co-operative. The average African farmer generally does not have the capital for all these aspects of farming and the society can get favourable loan terms from central banks and government organisations. In the *Gambia* produce marketing co-operatives handle 16 per cent of the groundnut crop. In *Tanzania* co-operatives began as early as 1925 among the coffee growers of Kilimanjaro and there are now over 1,400 registered societies marketing cotton, coffee, sisal, cashew nuts and vegetables. In *Zanzibar* the movement is fairly recent; the former Cloves Growers' Association is now a state enterprise and handles tobacco, chillies, and copra. In *Kenya* the government plans to develop and expand the co-operative movement (there are 1,000 societies in Kenya) and to establish a national co-operative federation and a co-operative bank.

In *former French territories* peasant co-operatives (paysannats) assist farmers in growing and marketing crops. In the *Central African Republic* both food and cash crops—coffee, cotton, groundnuts, sesame, gourds—are combined on the paysannats. African plantations of coffee, many of which were abandoned in the 1930s due to plant disease, began to be developed again in 1950. Today Africans own over 77 per cent of the total coffee acreage of 75,000 acres, the coffee being marketed through co-operatives. Four co-operatives in the C.A.R. also market, ginn and press raw cotton from African-owned estates.

The co-operative societies often work in close conjunction with the produce marketing boards of the various African states. The responsibility of these boards is to see that produce is shipped at economic rates, that fair prices are paid and that there is a steady development in the producing industries concerned. The boards ensure stable prices for producers, orderly marketing and improvement of quality, and they contribute large sums from their profits for development programmes.

Questions and Exercises are included at the end of Chapter Five on page 109. Students in Africa interested in conducting their own local land-use survey may find the following plan useful:

Local Study: A Simple Form for Use in Planning a Village Survey

Name of Village.............................

Administrative District.......................

Administrative Location......................

1 *SETTLEMENT*

  A *The Village Site*. Map based on local survey map if obtainable and roughly to scale showing:

    1 The general relief of the area.

    2 Village site in relation to water supply—rivers, streams, springs, bore holes, etc.

    3 Communications—roads, tracks, railways, rivers.

  B *The Village Layout*. Map or plan to scale showing:

    1 Houses or huts.

    2 Other buildings shaded or coloured according to function—shops, religious buildings, schools, etc.

    3 Grain stores.

    4 Cattle enclosures.

  C *Population*. Notes on the following aspects:

    1 The total population of the village; the number of male adults (say over 16); the number of female adults, number of children by sex; numbers of men absent from families and working elsewhere; origins of population if from outside village.

    2 Date of founding of village and its organisation.

    3 Analysis of a typical household, with plan of house or hut, layout of outbuildings, description of household activities.

2 *ECONOMY*

  A *Land Use*. Map roughly to scale showing:

    1 Land holdings of the village, divided if possible into plots on basis of ownership and type of crops grown, each plot coloured to show this. Houses and fields could be numbered, if possible, to show which family owns which fields.

    2 Grazing land outside cultivated area—near rivers or on higher ground.

    3 Amount of forest or trees and note whether these are of any economic use, e.g. oil palms, coconut palms, wattle trees, etc.

    4 Location of nursery beds, mills, quarries, water storage tanks, irrigation ditches, etc.

    5 Area of wasteland—bush, scrub, swamp, rain forest.

  B *Farming*. Notes on the following:

    1 Total cultivated acreage of all land owned by village; acreage under grazing; acreage under forest; acreage of waste land. These facts could be shown by percentage pie or bar graphs.

    2 Land tenure system—whether tribal or under title from Lands Office, how disposed of on death of owner, whether communally owned or individually owned, economic difficulties caused by system, e.g. fragmentation.

    3 The range of crops grown divided into subsistence and cash crops; the average acreage per family and the range of plot sizes; methods of agriculture describing range of tools used, methods to prevent soil erosion, use of fertilisers, methods of enclosure. A chart showing the activities carried on throughout the year in relation to rainfall seasons should be prepared if possible.

    4 Total numbers of cattle, sheep, goats, donkeys, camels, chickens, pigs, etc. kept by the villagers and average number per family. Types of cattle should be noted and particular problems in relation to keeping cattle such as diseases, lack of water, etc.

  C *Other Occupations*. Notes on occupations of those not engaged in farming, e.g. blacksmiths, tailors, cobblers, etc. Note light industries, if any, and numbers engaged.

  D *Trade*. Notes on the following:

    1 Cash crops and other commodities produced for sale and how and to where they are transported and sold.

    2 Commodities used by the villagers and where they are obtained.

CHAPTER FIVE

AGRICULTURE—MAN AND THE LAND (2)

External Influences on Agriculture in Africa

So far the use of Africa's soil by the African farmer has been discussed, but what of the land use by immigrant, largely European, farmers? Apart from the gradual spread of cultivation by the Boer farmer in South Africa from the seventeenth century onwards, real expansion began in European cultivation only towards the end of the nineteenth century. By the 1890s industrial Europe was looking for something more than mere territorial expansion in Africa; vast quantities of raw materials were needed—natural oils to lubricate machines, rubber for wheeled vehicles, and the growing populations demanded cheap foods requiring vast quantities of edible oils in their manufacture. Industrialists saw the rich potentialities of the African rain forests where there was scope for the plantation cultivation of oil palms, rubber, cotton, sugar cane, coffee and cacao.

The big industrial companies therefore sought concessions in Equatorial Africa from the governments ruling the new territories and plantations were carved from the forest belt. Elsewhere, individual farmers laid out estates in areas where it seemed land was unlimited and where climate was suitable for European settlement—the higher plateaux of East Africa and the Rhodesias.

The Advantages of Tropical Plantations

From the commercial point of view the plantation is much more economical than, say, the purchase of produce direct from local small-scale cultivators.

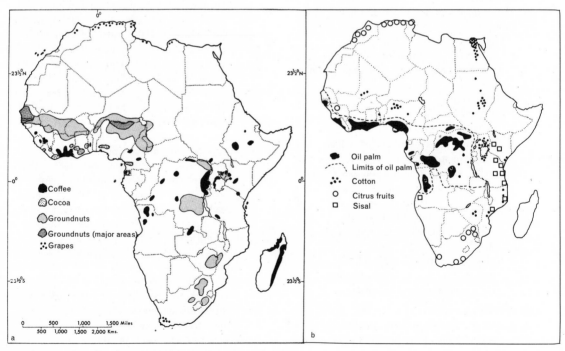

FIG. 1, a and b: Africa—distribution of some important cash crops

There are several reasons for this:

a The plantation is run by a company with tremendous financial reserves, efficient processing machinery, and control of a vast and efficiently-run marketing network.

b Strict control of plant growth, the breeding of improved varieties and the use of special fertilisers are easier operations for the large company. Plant products are easier to harvest than under natural conditions.

c The labourers, often transported great distances, are trained in the various aspects of plantation work and acquire specialised skills.

d Harvesting of the produce is carried out quickly, cheaply and efficiently, with economic transport to processing centres.

e Regular supplies of produce are guaranteed by the plantation system; this often justifies the erection of processing factories on the spot rather than exporting the bulky raw materials over long distances.

f Plantation organisation ensures no wastage; waste is used as fertiliser or as fuel.

The Disadvantages of Plantations

There are, however, certain disadvantages especially with smaller owners who adopt 'get-rich-quick' methods of exploiting land to its limits and leaving exhausted, overcropped soils. Often the labour, mostly young men, leave their villages and the cultivation of subsistence crops to the women and older folk, although some plantations do provide housing for families. Moreover, large plantations have much capital tied up in labour, machinery and marketing facilities and they are the first to suffer when prices for their produce fall on world markets. In contrast the small African farm can weather such economic storms and often produces substantial amounts of export crops when the plantations have reduced their exports, e.g. cotton and coffee production in Uganda. Some types of crops are more suited to the small farm, e.g. the rougher types of tobacco grown and cured by traditional methods in Rhodesia and the miombo woodlands of Tanzania. The small cocoa farms of Ghana need very little capital to begin and run and yet provide 65 per cent of the country's export produce; whether the plantation system would be more successful here is difficult to say.

Plantation Organisation

A plantation may be extremely large, covering thousands of acres and run by a huge company, usually European, or it may be much smaller and owned by a single man and his family, in which case it requires less capital to run. Whichever the type, the plantations will have certain things in common. They will be concentrating on cash crops, usually destined for markets outside the country of origin; subsistence crops will only be grown on a small scale to feed the workforce, and in some areas labour may have to be brought a considerable distance due to local scarcity, as in parts of the Congo rainforests. Many plantations increase their output by buying local produce. The plantation management provides housing, food and medical facilities and sometimes elementary education. Much revenue goes to the government of the host country through the taxation of the workers' wages, export duties on produce, and company land rents. Other benefits often accrue—roads and railways to and from the plantations will speed traffic generally and enable areas along their lengths to produce crops and market them more efficiently; factories are often set up and provide local employment, and bulk handling facilities at export ports are often financed by plantation companies.

The following examples illustrate the main types of plantation in Africa. The huge Unilever estates are good examples of large-scale organisation and huge capital investment; the Firestone plantations show the great support a country's economy receives from overseas investment, while many of the estates in the Kenya Highlands illustrate the smaller family-owned concern. Large company-owned plantations are seen again in Malawi (tea), Tanzania (sisal), and Natal, South Africa (sugar cane). Most of these sample studies lie within the tropical zone of Africa where plantation methods have flourished over the past sixty years.

Oil Palm Plantations

From small concessions granted by the Belgians to the Unilever Company of Great Britain in the early nineteenth century, plantations have spread throughout the Congo into Gabon, the Cameroons and Nigeria, producing vast quantities of palm oil, rubber, cocoa, bananas, coffee and smaller amounts of tea. The most important are the palm oil plantations which occupy 150,000 acres (79 per cent) of

Unilever's total concession of 191,000 acres in Africa (Fig. 5:2). Unilever was particularly successful in obtaining concessions in the Congo where the Belgians made every effort to expand the economy of the country, but in Nigeria plantation establishment had to be more selective since all land was African owned or held in trust or, in the most suitable area of south-east Nigeria, very densely settled.

The Creation of an Oil Palm Plantation

Site Selection and Preparation: Climatic conditions are most suitable for the oil palm between 5° north and south of the equator at low elevations; in the Cameroons cultivation has been successful up to 2,300 feet but not above this. Soils are usually poor, but better patches are indicated by richer vegetation and soil samples are taken and tested for optimum conditions. The oil mills need to be situated close to navigable rivers and on flat land to facilitate road building. Plenty of water is also needed for the various processes and for the workers' use.

Workers' accommodation is built and seed beds laid out in cleared forest patches. Within six months the six-inch tall seedlings are transplanted in a nursery in rows two feet apart. After two years they are finally bedded out and work is begun on the planned plantation layout. Roads are bulldozed on a rectangular pattern and the forest blocks gradually cleared. A cover crop is planted which suppresses secondary forest growth, yields precious nitrogen, scarce in tropical soils, and prevents the earth from being baked hard. The cleared timber is used for house construction or left to rot.

Planting and Harvesting: The young trees are taken from the nursery beds and planted in holes 30 feet apart in staggered rows. The workers control the growth of cover crops and secondary growth and, as the palm grows, they cut away the drooping fronds to make inspection easier. The African labour force is very skilled and a cutter must be able to judge when the fruit is ripe enough to yield high quality oil. This is important, since unripe fruit gives a lower yield and overripe fruit a good yield but of poorer quality, due to fatty acid development. Cutting goes on throughout the year, each tree bearing a fruit head once a week. The cutters use long knives attached to poles or, with taller trees, ladders or waist climbing ropes.

The fruit is often bruised by its fall or by handling, and processing is essential immediately. The fruits are carried in baskets or on poles to lorries or to steriliser cages pulled by a locomotive on a light railway. Lorries are preferred because they reduce carrying and can get closer to the rows of palms.

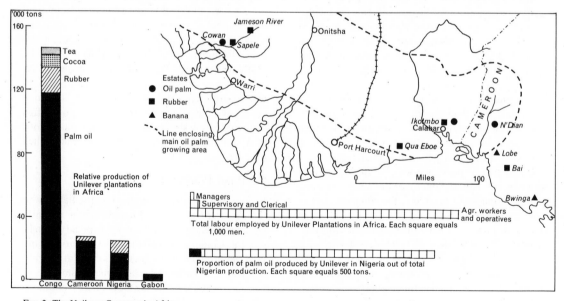

FIG. 2: The Unilever Company in Africa

92

Bulldozed roads are also less expensive to build and can reach all parts of the plantation, while railways are often uneconomic if harvests are small.

Processing: At the mill the fruit is weighed, sterilised under steam to arrest acid development, the stalks removed for fuel and the fruit reduced to a pulp which is passed through oil extracting machines. The oil is stored in settling tanks to separate impurities. The dried shells and fibre are used as fuel and the cleaned kernels graded and bagged.

Exports: The Congo produces about 25 per cent of the world's palm oil and large quantities of kernel oil and oil cake; about 80 per cent is plantation produced, the rest comes from wild palms.[1] Fig. 5:**3** shows the chief export routes. Rail routes run south from Port Francquie to Zambia, Rhodesia and South Africa and bulk oil goes by tank barge to Kinshasa and thence by rail tanker to Matadi where it is transferred to ocean-going oil tankers. There

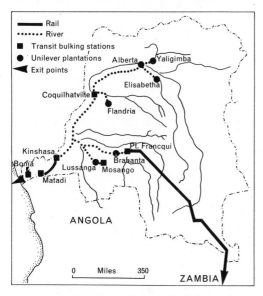

Fig. 3: Congo (Kinshasa)—exit routes for Unilever oil palm produce

are bulk oil transit stations at Coquilhatville, Mosango and Boma. The main countries of destination are the United States, Belgium, Holland, Germany and Italy with smaller amounts to Britain, Japan, Zambia, Rhodesia and France.

[1] Compare with Nigeria, where 94 per cent is produced on small farms and only 6 per cent comes from plantations.

Rubber in Liberia

Although palm oil is an important element in the Congo's economy there is also a wide variety of other plantation crops which helps to broaden the economy, for palm oil represents only 7 per cent of all exports. In contrast rubber has for years dominated Liberia's economy and in 1945 formed 96·6 per cent of exports. In 1965 rubber represented 16 per cent of exports but this does not represent a drop in exports; it is due to the increase in exports of iron ore (see page 168).

Plantation cultivation has developed in the coastal lowlands of Liberia where rainfalls exceed 100 inches a year with a long wet season (April to November) and a moist sticky 'dry' season. Relative humidities (up to 85 per cent) and temperatures (75 to 80°F [24 to 27°C]) are high. Under these conditions cocoa, coffee and citrus are plantation grown north-east of Monrovia and oil palm and cocoa in the central and southern coastal plains. But the largest plantations are those of the American Firestone Company located north of Harbel and at Cavalla in the south-eastern corner.

The history of rubber in Liberia goes back to 1910 when the British planted 2,000 acres at Mt Barclay near Monrovia but abandoned the project ten years later due to falling world prices. In 1924 there were only 1,000 acres producing £0·5 million worth of rubber. Physical conditions were examined by Firestone, which badly needed plantation concessions in view of Britain's monopoly of Malayan sources.[1] Firestone obtained 99-year leases in 1926 and rubber has since played a vital rôle in Liberia's economy. Housing estates, roads and dispensaries were built and by 1928 15,000 acres had been planted, rising to 55,000 acres by 1933. The Second World War stimulated production especially when Malaya was overrun by the Japanese. Today 25,000 workers (including 15,000 skilled tappers) tend 11·5 million trees producing 45,000 tons of dried rubber. This falls short of Firestone's aim of producing 200,000 tons annually and employing one-third of a million workers, and the plantations produce only 35 per cent of the company's needs. Research is constantly going on to find better yielding varieties.

Rubber is still a very large item in exports (16 per

[1] At this time Henry Ford established rubber plantations at Belterra and Fordlandia in the Amazon Basin; both failed due to labour problems, diseases and transport difficulties.

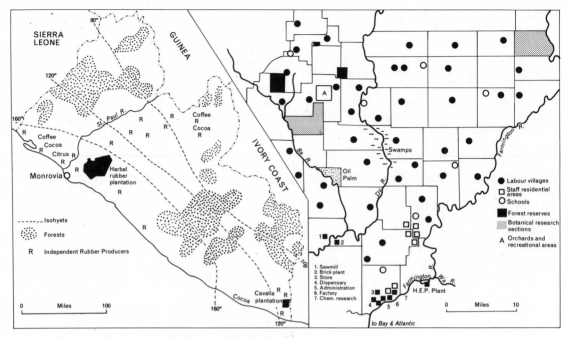

FIG. 4: Liberia—cash crop areas and the Firestone Harbel Rubber Plantation

cent) but its relative importance has decreased due to growing exports of iron ore. The main plantation is at Harbel on the Farmington River 15 miles from the coast, while a second plantation lies 25 miles inland on the Cavalla River which is only navigable for small craft owing to sandbars. Shallow draught barges navigate the bars and the liquid latex is pumped into the holds of tankers. There are storage tanks at Monrovia.

The Harbel Plantation is approached from the south-east along the Farmington River. The extreme southern section of this 85,000-acre estate is occupied by the processing factory, the clinical research laboratory, a dispensary, transport buildings and administrative offices. The remainder of the plantation is divided into 45 separate sections to facilitate administration and the orderly tapping of the trees. The whole plantation is crossed by a network of roads. Within the divisions are botanical research gardens, research and seed selection centres, rubber nurseries, sawmills, a brick factory, a club house, a hydro-electric power station, a soft drinks factory, a plant manufacturing rubber cups, sandals and soap, and a wireless transmitting station. The plantation is thus virtually self-contained.

The benefits to Liberia from such an economic enterprise may be summarised as follows:

Communications: Since 1926 300 miles of plantation roads have been constructed and 100 miles of

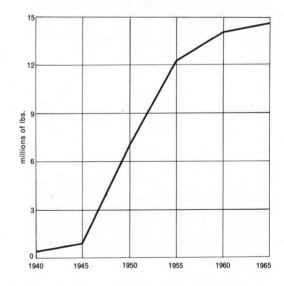

FIG. 5: Liberia—rubber production by independent growers

94

outside roads and bridges. These communications have stimulated local production along their lengths.

Agricultural Assistance: The company assists small-scale rubber growers (now numbering 3,000 compared with 150 in 1941) by supplying seeds, advice and by buying their entire rubber production. In 1941 independent rubber farmers sold 0·5 million lb. of rubber to Firestone; in 1951, 4·25 million lb., and the current sales are about 14·5 million lb. (Fig. 5:**5**).

Crop Research: The company also experiments with subsistence and cash crops suited to Liberia's soils and climate which are considered excellent for coffee, cacao, bananas, oil palm and rice. Experiments with livestock, poultry keeping and with many fruits—mangoes, papayas, pineapples, bananas, avocados, oranges, and grapefruit—are promising.

Medical Research: A company medical service provides two hospitals, 39 dispensaries, pre-natal clinics and a child care service. Research into tropical diseases and medical research costs £330,000 a year.

The Kenya Highlands—Small- and Medium-Sized Estates and Mixed Farms

The soils and climate of the Kenya Highlands are suitable for a wide range of commercially profitable crops such as coffee, tea, sisal, pyrethrum and pineapples. Sisal and pineapples are located on the drier eastern fringes (30 to 40 inches [762 to 1016mm] rainfall a year); coffee is grown north of Nairobi on the Aberdare dip-slopes (40 to 60 inches [1016 to 1524mm]); tea is found on the wetter plateau around Kericho (50 inches [1270mm] and over); pyrethrum needs the strong sunlight and coolness of the highlands for a good flowering head. These cash crops are mainly grown on large European estates although an increasing amount is being grown on small African shambas.

The moderate rainfalls, cool temperatures at 6,000 to 7,500 feet and rolling green pastures and shady woodlands are also ideal for herds of imported dairy cattle—Guernseys, Jerseys, Friesians and Ayrshires—and the Highlands are probably the foremost dairying region in the whole of Africa.[1]

The Highlands of Kenya thus form an economic heartland and original forest, savannah and bush has been converted in 70 years of European settlement into an agricultural concentration of stud farms, cattle ranches and plantations and estates covering 12,000 square miles. Many of these farms have been broken up into smaller units as we have seen and are being farmed by African cultivators. Thus, whereas in 1960 Europeans produced 80·3 per cent of the coffee they now only produce 68 per cent. Again, African farmers cultivate 12,700 acres of tea on small plots (average tea acreage 0·57) compared with approximately 26,000 acres on large estates. However, European estates and farms still figure largely in the economy.

A Coffee Estate

Coffee is the most important crop in Kenya (3 per cent world and 13 per cent Africa's output); it is the first export crop of Uganda (£34·8 million as against £15·3 million for cotton in 1966) and the third export of Tanzania. The main plantation zone is a broad belt 15 miles wide and 40 miles long extending north-east of Nairobi where there are several European estates. West of this area many small African shambas include coffee as a cash crop, producing 10,000 tons a year. Other coffee growing areas are found on the volcanic soils of Mt Elgon and the Cherangani slopes and the Mua hills.

The coffee estate shown in Fig. 5:**6** lies 35 miles north-east of Nairobi, and covers 513 acres of which 213 acres are under coffee. In this region, which is

[1] Other important dairy regions are found on the plateaux of Nigeria, in parts of Natal and Cape provinces and in Rhodesia.

TABLE 12
Kenya: Rainfall Figures for Sassa Coffee Estate

MONTH	JAN.	FEB.	MARCH	APRIL	MAY	JUNE	JULY	AUG.	SEPT.	OCT.	NOV.	DEC.	YEAR
Rainfall (inches) (mm)	1·7 43·2	1·1 27·9	4·2 106·7	9·1 231·1	3·5 88·9	0·2 5·1	0·3 7·6	0·8 20·3	1·5 38·1	5·4 137·2	9·5 241·3	6·3 160·0	42·4 1076·9

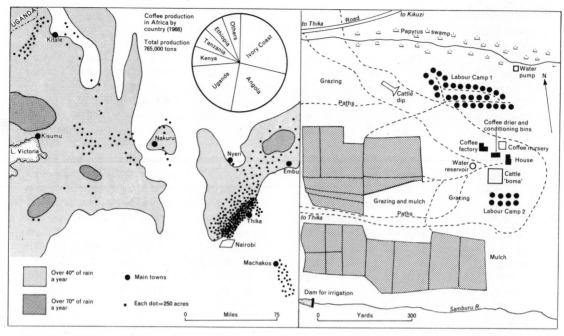

Fig. 6: Kenya—coffee production in the Kenya Highlands, and a coffee estate near Thika

Coffee production in Africa by country (1966)

Total production 765,000 tons

Over 40″ of rain a year

Over 70″ of rain a year

● Main towns

· Each dot=250 acres

marginal for coffee growing, the farmer keeps 50 Ayrshire cattle and 20 sheep and is experimenting with cotton. The landscape here is undulating, cut into broad flat ridges by dip-slope rivers of the Aberdares. Temperatures are modified by altitude (4,750 feet, 65°F [18°C] average) while rainfalls are moderate and fairly reliable as is shown by Table 12.

Work on the Estate: Before planting, the coffee seeds are dried in ash then planted in a primary nursery when six inches tall; later they are transplanted to a second nursery and left for two years. Then they are transferred to prepared fields and shaded by grass coverings which are later used for mulch. After two years the plants begin to bear and they reach maturity when ten years old.

Green oval beans appear on the bushes after the whitish, sweet-smelling flower has germinated and died. The beans develop in bunches and gradually turn a reddish brown. They are then hand-picked, taken to the plantation factory by lorry or in baskets and pulped to remove the skins and fleshy parts which are used as fertiliser. The beans ferment overnight and are then washed and covered with polythene sheets to prevent excessive drying by the sun.

After further washing and browning in the sun they are stored in conditioning bins prior to despatch to the roasting mills in Nairobi.[1]

A coffee estate is thus a concern unsuitable for a farmer in a hurry. Constant vigilance is needed against insects and plant diseases, bushes are sprayed constantly, weeding continuously carried on, and moisture retained in the soils by mulching. Production at the estate varies considerably with rainfall amount; in 1961 62 tons were harvested, in 1963, 150 tons and in 1964 70 tons.

A Dairy Farm

Dairy farming began in Kenya in 1911 and butter and cheese were first exported to London in 1921. By 1930 exports had increased thirty-fold and today dairy products are worth £5 million a year, of which £2 million worth are exported to Ethiopia, the Middle East, Uganda, Tanzania and Malawi.

The sample dairy farm north-west of Nairobi (Fig. 5:7) is fairly typical of the smaller types of

[1] The methods used are exactly the same as those on African coffee farms but in this case individual small-scale farmers belong to a central co-operative which collects, processes and markets their produce.

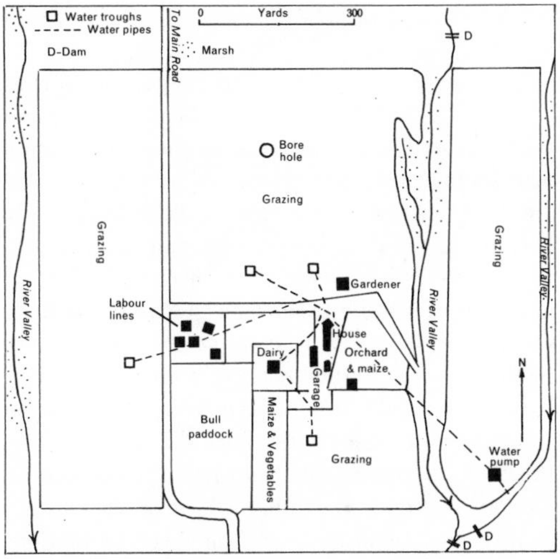

FIG. 7: Kenya—a dairy farm in the Highlands

farm. It covers 132 acres on the higher part of a broad ridge from which most of the forest has been cleared except for shade trees. Although a few subsistence crops are grown, practically the whole acreage is used to graze sixty Ayrshire cows and two bulls. The farm was originally used for coffee and pyrethrum and this mined the soils of minerals, but the use of fertiliser and inferior stock to clear the rank grass and provide manure helped the soils to recuperate. Many of the original cattle were lost through diseases such as East Coast Fever. Once the land was cleared better grades of cattle were introduced. Since dairy farming in Kenya suffers from droughts (November to March) farms must be near water supplies. On this farm a spring and small stream supply 2,000 gallons per day in normal periods and double that during droughts. The milk yield, usually 180 gallons a day, goes to Nairobi.

There are many other types of mixed farms in the Kenya Highlands, many still run by Europeans. Table 13 indicates the wide variety, sizes and uses

TABLE 13
Kenya: Sample European Farms in the Kenya Highlands

LOCATION	AREA IN ACRES	ALTITUDE IN FEET	AV. ANN. RNFL. (INS.)	SOILS	STOCK AND CROPS (*Figs. in brackets indicate acreage*)	WORKFORCE
1. *Nr. Kitale, Trans-Nzoia Plateau*	910	6,500	41 (28 Apr. to Aug.)	Red loams and Black Cotton	Coffee, oranges, rye, maize (350), sunflowers, wheat, tomatoes	40
2. *Nr. Kitale, Trans-Nzoia Plateau*	566	6,200	41	Poor sandy types needing much fertiliser	Maize (140), sunflowers, seed grass, apples, oranges. 150 pedigree Guernsey dairy cows	25
3. *Tana River region, south of Mt Kenya*	45,000	5,200	28 very variable	Black Cotton, sandy and red clays	Coffee (200), maize (200), pineapples, and lucerne. 3,500 Boran beef cattle	60
4. *Northern Highlands, north of Mt Kenya near Nanyuki*	9,000	6,300	25 very variable from 12 to 43	Black Cotton and red loams	1,000 Sahiwal and Ayrshire cattle, 60 sheep, 150 pigs, 300 laying hens	40
5. *Thika District,* 30 *miles north-east Nairobi*	1,020	5,000	32 variable	Red sandy and clayey types	Coffee, sisal, pineapples, apples, plums, cherries, vegetables	40
6. *Rift Valley, near Njoro,* 20 *miles west of Nakuru*	754	7,250	42	Dark-brown loams	57 Friesland and Jerseys, 25 pigs, 300 Hampshire Down, Cheviot and Romney sheep, 150 beef cattle. Maize (4), potatoes (10), wheat (250)	50

of these farms. It is very noticeable how the types of crops grown and the breeds of animals vary with location and with rainfall amount and reliability.

Sisal in East Africa

Sisal is found in the drier eastern fringes of the Kenya Highlands, in the coastal zone near Mombasa and in Tanzania, and along the main railways. There is a correlation between sisal distribution and the 40-inch isohyet (Fig. 5:**8**). The plant will grow on a wide variety of soils but red earths and those derived from coral limestone, the latter typical of East Africa's coastal plains, are best. The richer the soil, the better the fibre yields in quality and quantity, for sisal takes a heavy toll of soil minerals. The high temperatures, plentiful sunshine and rainfalls

between 27 and 47 inches [686 and 1194mm] are well suited to sisal.

Sisal was first introduced into Tanganyika in 1892 by Dr Richard Hindorf who brought Mexican bulbils from Florida and planted them at Kikogwe near Pangani; the first exports were made in 1900 and had reached 20,000 tons by 1913. Production fell during the First World War and in 1920 only 8,000 tons were exported. But since the 1920s sisal has figured large in Tanzania's exports, usually representing about 25 per cent and reaching a record of 60 per cent in 1951 with its use in the Korean War. It now forms about 3 per cent of exports (cotton 14 per cent, coffee 15 per cent) and employs one-third of all the people industrially employed in Tanzania. About £40 million is invested in Tanzania's sisal, a crop grown on large plantations seldom less than 3,000 acres in size. It has allowed areas unsuitable for most crops to be used fully.

In Kenya sisal makes a smaller but significant contribution to the economy, employing 25,000 men and representing 10 per cent of national income. It was introduced in 1907 when 1,000 acres were planted in the Thika District; in 1913 there were 7,000 acres and 1,000 tons were exported. The acreage rose to 60,000 in the mid-1920s and to 200,000 in the late 1940s.

A Sisal Estate

Sisal cultivation is largely in the hands of large companies, due to the considerable expense incurred in transport and specialised processing machinery. The Morogoro Sisal Estate (Fig. 5:**9**) belongs to the Central Line Sisal Estate Company and is one of a group lying 8 miles east of Morogoro. Here the land is flat or undulating with shallow valleys of intermittent streams and soils range from reddish-brown types to Black Cotton. Much of the original bush and scattered trees has been cleared. The rainfall is very unreliable and confined to a sharply defined season (December to April). In the last ten years annual rainfalls have varied between 22·23 inches [564·5mm] (1961) and 42·35 inches [1075mm] (1962) (see Table 14).

The weather is unpleasantly hot and humid during the rains with day temperatures in the 80s but August to September are pleasantly dry with clear, cloudless skies.

The whole estate covers 16,810 acres and the land is used as shown in Table 15:

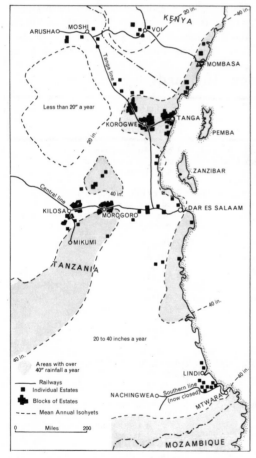

FIG. 8: Tanzania—distribution of sisal estates in relation to annual rainfall

TABLE 14
Tanzania: Average Monthly Rainfall Totals, Morogoro Sisal Estate

MONTH	JAN.	FEB.	MARCH	APRIL	MAY	JUNE	JULY	AUG.	SEPT.	OCT.	NOV.	DEC.	YEAR
Rainfall (inches) (mm)	4·96 125·9	4·45 113·0	4·39 111·5	4·87 123·7	2·44 61·9	1·00 25·4	0·71 18·0	0·91 23·1	0·86 21·8	1·85 46·9	3·26 82·8	3·46 87·5	33·16 838·2

TABLE 15
Tanzania: Land Use on the Morogoro Sisal Plantation

	MATURE	IMMATURE	NURSERIES	FALLOW	WASTE	ROADS, BUILDINGS
Pangawe	27%	4%	0·5%	2%	6·5%	2%
Kingolwira	34%	12%	0·5%	1%	7·5%	3%

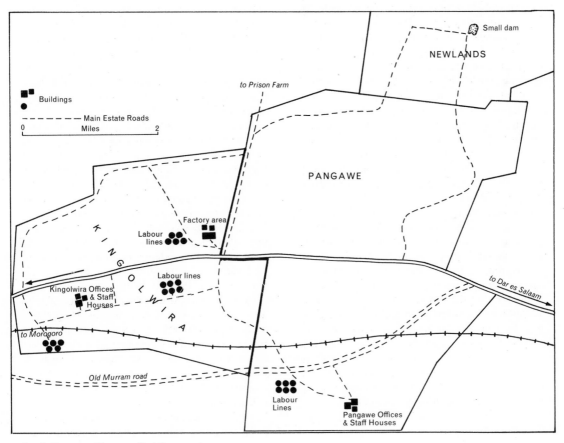

Fɪɢ. 9: Tanzania—Morogoro Sisal Estates

About 2,000 men are employed. There are ten Europeans, three Asians and the rest are African truck drivers, mechanics, sisal cutters and weeders. The estate is divided into blocks, each planted at staggered intervals so that the sisal is ready in stages. The blocks furthest from the processing centre are cut during the dry season to reduce carting during wet seasons over long distances. Each of the twelve blocks is worked on a nine-year rotation scheme.

African workers once planted maize and beans between sisal rows to keep down weeds but this was unsuccessful and a legume ('mbuki') was grown instead; this was an excellent cover crop providing nitrogen and shade, thus preventing soils from baking hard.

The sisal plants are well spaced out in rows to allow easy cutting. Each plant has a life span of from 8 to 14 years and there are between 2,000 and 2,500 plants per acre. The plant produces leaves for cutting when about three years old and yields up to 200 leaves during its lifetime. The leaves, like broad-bladed swords, grow five or six feet outwards from the bowl and are quite heavy, about 30 tons being obtained from one acre. Before it dies the plant sends up a 'pole' topped by a cluster of flowers and fresh bulbils which are used for seed.

While the plants are growing, regular weeding, insecticide spraying and soil fertilisation is needed. On some estates sisal has been grown for fifty years with satisfactory yields but there is evidence of soil decline and fertilisers are applied liberally every five years. The slashing of long grass to prevent shade and leaf-cutting are year-round occupations, each mature plant being cut once a year. The cut leaves are bundled, sent by lorry or locomotive to the processing factory and there stripped of their fibre before the plant juices become sticky. The leaves are scraped, washed, brushed and then fed into a decorticator at a rate of 600 a minute to remove, in running water, the softer tissues from the fibres. Waste fibre is recovered, dried, and made into 'flume tow' for padding. The main fibres are hung over wires to dry in the sun, brushed in machines, graded, baled and weighed. From Morogoro they are shipped to Dar es Salaam for export. The fibre is used to make rope, twine, sackcloth, bags, matting and other articles requiring a strong fibre.

Tea Plantations

While sisal can be grown on most soils, tea is more selective and needs deep, well-aerated soils which are permeable and well drained. Tea requires at least 60 inches [1524mm] of rain in tropical regions, well distributed throughout the year, and can flourish in temperatures as low as 55°F [13°C]. Such conditions are found in the highland areas of East and Central Africa—the western Kenya Highlands, the Paré and Usambara Highlands, the Udzungwa and Ufipa Highlands of Tanzania and the Mlanje Highlands of Malawi.

The first country to grow tea in Africa was *Nyasaland* (Malawi) where it was first planted near Blantyre in 1888. It spread to the coffee estates around Mlanje and soon ousted coffee as a commercial crop. In 1908, more tea estates were begun at Cholo and recently in the Nkata Bay area.

In *Kenya* the main tea area lies around Kericho, between 6,000 and 7,000 feet. Introduced in the early 1900s from Asia it is Kenya's second agricultural export by value and now covers about 25,000 acres in the Kericho area with smaller acreages at Nandi, Sotik, Limuru, Kitale and Molo. Africans are taking an increasing interest in this crop and it is not entirely grown on large estates. At Meru, near Mt Kenya, many African farmers have planted tea in $\frac{3}{4}$-acre plots and an African-run 500-acre estate supplies tea to a new processing factory.

Tea is also the third most important agricultural export of *Uganda*, a country ideally suited to the plant and where estate yields per acre are said to be higher than those of India and Ceylon. The Uganda Government has recently acquired several large estates from former European owners and has set up a training programme for African farmers.

In the Bamenda area of western *Cameroons* there are large areas suited to tea cultivation. The large Tole estate produced over 100,000 pounds in 1961 and there are plans to expand this to 1·2 million pounds by the early 1970s.

Other areas in Africa where tea is becoming an important commercial crop are in *Mozambique* where nearly 50,000 acres are now producing, the Eastern Highlands of *Rhodesia* with about 5,000 acres, and there are lesser producing areas in *Rwanda* and *Burundi* and the eastern *Congo* (Kinshasa).

A Tea Estate

The following account of the organisation and work on a tea estate would apply to practically any medium-sized estate in Africa. As on the sisal estate, growth must be regulated so that there is constant production; the most economical size for this is about 1,000 acres, which would need a workforce of about 600 women who are usually defter at the work than men and 70 general workers. The workforce is housed on the estate or travels to the estate each day. The usual facilities such as school, canteens and dispensaries are provided by the management.

The best land for tea is heavily forested land with slightly acid soils which are well drained. The larger trees are cut down and the stumps removed since they would attract termites. Grass cover and herbaceous growth are also removed and the slopes are then terraced to prevent excessive soil erosion in these heavy rainfall areas.

The young seedlings are transferred from their nursery beds after about two and a half years into prepared holes on the terraces, with three feet between each plant. During growth the bushes are constantly pruned so that they develop many short branches. After two or three years they begin to bear suitable leaves and picking is increased gradually until the mature bush can be picked every fortnight. Every four or five years the bush is pruned. Yields vary; in Malawi the average production of picked leaf per acre ranges from 800 to 900 pounds while in Kenya it is slightly higher. A thousand-acre estate would produce about three and a half million pounds of green tea annually.

The plucked leaves are taken by the pickers in baskets slung on their backs to a collecting point where they are loaded onto lorries and speeded to the processing factory. Here they are weighed, spread on racks and dried in warm air currents. The dried leaf is passed through rollers which crush it and free the natural juices; this helps in the next stage of fermentation. After the leaves have fermented for four hours they pass into the drying rooms and are then allowed to cool off before grading and packing in foil-lined chests.

Sugar Plantations

Sugar cane has a much wider distribution in Africa than either sisal, tea or oil palm. Its lower temperature limit is 68°F [20°C] which is easily attained in all lowland areas in tropical Africa, but it cannot be grown at high elevations without a considerable increase in the length of the growing season. Much sugar cane is grown by African farmers for their own use. In *Nigeria*, especially on the 'fadamas' (the riverine flats of the north) nearly 600,000 tons are produced each year and this is almost wholly consumed locally. Most of the sugar cane which enters commerce is grown on large plantations on the Natal coast of *South Africa*, the Kilombero Valley and coastal lowlands of *Tanzania*, the shores of Lake Victoria in *Kenya* and *Uganda* and on the islands of *Madagascar*, *Mauritius*, *Fernando Po* and *San Thomé*. Sugar cane is also produced in the *Sudan*, *Ethiopia*, the *U.A.R.*, *Swaziland*, *Ghana* and *Rhodesia*. Africa produces about 6 per cent of the total world production.

It is, however, in the coastal lowlands of Natal and Mozambique that plantation sugar cane is most important. In the *Natal region* it covers over half a million acres. Here sugar cane can be grown as far south as latitude 30° due to the southward drift of the warm Mozambique Current. But the rainfall is rather marginal, for sugar cane requires 70 to 100 inches [1778 to 2540mm] a year although it will grow in regions with rainfall as low as 40 inches. In the Natal coastal belt the south receives on average about 40 inches [1016mm], increasing northwards to about 57 inches [1448mm] with 70 per cent falling in the summer half of the year (October to April). The low rainfalls and their irregularity are compensated in many areas by the high water table levels. Since sugar cane cannot withstand frost it is confined to a rather narrow belt rarely more than ten miles wide from the coast, where cool season temperatures are moderated.

The soils within this belt are very variable. The best are the alluviums of the river valleys but space for cane is limited here since these are regions of intensive agriculture. The granitic soils of the south and some of the sandier soils are fairly good but need liberal doses of fertiliser. Many planters grow legumes for short periods between sugar plantings (once every nine years) and this returns some nitrogen. The keeping of livestock and the growing of other crops in rotation have been suggested to help maintain soil fertility but, like tea and sisal estates, the mills must be supplied with cane throughout the year if their running is to be economic.

Sugar cane was first brought to the Natal coast in the mid-nineteenth century and after 1860 expansion was rapid. Indentured labour was brought from India and many of these early plantation workers

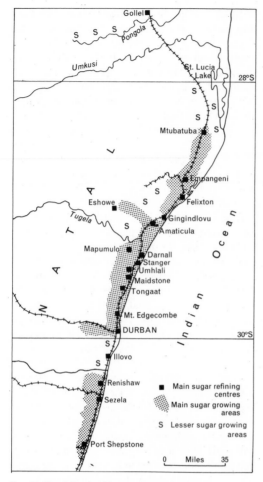

FIG. 10: Natal, South Africa—sugar growing regions

settled in Natal on completion of their indentured service. There are now few Asians working in the plantations and most of the cutting is done by Bantu labour.

Sugar cane is planted at staggered intervals so that production never ceases. The freshly planted cane takes from 18 to 20 months before it is ready for cutting and then another 18 months elapse before it is ready again. Cutting goes on for nine years and then the soil lies fallow for nine months under a legume. The cut cane is taken by lorry or rail to the factory and there weighed, chopped and crushed. Giant presses extract the juice and this is chemically treated, heated, clarified, brought to boiling point and then cooled, when the crystals separate from the brown molasses. The sugar is allowed to dry, and is then graded and bagged.

South Africa aims to become the fifth largest sugar producer in the world by 1970 and to produce 2 million tons annually. In 1967 there were 21 sugar mills—7 in northern Natal, 4 in southern Natal, 5 in Zululand, 2 in the Natal midlands, and 3 in eastern Transvaal.

Most of South Africa's sugar is produced in Natal and this amounts to approximately 1·4 million tons a year, which is rather more than South Africa consumes internally. Considerable amounts are exported to the United States, Japan, Canada and the United Kingdom, although the latter country gives preference to Commonwealth countries.

Tobacco and the Rhodesian Farmer

The amount of tobacco produced in Africa is only a fraction of world output, just over 5 per cent. Over a quarter of this is grown in Rhodesia which ranks seventh in world production, a position reached in a comparatively short period. In the 1945/46 season (Southern) Rhodesia produced 45 million pounds, in 1950, 105 million pounds and a record of 324 million pounds in 1964, most of it sold to the United Kingdom with smaller amounts to Australia and South Africa. The production and export of flue-cured tobacco has become the most important industry of Rhodesia and her economy relies heavily on it, tobacco representing over a third of the country's total exports in pre-sanction days and bringing more revenue than any other commodity.

Tobacco cultivation first began in Rhodesia in 1893 when a small amount was grown near Umtali, but it was not until 1911 that large-scale cultivation began at Marandellas, 50 miles east of Salisbury. The failure of cotton helped tobacco to establish itself in the north-eastern parts of Rhodesia a year later. In these early years the tobacco growers were assisted by the British South Africa Company which experimented with tobacco seeds, gave advice and generally encouraged tobacco growing. Following a short depression period high-grade tobacco production was greatly increased when the Imperial Tobacco Company of Great Britain began to buy regular and large amounts, and an export packing factory was opened at Masasa in 1927. There followed a series of legislative acts which led to Rhodesia's pre-eminence in the then Central

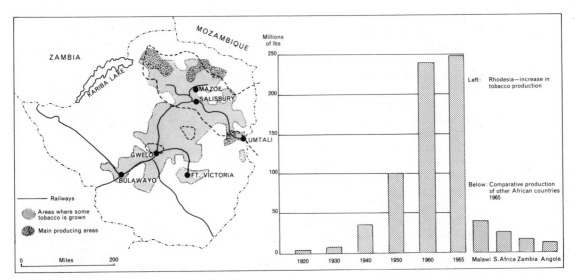

Fig. 11: Rhodesia—area of tobacco cultivation and tobacco production

African Federation in the production of flue-cured tobacco.

Today the crop is grown over a wide area especially in the north and east of Rhodesia near Salisbury, Marandellas, Makoni, Hartley and Lomagundi, with lesser areas at Mazoe, Umtali, Mrewa and Unrungwe. In these areas climate and soils are almost ideal for tobacco. The plant needs a constant and even annual rainfall of about 25 inches [635mm] at least, with no droughts or heavy rainy periods while optimum temperatures lie between 70 and 90°F [21 and 32°C]. Deep, well-drained and aerated sandy soils with rich organic content are best. These conditions are fulfilled in Rhodesia where, during the growing season (October to March), temperatures are in the 70°Fs [between 21 and 32°C] with a small range of 3°F [1·7°C], humidities rarely fall below 60 per cent and there is plenty of sunshine. The lighter, sandy veld soils are well drained and very suitable for tobacco although tobacco is also grown in regions with poorer and more varied soils.

In the early days land was freely available and farmers could afford to crop their fields with tobacco for two years, then the land reverted to fallow or natural grass for periods of up to twenty years. As land became scarcer with the influx of settlers and tobacco demands increased the fallow period was reduced to ten years. This caused serious soil deterioration and erosion but a liberal use of ferti-

liser, the ploughing in of green crops and soil conservation methods checked this. A rotation system evolved with two out of every three fields kept constantly under crops. Later, a less exhaustive system was used involving the grazing of cattle on improved pastures and the growing of alternative crops such as maize and nitrogen-rich legumes. The following account, slightly abridged, gives a clear picture of the methods of growing tobacco in Rhodesia and the special problems with which the tobacco farmer has to contend.

. . . tobacco is not a planter's crop, but a farm crop which fits into a definite rotation—one year of tobacco followed by three or four years of improved grass ley and back to tobacco for one year only. It is the most expensive and risky crop on the farm, the most difficult and tiresome one to produce, which requires constant attention for eleven months in the year. The farmer must prepare his seed beds, probably some two acres on the average tobacco farm, and fumigate them against eelworm; if he has any irrigated tobacco he will begin sowing his beds in the first week in July and then has to protect them against sunburn and water them twice daily, and they must also be sprayed regularly against a variety of possible diseases.

103

Sowing goes on for two months, and transplanting the seedlings to the fields takes place two to three months later. Before any land can be planted it must be ridged up and fertilised with phosphates and potash.

Planting is done by hand, and a mixed fertiliser, predominantly nitrogenous will be added. The land will need to be cleaned twice; plants which have failed will be replaced; a top dressing of nitrogen may be required if there has been excessive rainfall. Suckering of the plants is the next task—the picking off of little shoots which grow off the stem. After that topping must be carried out so that the plant does not run to flower. Reaping will begin about two months after the land has been planted up, the bottom leaves first and so on up the plant until each plant has been re-visited and reaped at least six times in all over a period of some two months. Reaping will continue into April.

With each reaping the tobacco is carried into the barns for curing and one barn is needed for every six or eight acres of tobacco grown. Curing takes about a week, and the crop can easily be ruined by lack of attention to temperature control. After curing the tobacco is taken into the bulking shed and stacked, and after a while it will be graded by the farm labour into colours and sizes, probably at least twelve different grades in all. Finally it will be packed into special waterproof paper and hessian and the bales will be transported to the auction floors in Salisbury.[1]

Tobacco is thus a difficult crop and the farmer is never sure of his amount of profit; for example, the 1964 record harvest season was a poor one for prices as is shown in Table 16:

Despite these fluctuations the profits from tobacco have gone a long way in forming the base on which the whole of agricultural production in Rhodesia rests. Tobacco in 1965 totalled nearly £45 million in value (1964 £39·2 million) or nearly 33 per cent of the total value of exports. In view of recent sanctions, however, many Rhodesian farmers are increasing their acreages of foodstuffs in local demand —animal fodder, maize and wheat.

Viticulture, Fruit and Mixed Farming in the South-West Cape

While dairy and mixed farming are important in the Kenya Highlands, citrus fruits (oranges, lemons, grapefruit and naartjes) have never been significant crops there. Citrus fruits suffer from the reduced temperatures at these altitudes and from frequent cold spells experienced in June and July; deciduous fruits grow continuously throughout the winterless year and are generally of poor quality.

In contrast, wheat and fruit cultivation are two important occupations of the white farmers of the south-western Cape Province of South Africa. Here, in the broad valleys and flat coastal plains in the Cape Town hinterland, stretches a broad arc 200 miles long and from 20 to 80 miles wide of small farms varying from 40 to 300 acres in size.

Stock rearing is of minor importance and cattle are often kept merely for manuring the soils, but fruit farming is one of the most intensive uses of the soil to be found in Africa. In the valleys to the east of Cape Town viticulture—the growing of grapes for wines— is most important, with small areas of

TABLE 16
Rhodesia: Seasonal Production, Sales and Prices of Tobacco

ITEM	SEASON 1962	1963	1964
Weight sold in lb.	230,791,000	194,780,000	323,836,000
Value	£33,622,985	£33,778,661	£35,002,297
Seasonal average per lb.[2]	35·01d	41·61d	25·94d

[1] The Rt Hon. Lord Hastings—Farming in the Rhodesias, Rhodesia and East Africa, pages 94–95.

[2] In view of restrictions on production, the Rhodesian Government fixed the price paid to tobacco growers at 28d in 1967 and 22d in 1968.

citrus especially along the Breede River Valley. On the cooler, higher plateau of the interior deciduous fruits—peaches, apricots, apples, table grapes, pears, plums and prunes—are the main fruits grown. Wheat is also important in the south-west Cape and is grown in two broad regions stretching from Paarl to Het Kruis north of Cape Town (the Swartland wheat belt) and south of a line from Caledon to Swellendam (the Ruens wheat belt).

The importance of fruit in South Africa's economy may be judged from the figures in Table 17; a comparison is made with wool values which are second only to gold in production and export values. These figures show that the combined value

was mainly with Britain and Western Europe, where winter supplies of fruit are limited during the summer harvest seasons at the Cape. The trade was curtailed during the Second World War but after 1945 new plantings were carried out which have lead to the present huge output.

Viticulture

The main vineyards of the south-west Cape lie within a radius of approximately 100 miles of Cape Town, where nearly 60,000 acres are planted with 90 million vine plants. This region produces on average some 80 million gallons of wine each year, but exports have suffered in recent years with the

TABLE 17
South Africa: Average Production and Export Value of Wool and Fruit, 1962–64

ITEM	PRODUCTION	EXPORT	EXPORT VALUE AS PERCENTAGE OF PRODUCTION VALUE
Wool	£46 million	£41 million	90%
Citrus Fruits	£17 million	£15·5 million	91%
Deciduous Fruits	£13·5 million	£13·0 million	96%
Wine	£8·5 million	£2·0 million	23·5%

of fruit production averages £39 million a year and brings some £30·5 million from external sources. In 1966, Britain purchased £6·0 million worth of citrus fruit, £7·7 million worth of deciduous fruit and £1·2 million worth of wine from South Africa.

The cultivation of fruit is probably the oldest agricultural activity in South Africa, originating to supply passing ships of the Dutch East India Company especially with citrus to prevent scurvy amongst the crews. But interest soon shifted to grapes which grew better in the Mediterranean-type climate and which, converted to wine, withstood long sea journeys; citrus fruits were grown mainly for local markets. When the Boer farmers trekked from the Cape to the Transvaal they took with them citrus fruit seeds and with the opening of the Rand goldfields in the late nineteenth century demands for fruit increased. Farmers in the Cape were also able to supply the mines when trunk railways were completed. The export trade in fruit increased in the early twentieth century with the establishment of regular sailings of refrigerated vessels. This trade

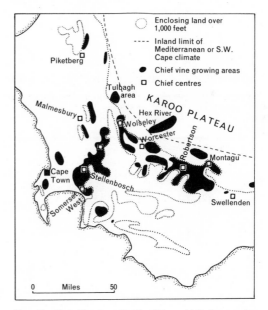

FIG. 12: Cape Province, South Africa—chief vine growing regions

reduction of the British market due to Commonwealth preference, and over-production has resulted in a quota system limiting farm output.

The vine does best in the winter rainfall area in the south-west Cape and the chief centres are at Stellenbosch, Paarl, Worcester, Tulbagh and Robertson. The slight climatic variations result in different types of wine; the cooler, higher slopes with lower temperatures (65 to 75°F) [18 to 24°C] are best for dry wines, while in the valleys with summer temperatures over 80°F [27°C] heavier, sweeter wines are produced. The summers must be dry since the vine is very subject to fungoid diseases and rainfall from January to April should not exceed 2·5 inches [63·5mm]. The annual amount of rainfall needed is about 25 inches [635mm] and this is received in the western coastal zone and in the Tulbagh and Ceres Valleys. But east of Worcester in the Breede and Hex Valleys the annual totals often fall below 20 inches [508mm] and vineyards must be irrigated; about 55 per cent of the annual crop comes from irrigated vineyards. The best sites for vineyards are on the eastward-facing slopes of the highlands where soils are deep, well drained and fairly fertile sandy loams and better types weathered from granitic rocks. The variations in size of farms and the crops grown with vines are shown in Table 18.

Mixed Farming—The Elgin Basin
South of a line between Elgin and Swellendam the relatively cool summers and the risk of cool season frosts virtually exclude the growth of the vine except in most favoured localities and a more mixed farming economy based on deciduous fruits, vegetables and dairying is found. The Elgin Basin 40 miles east of Cape Town is probably one of the most intensively farmed regions in the whole of Africa. This is the chief apple-growing region in South Africa and produces over half the annual apple crop. Unlike the Kenya Highlands the cool season here is sufficiently cold to produce a high quality apple for export. Farmers take advantage of air drainage and plant the apple trees on the lower slopes of valley sides while peaches, requiring warmer conditions and lighter soils, are found near the tops of ridges. Other fruits include berries and pears and a wide range of vegetables is grown—cauliflowers, cabbages, carrots, onions and potatoes. Most farms have pastures for grazing dairy cattle and the produce is sold locally or in Cape Town. During the summer months most crops are irrigated and each farm has a small dam to store the winter-season rainfall of 35 to 40 inches [889 to 1016mm]. The slopes surrounding the Basin are planted with pines as are all areas of land unsuitable for cultivation.

TABLE 18
South Africa: Sample Vineyards, South-West Cape Province

LOCATION	AREA IN ACRES	ALT. IN FEET	AV. ANN. RAINFALL	SOILS	TYPES OF FRUIT WITH ACRE- AGES IN BRACKETS WHERE AVAILABLE
1. *Nr. Paarl*	50	485	24 ins 610 mm	Fertile granitic	Table grapes (23), wine grapes (4), apricots, peaches. Irrigated only during severe droughts
2. *Nr. Stellenbosch*	157	400	24 ins 610 mm	Sandy with clay loams	Wine grapes (15), deciduous fruits (35)—plums, prunes, pears
3. *Nr. Tulbagh*	75	475	21 ins 533 mm	Grey sandy soils	Wine grapes (30), deciduous fruits (20)—prunes with small acreages of apricots, peaches and plums; partly irrigated. Wheat important
4. *Hex River Region*	75	1,500	11 ins 279 mm	Sandy	Table grapes (39), wine grapes (½). Wholly irrigated

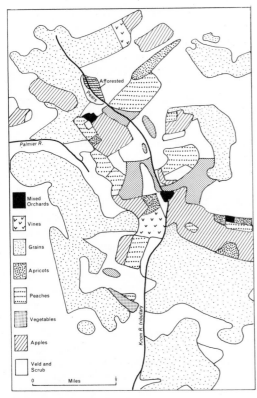

Mixed
Orchards

Vines

Grains

Apricots

Peaches

Vegetables

Apples

Veld and
Scrub

0   Miles

Afforested

Palmier R.

Pearls

Krom R. tributary

FIG. 13: Cape Province, South Africa—land use in the Elgin Basin

Conclusion—Some Comparisons between African and European Farming in Africa

We are now in a position to draw some comparisons between African and European methods of farming. As we have seen, European farming on an intensive scale tends to be concentrated in certain regions of the continent—coastal Algeria, the Kenya Highlands, Rhodesia, the south-west Cape and Natal. The soils and climate of these regions are ideally suited to the transplantation of European cultivation techniques and farming systems direct from Europe—strict crop rotations, liberal use of fertiliser, enclosed pastures, high-class dairy and beef herds, electrification and mechanisation. In particular, in areas such as the Kenya Highlands some 60 years of European adjustment and experimentation had laid a firm economic base for the country and provided an excellent basis for the future development of African farming. It must be noted, however, that the very existence of European settlers in Kenya for a long time hindered the development of cash crop farming by the African.

Most European farming tends to produce cash crops for the overseas markets and is thus of an extractive nature, while crops grown for African subsistence cover a relatively small proportion of land on such farms. On the African farm the reverse is usually true, a considerable proportion of the land being devoted to subsistence crops and usually less than one-third given over to cash crops.

European farming has nearly always had the advantage of capital backing both from private or from government sources as in Rhodesia, whereas one of the greatest limitations which has hindered the African farmer has been the lack of capital. With such capital backing the European could afford to experiment while it was more difficult for the African farmers to change from their proved traditional cultivation methods to new and probably risky ideas. Nevertheless, the African cultivator has frequently adopted European techniques within his own cultivation system especially in relation to cash crops such as coffee, tea, pyrethrum and tobacco.

European farms in Africa, unlike those generally to be found in Europe, tend to be on a large scale in contrast to the small size of traditional African farms. Such farms, as we have seen on page 77, support a much lower population density than those of the African and, although producing large amounts of cash crops for export, tend to produce little that is immediately useful in supporting African populations. Some of the settlement schemes in East, Central and North Africa are designed to break down such large estates into more viable units suited to the African's needs, to support a larger population per acre but also to maintain cash crop production for export by more intensive cultivation of the soil.

From the point of view of quality it is often assumed that the estate method of farming produces a higher quality crop but this is not always the case. Where the African farmer produces a cash crop for sale to local factories or estate processing plants the quality often surpasses that of the plantation, since the farmer cannot afford to lose money on crops which he has carefully tended for several years on land which could have been devoted to subsistence

107

crops for his family. In Kenya, for example, it is in the new tea areas opened up by African cultivators that the better quality tea is produced.

The cultivation of the small-holding is the more natural form of agriculture for the African farmer. The retention of such small holdings within the framework of a co-operative, the intensification of research into cultivation methods, the granting of increased credit facilities by both national and international bodies to deserving cases, and the aim to produce an economic balance between cash crop and subsistence crops production seem to be the major trends in African agriculture today.

New Ideas in African Agriculture

In many parts of the African continent African farmers are beginning to adopt a fresh approach to crop cultivation and animal husbandry, turning from the limiting ideas of tribal agriculture to more scientific methods of cultivation. Evidence of this new approach can be seen in two of the more important schemes currently operating in Africa and which are promoting a new outlook among African farmers—the African Purchase Area scheme in Rhodesia and the adaptation in many African countries of agricultural co-operative farming on the lines of the Israeli kibbutz system.

The Rhodesian Purchase Area Scheme is an attempt to bridge the gap between traditional African cultivation techniques and modern scientific farming. Agricultural production forms nearly one-quarter of the gross national product of Rhodesia but over 65 per cent of this agricultural output comes from the 6,200 European farmers who produce large amounts of tobacco (see page 102) and other cash crops; the remaining one-third comes from nearly half a million African cultivators (including 8,000 Purchase Area farmers) who are more content to produce mainly subsistence crops.

The Purchase Area farms are similar in many ways to the land resettlement farms in Kenya but they are not on former European land now subdivided; they occupy land which has been set aside since 1929 for use by Africans only. The African Purchase Areas cover over 8 million acres of land adjoining traditional tribal areas. African farms in these zones are not the five or ten acre holding of the tribal areas but range from 100 to over 1,000 acres in size, the average being 250 acres. An African can buy land here at very low prices, the

cost being spread over a period varying from 10 to 25 years. Only farmers of proven worth are accepted for this scheme; they must, for example, possess a Master Farmer's Certificate which means they are progressive in their methods, be able to provide capital up to £600, and have some degree of governmental agricultural training. Even then, the farmer holds the land he wishes to purchase on trust for three years, during which time he must prove himself a successful farmer. Credit can often be obtained from the Land Bank of Rhodesia or from the growing number of African co-operative societies.

The type of farming in the Purchase Areas varies with the climatic location of the farm. Nearly a third of the farms fall within Rhodesia's dry zone and here cattle ranching is the chief occupation; in areas of higher but erratic rainfall cattle are important but are combined with crops of maize, fodder and other crops when possible; nearly 40 per cent of the Purchase Areas lie in a reliable rainfall zone receiving between 20 and 25 inches annually and these farms support an intensive mixed farming economy. Labour is mostly provided by the farmer's family although this is often inadequate and labour has to be hired. Such farms produce about £250 a year on average and yields of maize at 20 bags an acre, although not as good as the 30 bags of more scientific farms, are a great improvement on the 4 or 5 bags per acres of the tribal reserves.

Another interesting experiment which may revolutionise African farming is the adoption by a number of African governments of the *kibbutz* method of farming which originated in Israel. The *kibbutz* is a collective farm (on a smaller scale than those found in Russia); all members are equal, all property commonly owned, the individual works for the community as a whole, and the organisation and decisions are on democratic lines. Facilities for eating, laundrying, washing, etc. are pooled. The *moshav* is another type of co-operative village but in this case the farmer lives in his own house with his family and farms his own plot of land. Each piece of land is equal in size and is cultivated only by the farmer and his family; but marketing and supply and the use of farm machinery are communal.

Several African states are now experimenting, with assistance from Israeli experts, in adapting these systems to African agriculture. *Tanzania* has begun a pilot project at Kitete village near the

Ngorongoro Crater, the home area of the Wambulu people. Each family has a three-acre shamba of its own but also works the communal fields on a co-operative basis. The village possesses its own school, communal store and social centre. A further sixty co-operative villages are planned within the next five years. The *Malagasy Republic* has a *moshav* at Mandabe; there are two in the *Cameroons* under Israeli supervision; *Togo's* first co-operative village is at Togodo and now has nearly 400 inhabitants; the Central African Republic has now six *moshavs*. Other nations in Africa where co-operative villages have been formed or who have trainees in Israel include Zambia, Dahomey, and Niger. Although these are as yet in the experimental stage, the growth of the co-operative village may become one of the major methods of farming on the continent since it seems particularly well adapted to the African rural way of life.

Questions

1 Compare and contrast the methods of production of any *two* cash crops grown in Africa (*a*) on plantations; (*b*) on small African-owned farms.
2 What are the main advantages and disadvantages of African small-scale cultivation? Illustrate your answer with reference to examples familiar to you.
3 The nomadic herdsman makes the best possible use of the desert and semi-desert regions of Africa. Discuss this statement with reference to specific peoples.
4 It is rainfall and not temperature, soils and relief which exerts the greatest influence on the distribution and range of crops grown in Africa. Discuss this statement with reference to particular crops.
5 What proposals would you suggest to improve African small-scale cultivation generally? Answer this question with reference to any improvements being made in your own country or in an area familiar to you.
6 The cash crop is of vital importance to the economy of many African countries. Select a country where this statement is valid and prove the statement by showing how cash crops form a large proportion of the exports and dominate the general economy of the country.

7 Compare and contrast two areas of European small-scale farming in Africa.
8 What is meant by shifting cultivation? What is the basic difference between shifting cultivation and bush fallowing? Illustrate your answer with specific references to particular peoples in Africa.
9 How is land fragmentation caused? Describe, with specific reference to particular schemes, how land fragmentation can be solved.
10 Describe any land re-settlement scheme known to you. Explain the advantages and disadvantages of such schemes for the African farmer and the economy of the country in general.
11 Discuss, with reference to West Africa, the rôle of the small farm and the large plantation in the production of (i) palm oil, and (ii) cocoa.
12 Where and under what conditions is *one* of the following commodities produced in Africa: cocoa, palm oil, tobacco, sisal, cotton, tea?
13 Review the types of farming to be found in *either* East Africa *or* Zambia, Malawi and Rhodesia and comment on their distribution in the area you have chosen.
14 Where and under what conditions is transhumance practised in Africa?
15 With reference to specific examples discuss the decline of nomadism in and around the Sahara.

Practical Work

A typical question on practical work in the agricultural field of geography might be:

Describe the farming methods and the relationship of agriculture to relief, climate and soils in any one small area with which you are familiar.

The following topics are suggested as vacation work which a student might find interesting and profitable:

1 A geographical description of an African- or European-owned farm, plantation or estate. The account should include:
a a location map; *b* large-scale map of the farm; *c* climatic statistics; *d* soil profiles; *e* history of the farm's development; *f* a list of crops grown and their suitability for that particular area; *g* methods of cultivation; *h* processing of the crops; *i* marketing.
2 A selection of a particular crop of the country and the plotting of its distribution from the latest data

obtainable from agricultural departments. Dots or shading may be used to show the crop's distribution on a map and isohyets may be drawn to show any significant climatic relationships. Details of the crop's requirements, methods of production and marketing might also be collected and graphs prepared to show the increases (or decreases) in production.

Discussion Topics

The following is a list of topics which would provide a basis for group discussion, essays or additional notes:

1 Shifting agriculture as practised by one African people other than the ones described in Chapter 4.
2 The decline of nomadism in the Sahara and its fringe regions.
3 The agricultural system of any one particular region.
4 The settlement and agricultural development of Algeria by the French.
5 The relationship of farming practices to climatic regimes, e.g. sheep, cattle and maize in South Africa, the agricultural zones of Nigeria, the importance of groundnut cultivation in the drier parts of West Africa.
6 The climatic and soil requirements, development, cultivation, processing and export of any one of the following crops:
a cloves in Tanzania (Zanzibar and Pemba); *b* olives in Tunisia; *c* dates in a Saharan oasis, e.g. Touggourt.

Statistical Exercises

Either in your notebooks or on large sheets of paper to act as wall charts draw pie, bar or simple curve graphs to illustrate the following statistics:

1 Niger Republic: Production of Groundnuts: 1965/6 season—158,000 tons; 1964/5—105,000 tons; 1963/4—114,000 tons.
1966 exports—125,000 tons to France; 33,000 tons to international market.
2 Senegal: Groundnuts and grains production: Groundnuts (1965/6 season)—1·1 million tons, of which 950,000 tons were marketed (839,000 tons in 1964/5 season).
Rice (1964/5)—106,000 tons; 1965/6—120,000 tons.
Millet and Sorghum—532,000 tons; 590,000 tons.
3 The Gambia: Groundnuts Production: 1965/6—118,500 tons; 1966/7 estimate—105,000 tons.
Niger Republic: Groundnuts Production: 1965/6—105,000 tons; 1966/7 estimate—158,000 tons.
4 Coffee Production in Selected African States (1965):
Sierra Leone—10,000 tons; Ivory Coast—275,000 tons; Tanzania—51,000 tons; Kenya—70,000 tons.
5 Cotton Production in Selected African States:

	1963/4 season	1964/5 season
Sudan	940,000 bales	799,402 bales
Uganda	437,000 bales	400,000 bales
South Africa	95,000 bales	83,000 bales

6 Sugar Production in Selected African States:

	1964/5 season	1965/6 season
South Africa	1,412,000 tons	1,001,784 tons
Uganda	123,551 tons	115,669 tons
Mauritius	520,000 tons	664,460 tons

7 Coffee Quotas set by International Coffee Council for the 1967/8 Season:

NON-AFRICAN PRODUCERS COUNTRY	NO. OF BAGS	AFRICAN PRODUCERS COUNTRY	NO. OF BAGS
Brazil	20,926,000	*OAMCAF (African group of smaller producers)*	5,322,000
Colombia	6,900,000	*Uganda*	2,379,000
Portugal	2,776,000	*Kenya*	825,000
El Salvador	1,900,000	*Tanzania*	600,000
Guatemala	1,775,000		
Mexico	1,719,000		
Indonesia	1,357,000		

CHAPTER SIX

SETTLEMENT—VILLAGES, TOWNS AND CITIES IN AFRICA

In Chapter Two we saw some of the great urban centres developed in Africa as centres of industry and trade as long as 2,000 years ago. In this chapter we shall be largely concerned with more recent developments. Despite the phenomenal growth of towns and cities in Africa the village still retains an important position in the evolving pattern of settlement on the continent. Even though many people live and work in towns, most of them regard their villages as their true homes and look forward to retiring there later. Industrial workers try to save some money to build near their village and keep up their contacts by frequent visits. Very often however, they come to prefer the life of the towns and become townsmen.

A: Villages

Factors Affecting the Growth of Villages

The presence of good soil is one of the chief considerations influencing the choice of site of a village. Others are nearness to water supply, proximity to routes to maintain contact with other people and to export products and, in troubled areas, the value of the site for defence.

But settlements will only flourish in response to political, social or economic influences. Villages may develop because they are the site of a chief or because officials feel the site a good one for administration. Again, local mineral deposits will attract companies who use the village as a base and employ male workers. Commercially useful crops may help development as a marketing and collecting centre. Conversely, some villages decline because the menfolk go to work in towns, the demand for the villagers' crops decline as new substitutes are found or routeways are built which divert trade away from the settlement.

Factors Affecting the Site and Settlement Pattern of Villages

It is not always easy to explain the pattern of village settlement or why one village has flourished and another declined. Villages tend to be nucleated and lie fairly close to each other to maintain mutual links; it is rare to find single scattered homesteads except where people felt remote or strong enough to resist invasions. The major considerations affecting the settlement pattern of rural communities in Africa are:

a Defence, producing small nucleated hamlets on high vantage points.

b Water Supply, especially important in savannah and semi-desert regions where villages congregate near water sources in valleys. On the plateau settlement is usually more scattered.

c Good Soils attract settlements while poor soils or dry regions are neglected; pastoralism becomes more important and villages rare.

d The Tsetse Fly is a contributory cause to villages being centred in large clearings in bush country and settlements are nucleated and often far apart.

e Good Communications are essential in cash crop areas to speed crops to processing centres and export routes; villages will lie near to them. In tropical rain forests villages usually lie close to routes along interfluves.

f Political and Administrative Considerations—a village may become the residence of a chief, or develop as the regional headquarters of the central government.

g Modern Influences—the establishment of a mine or plantation will attract people and villages and shanty towns may spring up. Later, specially planned settlements develop.

Examples of Village Settlements

The following examples of village settlements in Africa show the variety of influences on choice of site and the settlement pattern. Often more than one of the above factors have had a combined influence.

The Jos and Bauchi Plateaux of central Nigeria were the favourite hunting grounds of slave traders and the sites of many battles between rival peoples.

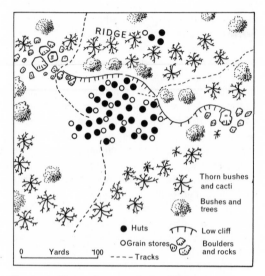

FIG. 1: A village settlement on the Bauchi Plateau

Villages were built in secluded spots hidden by rocky ridges, dense bushes and cacti thickets. Huts were clustered to help easy escape along narrow alleyways and one hut would be built on higher rocks to warn of danger. Enclosed cultivated fields were close, enabling the villagers to return quickly to their homes. Thus villages on the Nigerian plateaux are often nucleated but well spaced from one another, although with more peaceful times isolated settlements are found in more open country.

In the Kikuyu zone of the *Kenya Highlands* the effect of defensive measures is seen more recently. Kikuyu cultivation methods led to an open settlement pattern, the thick forests providing protection. As the population grew and more patches were settled this basic pattern remained, resulting in few villages but many scattered homesteads. In the Emergency of 1952–1960 the colonial authorities concentrated the Kikuyu in large villages surrounded by defensive walls. By 1956 almost the entire rural population of Kiambu, Fort Hall and Nyeri Districts had been moved into villages. Over 170,000 new huts were built, each village averaging 1,500 huts. About 830,000 people were moved and land consolidation was made easier. Villages were generally placed on top of broad ridges (Fig. 6:**2**a).

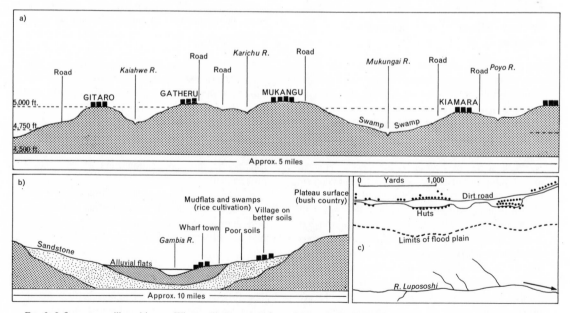

FIG. 2: Influences on village siting—*a* Kikuyu villages on interfluves, Murang'a (Ft Hall) District, Kenya; *b* village siting in Gambia; *c* linear settlement near Lupososhi River, Zambia

In *Malawi* villages tend to be small, about thirty huts occupied by related members of a family group, the numbers carefully limited so that field boundaries do not extend too far from the village. In parts of the Lilongwe Plain early villages were near springs at the foot of valleys while the more level plateau surfaces were used for grazing or shifting cultivation. Later, more war-like peoples set their villages on rocky outcrops for defence, but with the decline of warfare the earlier sites were re-occupied and today many villages are found near springs.

Further south live the *Shona* of south-eastern Rhodesia. The land here lies between 2,000 and 4,500 feet and has a rather level surface broken here and there by isolated granitic hills. Little natural

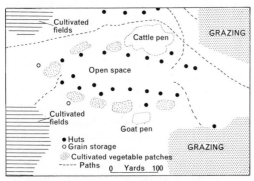

FIG. 3: North-east Rhodesia—a Shona village layout

woodland is left except patches of forest and the region displays the long dry season (May–October) and low rainfalls (20 to 30 inches) [508 to 762mm] of the savannah areas of Rhodesia. Springs are few and rivers empty during the dry season. Villages are small and cultivated fields lie close by, often abutting onto those of a neighbouring village. The settlements extend on both sides of a wide open space or roadway and the larger the village population the greater the village extent. All the fields are separated from those of the neighbouring village by low thorn hedges. The form of village settlement is thus not nucleated but elongated and villages tend to be fairly close together.

In *Pemba* and *Zanzibar* there is often a close relationship between relief, rock type and water availability (Fig. 6:**4**). Villages are situated at the foot of a central coral ridge with a thin soil cover. On the

lower slopes are springs and deeper soil and settlements here string out along a line. The central ridge is also avoided because it is deeply cut by streams and the soils are thin. Settlements avoid the flat coastal marshes because of floods and insects but there are isolated fishing hamlets. There is no settlement on the coral platform to the east. Natural

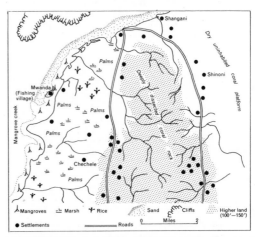

FIG. 4: The influence of relief on village siting, north-east coast of Zanzibar

conditions have thus produced an elongated village settlement pattern.

In the *Gambia* village sites are influenced by both physical features and commercial interests. In the upper river course where the waters have deeply incised themselves into the soft sandstone, the valley is narrow and there is little swampland. The villages lie on the high plateau above the bluffs. In the middle course the Gambia River has a wider valley and is flanked by flat swampy lowlands (the banto faros) flooded during the rains and infested with insects. Here two types of settlement are found; on the plateau are the chief groundnut areas, in the banto faros the patches of swamp rice. To reach both sets of fields easily villages extend along the middle slopes, each village surrounded by small patches of vegetables (Fig. 6:**2b**). Small hamlets have grown near the river's edge where goods from downstream and groundnut exports are handled.

The *Southern Ashanti District of Ghana* illustrates clearly the effect of cash crop farming on settlement distribution and the need for villages to be near

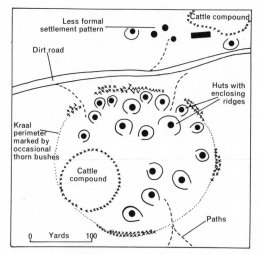

FIG. 5: Traditional defensive layout of Zulu Kraal in northern Natal, South Africa

communications. This region is densely populated with villages only a few miles from one another, and small townships have grown as collecting centres for cocoa and vegetables. These settlements string out along the main roads while outlying farms are connected to marketing centres by tracks (Fig. 6:**6**).

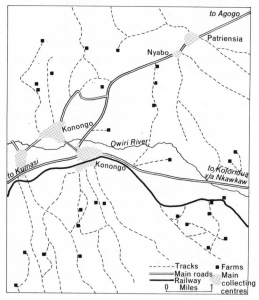

FIG. 6: Marketing centres in the cocoa regions of Ghana

Most farms and settlements south of Konongo have been established within the last thirty years and Konongo has grown from a small hamlet to an important market centre. Away from the main roads many villages are stagnating because of transport difficulties over the rugged terrain.

B : Towns

The Growth of Towns

If a village is particularly fortunate in its natural and economic advantages it may develop into an important township or city. Factors which may aid this growth include:

a Defence: Peninsulas, islands and hills offer good defence and excellent examples are found in Lagos and Mombasa (islands), Tunisia (isthmus), Kano and Kampala (hills).

b Strategic Considerations: Ports like Dakar, Freetown and Cape Town occupy strategic positions commanding ocean trade routes and have grown as important naval bases; Suez and Port Said command the approaches to the Suez Canal.

c Routes: Where routes meet or cross settlement tends to develop to handle the trade and the site is often a good defensive one. Khartoum on the White and Blue Niles, Algiers on the Mediterranean sea lanes and coastal land routes, Bulawayo at the junction of major roads and railways, Tabora, Dodoma and Kilosa (Tanzania) on former Arabic slave and modern routes are good examples.

d Administration: Some sites were chosen by officials as good places from which to govern. The marshy and insanitary site of Bathurst was an excellent spot from which to control the Gambia mouth; Nairobi's physically poor site was chosen for the central government; Addis Ababa is virtually in the geographical heart of Ethiopia.

e Industry: Towns grow rapidly with the establishment of industry and industry usually lies close to power supplies. Jinja in Uganda, Tema in Ghana, and the Rand cities in South Africa have developed rapidly due to industrial establishment. Towns grow up on the sites of mineral deposits and flourish with continuous production and demand—the copper belt towns in Zambia and Katanga, Johannesburg and its neighbours, Enugu in Nigeria and others owe their origins to mineral discoveries.

Stages in the Growth of a Town

A well chosen village site may form the base for the development of a town, but unless some important mineral is discovered nearby the progression from village to township to town is a gradual one, perhaps speeded by industrial establishment. The following stages apply to many towns in Africa:

1 An African people selects a village site and the village grows as a market centre. A town may develop if the site is on major trading routes, as did many of the urban centres of West Africa.

2 Sometimes colonial officials chose the site for administrative purposes. This often happened in East and Central Africa.

3 Traders, often Asians or Levantines, arrive to serve the basic needs of the Africans and Europeans.

4 Roads to the village are improved, schools and better houses built.

5 Industrialists may see the possibilities of establishing a factory, especially if the village is a collecting centre for raw materials. A trained workforce often becomes a settled community with purchasing power to form a good market.

An Example of Town Growth

The stages outlined above are well illustrated by the growth of Thika, a flourishing industrial and commercial centre 28 miles north-east of Nairobi on the eastern edge of the Kenya Highlands. At the end of the nineteenth century Thika was a small African village, a resting place for travellers and an administrative 'boma' of the British colonial government. The local tribes—Kikuyu and Wakamba—traded here because it lay between their reserves and a small market developed. Asian traders settled in the village and set up dukas (shops) to sell personal items to the Africans while bigger stores catered for European farmers from the surrounding coffee, sisal and pineapple plantations. The African market flourished and the sale and purchase of fruit and vegetables grew steadily.

A wattle extract factory was attracted in 1932 followed by a leather tanning factory in 1942. By 1945 Thika had 2,000 Africans, 2,000 Asians and 100 Europeans. The improvement of road conditions, the low land costs, the government's policy of decentralising industry, the good water supply in the nearby Thika River and the large numbers of local Africans seeking work helped attract more

industry—a metal box factory (1952), a fruit and vegetable canning plant (1952), a paper mill (1958) and three textile factories (all after 1960). Many Africans came to work in Thika from the Kikuyu and Kamba reserves and from the Luo regions near Lake Victoria. New housing estates were set up,

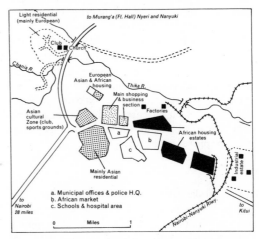

FIG. 7: The functional zones of Thika township, Kenya. (*Simplified*)

training schools built, a walled market constructed and the old village swept away for new improvements.

Today Thika, the present estimated population of which is 25,000, has an African workforce of 5,000, several of whom occupy important posts in the British, Japanese and Asian owned firms. With a population growth rate of approximately 12 per cent per annum, Thika may become part of the growing urban complex of Nairobi within the next 25 years. The map (Fig. 6:7) shows the present layout of this growing township.

Towns, Cities and Ports in Africa

One of the most striking features of the growth of population in Africa is the rapid expansion of urban communities. The populations of cities and towns are now increasing at the annual rate of 3·5 to 4·5 per cent (up to 8 per cent in some cases) while the annual growth of Yaoundé in the Cameroons has doubled in the past seven years, and that of the Guinean capital, Conakry, has quadrupled; the population of Dar es Salaam, Tanzania's capital, has nearly doubled since 1956, and the population of the capital of Ghana, Accra, has more than trebled.

115

Urban development may take place in the most unlikely spot—Nairobi developed on a most unfavourable site but unlikely physical conditions were overcome by later commercial and political advantages. Man is thus able to choose a spot for settlement for purely administrative and social reasons and if other factors, especially economic, are favourable, the settlement will flourish. If these factors are absent the settlement may decline.

In the classification of towns we used earlier, the importance of defence of the situation on routeways was stressed and these give a settlement an initial impetus. Later, considerations such as defence become less important and towns take on new functions as marketing centres, industrial nodes and regional capitals, many towns combining several of these spheres of activity.

Ports

Ports lie at the junction point of sea and land routes and handle the produce of overseas territories and their own hinterlands. They are entrepôts—points through which exports and imports pass—and they often become large store houses for raw materials.

Later they may acquire industries based on these raw materials, become regional capitals or route nodes for the regions in which they stand. The following examples of ports in Africa are described with reference to the dominant influences which have most aided their development.

Three Ports of the Maghreb—Algiers, Casablanca and Tangier

The ports of North-West Africa have been greatly influenced by their commercial and political ties with Europe. Many of their sites were chosen by the Romans as military outposts or collecting points for their Mediterranean empire. Later Arab occupation brought a new style of architecture in the narrow streets of the medina and the small market places. European colonisation encouraged extensive building development, industry and trade, and population, both European and African, grew. Casablanca grew from a small village in 1900 to a city with over one million inhabitants and the same is true of Algiers (900,000) and Tunis (680,000).

A Capital Port with Many Functions: Algiers
Algiers is the capital and the largest administrative,

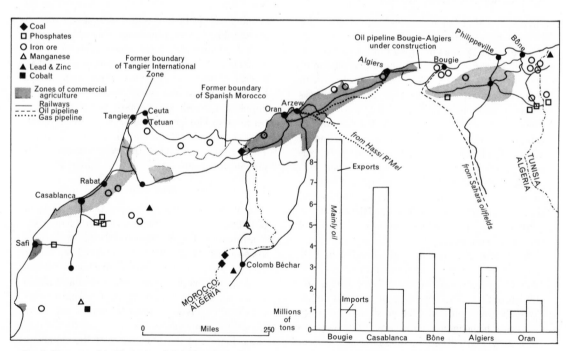

FIG. 8: The ports of the Maghreb and their hinterlands. The inset bar-graphs show the tonnage handled by the five major ports

commercial and industrial centre of Algeria, serving the whole of the Algerian coast and much of the country's hinterland. Its site was selected by the Romans for defence and it attracted the Arabs at a later date. Algiers was later occupied by the Spaniards, the Turks and the Barbary pirates, the latter holding out against the French, British, Danish and Spanish fleets but finally succumbing to the French in 1830.

The port was then developed to serve both Algeria and France and a $2\frac{1}{2}$-mile long harbour was constructed enclosing four smaller harbours which have facilities for handling oil, grain, ore and coal. The port is well served by rail which brings the products of the Metidja and the hinterland for export—cereals, wine, olive oil, esparto grass, sheep, wool, iron ore, phosphates, gypsum and coal, most destined for France. The port handles large imports of coke, timber, manufactured goods, chemicals and foodstuffs and is the chief passenger port in the country.

Algiers has excellent road and rail connections with Oran, Constantine and Blida and has become the largest collecting and industrial centre in Algeria. Most of the industries are concentrated in the southeast sector and include flour-milling, fish canning, engineering and cement, beer and soap manufacture. Other concerns produce wine barrels, tobacco and cigarettes, superphosphates, chemicals, bricks and tins and there are railway workshops and ship repair yards.

The chief factors which have led to Algier's growth may thus be summarised as:

a its early selection as a defensive site;

b its maritime connections with Europe and the development of routes by the French to tap the hinterland;

c its selection as an administrative capital;

d its growth as an industrial centre based on the bulky products which it handles.

The Effect of Political Change: Casablanca and Tangier

A comparison between the rates of growth of Casablanca and Tangier illustrates the influence of physical position and political measures. Casablanca is the largest city in Morocco and the most important port in north-west Africa. Its fantastic growth is shown in the following population figures:
1900—20,000; 1926—106,608; 1946—500,000;

1952—682,388; 1960—965,277; today—over 1 million.

The city's rise to importance is due to:

a its strategic position in relation to Atlantic shipping routes.

b French government stimulation during the French occupation of Morocco; the port was developed to serve the French sphere of control at the expense of Tangier which was converted into an international port.

c The fairly deep harbour which does not suffer from riverine silting as do many of Morocco's ports.

d The tremendous flow of goods from the vast hinterland which includes virtually the whole of Morocco. Casablanca handles about 75 per cent of Morocco's trade, importing manufactured goods (cars, trucks, machinery) and exporting phosphates, manganese ores, grains, vegetables, fruits, fish and sugar. The tonnage handled has grown from 200,000 tons in 1914 to 7 million tons in 1948 and today it has topped 9 million tons.

e The development of the city at a natural focal point of routes. Electrified railways run south to Marrakesh and the phosphate deposits of Ben Guerir, with a branch line to the Wed Zem phosphate mines in the east, to Rabat and Kenifra on the coast to the north and further north to the productive Fez-Meknes agricultural region.

f The growth of industries based on the bulky raw materials. Casablanca now has 53 per cent of Morocco's industrial concerns, many supplied with power from a huge electric power plant. Industries include flour milling, grain conditioning, oil milling, fish canning, soap, cement and superphosphate manufacture and sugar refining.

While Casablanca was designed to serve the needs of Morocco as a whole, Tangier (150,000) displays the adverse effects on port growth which a physically limited hinterland and political changes may have. In 1900 Tangier was a small village of about 5,000 people but it grew rapidly with developing Mediterranean trade and its harbour was greatly improved. The seaward aspect of the site is an excellent one for several major shipping lines focus here. But the hinterland is limited by the barrier of the Rif Mts and its interior trade is low. In 1925 the port was made an international one, the new boundaries cutting off Tangier from the rest of Morocco and reducing its land trade to no more than 2 per cent; more trade passed to the nearby Spanish port of

Ceuta. Although now part of Morocco again, Tangier's rate of growth has been checked although the city is still an important centre for international trade and for banking, commerce and tourism.

Three Ports of West Africa—Freetown, Lagos and Tema

The coast of West Africa is limited in the number of good natural harbours suitable for major port development. Dakar is an artificial construction but it has the protection of a rocky promontory, but south-eastwards from Dakar to Cape St Ann the coast is a drowned one providing many natural inlets and good harbours. From Cape St Ann eastwards to the Niger delta the off-shore water is shallow with numerous sandbars backed by lagoons. There are one or two larger inlets as at Lagos but many of the ports are artificial—Takoradi, Abidjan, Sekondi, Tema—and most harbours must be constantly dredged.

A Natural and Strategic Port—Freetown

The Sierra Leone estuary provides a deep, well-sheltered and easily entered harbour for the largest of ocean-going vessels, the site easily recognised by the Colony Mts which rise up steeply behind the port to over 2,500 feet.

Freetown was founded in 1792 as a settlement for freed slaves and by 1800 had about 3,000 inhabitants. When the peninsula became a crown colony of Britain in 1808 the port was developed as a naval base because of its strategic importance in suppressing the slave trade and for the bigger rôle of policing the Atlantic approaches to West Africa. In 1899 Freetown was linked by railway to the interior as far as Songo and later as far as Pendembu and this enabled the port to take over much of the trade of smaller ports such as Sulima and Bonthe. Freetown soon became the chief British settlement along the West African coast and took over administrative responsibility for other British-controlled territories. The population grew slowly

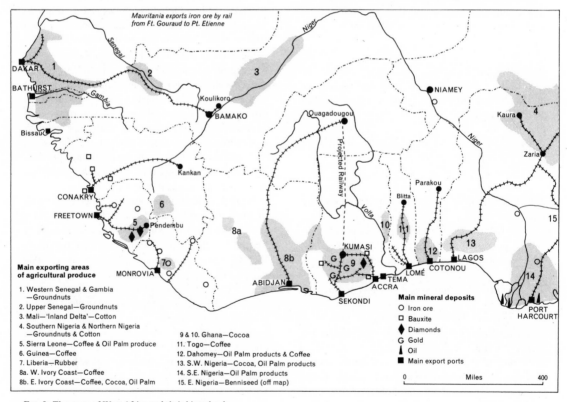

FIG. 9: The ports of West Africa and their hinterlands

118

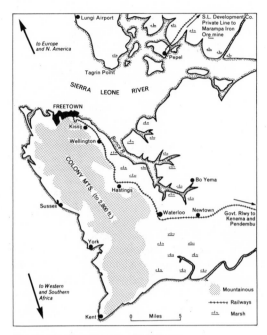

FIG. 10: The site of Freetown, Sierra Leone

it was first settled as a defensive site by the Yoruba in the fifteenth century and later became a flourishing trading centre for the Benin people and the Portuguese. Although badly drained and malaria-ridden, Lagos was used extensively by slave traders because of its easily defended position. Slaves were brought along the coastal lagoons up to 1861 when the British occupied the site and developed a less obnoxious trade. In 1867 there were 22 European traders and by 1898 there were 200 British residents, most of them concerned with shipping palm oil to Europe.

From 1900 the town developed rapidly. A canal was cut across Lagos Island to create Ikoyi Island in the east where a European settlement grew. In 1901 the railway to Ibadan was opened and in 1912 it was linked to Kano and rail and road bridges built to connect Lagos to the mainland. The narrow channel leading to the port was dredged in 1914 to admit ocean-going ships and the port capacity was further increased by the completion of the Apapa wharves in 1926. Today the port provides sixteen berths and anchorages suitable for ocean-going vessels with modern loading and discharging facilities. Lagos now handles 60 per cent of Nigeria's exports—

to 64,576 in 1948 (46,081 Africans, 17,331 Creoles, 792 Asians and 372 Europeans); by 1960 this had risen to 90,000 and is about 125,000 today.

The harbour was greatly improved in 1953 by the completion of the Queen Elizabeth Quay which can accommodate large ocean-going vessels, for previously ships had to anchor off-shore. Freetown handles virtually all (except iron ore, which goes through Pepel) of Sierra Leone's products—diamonds, chrome ore, palm kernels, cocoa beans and piassava—and practically all the imports—sugar, rice, grain, flour, meat, fuel oils, chemicals, machinery, transport equipment, cement, clothing and footwear. Over 800 vessels call and half a million tons of goods are handled annually.

Freetown has few industries but they are growing in number—railway workshops, groundnut and rice mills, cigarette manufacture, brewing, liquor distilling, and paint, nail, cement, shoe and clothing manufacture. But its development has largely depended on its strategic position and its rôle as an entrepôt for Sierra Leone.

A Trade Focus and Federal Capital—Lagos
Lagos is the federal capital, largest city and best port of Nigeria. A trading centre from the earliest times,

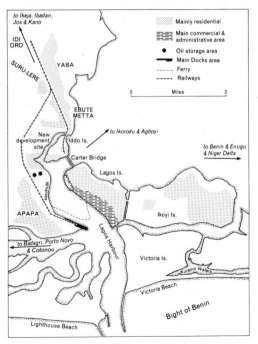

FIG. 11: The site of Lagos, Nigeria

cocoa, groundnuts, cotton, palm kernels, rubber, hides, skins, benniseed, groundnut and palm oils. Imports include cars, electrical machinery, lorries, construction equipment, cotton goods, jute bags, tyres, constructional steel, fuel oils, salt, sugar and fish.

As an entrepôt for raw materials Lagos has attracted the greatest concentration of industry in Nigeria with over 400 factories of all sizes. Most are near Apapa where large plants produce carbon dioxide, bitumen, soap, beer, metal containers, vehicles, margarine, mineral waters and flour. There are also a steel fabricating factory, a joinery works, metal workshops, and printing, weaving and furniture concerns. Bulk palm oil, mineral oil depôts and large railway workshops are found at Ebute Metta and more factories further north-west at Yaba.

Lagos is linked by air services to all major towns in Nigeria and to other West African countries. Eleven international airlines use Ikeja Airport 14 miles from the city centre. Two trunk roads connect with Nigeria's national road network via Ibadan.

The city is expanding and new estates have been built to the west of Apapa at Ebute Metta and Surulere. Lagos is the seat of the federal legislature and the natural location for the head offices of leading business and financial houses.

A Modern Industrial Port—Tema

Tema is an ambitious attempt by Ghana to combine a modern port to serve the eastern regions of the country with the rapid growth of industry which the huge power potential of the Volta Scheme makes possible. The plan for Tema includes a modern city surrounded by irrigation schemes and agricultural projects. Tema will greatly reduce the strain on ports such as Takoradi which have found Ghana's increasing volume of exports difficult to handle.

The site of the new port is 17 miles east of Accra. This was the home of the Ga people who had settled in this area in the sixteenth century or before, and some 4,000 of whom fished the waters where the new harbour was to be constructed; they were later settled into a new fishing village east of Tema. The site was chosen because it was close to the Volta Project, with suitable building stone in the nearby Shai Hills and comparatively deep off-shore water which would reduce the amount of dredging needed.

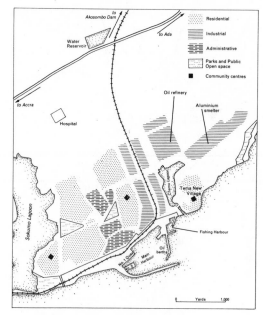

FIG. 12: The site of Tema, Ghana

Tema had to be integrated with Ghana's major road and rail network and rail connections were built to Accra and Kumasi via Achimota and to major road routes by 14 miles of new trunk roads. Tema harbour was built to accommodate one million tons of shipping and it covers 500 acres. Cocoa storage sheds, a modern railway station, a lighthouse, offices, a ship repair dockyard and servicing and oil berths for 35,000-ton tankers are the main features of the harbour installations.

Tema city consists of community estates containing 3,000 to 5,000 people. Each estate has its own shops, market, churches, and schools, and a group of four estate units has a clinic, secondary schools, nurseries and service industries. Tema's population is rapidly increasing, and plans envisage a population of 200,000 by 1985.

Tema is destined to become the foremost industrial centre of Ghana, if not of West Africa, using power from the Akosombo Dam. A well-planned estate of over 1,000 acres with 2,800 acres reserved for expansion has been laid out and has attracted many industries. The Valco Aluminium Co's smelting plant will go into production in 1967 with a capacity of 180,000 tons annually, and industries already established include oil refining, block and pre-cast concrete manufacture, lorry assembly and

120

sheet metal, corrugated iron, suitcase, paint, cement and insecticide manufacture. Fish canning, fish cold storage, metal utensil manufacture, a mattress works, an angle steel plant, a radio and electronics concern and a large chocolate factory are all well established. Two recent concerns are a large textile plant and a chemical factory.

Tema is thus a flourishing industrial centre and a modern port. Two factors have lead to its success—the need of Ghana for a modern outlet for increasing exports and the rapid growth of industry attendant on the Volta Power Scheme.

Sub-Equatorial Africa—Three Ports of the West Coast

For 3,000 miles from the eastern border of Nigeria to Great Paternoster Point north of Cape Town

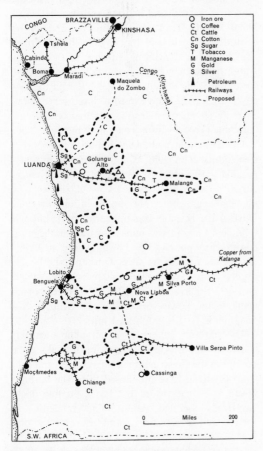

FIG. 13: The ports of Angola and their hinterlands

there are no large ports except for Luanda. There are several reasons for this. The coast here is unusually straight with few deep harbours suitable for large vessels. Moreover, for 1,400 miles southwards from Benguela the coast is backed by desert, semi-desert, scrub and dry savannah. The existing ports also suffer from the diversion of interior trade by routes leading to eastern and south-eastern coasts of Africa.

Luanda (250,000) is the largest port and the capital of Angola. Established for defence by the Portuguese in the seventeenth century the town stagnated until its planned rebuilding began in 1938. The port serves the whole of northern Angola handling coffee, palm oil, palm kernels, cotton, hides, sisal and sugar. Manganese and iron ore are brought by rail from Malange. An industrial estate served by rail lies to the east with railway workshops and a brewery and there are plans for a textile mill, an oil refinery, a cement plant and numerous processing industries.

Lobito (40,000) is a railhead and terminus port which handles the copper of the Copper Belt. The British-built 840-mile long railway links the Zambian and Katangan copper belts via Lubumbashi (Elizabethville) to Lobito. Little Katangan ore has gone down this route, the Belgians preferring the Port Franqui-Matadi route until 1956. Since the Congo's independence Lobito has acquired more of this trade and handles Angolan ore from Cassinga and Cuima mines and maize, hides, skins, groundnuts, sugar cane and sisal from its own hinterland.[1]

Matadi lies at the head of ocean navigation on the Congo River and was developed by the Belgians, despite a difficult natural site, to act as an outlet port for the vast hinterland of the Congo Basin. The port occupies a narrow stretch of land on the south bank of the Congo River, the wharves having been blasted from the rock. A whirlpool makes the approach difficult and installations were built at Ango Ango to the south-west on land purchased from Angola. Interior produce arrives at Matadi by rail or river via Kinshasa (Leopoldville)—palm oil and kernels, cotton, sugar, cocoa, coffee and rubber and Katangan mineral ores.

[1] The construction of the proposed Cubal variant railway would greatly increase traffic to Luanda (see pages 166–167).

Two Ports of South Africa—Cape Town and Durban

South Africa does not possess any really good natural harbours and her major ports are largely artificial creations developed to serve the Republic's expanding economy. Cape Town was for a long time the only major port, administration centre and entry point for settlers. Later, as the south-eastern parts were opened up and settled, Port Elizabeth, East London and Durban grew to importance.

A Strategic Port—Cape Town

Cape Town dates from 1652 when Jan van Riebeeck established a victualling station to supply fresh produce to Dutch East India Company vessels on their way to the East. The harbour was ill-protected from gales (over 300 vessels have been wrecked) and cargo had to be lightered ashore. It was only in the 1870s that real protection was achieved with a long breakwater and the Albert Dock.

The strategic position of Cape Town between the Atlantic and Indian Oceans, the development of the fruit and grain trade, and the economic growth of South Africa led to extensive improvements so that Cape Town's 365-acre harbour is now one of the best in the world. Pre-cooling sheds, a 30,000-ton capacity grain elevator, coal and oil bunkers, ship repair yards and modern cranage have been installed. The 29-acre Duncan Dock has made possible the reclamation of 360 acres of foreshore where a new city section has been built.

Cape Town serves most of the Republic and also Rhodesia but its immediate hinterland is limited (Fig. 5:15). The chief exports include fruit, wine, wool, hides, skins, mineral ores and general cargo. Cape Town is now an important oil and coal bunkering port and handles over 1,500 vessels annually. A new oil-tanker basin has just been completed and the unreliability of using the Suez Canal will increase the use of Cape Town as a port-of-call for vessels carrying Middle East oil (see caption, Fig. 10:5, page 198).

The city is the focus of road and rail routes. National highways give speedy access northwards to the Swartland, north-eastwards to Paarl and Worcester, and eastwards through the Elgin Basin to Swellendam. These national routes penetrate to the interior and east coast and are duplicated by major rail routes. The city is well served by the D. F. Malan Airport 12 miles to the east.

Cape Town (807,221) has developed port industries and others based on hinterland produce—grain milling, fruit and jam canning, tobacco processing, tanning, textiles and woollen goods, general and electrical engineering and the manufacture of footwear, paints and varnishes and building materials.

The city thus owes its importance to:

a Its strategic position commanding ocean routes and the major feeder routes from the hinterland.

b Its growth as an entrepôt for both passengers and the produce and imports of the Republic.

c Its later growth as a commercial, banking, administrative and industrial centre.

A Regional Capital and Great Entrepôt—Durban

In comparison, Durban did not achieve the early importance of Cape Town but developed with the growth of agricultural and mineral production of Natal and the Transvaal. Established in 1824, its early development was hindered by hostile tribes and the rather dangerous entrance to the Bay of Natal. In the early days it served as an entry port for the growing colony of Natal but with the discovery of Rand gold it leaped to importance. Now covering 80 square miles the city had 681,492 inhabitants (196,398 Europeans) in September 1966.

The Transvaal and Natal hinterlands export a tremendous tonnage of coal and mineral ores (especially manganese), wool, sugar, dairy produce, citrus fruits, maize and tobacco. Oil, timber, and miscellaneous goods are the main imports and Durban also acts as a coal bunkering port although it has lost a lot of its oil bunkering trade to the more conveniently placed Cape Town. Due to the bulkiness of the cargoes handled, Durban imports and exports more tonnage than any other South African port—22 million tons in 1967, 53 per cent of all traffic (Cape Town—6·2 million, Port Elizabeth—5·1 million, East London—1·1 million).

The harbour suffers from silt almost entirely caused by the action of longshore drift along the coast, but the construction of breakwaters and constant dredging have minimised this. The harbour covers six square miles and has a floating dock, electrically operated coaling points, numerous oil fuelling and storage sites, a grain elevator and pre-cooling and storage sheds. There is a whaling station and whale processing factories at the Bluff.

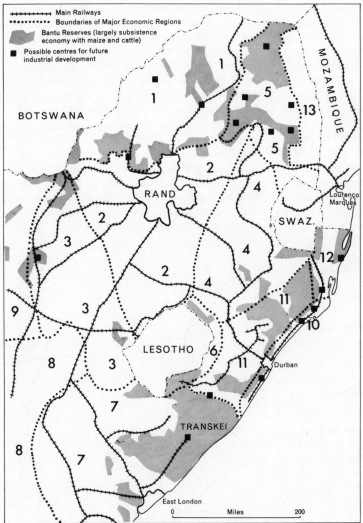

Main Railways
Boundaries of Major Economic Regions
Bantu Reserves (largely subsistence economy with maize and cattle)
Possible centres for future industrial development

BOTSWANA

MOZAMBIQUE

RAND

Lourenço Marques

SWAZ.

LESOTHO

Durban

TRANSKEI

East London

Miles 0 200

FIG. 14: Durban, East London and Lourenço Marques—their major hinterlands

Miles 0 5

Major Roads
Built up area
Mountains

TABLE BAY

Mouille Pt.

Signal Hill

Table Mt.

Twelve Apostles

Houf Bay

Chapmans Bay

Airport

Airport

Lakes

FIG. 15: Site and functional zones of Cape Town

1. Dock area.

2. Central commercial core.

3. Industrial area.

Routes:
a To Malmesbury.
b National road to Paarl and north.
c To Somerset West, Strand and Caledon.

1. Northern Transvaal: Mainly cattle ranching.

2. Johannesburg-Northern Orange Free State-Southern Transvaal: Manufacturing, mining, sheep, cattle, dairying, maize.

3. Western Orange Free State: Sheep, cattle, dairying, maize.

4. Eastern Transvaal and North-Eastern Natal: Sheep, cattle, maize, dairying, timber, mining, some manufacturing.

5. North-Eastern Transvaal: Fruits, vegetables, timber, African cattle, maize and subsistence crops.

6. Lower slopes of Drakensberg: Sheep and cattle ranching.

7. Eastern Cape: Bantu subsistence and cattle in north; dairying, citrus fruits, sheep and cattle by Whites in south and south-west.

8. Cape Interior: Beginnings of large-scale pastoral economy based on sheep and goat rearing with some cattle.

9. Northern Cape: Cattle ranching on extensive scale.

10. Natal Coast: Sugar cane, sub-tropical fruits, timber.

11. Natal Interior: Mainly timber and dairying with some Bantu subsistence.

12. North-Eastern Zululand: Largely Bantu subsistence economy based on cattle and maize with some cotton, sugar and timber.

(Map based on material supplied by the State Information Office, Pretoria.)

123

Some 500 acres of dunes and swamps are being reclaimed for the establishment of a major shipbuilding industry.

Durban is an important industrial, commercial and holiday centre. The city has spread in a wide arc around the harbour between the Umlaas River in the south and the Umgeni in the north. The industrial zones contain factories making rope, paper, soap, matches, tyres, blankets, glass, plastics, clothing, enamelware, furniture, paint, chemical products, toilet articles, confectionery, jam and processed foodstuffs. There are also oil and sugar refineries, an important engineering works and large railway workshops. Margarine, biscuits and fertilisers are also manufactured.

Durban undoubtedly owes its importance to:

a Its comparatively good harbour which has been greatly improved artificially.

b Its nearness to the Transvaal and the agricultural importance of its hinterland; Durban acts as an entrepôt for the whole of the south-east and much of the interior.

c Its growth as a collecting centre which has led to its development as one of the foremost industrial areas of the Republic.

Two Ports of Mozambique—Lourenço Marques and Beira

Mozambique has plenty of small shallow harbours along her 1,700-mile long coast but only two ports, Lourenço Marques and Beira, have harbours suitable for large-scale international trade. These two ports are more important as outlets for inland territories than for Mozambique itself.

A Capital Port and International Entrepôt— Lourenço Marques

Lourenço Marques (185,000) owes its importance to the vast hinterland it serves—the Transvaal, Rhodesia and southern Mozambique. Delagoa Bay was first discovered in 1502 and forts were built in 1544 and 1787 to protect the slave and ivory trade and to control the entrance to the Esperito Santo River. Once one of the most unhealthy sites in Africa, Lourenço Marques is now a pleasant city with broad, tree-lined avenues, spacious parks and modern buildings.

Although the capital since 1907, Lourenço Marques is badly situated in the south of Mozam-

bique with poor connections to the rest of the country, there being no good road connection to Beira until recently and no railway to northern Mozambique. Most services were run by air and the shipping lines. The railway system originally extended only as far as Rossano Garcia on the Transvaal border. With the linking of the port to the Rhodesian system via the Incomati and Limpopo valleys to Malvernia a vast new hinterland was opened up and both Zambia (until recently) and Rhodesia use this line extensively.

The port thus handles Zambian copper, Swaziland iron ore along the rail extension to Bomvu, the ores, fruit and wool of the Transvaal, Rhodesian tobacco and minerals and Mozambique cotton, sugar, cashew nuts and copra. The effect of recent

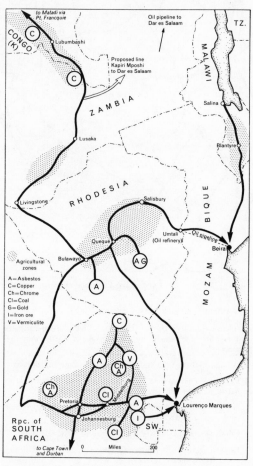

Fig. 16: The hinterlands of Beira and Lourenço Marques

economic sanctions against Rhodesia has reduced or eliminated Zambian copper and Rhodesian tobacco and minerals. But Lourenço Marques has gained at the expense of Beira; official statistics show that the annual turnover of Beira harbour fell from 4,383,038 tons in 1965 to 3,315,726 in 1966, while Lourenço Marques' turnover rose from 8,217,035 tons in 1965 to 8,867,216 tons in 1966, and reached an all-time record of 11·5 million tons in 1967. The bay is 25 miles long and 22 miles broad and protected by the Inhaca Peninsula. The port facilities have a shed storage capacity of a quarter of a million tons and the modern cranage can handle fifteen vessels at once. There are fruit pre-cooling sheds, fish-freezing plants, chrome, iron ore and timber wharves, while at Matola is a modern bulk oil discharge quay. The harbour can deal with 9 million tons; exports now amount to 5·2 million tons and imports to 4 million tons annually. Constant dredging of the harbour is necessary, however, especially around the Matola dock since ore vessels have deep draughts. Altogether, 1,800 vessels call here each year.

Lourenço Marques has attracted a great number of industries the chief being those making cement, furniture, cigarettes, pottery, beer, footwear, soap, oils, radios, railway wagons and river barges. There is an important oil refinery and a rubber processing plant.

A Regional Capital and Outlet Port—Beira

Beira's harbour is not as good as Lourenço Marques' for the Pungue River has strong tides and has deposited huge shoals of silt (three dredgers are constantly at work). But Beira (66,000) achieved importance as the main outlet for the Rhodesias and Malawi and to a lesser extent for Katanga. It is another good example of a port which serves a wide hinterland beyond the borders of its own country.

Formerly the capital of the territory administered by the Mozambique Company, Beira grew to importance towards the end of the nineteenth century. With the completion of the line to Salisbury via Umtali and later to the Copper Belt, Beira became the most convenient outlet for mineral ores and agricultural produce. But the small harbour was unable to handle the huge volume of post-war traffic and much trade was diverted along the Limpopo line to Lourenço Marques.

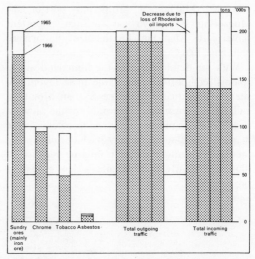

FIG. 17: Beira—trade comparisons for the first five months of 1965 and 1966

The traffic problem has partly been solved by extending the deep water wharf, constructing special ore-loading terminals and installing modern cranage, bulk oil and chrome ore-loading bays. Beira handles 3 million tons of ores, liquid fuels (by pipeline to Umtali) and general cargo each year and over a thousand ships call annually.

But while Lourenço Marques is assured of a steady trade with the Transvaal and Swaziland the future is not so certain for Beira with the diversion of much traffic along southerly routes and the port is acquiring other functions. Its wide sandy beaches and luxury hotels attract tourists from Rhodesia and Zambia; numerous small factories manufacture beer, pottery, tiles, mattresses, bricks and cigarettes, and there is an oil extract plant. Factories at Manga, six miles away, make electric cables and jute fibre articles.

Three Ports of the East African Coast—Mombasa, Dar es Salaam and Tanga

The ports of East Africa were founded by Oman and Hadramaut Arabs from Arabia, some as early as the first century A.D. They grew as embarkation points for slaves, defensive sites and marketing centres, and administrative headquarters. They handled cargoes from the Middle East, India and China. By the fourteenth century there were many flourishing centres—Kilwa with three hundred mosques; Malindi, a prosperous port-of-call; Mogadishu, Bagomoyo and Zanzibar, important slave centres. Many have lost their early importance and some, like Gedi, are now empty ruins.

With the development of the hinterland in the colonial era port growth at the most favourable sites was accentuated—at Dar es Salaam, Mombasa and Tanga. These became termini for the railways and import points for the growing colonies. The map (Fig. 6:**18**) shows the way in which railways tap the economically important interior regions. It illustrates clearly how Mombasa has grown to pre-eminence.

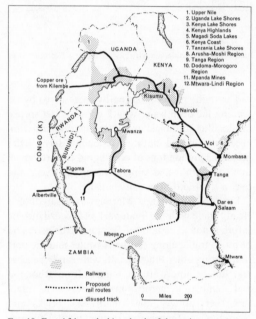

FIG. 18: East Africa—the hinterlands of the major ports

A Regional Capital, International Entrepôt and Industrial Port—Mombasa

Mombasa's early development was due to its deep, well-sheltered harbour and its excellent defensive position on an island. Founded in the tenth century, occupied by the Portuguese in the sixteenth century, it again became an Arab capital until 1832 when the court moved to Zanzibar. Mombasa's site was well chosen. The old city lies on an island 2½ miles wide and 3 miles long, opposite a break in the off-shore coral reef. To the north lies Tudor Harbour

approached by a narrow channel guarded by Portuguese-built Fort Jesus. The channel, Mombasa Harbour, is still used by Arab dhows but is too shallow for bigger vessels. West and south-west of the island is the wider and deeper Kilindini Harbour which has undergone extensive improvements until it has become one of the finest of Africa's harbours with fourteen deep-water berths, modern loading quays at Kipevu, and bulk petroleum wharves at Shimanzi and Changamwe.

Mombasa's hinterland includes Kenya, Uganda, northern Tanzania (from where much trade has been diverted from Tanga), Rwanda, Burundi and parts of the eastern Congo (although trade with the latter only amounts to about 25,000 tons annually). The port handles Kenya's coffee, sisal, tea, pyrethrum, sodium carbonate, cement and meat, Tanzania's sisal, coffee and tea, and Uganda's copper, coffee, cotton and tea as well as packaged oils, wattle extract, maize meal and cattle cake.

Mombasa handles three million tons of goods annually compared with Dar's one million; petroleum fuel equals half of all imports but coal imports have declined with the cessation of South

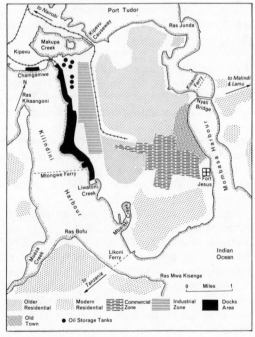

FIG. 19: The functional zones of Mombasa

126

African trade and the switch to oil fuels. There are many miscellaneous imports—cars, machinery, radios, machine tools and spare parts—the majority destined for Kenya's secondary industries. Vessels of 24 shipping lines use the port and over 90,000 passengers pass through each year. However, Mombasa handles less coastal trade than the Tanzanian ports. Coastal cargoes include mangrove poles, copra, cotton, cashew nuts, citrus fruits, sisal, cattle, skins, vegetables, ivory and fish. About 100 dhows bring carpets, dates, dried figs, fish, firewood and pots from Arabia, returning with loads of cement, paraffin oil, coffee, tea, copra, coconuts and mangrove poles. This trade is a dying one for today only 300 dhows ply along the East African coast compared with 1,000 twenty-five years ago.

Despite the tendency for industries to concentrate up-country, Mombasa has many factories producing metal goods, soap, matches, furniture, glass, metal containers, bottles and light clothing. There are light engineering and railway workshops and ship repair yards, while a modern oil refinery at Changamwe has a refining capacity of two million gallons of crude oil annually.

The map (Fig. 6:**19**) shows the layout of the port. In the 1920s Mombasa contained only 20,000 people but this had increased to 54,000 before the war; in 1948 it was 84,750 and it is now 180,000 (112,000 Africans, 44,000 Asians, 18,000 Arabs, 5,300 Europeans). Any future expansion must take place on the mainland and a master plan has been drawn up to provide housing and facilities for a population of a quarter of a million people in 1980.

A Modern Capital Port—Dar es Salaam

Unlike Mombasa, Dar es Salaam was never fully developed under the Arabs and was largely overshadowed by Bagomoyo as a slaving port. Dar's development is therefore more recent. Its site lies near Mzinga Creek which, though well protected, could never accommodate as many vessels as Kilindini. The town itself has developed round a swampy lowland.

The Germans and British gave Dar more attention than the Arabs, connecting it by road to the end of Lake Nyasa in the 1870s and in 1891 the Germans transferred their headquarters from Bagomoyo to Dar since it was a better anchorage. A railway, largely for administrative purposes, was built from Dar directly westwards reaching Kigoma on Lake Tanganyika in 1914 and a later British-built branch line was constructed to Mwanza on Lake Victoria.

Dar handles only 22 per cent of East Africa's trade (Mombasa, 70 per cent) because of a more limited hinterland. On average, however, Dar receives more trade from the Congo, between 65,000 and 90,000 tons a year. The railway brings sugar, cotton, sisal and diamonds from the Mwanza region, lead from Mpanda, and groundnuts, grains and sisal from points along the line. The total value of these exports is approximately £55 million while imports are worth £37 million, reflecting Tanzania's small demand for expensive articles. The port also handles a large coastal trade carried on by dhows carrying mangrove poles, copra and sisal.

But Dar es Salaam is not an international port like Mombasa. It is a port-of-call, a route focus, an administrative capital, a commercial, domestic marketing and tourist centre. Like Mombasa, however, it is attracting a great deal of industry: meat processing, canning, grain and oil milling, brewing, paint manufacture, dyeing, soap making, textiles, printing, sisal spinning, cigarette making and furniture and shoe manufacture. Most industry is located on an estate in the south-west of the city. A large oil refinery was completed in 1966.

Dar es Salaam's present population is 132,000 (including 28,000 Asians and 4,500 Europeans) a spectacular increase over the 5,000 of 80 years ago. Dar's growth has been partially overshadowed by Mombasa and competition from Tanga, Lindi and Mtwara (which together take about 8 per cent of trade). But if the proposed railway from the Zambian Copper Belt (see page 166) is completed Dar es Salaam may experience a great expansion.

The Effect of Competition—Tanga

Tanga (40,000) is the second largest urban area in Tanzania and again shows the importance of railway connections. The Germans built the railway from Tanga to Arusha-Moshi for administrative purposes and to tap the sisal- and coffee-producing regions. The line, 219 miles long, carries grain, timber, wattle, sisal, coffee and gypsum for export through Tanga. At one time Tanga's trade was greater than Dar's, but it has now been overshadowed by Mombasa and Dar. Tanga has a good though small harbour which can accommodate four ocean-going ships and several smaller vessels; about 700 vessels call each year. A soap factory and oil mills use power from Pangani Falls. But, sandwiched between Dar and Mombasa, Tanga is limited in its economic expansion.

Lake Ports

Large lakes like Lakes Victoria and Nyasa and the huge artificial lakes of Kariba, Volta and Nasser, often act as contributors to the existing communications network and link areas differing widely in their economies. Around Lake Victoria several ports have developed to handle the produce of their hinterlands—*Bukatata* serves the north-western area and exports cotton and coffee; *Port Bell*, Kampala's outport, handles the sugar of the northern lowlands; *Mwanza* in the south-east is more important as a focal point of trade from both Uganda and Kenya and is the only large lake port in Tanzania. Mwanza has a considerable cross-trade in rice, groundnuts, cotton and sisal with Bukoba and possesses several industries based on this trade—cotton seed oil milling, soap manufacture, cotton ginning, tanning, flour milling and ship repair.

Kisumu (24,000) has risen to pre-eminence among Africa's lake ports largely because it is a focal point for both rail, road and lake routes. In the late nineteenth century Kisumu, then called Ugowe, was only a small African fishing village and a staging point on caravan routes. Later called Port Florence. it became a survey headquarters and a small garrison town. But its real importance dates from 1901 when the railway from the coast created it a railhead port and it then grew as a collecting centre for cotton and other products of the lake shores.

Kisumu is now a flourishing port situated on the main road from Nairobi with regular steamship services across the lake. It is the administrative headquarters of Nyanza Province and a market centre for local agricultural produce. There is plenty of local labour to work in the large industrial estate and power comes from Owen Falls. Kisumu's industries include the manufacture of soft drinks, textiles, footwear, cement, confectionery, soap and furniture, and there are saw mills, flour mills, fish-filleting and freezing plants and a hides and skins preparation plant. Small vessels can be repaired in dry docks.

The port owes its importance to lake trade development and to the focal position for rail and road routes. Although Kisumu lost some of Uganda's trade when the northerly rail route was completed, the port has an assured growth as the regions bordering Lake Victoria develop and as more industry is attracted.

Towns and Cities

While ports function as entrepôts for their hinterlands and their sites are largely dictated by natural features, the sites and functions of interior settlements are not always easy to explain. In the following examples the majority of the urban centres have developed complicated relationships with the regions which they serve.

A Commercial Centre and Trade Focus—Kano
Kano (150,000) in northern Nigeria, owes its importance to several factors. It lies on the great trading routes which cross the Sahara and has become an important commercial centre lying between Equatorial West Africa and the Mediterranean North. The surrounding countryside supports one of the densest agricultural concentrations of populations in Africa and Kano has thrived as a marketing centre. The British also chose nearby Nasarawa as a governmental headquarters in view

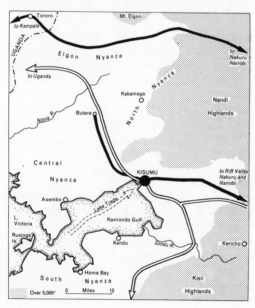

FIG. 20: The location of Kisumú, Kenya

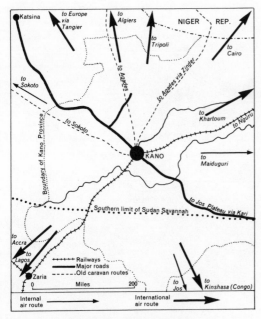

FIG. 21: The regional setting of Kano, Nigeria

of its central position in Northern Nigeria and later it attracted many industries. It is also a focal point for international and local air routes.

Kano lies in the savannah zone of West Africa roughly half way between the Sahara proper and the great southern forest belts. The site was first chosen because the rocky hills of Dalla and Goron Dutsi gave a commanding view over the surrounding plains, a small stream existed and local ironstone attracted smelters. The settlement grew rapidly as a terminus of trans-Saharan trade routes (see Chapter Two, page 46). The huge walls, enclosing 14 square miles of houses and grazing land, were looked on as a refuge in troubled times.

The city entered a new phase of development when the British arrived in 1903. Headquarters were first set up outside the old city walls at Bompai to the east and later moved to Nasarawa near the emir's palace. In 1912 the railway arrived from the coast and commerce was stimulated with the arrival of numerous Asian traders.

Today Kano consists of ancient and modern sections. The city is the centre of a metropolitan area covering 16 square miles with 250,000 people and is the headquarters of Kano Province (population 4·3 million). Within a radius of 30 miles of the city

live 1·8 million people, an increase of about one million over the 1956 figure. This large increase is due to industrial growth resulting from improved transport and marketing conditions. Industries include the manufacture of furniture, soap, tiles, cosmetics, soft drinks, confectionery, groundnut oil, rubber shoes, cotton goods, fertiliser, metalware and leather articles; tanning, food processing, tyre retreading and weaving are other occupations. Kano also retains a tradition of ancient crafts—brass, silver and leather working, mat and rope making, cloth dyeing and tailoring.

The Importance of the Railway—Nairobi, A Capital City

Nairobi, Kenya's capital, illustrates clearly several factors influencing urban growth in Africa. Once occupying a site with no particular advantages the city has become a regional centre for the whole of East Africa, an important collecting centre and an industrial and communications node.

In 1899 the railway to Lake Victoria from Mombasa had passed through 300 miles of dry bush to reach the flat Athi Plains, the approach to the fertile Kenya Highlands. It was a good place to halt before pushing on up the steeper gradients towards the Rift Valley and it formed a convenient storage point roughly half way towards the proposed terminus at Port Florence (Kisumu). Railway headquarters were moved from Mombasa, workshops were set up and government offices moved from Machakos. Nairobi became a natural resting place for travellers moving up-country. By 1902 the population was 4,300 (100 Europeans) and the settlement attracted many Africans thrown out of work by the railway's completion. An ugly shanty town developed and diseases were rife. But the settlement persisted and the development of the 'White Highlands' by European farmers and the flow of agricultural produce through Nairobi assured its economic growth. The site was a good one for administration of the large Kamba, Kikuyu and Masai tribes. A branch railway was constructed northwards to Thika and later extended to Fort Hall and Nanyuki.

From a collection of shacks at a temporary railhead Nairobi has developed into a modern city with a population (1962) of 266,794 (156,246 Africans, 86,453 Asians and 21,477 Europeans). The controlled planning of the city, its pleasant climate at 5,500 feet, and the spacious parks and gardens make

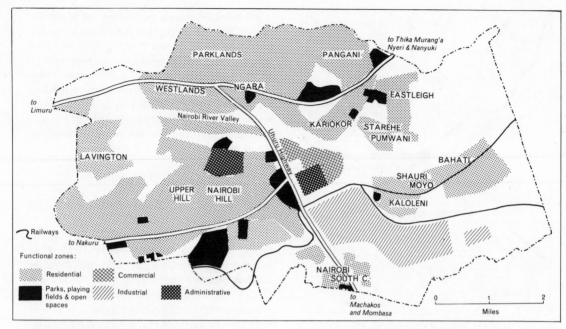

FIG. 22: The functional zones of Nairobi, Kenya

Nairobi one of the pleasantest capitals of Africa. Its layout is seen in the map (Fig. 6:**22**).

Nairobi has all the functions of a modern capital and until recently many aspects of administration of all three East African territories were carried on in the city.[1] Many commercial firms have headquarters here and the city has become a cultural centre with several schools, colleges and theatres. It is an important tourist centre with several first-class hotels and safari organisations.

Nairobi has the heaviest concentration of industry in East Africa, the oldest connected with the railways while others are mainly of the processing kind —coffee and flour milling, cigarettes and tobacco processing, tanning and hide preparation, timber cutting and furniture making and the manufacture of boots, shoes, soft drinks, beer, bricks and tiles. Other concerns include general engineering, motor car servicing, paper bag manufacture, printing and tyre retreading.

Modern tarmac highways link Nairobi with all parts of the Highlands and railways lead to Uganda, Nanyuki and Mombasa. There are two small air-

ports and a large modern international airport at Embakasi eight miles to the south-east.

Nairobi has benefited from judicious planning unhampered by restrictions of site. The factors leading to its rapid growth over the last sixty years are:

a Human persistence at a site which, although initially unfavourable, later received the full benefit of the economic development of the country as a whole.

b Its early selection as an administrative centre and the widening of the administrative field to include Uganda and Tanganyika (Tanzania).

c The position at the southern edge of the fertile Highlands and the channelling of agricultural produce from there and Uganda through the city to the coast.

d The key communications position halfway from coast to lake with major routes into the Highlands and southwards via Namanga to Tanzania.

e The early establishment of industry connected with the railway and the suitability of the site for raw material collection and processing industries.

A Communications Node—Bulawayo

Bulawayo is perhaps the best example in Africa of the rapid growth of a town at a focal point of

---

[1] The headquarters of the newly formed East Africa Community has been moved to Arusha in northern Tanzania.

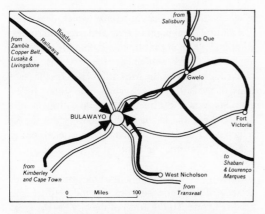

FIG. 23: A communications node—Bulawayo, Rhodesia

routes. From a small settlement in 1893 Bulawayo has grown into the second largest city after Salisbury with a population of 200,000 (50,000 Europeans). In 1897 the railway from South Africa reached Bulawayo and extensions were built to Salisbury and Beira, to Wankie, Livingstone and Lusaka, the Copper Belt and Elizabethville (Lubumbashi), thus placing Bulawayo at a strategic junction of major routes. A branch line runs from Heany junction east of the city southwards to West Nicholson, an important cattle rearing area and gold and asbestos mining region. At Somabula 80 miles to the north-east another branch line runs to the asbestos and gold mines of Shabani and 100 miles north-eastwards lies Gwelo junction.

Major roads converge on Bulawayo from Beit Bridge on the South African border in the southeast, from Blantyre via Salisbury from the northeast and indirectly from Umtali and Beira to the east, and from Lusaka and Livingstone in the northwest. Local air services link the city with Salisbury, Livingstone, Lusaka, and Johannesburg with indirect services to Blantyre, Beira, Ndola and Lubumbashi.

The city is the natural headquarters of the Rhodesian Railways and because of the ease of assembling raw materials it has developed steel, iron and brass, engineering, electrical, and rubber tyre industries. There are factories making clothing, soft drinks, beer, agricultural implements, processed foods, tin, cement and asbestos goods.

A River Confluence Settlement—Khartoum

Rivers are often arteries of trade, goods being transported along the river or on roads and railways following the river valley. Where rivers join a settlement often develops because the site is a natural node and easy to defend because of the water barriers. A good example is Khartoum, the capital of the Sudan Republic.

Khartoum (320,000) stands at the confluence of the White and Blue Niles, the two rivers joining and flowing northwards as the main Nile River. It is not an ancient city, being founded in 1824 by the Egyptians who saw its defensive possibilities. By 1840 the population had grown to 15,000. The town was later destroyed by the Dervishes who were, in turn, defeated by Kitchener who set about rebuilding the town.

Khartoum developed, however, as three separate townships, the Nile acting as a barrier to unified growth. On the left bank Omdurman remained as the old native city while the more modern Khartoum developed to the south in the angle between the two Niles. On the north bank of the Blue Nile Khartoum North grew as a separate settlement. The city was not unified until bridges were built across the rivers in 1909 and 1928.

The construction of railway lines strengthened Khartoum's rôle as a route focus. The line from

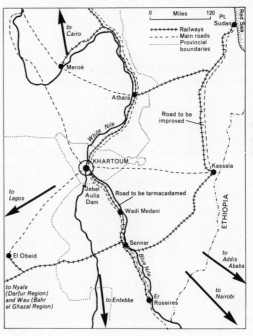

FIG. 24: The regional setting of Khartoum, Sudan Republic

Egypt via Wadi Halfa reached Khartoum in 1899 and a branch line to El Obeid was completed in 1912. Later, branch lines ran from Atbara to Port Sudan on the Red Sea coast and the northern line was continued southwards in 1955 to Er Roseires. A line links Sennar to Port Sudan via Kassala, thus placing Khartoum on a circular rail route encompassing the Province of Butana.

Khartoum is now the capital, the seat of the central government, and the headquarters of foreign legations, banks and commercial houses. It is a university city which is expanding, especially towards the south where new housing estates have been constructed. It is a market centre for livestock, cloth and spices and many camels, goats and sheep are sold here and transported to Egypt. Omdurman has still retained its native Sudanese character although many of its inhabitants work in other parts of the city. Most native craft industries are found in Omdurman—the manufacture of furniture, beds, glassware, pottery and metalware. Modern industry is located in Khartoum North where there are ship repair facilities along the Nile, grain storage houses, light engineering concerns, the Mint, an ordnance factory, a large tannery and a brewery. The city's airport is situated on the main European air line routes serving Africa.

A City at a Focal Point of River and Land Routes—Cairo

Cairo (3·5 million) is the largest city of Africa and the Arab world and is a superb example of a great religious and commercial capital which developed at a natural focal point of river and overland routes. Built in 969 A.D. at the site of a Roman fortress and an earlier Greek settlement, the city has spread along a low spur of the Mokotam Hills on the right bank of the Nile to cover nearly nine square miles. The city was a centre of Moslem culture in the Middle Ages and in the twelfth century during the religious crusades it was a great citadel under Saladin. It became the national capital of Egypt in 1863.

Cairo grew rapidly as a trading centre, indeed, because of natural conditions it could hardly avoid becoming one. To the north of the city lies the great triangular delta of the Nile, its many distributaries making it difficult to traverse by trade routes. From the south the Nile Valley forms a long corridor linking Upper and Lower Egypt. Thus the great trading routes from Tunis ran along the northern coast of Africa and on reaching the delta ran south-eastwards to skirt it. Here they met the great caravan routes from Jerusalem and Asia Minor and the natural artery of the Nile.

The ancient pattern of trading routes was accentuated during the railway age. Lines were constructed along the Nile corridor as far as Aswan, then on to Wadi Halfa and later to Er Roseires, 1,400 miles from Cairo. Another line runs north-eastwards through Israel to Turkey via Aleppo, and the western coastal route reaches the Libyan border. Other railways and modern motor roads link the major settlements of the delta—Suez, Port Said and

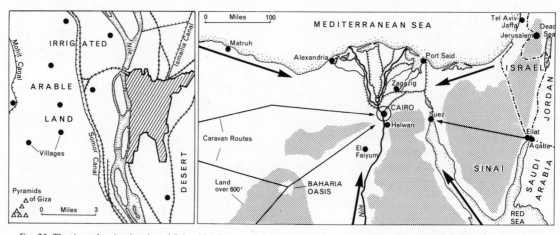

Fig. 25: The site and regional setting of Cairo, U.A.R.

132

Alexandria—with Cairo. Cairo airport stands at the junction of routes from Europe, the Middle East, India, Asia and the Soviet Union and from all parts of Africa. A system of national air routes connects with Luxor, Port Said and Aswan.

Cairo is the administrative centre for the United Arab Republic and the great political centre of the Arab world. The modern section of the city lies in the west and near to the river where there are large blocks of commercial and government offices, European residences and public buildings. The eastern half of the city still retains its oriental character and contains the Mohammedan and Jewish quarters. Many parts of the city are congested and there is an absence of wide spacious planning found in other African cities. Cairo has also attracted several industries—grain milling, cotton and wool weaving and spinning, brewing and cement manufacture.

Agricultural Collecting Centres and Market Towns—Kumasi and Nakuru

A settlement in the middle of a rich agricultural region often becomes a natural collecting point for the agricultural produce which may either be processed in the town or sent to other centres. The following two examples, Nakuru in the Kenya Highlands and Kumasi in the Ashanti region of Ghana, lie in two contrasted agricultural zones— one greatly influenced by the European and one exclusively African.

Nakuru grew with the development of the former 'White Highlands', being little more than a Masai manyatta in the 1890s. It became a temporary railhead in 1900 when the railway from Nairobi reached it. As European settlers began to farm the surrounding highlands, tracks were constructed to link Nakuru with the farming districts of Eldoret and Kitale, Thomson's Falls and the Londiani-Lumbwa region. Goods needed by the farmers were railed from Mombasa through Nairobi or brought by bullock cart.

Nakuru became a centre where farmers met to buy goods, discuss business and market their produce. By 1924 there were 24 firms connected with the purchase and export of agricultural produce. The continuation of the railway to Kisumu brought a steady flow of trade from the lake region and the town became a junction with the completion of the line to Kampala. Local roads and the main Nairobi

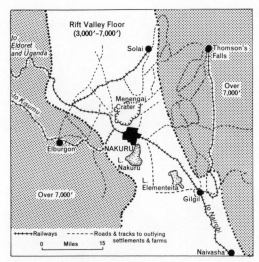

FIG. 26: The site of Nakuru, Kenya

road were improved and Nakuru became an important marketing centre, a headquarters of agricultural co-operatives and a regional administrative centre.

Nakuru is now the third largest town in Kenya and has experienced a rapid growth in post-war years—1945 population, 11,032 (455 Europeans); 1952, 21,659 (1,159 Europeans); 1962, 38,181 (1,414 Europeans, 6,203 Asians, 30,189 Africans). This increase is due to the growth of Nakuru's many industries based on local produce—the manufacture of animal foodstuffs, flour milling, a large creamery, a blankets factory, soap, leather goods, tobacco and vegetable canning concerns. The town has a modern marshalling yard to handle increasing rail traffic.

Kumasi is a much larger urban centre than Nakuru but shows a similar pattern of recent development growing to a regional collecting centre and market town and a focus of roads linking with agricultural districts with good rail connections for the speedy export of goods. There the similarity ends for Kumasi was first and foremost the seat of rulers of the powerful states of Ashanti and has become a great cultural, political and commercial centre.

Kumasi is the rapidly growing capital of the Ashanti region of Ghana and has attracted a large number of people from the surrounding area. In 1900 its population was 3,000; by 1911, 18,850; in 1921, 23,700; in 1931, 35,800; in 1951, 80,000, while today it is over 220,000.

133

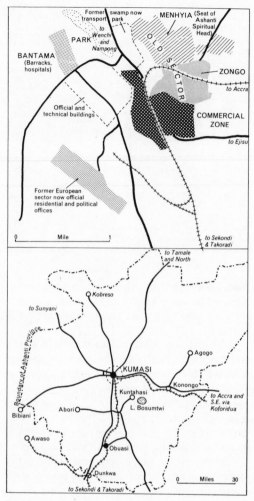

Labels within the figure:

Former swamp now transport park

to Wenchi and Nampong

PARK

BANTAMA (Barracks, hospitals)

MENHYIA (Seat of Ashanti Spiritual Head)

OLD SECTOR

ZONGO

to Accra

Official and technical buildings

COMMERCIAL ZONE

to Ejisu

Former European sector now official residential and political offices

0   Mile   1

to Sekondi & Takoradi

to Tamale and North

Kobreso

to Sunyani

Boundary of Ashanti Province

Agogo

KUMASI

Konongo

Kuntahasi

to Accra and S.E. via Koforidua

Abori

L. Bosumtwi

Bibiani

Awaso

Obuasi

Dunkwa

0   Miles   30

to Sekondi & Takoradi

FIG. 27: The functional zones and regional setting of Kumasi, Ghana

No more than a small town at the beginning of this century, Kumasi experienced a rapid expansion with the arrival of the railways linking it to Sekondi on the coast (1903) and the capital, Accra (1923). A network of roads was constructed connecting the town with the surrounding cocoa-growing areas, with Takoradi and with the northern areas of Ghana. Thus its position as a collecting centre for cocoa and a redistribution point for imported goods was strengthened. Besides this Kumasi is a great cultural, commercial and administrative centre with a market for the shea butter, poultry, sheep and goats, yams and other products of the northern

regions. The map (Fig. 6:27) shows the present layout of the town.

Administrative Centres—Entebbe and Addis Ababa

The administrative capital of a country is not necessarily the largest city and its site, especially in hot tropical regions of Africa, may have been chosen for its coolness rather than for its relation to economic resources. A central position and good communications are necessary if the centre is to fulfil its functions of administration. Examples of such capitals include Pretoria (page 182), Entebbe and Addis Ababa.

Entebbe (11,000) was the administrative capital of Uganda in colonial times but has since lost most of this function to Kampala. Climate played a large part in the selection of the site at the end of a peninsula jutting into Lake Victoria, for the cool lake breezes gave a pleasant relief to the high monotonous temperatures of Uganda. Founded in 1893 the town was almost wholly populated by civil servants and was situated in beautiful grassy parklands. It gained other importance in the 1920s and '30s as a seaplane landing base on British Imperial air routes, and it is now a major stopping point on air routes from Europe although some of this traffic has been lost to Nairobi. The little town has not attracted any industry but has become a residential centre for the President and the heads of government departments. It is connected to Kampala by a 22-mile long road and to Kisumu by steamer service.

Addis Ababa (475,000), the capital of Ethiopia, is not an old city for its site was selected by Menelik II in 1800. The site was an obvious one from which to govern the rugged and turbulent territory of Ethiopia for it lies in the heart of the central province of Shoa and from here the emperor's rule was extended over the Harar and Ogaden Provinces. The city was difficult to attack because of its high elevation (8,000 feet) on the Ethiopian Plateau.

In 1926 Addis was linked by rail to Djibouti, the chief outlet on the Red Sea and, during the Italian occupation (1936—1941), its administrative rôle was enhanced by the construction of 4,300 miles of tarmac and dirt roads leading to Asmara, Jimma, Dire Dawa and Neghelli (Fig. 6:28). The Italians made Addis their headquarters and the European population greatly increased.

The city has many fine modern buildings—the

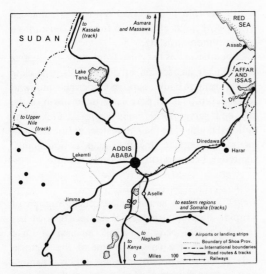

FIG. 28: The regional setting of Addis Ababa, Ethiopia

Jos (40,000) grew with the development of the tin mining area on the Jos Plateau. Tin was first discovered in commercial quantities in 1895 but had been known to the local Africans much earlier than this. A deposit was discovered near the Delimi River to the east of Jos and a mining camp was set up. The mining progressed only slowly until the railway from Zaria to Bukuru 8 miles to the south was completed and later extended to Jos in 1914. In 1927

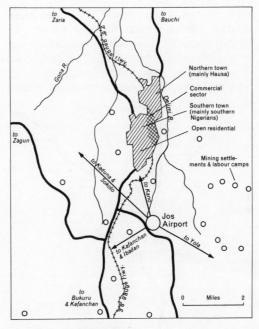

FIG. 29: The site of Jos, Nigeria

Ethiopia and Ghion hotels, the Stadium, Parliament House, the University, the Commercial Bank and the New Africa Hall where the heads of African organisations meet. The broad boulevards contrast with narrow side streets and their tin-roofed houses.

There is little industry except for the processing of local produce and local crafts such as leather and gold working. The city's airport serves local and international flights, air connections being of vital importance in a country with so few good roads.

Mining Towns—Jos and Lubumbashi (*formerly Elizabethville*)

The presence of metalliferous ores, diamond deposits, and fuel supplies in large quantities will almost invariably lead to the growth of a mining settlement if communications are good and economic mining feasible. A mining town grows rapidly and just as quickly disappears with the exhaustion of the mineral. But where there are numerous minerals in a region the mining settlement may grow into a township or a city such as Johannesburg (page 182) eventually merging with other settlements to form a conurbation of which only one exists in Africa at present—the Witwatersrand conurbation. Mwadui (page 174), Jos in the tin mining area of Nigeria, and Lubumbashi in the Copper Belt of Katanga are good examples of mining settlements.

facilities for tin export were improved by the completion of the line linking Bukuru and Jos to the main Eastern Line of Nigeria and the cost of tin transport was greatly reduced. Coal supplies were railed from Enugu although local hydro-electric power was already in use. Jos became the leading mining administrative centre on the plateau, a regional headquarters and an important route centre with roads leading north to Kaduna and Zaria, south to Makurdi and Enugu, and north-west towards Bauchi. Internal air services connect Jos with Zaria, Kaduna, Kano, Sokoto and Enugu. Jos has become something of a tourist centre because of its pleasant climate and position. There is a large tin smelting plant nearby.

135

Lubumbashi (*Elizabethville*,[1] 190,000 with 14,000 Europeans) developed on much the same lines as Jos, beginning as a small copper mining settlement and then developing with improved rail communications as the administrative centre of the regional government of Katanga Province (Congo Kinshasa). It lies at approximately the same height as Jos (4,035 feet) and first began as a collection of tents and shacks of the European mining community. The pleasant climate encouraged further European settlement.

The opening of the Star of the Congo Mine attracted African workers from the Congo and Rwanda, Burundi and Zambia (Northern Rhodesia). Development was fairly rapid after the completion of the railway to Elizabethville from Rhodesia in 1910, the copper then being shipped south; after

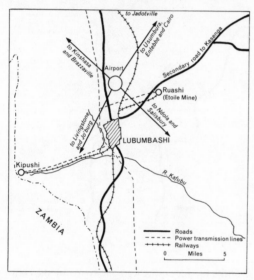

FIG. 30: The site of Lubumbashi, Katanga

1928 most ore went through Port Francquie to the north and some passed through Elizabethville along the Benguela Line. Elizabethville was thus placed at an important rail junction and at the terminus of the Voie National—the Congo's own outlet.

New mining centres developed at Kolwezi, Jadotville and Kipushi, and Elizabethville took on a new importance as a regional and commercial

[1] The name was changed on 1 July 1966, the sixth anniversary of the Congo's independence. Léopoldville is now called Kinshasa, and Stanleyville, Kisangani.

centre. Its rôle as a political centre was enhanced with recent political trends to form Katanga into a semi-autonomous state.

Lubumbashi has benefited from modern spacious planning. It has several broad avenues, first-class hotels, six large banks, parks, a modern hospital and several clubs. The airport lies 8 miles north of the city and serves local, inter-territorial and international flights. The main industries at Lubumbashi include copper ore smelting, soap, cotton goods, cigarettes, beer and soft drinks manufacture.

An Industrial Centre—Jinja

Jinja (32,000) in Uganda is an excellent example of a rapidly developing industrial centre. The town lies at the head of Napoleon Gulf, an arm of Lake Victoria and at a crossing point of the Victoria Nile. It has thus developed as an important transport node with routes converging from Kenya and from the Nile and western Uganda. Numerous minor roads also converge here, tapping the agricultural resources of the productive zone in which Jinja lies. Jinja is thus a route centre, a market town, a port, a collecting centre and a rapidly expanding industrial township.

Communications played an important part in Jinja's early development. The Busoga Railway was opened in 1912 to tap the cotton-growing areas of Busoga and in 1928 Jinja was connected to the main Kenya railway which gave it an outlet through

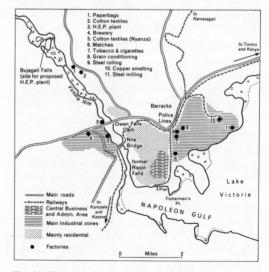

FIG. 31: The functional zones of Jinja, Uganda

Mombasa; later in 1931 this line was continued westwards to Kampala and northwards to Tororo and Soroti. A recently completed extension also links Jinja with the Albert Nile region via Pakwach. Jinja's port also developed rapidly and now handles over 70,000 tons of goods annually.

But real growth only began with the completion of the Owen Falls Dam on the Victoria Nile in 1954 which lead to a tremendous upsurge of commerce and industry. The biggest user of Owen Falls power is the large copper smelter completed in 1956 which now has an annual output of 16,000 tons of blister copper, the ore being railed from Uganda's western Kilembe Mine; the Nyanza Textiles concern produces nearly 30 million yards of cloth each year.

The most noticeable aspect of Jinja's industries (see Fig. 31) is that they are not heavy industries but are largely of the processing kind using local raw materials—timber, cotton, tobacco and minerals. This type of industry is typical of many urban industrial centres in Africa.

Summary

The pattern and nature of urban settlements in Africa is the result of many historical and economic factors which the foregoing sample studies have attempted to show. Although the urbanisation of African populations is proceeding at a rate faster than that of any other continent it still remains true that, except for South Africa and Egypt, the rural populations of most African countries is still very high, generally 70 per cent of the total. Even in Nigeria where there has always been a relatively high concentration in urban areas, nearly 90 per cent of the population live in towns of under 30,000 which would be considered small in Europe.

Approximately 40 per cent of urban populations live in the large ports while, except for South Africa, there are few countries with sea coasts which have large cities inland. Exceptions to this are South Africa (the Rand region), Kenya (Nairobi), Nigeria (Kano), Sudan (Khartoum), Ethiopia (Addis Ababa) and the Congo (Kinshasa). This is largely due to the early development of trade with Africa which was largely confined to the coasts right up to the end of the nineteenth century. Arabs in East Africa and Europeans elsewhere built their trading stations on the coast and economic movement of trade tended to gravitate there. Later the railways and to a lesser extent the road routes led directly from such early settlements inland and this maintained the trade flow towards the coasts. The political division of the continent between the various colonial powers and the development of rival economies hindered interterritorial trade but fostered movement to separate ports on the coast even though these were often close to one another, e.g. Tanga and Mombasa (German and British), Lomé and Porto Novo (German and French).

The next stage of urban development began in the early twentieth century as minerals were discovered and exploited and where suitable farming areas were developed by the Europeans. These areas became centres of attraction for African workers and for European and Asian immigrants; as commerce developed these interior regions became collecting centres for the transhipment of produce to the coast for export.

Other towns and cities have grown at the crossing or convergence points of routeways. These too became collecting centres or secondary industrial centres where raw materials could be assembled easily and cheaply. As we have seen, in some cases the climate had an influence in site selection and many large cities have developed where the altitude reduces temperatures—Nairobi, Salisbury, Nova Lisboa, Bulawayo and Umtali were all early centres of European settlement.

Some cities and towns have grown as transhipment points where natural routes along rivers have been broken by rapids and waterfalls; the best examples are Port Francqui, Kinshasa, Brazzaville, and Kisangani. Other large inland ports where products tend to gravitate for shipment to the coast are at Fort Lamy, Bamako, Niamey, Bangui and Khartoum.

Once an urban centre is well established, amenities and services are improved and this in turn tends to attract more people. Such centres are attractive markets for industrialists and attract much secondary industry, much of it consumer-orientated. Again, as the centre grows even larger more and more governmental departments will be situated there. Thus the most likely trend in urban development in the future is for the already existing urban centres to grow even larger. It may be that future discoveries of minerals, the construction of hydro-electric power stations, or the improvement of agricultural regions will create the need for new towns. But it is probable that the present pattern of urban settlement will persist and will be accentuated with further growth.

Questions

1 Discuss the factors which lead to the choice of site of village settlements in Africa. Confine your answer to specific examples.
2 With the aid of specific examples describe the main factors which lead to the development of towns in Africa.
3 Select a good example from urban settlements in Africa to explain the following urban definitions: *a* an entrepôt port; *b* a transport node; *c* an administrative centre; *d* a collecting centre; *e* a federal capital; *f* a railhead; *g* a river confluence town.
4 Discuss the importance of railways in the development of urban centres in Africa.
5 Describe and account for the growth of Casablanca as the largest port in Morocco.
6 Show how the relative growth and extent of Durban, Cape Town, Port Elizabeth and Swakopmund have been influenced by their position.
7 Describe the physical setting, foreign trade and development of Freetown, Abidjan, Dakar, Lagos, Takoradi and Tema.
8 Write an account of the importance of site and communications in the growth of *a* Mombasa; *b* Dar es Salaam; *c* Tanga.
9 How far is it true to say that in each of the countries of West Africa communications and trade are dominated by one port?
10 Attempt to explain why *a* Johannesburg is the largest city in the Republic of South Africa, *b* Durban is the leading port for bulk commodities.
11 Suggest reasons for the relative sizes of the towns listed below:

September 1966

Johannesburg	1,152,525
Cape Town	807,221
Durban	681,492
Pretoria	422,590
Port Elizabeth	290,693

12 Examine the situation and describe the importance of the following Portuguese African ports: Beira, Lobito, Lourenço Marques and Luanda.

13 Show how the location of mineral deposits has lead to the growth of towns in Africa, illustrating your answer with examples from the Congo, South Africa and any one country in either East or West Africa.
14 Discuss the factors influencing the growth of towns in East Africa (Kenya, Uganda and Tanzania).
15 Discuss the influence of trading routes, both ancient and modern, on the growth of *a* Kano; *b* Cairo; *c* Khartoum.

Practical Work

Typical practical questions on urban geography might be:
1 Describe some particular piece of field-work you have carried out in connection with a study of village settlements.
2 In connection with any rural or urban survey in which you have taken part, outline *a* the aims, *b* the methods of procedure, and *c* the results.
3 Comment on the site, position and functions of any one town in Africa south of the Sahara of which you have first-hand knowledge.

The following topics are suggested as vacation work which the student may find interesting and profitable:
1 A geographical description of the town or city in which the student lives or one with which he is familiar, using the following plan:
a Location map; *b* larger scale map to show functional zones of the settlement, e.g. residential areas, the industrial sector, the commercial area, etc.; *c* the site; *d* the historical growth; *e* communications, marketing and trade; *f* industries; *g* population growth; *h* future trends.

Sources of information may include town planning offices, factory and town tours, town council handbooks, local libraries.
2 The mapping of village layouts and the general settlement pattern in rural areas by visits and survey map consultation.

Discussion Topics

The following list of topics provides a basis for group discussion, essays or additional notes.
1 The importance of Arabic and European influence on the growth of towns in Africa.

PORT	EXPORTS (MILLIONS OF TONS)	IMPORTS	PORT	EXPORTS (MILLIONS OF TONS)	IMPORTS
Alexandria	1·5	3·5	Takoradi	2·5	1·3
Suez	2·2	3·0	Dakar	1·3	1·7
Djibouti	1·25	1·25	Safi	2·2	0·3
Port Harcourt	2·7	0·8			

2 The relative importance of *a* agricultural and *b* mineral production in the growth of ports in Africa.

3 The major influences which have led to the growth of those cities in Africa with over a million inhabitants.

4 The importance of road, rail and air communications in the growth of major cities in Africa.

5 Ports and their hinterlands in Africa.

6 Notes on the historical development and present functions of the following towns and ports: Alexandria, Oran, Dakar, Abidjan, Bathurst, Swakopmund, East London, Port Elizabeth, Kinshasa (Leopoldville), Salisbury, Walvis Bay, Ibadan, Port Said, Suez, Kampala.

Each account should be illustrated with a map showing the location of the port or town and the main factors which have helped its growth such as communications, mineral deposits, and agricultural production.

7 'The location and siting of towns can rarely be understood without reference to past conditions.' Discuss this statement with reference to the towns of any *one* country in Africa.

Statistical Exercises

Either in your notebooks or on large sheets of paper to act as wall charts draw pie, bar or simple curve graphs to illustrate the following statistics:

1 Relative Import and Export Tonnages of Major African Ports (Figures based on 1961–64 average totals): see table above.

Statistics for other ports are included in text.

2 For your own country obtain the population figures for all major towns and draw a map showing the location of the towns by means of circles proportionate to the population size.

3 Using the statistics provided for the capitals of countries in Appendix I draw a series of bar graphs to show their relative population sizes.

4 Draw a large-scale base map of the Republic of South Africa showing the provincial boundaries. On this base map, by means of proportional divided circles (pie graphs), illustrate the following statistics for the twelve major cities in the Republic: see table below.

URBAN CENTRE	WHITES	BANTUS (AFRICANS)	COLOUREDS	ASIATICS	TOTAL
Johannesburg	413,153	650,912	59,467	28,993	1,152,525
Cape Town	305,155	72,200	417,881	8,975	807,221
Durban	196,398	221,535	27,082	236,477	681,492
Pretoria	207,202	199,890	7,452	8,046	422,590
Port Elizabeth	94,931	123,183	68,332	4,247	290,693
Germiston	86,314	121,496	4,194	2,389	214,393
Bloemfontein	63,046	75,944	6,281	2	145,273
Springs	38,217	100,797	1,545	1,384	141,943
Benoni	41,992	90,236	5,566	2,996	140,790
Pietermaritzburg	40,065	55,991	5,715	26,827	128,598
East London	49,295	56,603	8,431	1,727	116,056
Welkom	27,096	70,230	288	0	97,614

CHAPTER SEVEN

WATER FOR POWER AND IRRIGATION

Africa's Water supply and its Distribution

Annual rainfall maps of Africa suggest that about half of the continent from latitude 14°N to 17°S receives a rainfall of over 20 inches [508mm] a year, increasing to 40 inches [1016mm] in the core of this region and reaching a maximum of over 100 inches [2540mm] in the Cameroons and Sierra Leone.

These totals would appear adequate for most types of farming but the seasonal rainfall maps (page 25) quickly dispel this favourable impression. In January, the southward shift of the north-eastern trade wind belts brings dry parching conditions to most parts of West Africa, the northern Congo and the southern Sudan. By April, with the sudden swing northwards of the rain belts, the southern third of the continent is beginning to experience drier weather which reaches its maximum extent by July.

Only in a narrow equatorial belt is there continuous and reliable rainfall and here the danger is rather from too much water than from too little. But outside this zone lie regions seriously affected by a seasonal lack of rain, by rainfall unreliability, or by a complete lack of rainfall for several years.

Thus one can recognise three general climatic divisions of Africa based on the amount and occurrence of annual rainfall:

a The rain forest belt of equatorial Africa which experiences no shortage of water supply.

b The semi-circular savannah region flanking the equatorial zone with a season of irregular and deficient rainfall varying in length according to location. The Mediterranean regimes along the northern coast of Africa and in the extreme south-west Cape also experience short periods of rainfall deficiency.

c The desert regions with hardly any rainfall— the Sahara, the Kalahari and Namib and the semi-deserts of Somalia and Eritrea.

Unfortunately, many of Africa's major rivers— the Niger and the Congo particularly—flow away from those regions which need water most and per- manent rivers with an even volume of flow are practically non-existent outside the Congo Basin. The Nile and the Orange are the only major rivers which pass for much of their middle and lower courses through desert and semi-desert regions while the Niger, the Volta and the Limpopo pass for only parts of their courses through dry regions. There are numerous medium- and small-sized rivers such as the Tana of Kenya which are also being developed, not only for irrigation but also for hydro-electric power. But all these rivers have one thing in common—they experience wide variations in their annual rate of flow which makes the harnessing of their potentialities difficult. The new African nations realise that water is a vital key to economic development and over the last ten years several major schemes have been planned and completed in an effort to make fuller use of this asset.

Africa's Hydro-Electric Power Potential

The rivers of Africa have a hydro-electric power potential greater than that of any other single continent in the world except Asia. If fully developed Africa's rivers could supply 23 per cent of potential world hydro-electric power, but at present Africa produces only 1 per cent of the world's installed capacity. Although Africa is short of water its rivers have a tremendous head of water essential for power development—the Orange drops over 10,000 feet from source to mouth, the Congo and its tributaries over 6,000 feet, the Nile over 6,000 feet from Lake Tana and nearly 4,000 feet from Lake Victoria, the Niger over 3,000 feet. But of these rivers the Congo is the only one which possesses a regular and continuous flow ideal for hydro-electric power development.

In contrast the other rivers do not possess such a regular natural flow but man-made dams are helping to adjust this. In the following sample studies of man's efforts to harness Africa's rivers, both larger schemes and smaller ones are discussed, and

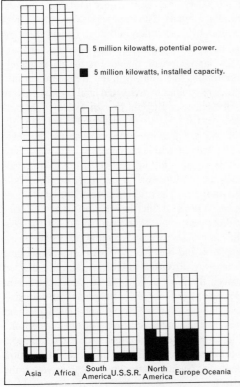

☐ 5 million kilowatts, potential power.

■ 5 million kilowatts, installed capacity.

Asia Africa South America U.S.S.R. North America Europe Oceania

Fig. 1: Africa's installed and potential hydro-electric power compared with other countries

consideration is given to the use that is being made of them for both power production and irrigation.

The First Great Project—The Gezira Scheme of the Sudan

The Gezira Scheme together with its western Manaqil extension lies in the huge wedge of land between the Blue and White Niles. This is a region of flat or gently sloping land covered with dark-brown clayey soils, dusty and cracked in the dry seasons and sticky during the rains, which formerly supported vast expanses of Sudan grass, scattered trees and, in the north, semi-desert bush and scrub. Rainfall varies from 18 inches [457mm] a year at Sennar to 6·5 inches [165mm] at Khartoum, mainly falling between May and October while from November until April no rain falls over the parched plains. This region was once the home of people who cultivated poor cereals in the rains; if the rains failed they suffered extreme famine.

After the destruction caused by the wars between the Mahdi and the British it was realised at the beginning of this century that if Anglo-Egyptian

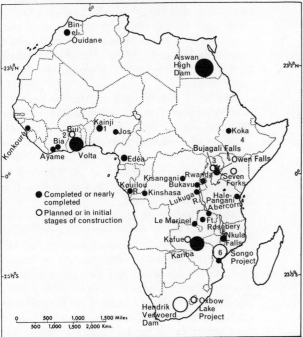

● Completed or nearly completed

○ Planned or in initial stages of construction

Fig. 2: Some of the major hydro-electric power schemes in Africa

1 NIGERIA: Kainji Project is to cost £80 million and is now in its second phase. When complete it will generate 880 MW—enough to satisfy the anticipated power requirements of Nigeria until 1980. A £3·5 million transmission network is being constructed. Work on the project has been suspended during the civil war

2 GHANA: Work on the Bui Dam is suspended owing to lack of finance. The dam lies on the Black Volta and would cost £19 million

3 UGANDA: The Bujagali Falls Project has been agreed on and a dam is to be built 4 miles downstream from Owen Falls. Its potential will be 18,000 K W

4 ETHIOPIA: The Fincha H.E.P. Project at Wolleja will take 5 to 6 years to complete, cost £10 million, and generate 100,000 K W

5 MALAWI: The £2·5 million Nkula Falls H.E.P. station was opened in July 1966 on the Shire River. It will generate all the power required by the Southern Region of Malawi. Another H.E.P. station on the Shire is to be completed by 1971

6 MOZAMBIQUE: The Songo Project entails the damming of the Zambezi River at the Cabora-Bassa gorge some 45 miles upstream from Tete to form a lake 150 miles long. South Africa is to contribute to the £66 million total cost

141

administration was to be successful the country's economy had to be revitalised. The soils, landscape and climate of the Gezira had been proved ideal for the cultivation of long staple cotton under irrigation from the Blue Nile and work began in 1913 on the Sennar Dam. The Government formed a syndicate with the private Sudan Plantations Company to administer the scheme and took over complete control in 1950 through the Sudan Gezira Board.

Canal construction on the flat plains was fairly easy. The main irrigation canal was cut along the eastern edge of the region and from this water flowed along the westward dipping gradients of the branch canals, the flow controlled by the Sennar Dam. The first flood waters on the Blue Nile reach Sennar in June and the gates are closed to allow sufficient water to rise and flow into the main canal while that not required passes through to the White Nile and Egypt. The reservoir reaches maximum capacity by late October and this stored water is slowly released to the fields of the Gezira. In December the remainder is allowed to flow through to Egypt. Egypt's demands on Sudan's water, however, will be greatly reduced by the increased storage capacity afforded by the Aswan High Dam (page 144). Water from the

Sennar reservoir is released once a fortnight into the subsidiary canals. The impervious clayey soils prevent loss by percolation, although during the rains this same imperviousness causes flooding.

The landscape of the Gezira is an extremely monotonous one—flat, with few trees, and cut into regular rectangles of cultivated land broken only by small villages and tenant houses. Each tenant possesses between 20 and 40 acres subdivided into four fields, a large area by African standards. But there is still plenty of land in the Gezira and crop rotations include regular fallow periods at short intervals which are unthinkable in the more crowded Nile lands of Egypt. The rotation system year by year is—cotton—fallow—millet or sorghum—fallow—beans—fallow—cotton—fallow, and so on. Of the peasant's four fields two will be fallow, one will be growing cotton and one millet or beans at any one time of the year. Profits from cotton sales are divided between the Government (42 per cent), the tenant (42 per cent) and the Gezira Board and other departments (16 per cent) which run welfare schemes and supervise the whole operation. The tenant keeps the millet crop but he pays for seeds, tools and transport costs to the ginnery. In return for growing the cotton essential to Sudan's economy he obtains water, the use of large-scale machinery, expert advice and full ownership of up to 40 acres of land. The Gezira tenant is one of the richest of Africa's native farmers and although many still prefer to live in traditional mud-brick houses their profits are used to purchase a better education, radios, sewing machines, bicycles and cars.

The Gezira Scheme with the Manaqil extension completed in 1961 covers over 1·8 million acres. The Manaqil region receives its waters from the new Roseires Dam; here the farms operate a three-years rotation of millet, beans and cotton on 15-acre farms. A further 1·2 million acres are to be irrigated with Roseires Dam water in the Kenana Extension Scheme.

The Gezira Scheme plays a very important part in the Sudan's economy, its cotton crops providing nearly 50 per cent of the Sudan's total revenue. But the Government has become alarmed by several factors—the fluctuations in cotton prices on world markets, the need to grow more subsistence crops for a rapidly growing population, and the low yields on the Gezira's rather poor soils despite fertilisation and regular fallowing. To attempt to solve these

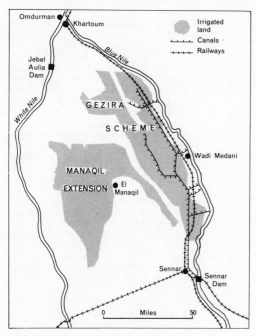

FIG. 3: The Sudan—the Gezira scheme and Manaqil extension

problems the Government has embarked on a scheme of diversification in agriculture and the encouragement of secondary industries where possible.

TABLE 19
Sudan: Cotton Exports 1963–67

YEAR	QUANTITY EXPORTED (BALES)	VALUE (£)
1963	938,045	45,400,000
1964	618,748	33,200,000
1965	546,749	30,400,000
1966	763,197	34,800,000
1967	833,700	38,500,000

The Kariba Dam—An Economic Necessity

The post-war years saw in Central Africa a vast influx of people to the developing Copper Belt and to the mines and farms of (Southern) Rhodesia. Secondary industry was expanding and the market for consumer goods was growing. Rhodesia's population leaped from 1·3 million in 1936 to nearly 2·5 million in 1956—almost double in twenty years. This rapid growth placed a great strain on fuel resources and the existing rail network was unable to move the increasing amounts of coal from the Wankie field. Coal had to be imported from South Africa and the United States and local wood, three times as expensive as coal, was being removed from forests at an alarming rate. In the 1950s the annual demands of the Copper Belt—80,000 to 100,000 tons—were unable to be met by Wankie and factories had to limit production according to coal supply. Moreover the demand for energy was increasing (Fig. 7:**6**) and by 1955 the annual rate of increase of electricity consumption had reached 11 per cent.

Several alternative solutions were put forward to meet the increasing energy demands:

a The construction of an atomic power station similar to those being pioneered in Britain was not thought feasible because such stations were then in their infancy and at that time their production costs were higher than the normal hydro-electric power station; fuel had to be imported, waste products disposed of and highly specialised staff employed.

b An increase in the number of thermal power

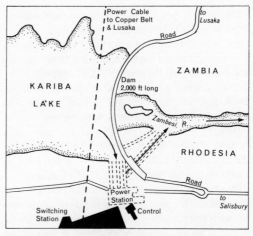

FIG. 4: Rhodesia-Zambia—site of the Kariba Dam

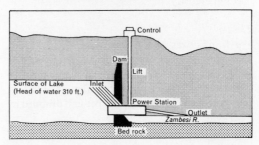

FIG. 5: Rhodesia-Zambia—cross-section of the dam site at Kariba

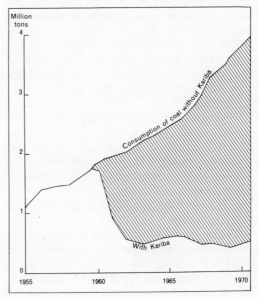

FIG. 6: The economic importance of Kariba

143

stations was suggested but this would have cost almost as much as Kariba (£114 million) and smaller stations might not have attracted overseas capital. The stations would have placed a big strain on railways and drained the country's coal reserves.

c An alternative site at Kafue was suggested but knowledge of that river was not as complete as Kariba. The Kafue Scheme is receiving more attention now, due to the political and economic split between Zambia and Rhodesia. The hope that the dam would help to bind the former Central African Federation more closely has proved a failure.

A large hydro-electric power station and dam was the answer to central Africa's power problems. Water is not a wasting asset like coal and its power is always on tap and can be regulated to the varying needs of industry.

The Results

a Kariba was an economic necessity. This is shown in Fig. 7:**6** which indicates the reduction that Kariba will produce in the price of energy over the years. In 1964/65 the overall consumption of H.E.P. rose by 10 per cent and the price per unit dropped by 9 per cent.

b The Dam will provide plenty of power for any industrial expansion envisaged in central Africa. Mining, secondary industries and other users of electrical energy can expand in the knowledge that there is almost unlimited energy to be had over the next ten years at least.

c A great burden has been lifted from the railways. They no longer have to carry huge supplies of coal to industrial areas. Moreover, imports of coal have now virtually ceased, thus saving valuable foreign capital.

d Control of the Zambezi, a very turbulent river subject to heavy flooding (it twice overtopped the dam during construction), is assured. The lake now provides a safe method of communication and a shipping service is in operation. Navigation on the lower Zambezi is now safe.

e The lake itself provides fish and is a great tourist attraction.

Kariba was the first of the big modern projects which have sprouted up all over Africa. It was taken as a model by many African states and thus has indirectly stimulated and helped the greater control of Africa's rivers. Despite present troubles the water still flows through Kariba at the rate of 90 million

gallons a minute producing 600,000 KW. of electricity, 48·9 per cent of which was used by Rhodesia in 1964/65 and 51·1 per cent by Zambia. Zambia, however, is hoping to make herself independent of Rhodesian supplies and is considering a planned barrage near Victoria Falls.

The United Arab Republic's Huge Project—the Aswan High Dam

The United Arab Republic's Sadd-el-Aali project—the construction of the Aswan High Dam with Soviet technical and financial aid—is a tremendous undertaking. It entails the holding back of the Nile's waters in a huge lake extending southwards from five miles upstream from the old Aswan Dam to beyond Wadi Halfa, a distance of 312 miles. This will be the world's second largest man-made lake after Kariba, held by a 500-foot high dam, the top of which will carry a $2\frac{1}{2}$-mile long highway. A diversion tunnel on the east bank will channel the Nile's waters through six spillway tunnels to a downstream hydro-electric power station housing twelve generators with a total capacity of 2·1 million kilowatts. Lake Nasser will store 157,000 million cubic yards of water for perennial irrigation and land reclamation. The right wing of the dam has already been completed and lake waters have already engulfed Wadi Halfa. The whole structure will be completed in the early 1970s and electric power already flows to Cairo. The dam and its subsidiary projects will cost over £400 million.

The Importance of the Nile to Egypt

The Nile, 4,060 miles long, was a wonder of the ancient world, for its summer floods occurred when other rivers were at their lowest levels. This inundation is caused by the summer rains of the Ethiopian Highlands swelling the Nile's tributaries—the Blue Nile, the Atbara and the Sobat.

These rivers vary greatly in their contributions to the Nile's volume and regularity. The Sobat is slow and sluggish because of the thick growths of sudd[1] along its course. It rises in May but its maximum floods are not felt in its lower reaches until November. These floods pond back the White Nile's waters

[1] Masses of grass, reeds and weeds near the banks which spread onto the water surface and break away to form floating islands.

in the Bhar el Ghazal swamps to the south-west and this causes much loss by evaporation from the swamp surface. The Blue Nile flows throughout the year, fed from ice-blue Lake Tana. Its rise begins in June and goes on throughout July and August to reach a peak in September; again it causes ponding back of the White Nile above Khartoum. It subsides in November and December. The Blue Nile is the main cause of the Nile's summer floods, bringing irrigation water just when needed and thick layers of rich silt. The Atbara adds to the Blue Nile's waters in summer and early autumn but dwindles to a series of shallow water holes in the winter months.

Africa's greatest lake, Lake Victoria, provides little of the water which flows along the Nile's lower course and most is provided by the tributaries whose flood waters reach their maximum at Khartoum by September and in the delta by October. By January the Blue Nile is almost exhausted and the White Nile provides much of the volume until late May and June.

Life in Egypt is geared to this uneven flow and successful cultivation depends on the summer floods. Egypt faced an increasingly acute problem: her population had increased at an alarming rate but the Nile's waters could not be controlled sufficiently to supply regular and increasing water supplies to enable irrigated areas and food production to be expanded. Thus although Egypt covers 386,000 square miles, only 14,000 square miles were fully cultivated. In the narrow strips flanking the Nile are crowded 26 million people, and in some

parts densities reach 1,000 per square miles rising to 1,500 in the delta.

Early Attempts at Solution

To provide a more reliable regime on which to base agriculture, dams and barrages have been constructed to provide perennial irrigation so that water could be held back and released slowly throughout the drier months; this enabled extra crops to be grown before the natural floods. The barrages and dams are shown on the map (Fig. 7:**8**). But the accumulation of silt on the river bed behind the barrages steadily reduced the amount of water able to be stored and the old Aswan Dam was twice heightened to improve water capacity. Its sluice gates were partially closed in late November when the Nile is comparatively free of silt and when lower Egypt has still plenty of water, and then reopened three months later for careful distribution to the cotton fields. Thus storage capacity was limited to when the Nile was falling and was seriously reduced when the Nile failed to produce its usual volume. The storage of sufficient water could thus never be guaranteed.

There were two solutions: the construction of a series of dams on the Nile and its tributaries to give greater control along the whole course, or one huge dam which would store all water needs from one year to the next and make provision for silt accumulation. The U.A.R. chose the second of these two alternatives.

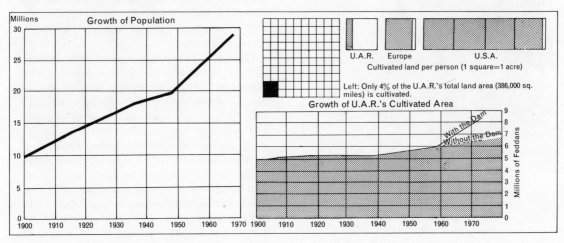

FIG. 7: The U.A.R.—population growth and growth of cultivated areas

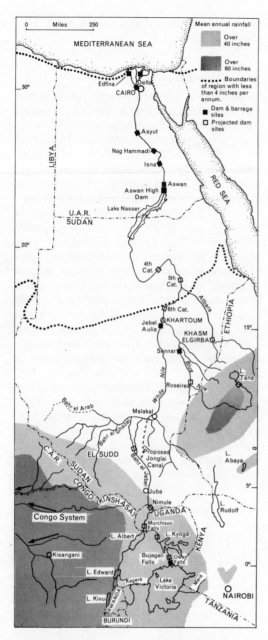

FIG. 8: The Nile—completed and projected schemes

The Results

Undoubtedly the Aswan High Dam is a very expensive undertaking, an expense which was not thought worth the risk by the World Bank and Western Powers. But the benefits are great and the U.A.R. claims the following results:

a An additional 1·7 million acres of cultivated land; 700,000 acres able to be converted from basin to perennial irrigation, thus increasing the U.A.R.'s irrigated area by 25 per cent; guaranteed water will increase crop yields especially for a planned one million acres of rice.

b Complete control of the Nile will eliminate floods; money will be saved which was formerly spent on flood damage repair; labour involved can be diverted to food production.

c The lake will improve navigation since former dangerous bends and shoals are completely covered.

d A regular water flow for hydro-electric power production. It is hoped to double the present power capacity of the Old Aswan power plant and to establish several industries there.

e A guaranteed flow of water for the barrages on the lower Nile. Future H.E.P. stations can be constructed should Egypt need them with no fear of irregular water flow. The U.A.R. plans to use the Nile cataracts for H.E.P. as soon as the Aswan Dam is completed.

f The power from the dam will mean a five-fold increase in Egypt's power potential. The need for solid fuels in industry will be reduced by 2·5 million tons annually. Three of the twelve generators are now in operation.

The Sudan will be able to expand her agricultural schemes knowing that there will be an increased amount of water now available; water can be stored more freely which will mean clearer water and less sediment in Sudan reservoirs; more water, formerly used for irrigation, can now be diverted to hydro-electric schemes.

But there were problems, especially the displacement of people who had lived in the area now covered by Lake Nasser. By July 1965, the population of the border town of Wadi Halfa and of 13 villages to the north—some 42,000 people with their livestock—had been evacuated 800 miles by rail across the Nubian Desert to Khasm El Girba, a small settlement 40 miles from the Ethiopian border on the River Atbara. Here the peasants were given double their former acreage and tenant cultivation rights on government-owned land in blocks of 15 acres on which wheat, cotton and groundnuts are grown on a three-year rotation system. Khasm El Girba, a small administrative and market centre

146

lying in a region where semi-nomadic tribesmen grazed their herds of cattle, camels and sheep, has had its population doubled to 6,000. Surrounding it are 26 new villages of 250 houses each. Irrigation and electric power come from a new dam.

In Egypt 75 new government townships have been built. Forty miles north of the Aswan Dam the new township of Kom Ombo is flourishing, surrounded by 30,000 acres of new cropland divided into 5-acre plots.

It appears therefore that the dam is already stimulating great agricultural development. But whether all the claims made by the U.A.R. will be fulfilled and whether the expense involved will be justified remains to be seen. There is a limit to the amount of Egyptian desert that can be irrigated but apparently no limit to the rapid rise of population. Moreover, Egypt's industrialisation programmes will take a long time and much of the potential power may not be used for some time to come.

Ghana—The Volta River Project

Until 1962 the hydro-electric power and irrigation potential of Ghana's rivers had been little developed despite the country's heavy annual rainfalls in the south-west and the numerous deep valleys suitable for dam sites. This lack of development was largely due to the extreme variations in the seasonal flow of Ghana's rivers.

Although Ghana has numerous short rivers in the well-watered south-west—the Tano, the Pra, the Ancobra and their tributaries—her major river systems, the Volta, the Black Volta, the White Volta and the Oti, derive their waters from savannah regions covering the northern two-thirds of the country. Here the long dry season (October to March) is followed by heavy rains brought by south-westerly air currents: see below.

During the dry season the rivers of northern Ghana dwindle to mere trickles, their courses marked by water holes. The Volta itself experiences a great reduction in its volume despite contributions by its more southern tributaries—the Puru and Afram. But in the rainy season the rivers become roaring torrents frequently overflowing their banks and flooding large areas. Practically all the surface water of the northern half of Ghana is channelled into the Volta—during the Akosombo dam's construction record-breaking floods occurred unequalled over 50 years.

The Reasons for the Volta Project

Why was this great project costing £60 million embarked upon? Ghana possesses considerable reserves of bauxite, the aluminium ore, vital in the construction of modern aircraft, motor cars, railway engines and coaches and household utensils. The large-scale production of hydro-electric power would make the cost of smelting the ore before export economically feasible, and refined aluminium would be less expensive to ship than the bulky ore. Aluminium exports would lessen the reliance on agricultural exports, particularly cocoa (page 77). The cheap power would also encourage the establishment of secondary industries and broaden Ghana's economy which relies too much on mineral extraction and agriculture. Moreover, the Ghanaian Government had pushed on with the construction of the £35 million port of Tema (page 120) designed to handle the expected increases in exports and the inflow of constructional equipment. Tema is now the site of the Valco aluminium smelter, instead of Kpong near the dam site at Akosombo. This saved the cost of constructing a new settlement at Kpong. Ghana is providing half the cost of the Volta project with the remainder supplied by the United States, Britain and the World Bank.

TABLE 20
Ghana: Rainfall Figures for Navrongo

MONTH	JAN.	FEB.	MARCH	APRIL	MAY	JUNE	JULY	AUG.	SEPT.	OCT.	NOV.	DEC.	YEAR
Rainfall *(inches)*	0·0	0·0	0·85	3·91	5·72	4·06	7·78	8·78	8·42	0·0	0·0	0·0	39·52
(mm)	0·0	0·0	21·6	99·3	145·3	103·1	197·6	223·0	213·9	0·0	0·0	0·0	1003·8

The Dam[1]

The building of the dam at Akosombo, although a more difficult site than the one originally proposed at Ajena, reduced construction time by four years and increased the potential amount of power that could be generated. Already the great lake which will eventually cover 3 per cent of Ghana and stretch 200 miles is growing and will expand to drown 3,375 square miles—the world's third largest man-made lake. A power house generating nearly 600,000 kilowatts of hydro-electric power through its four turbines will distribute electricity over a 500-mile long transmission network. The dam rises 440 feet above the river bed and its crest is 2,200 feet long.

The Results

While some critics have pointed out that it might have been wiser to sink the money into several smaller schemes on the many dam sites available in Ghana and thus spread the benefits of power and irrigation water over a wider area, there is no doubt that Ghana will receive tremendous economic benefits from the Volta Project. These include:

a Large supplies of cheap power for Valco, the mining and secondary industries. This will reduce Ghana's consumption of thermal power which has jumped over the last ten years from 40 million kWh to 200 million kWh.

b Large benefits to agriculture. Irrigation experiments are being carried out on state farms north of the lake and on the Accra Plains, particularly with paddy and sugar cane. Downriver from the dam an area once devoted to shifting agriculture is being converted into small farms and state-owned plantations. Some 8,000 acres of sugar cane, 11,000 acres of rice, and 2,000 acres of groundnuts, maize, tobacco, vegetables and other crops are being laid out. The experimental area lies only 100 miles east of the large Accra market and stretches for 50 miles inland from the coast.

The lake itself will yield an estimated 25,000 tons of fish a year, while the annual rise and fall of the lake surface along its 4,500-mile long shores will expose much fertile grazing land.

c The economic development created by the dam will be felt throughout Ghana. The operations at Tema and Akosombo have created a skilled body of workers who are a valuable asset. The building of

[1] For map showing location of dam and lake see Fig. 9:7, page 185.

trunk and feeder roads to serve both the project and Tema is already stimulating economic activity in interior Ghana.

d The lake will become an inland waterway. New ports are planned and a lake service designed to transport goods and passengers. The lake will provide a great attraction for tourists.

As with the Aswan High Dam, the Volta Project has made a great change in many people's lives. Some 80,000 people have been moved to 54 well-planned townships and have been introduced to modern co-operative methods of cultivation. Originally living in isolated villages and producing subsistence crops, they are now contributing to the national economy. The Volta River Authority (V.R.A.) and the Ghanaian Ministry of Agriculture plan to resettle 42 per cent of the people as arable farmers. Some 7,000 families have been given 42,000 acres in plots of six acres; of these 3,000 families will concentrate on pineapple growing, others on vegetables, tree crops and pastoral farming.

The Republic of South Africa—The Orange River Project

The Republic of South Africa suffers from a very uneven distribution of its water resources. The main watershed of the country—the well-watered arc of the Drakensbergs and Maluti mountain ranges of the south-east—lies only 100 miles from the shores of the Indian Ocean but over 700 miles from the South Atlantic. The map (Fig. 7:9) shows how this watershed divides the drainage system of South Africa. To the east and south down the steep escarpment face and across the coastal plain flow many short rivers—the Tugela, the Umkomaas, the Umzimvubu, the Great Kei, the Sundays and the Olifants. These rivers depend entirely on annual rainfalls on the Drakensberg and associated highlands. During the rainy periods in the early and late parts of the year the rivers are rushing torrents; in the drier months they are sluggish and irregular, their levels dropping considerably.

Westwards from the Drakensberg flow the long rivers—the Orange and its tributaries the Hartz, the Vaal, the Modder and the Caledon. The Orange, flowing for 1,300 miles to the desolate west coast near Alexander Bay also suffers from seasonal rainfall variations, varying between a rushing, muddy torrent and a trickle. The South African Government is now attempting to harness the vast power and irrigation potential of the Orange.

The Republic has several schemes, mainly for irrigation on the Sundays, the Great Fish and the Kei and also on the main tributaries of the Orange. The biggest scheme is on the Vaal where the Vaal-dam reservoir provides water for the densely settled mining and industrial complex of the Witwaters-rand. This water is also used to feed many other towns and irrigation projects including the Vaal-Hartz irrigation settlement. Although the Vaaldam's capacity was doubled in 1956 the ever-increasing demands of the Rand cities and mines has placed a severe strain on the river's resources. The Orange River irrigation and hydro-electric power scheme, which will take thirty years to complete, will greatly ease this burden.

The Orange River

The Orange is South Africa's largest river with a flow of water equal to all the other rivers combined. It drains 330,000 square miles of Lesotho, Botswana, South-West Africa and the Republic. Its upper course lies in the well-watered (80 inches [2032mm] a year) Maluti mountain ranges where there are plans for several independent schemes, e.g. the Oxbow Project, which entails the joining of the numerous headwaters of the Orange by a series of tunnels and canals and channelling the water through several power stations leading down to the Caledon River.

From this highland zone the Orange drops from 11,000 feet and crosses the flatter interior plateau between 4,000 and 5,000 feet forming the southern boundary of the Orange Free State; 450 miles from its source it is joined by the Vaal. The Orange then flows south-westwards, skirts the southern highlands of Griqualand and then turns sharply north-wards at Prieska, where annual rainfalls drop from about 25 to 10 inches [635 to 254mm] and evapora-tion rates rise enormously. The three hundred-mile stretch from the Caledon junction to the bend at Prieska is the vital section of the scheme for it is here that the Orange receives over half of the total run-off of the whole drainage system.

Westwards from Prieska the Orange drops steadily to 2,000 feet in a 250-mile long stretch where rainfall totals fall to 5 inches [127mm] in the west and evaporation rates rise to over 100 inches [2540mm] a year. The Orange has here formed wide plains of fertile soils which, with irrigation, could support good crops. The river then topples through the Aughrabies Falls (475 feet) then flows through

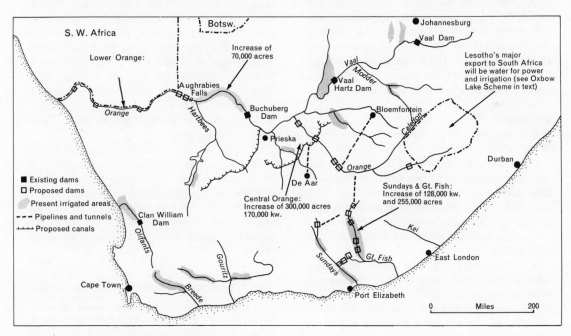

Fig. 9: South Africa—the Orange River Scheme

149

rugged desert country for 300 miles before reaching the Atlantic.

The Scheme

The main aim of the Orange River Scheme is to make full use of the irrigation and hydro-electric power potential of the river and provide a sound basis for agricultural and industrial development. The total cost will be £225 million over the next thirty years. The scheme will enable a further 700,000 acres to be irrigated and will be carried out in six phases. The main control dam (225 feet high) in the Ruigte Valley downstream from Bethulie will store 360,000 million gallons; the Van der Kloof Dam downstream will provide more storage water for the interior plateau and water will be pumped into irrigation canals leading to De Aar and the Riet, Brak, Ongers and Carnarvonleegte Valleys. A third dam at Torquay will provide irrigation water for land flanking the Orange as far as Prieska. All these dams will control the Orange River's water as far as its mouth, where there are great irrigation possibilities. A 51-mile long tunnel will lead from the Ruigte Valley through the southern mountains to the upper Great Fish River and thence by canal to the lower Sundays Valley; this will improve existing irrigation and power facilities and help expand the area devoted to sheep and fruit farming.

Work has already begun on the Hendrik Verwoerd Dam which will cost £30 million and is to be completed by June 1971. This is one of the three major dams in the Orange River Scheme and when completed it will be the fifth largest in the world.

The Results

The Orange River Project will benefit South Africa in the following ways:

a The 700,000 extra acres of irrigated land will mean a crop increase of 25 per cent over the present crop value especially of fruits, vegetables, hay, stockfeed, maize, wheat, groundnuts and cotton. The dangers of severe droughts over a large area of the interior will be reduced and wool production will increase.

b A wide measure of flood control will reduce damage and stabilise water supplies for new and existing irrigation schemes.

c Existing irrigation and power schemes whose efficiency has been reduced by silting will be revitalised by fresh water supplies.

d In the long run, primary and secondary industries will be stimulated. Agricultural expansion will attract more fruit and vegetable canneries, wool scouring, washing and combing plants, textile and agricultural machinery factories. The cheap power will aid mining and communications development and textile and chemical factories needing large supplies of water will benefit.

e By this scheme the Government plans to adjust the present economic imbalance in South Africa. South African industry is heavily concentrated in a few major regions—the Rand, Durban, Cape Town, Port Elizabeth and East London. New industry can now move away from these concentrations and stimulate the economy in less favoured regions. Existing water supplies, as at the Vaal reservoir, will be relieved. In general there will be a loosening up of the country's economic structure.[1]

Three Smaller Schemes—The Limpopo, Tana and Owen Falls
Mozambique—The Limpopo Valley Scheme

The Limpopo is small by African standards, being only 600 miles long but its lower reaches, about 75 miles north of Lourenço Marques, have riverine lowlands of some of the richest soils in Africa, varying from light sandy soils along the valley margins to rich black silts along the river banks. Irrigation is necessary here despite 30 inches [762mm] of rain a year, for there is a dry period from June to September. Until fifteen years ago little had been done to organise native and European agriculture. A few farmers grew small patches of rice and cattle were grazed on the lowlands and moved to higher pastures during floods.

Development was hindered by malaria, inadequate transport facilities, fear of floods and the lack of a local market. An anti-malaria campaign resulted in the practical elimination of the disease and a dam, 210 feet high, was constructed 14 miles above Guija to control floods and conduct the Limpopo's waters through 125 miles of irrigation canals.

[1] South Africa is also interested in the prospect of importing water and power from Lesotho. An industrial consortium is to construct a dam at Oxbow Lake which will produce 400 million kilowatt hours per annum; water for industry will be sold to South Africa. The plan will cost £30 million and envisages the possibility of a 300-mile long pipeline to Vereeniging.

The Limpopo Irrigation Scheme lying in an area 60 miles long by 10 miles wide is a series of small-holdings farmed by Europeans and Africans. Over 1,500 Europeans from Portugal, the Azores and Madeira, and 800 African farmers are now working plots of 10 to 25 acres and a further 1,500 are being trained in farming methods. The main section of the scheme has thirteen government-built self-sufficient villages laid out on rectangular plots close to the irrigated areas, each house having its own small cultivated patch.

The rich soils of the flat Limpopo plain are now a patchwork of rectangular fields yielding rice, wheat, maize, long-staple Egyptian cotton, potatoes, tobacco, beans, peas, tomatoes, onions, cabbage, cauliflower and carrots. In addition to the 800,000 acres available for cultivation there are 500,000 acres for grazing dairy cattle. Each settler keeps a small number of livestock, a compulsory part of the scheme; these include hens, a milking cow, pigs, calves and ploughing oxen.

The government has constructed several processing factories in the area and exports the produce to inland markets via the railway from Lourenço Marques. There is a good market in this port and in Rhodesia, particularly for supplies of fresh vegetables which are in season in the Limpopo Valley before the crops on the cooler plateaus.

Other schemes on the Limpopo include the Inhamissa area near the river's mouth where swamps have been drained for 2,500 families to grow rice, maize, beans and wheat as cash crops, and bananas, vegetables and tobacco for their own use. In the drier sandier soils cassava and groundnuts are cultivated and herds of cattle and goats reared.

The irrigation of the fertile lands of the lower Limpopo and its settlement by European and African farmers is a good example of a government-sponsored agricultural scheme of an intensive type in a region which, fifteen years ago, was a fever-ridden wilderness.

Mozambique is also planning another large scheme. This entails the construction of a £66·5 million dam at Songo, where the Cabora-Bassa Pass narrows to about 87 yards. Large tracts of land are to be irrigated and the scheme will provide enough H.E.P. to fulfil all Mozambique's requirements. Power will be exported to South Africa via Rhodesia by overhead transmission cables.

Kenya—The Tana River Development Scheme

Although the Tana is also a comparatively small river it is of great importance to Kenya's economy. Little more than a third of Kenya's 225,000 square miles—the coastal strip, the highlands above 5,000 feet and the Lake Victoria shores—have sufficiently reliable rainfalls to support good crops and healthy cattle. The remaining two-thirds is semi-desert, bush and scrub. With irrigation things could be different.

But Kenya is unfortunate in its rivers. The highlands, with annual rainfalls of 40 to 70 inches [1016 to 1778mm], act as a watershed. Down their western slopes the Sondu, Nyanda and Nzoia Rivers flow only fifty miles through well-watered country towards Lake Victoria. The rivers flowing eastwards to the Indian Ocean have more difficult courses. Hundreds of streams flow down the dip-slopes of the Aberdares and from Mt Kenya to join the Tana, Ewaso Ngiro and Athi (which later forms the Galana). Only two, the Tana and Athi-Galana, reach the sea across the 300-mile wide Nyika, for the Ewaso Ngiro drains to a halt in the Lorian Swamp.

Kenya is making great efforts to use these limited water resources to best advantage. With a rapidly

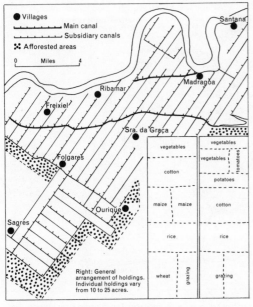

FIG. 10: Mozambique—part of the Limpopo River Scheme

151

growing population (5·4 million in 1948, 8·6 million in 1962) it is vitally important to increase the acreage of productive land and to develop power to expand existing industries and attract new ones. Apart from several small power plants there is no major power station in the country and with no coal Kenya must rely on electric power from Owen Falls and fuel oils from overseas. Projects so far completed (for irrigation)—the Perkerra Scheme on Lake Baringo, the Yatta Furrow, and projects near Taveta—are all on a small scale. But the Tana offers good opportunities for the irrigation of large areas and the production of a substantial amount of hydro-electric power.

The Tana is approximately 400 miles long and drains 40,000 square miles (equal to the area of Liberia). But rainfall over this catchment area is badly distributed with great variations from year to year and except in the highlands annual totals do not exceed 20 inches [508mm]. Evaporation rates are high (Garissa—rainfall 8 inches [203mm], evaporation 120 inches [3048mm]). Moreover, the rain falls in two short seasons, October to December and March to April. The Tana thus experiences wide

variations in its levels, but even so it is the only river which possesses a considerable potential. Already this potential is being tapped in the following schemes.

Irrigation Schemes

a The Mwea-Tebere Scheme The area of plateau land fringing the Aberdares and Mt Kenya and drained by the Tana and its tributaries is one of the richest agricultural areas in Kenya. Here, at about 4,250 feet there is enough water to serve the many coffee farms in the west, the new resettlement schemes and to irrigate some 20,000 acres. The black, sticky impervious soils make the flatter parts ideal for rice cultivation and on the Mwea-Tebere plains is Kenya's large rice scheme, irrigated by the Nyamindi and Thiba tributaries, which will eventually cover 12,000 acres. Some 10,000 people live on planned four-acre farms and in 19 new self-contained villages. Here annual rainfalls vary from 25 to 30 inches [635 to 762mm] a year with long dry periods, so irrigation is essential. Sindano type rice gives high yields (40 bags per acre) exceeded only by Australia and Ethiopia. The scheme reduces Kenya's

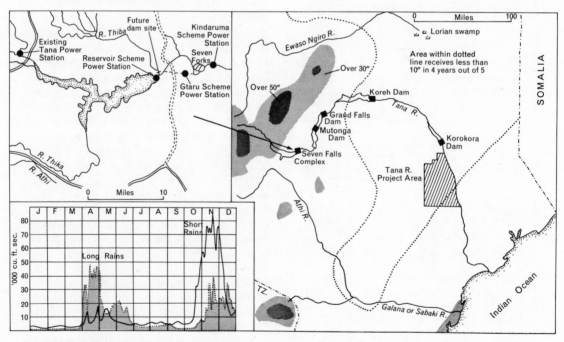

Fig. 11: Kenya—the Tana River Scheme. The graph shows the extreme variation in volume of the River Tana during Kenya's two rainy seasons between 1953 and 1965

reliance on imports by producing 12,000 tons of rice annually, worth £250,000.

b The Galole Pilot Scheme Below the great bend of the Tana at Galole is an irrigation scheme which may be the forerunner of a much vaster operation. This is the dry (15 inches [381mm] a year) country of the Pokomo who, unlike the neighbouring pastoral Somali and Galla, cultivate poor grains and root crops in the silt at falling flood times, often enduring famine when the rains fail. Here on the right bank is an irrigation settlement covering 1,200 acres, to which water is pumped through an 11-mile long canal. Cotton, groundnuts, soya beans and rice are grown entirely by irrigation and this small scheme has proved that good yields (1,000 to 1,500 lb. of cotton per acre) can be obtained from irrigated desert soils.

c Future Prospects—Plans for the Lower Tana Basin With the success of the Galole Scheme a large area flanking the Tana between Garissa and Garsen covering three million acres has been aerially surveyed with the object of selecting 300,000 acres for irrigation. Such an area would be sufficient to settle 75,000 families or nearly a third of a million people. Its gross agricultural production would amount to £24 million a year of which £15 million would come from cotton. Extra employment would be created by cotton ginneries to be set up in the area.

Hydro-Electric Power—The Seven Forks Scheme
Three miles downstream from the Seven Forks Rapids the Kindaruma Dam will create a lake 30 miles long by 8 miles wide. From this reservoir two power stations will produce enough power to supply electricity to the whole of Kenya and when completed the scheme will have a capacity of 240 Megawatts (Owen Falls generates 150 Megawatts). The lake will provide a large inland fishery and will be a tourist attraction. As Kenya's industrial and domestic demands for power increase there are plans for future power plants at Mutonga, Grand Falls and Koreh.

The Results
The development of the Tana River's potential, although small compared with the Volta, Zambezi and Orange schemes, will bring considerable economic benefits to Kenya, the most important being:

a Kenya's dependence on imported fuel and local wood will be greatly reduced. Kenya bought 190 million electricity units out of a total of 332 million produced by Uganda in 1965. Power lines will eventually run to all settled areas including Mombasa which now imports electricity from Pangani in Tanzania.

b The industrial potential of the country will be increased by the great reserves of cheap power. More factories will be needed to process the products of the new irrigated areas.

c The irrigation schemes will eventually provide settlement for over a third of a million people who will support themselves; grow food crops for Kenya's growing population, and supply raw materials for industry.

Uganda—The Owen Falls Dam

In 1862, as a result of the journey of John Hanning Speke, the source of the Victoria Nile, the narrow outlet for the waters of Lake Victoria, became known to the outside world. Here, the waters of the world's third largest lake poured over the Ripon Falls to enter marshy Lake Kyoga to the north and eventually find their way via the northern tip of Lake Albert and the western arm of the Rift Valley to the main drainage system of the Nile. In 1907 Winston Churchill saw the huge possibilities of the tremendous volume of rushing water when he stated, 'It is possible that nowhere else in the world could so enormous a mass of water be held up by so little masonry.' But it was not until 1954, 92 years after Speke's journey, that the waters first produced hydro-electric power.

Unlike Kenya and Tanzania, Uganda is fortunate in her water supplies. Roughly one-seventh (13,700 square miles) of Uganda's total area (94,000 square miles) is covered by water. Rainfalls throughout most of the country are reliable and plentiful and few regions receive less than 40 inches [1016mm] a year. Combined with the warm humid atmosphere and the deep soils found over much of the country the land supports a dense population and a wide variety of crops—cotton, sugar cane, tea, groundnuts, tobacco and tropical fruits.

But until 1954 the country had one major problem—the lack of power for industrial development. There are no coal deposits in Uganda and no major oil fields. Fuel imports, hauled 650 miles from the sea, were expensive and without cheap power a severe limit was set on industrial expansion. The government was anxious to develop industries for several reasons. The population was growing

153

Fig. 12: Uganda—Owen Falls and the distribution of power

The dam can accommodate ten turbo-alternator sets but when opened in 1954 only six were installed until the demand for power increased. Today all ten are in operation producing a total of 150,000 Kilowatts—a sixteenth of Uganda's power potential. Today the Owen Falls Dam is the chief supplier of electricity in Uganda and much is exported via high-tension wires to Kisumu, Nakuru and Nairobi.

The Results

The supplies of cheap power from the Owen Falls Dam benefit Uganda in the following ways:

a The overall planning of the national economy need no longer be restricted by fears of lack of energy. There is now ample power for Uganda's present and future needs especially now that Kenya is developing its own power supplies.

b Industrial growth has been greatly stimulated. Jinja (page 136) has become the industrial hub of the country and using the power are cement and asbestos factories at Tororo and a whole range of industries in several towns—Kampala, Port Bell and Mbale.

c There has been an immense reduction of oil imports for the thermal power stations in Uganda. Only one of the turbo-alternators saves 4,000 tons of oil a year.

Questions

1 Examine the distribution of the major water resources of Africa south of the Sahara and discuss the attempts by man to harness them.

2 With the aid of well-chosen examples, discuss the factors which have generally hindered the use of rivers in Africa for power and irrigation purposes.

3 In what ways are rivers helping the economic development of nations in Africa? Confine your answer to specific projects.

4 Discuss the various factors which prompt governments of African nations to develop their river potential for power and irrigation purposes.

5 Consider the factors which affect the regimes of the Congo, Niger, Zambezi, Tana, Volta and Nile.

6 Choose any *one* of the following river schemes and for the one chosen:

a Outline the reasons for its undertaking; *b* Describe the site and construction briefly; *c* Discuss the benefits, both industrial and agricultural, which will result from its completion.

Ghana: The Volta River Project; United Arab

rapidly (3·5 million in 1931, 5 million in 1948) and large areas of agricultural land were already reaching their limits of production. New industries would help broaden the economy and provide alternative employment. Again, Uganda possessed other advantages—an increasing supply of raw materials for secondary industry (cotton, tea, sugar, coffee); a large supply of unskilled labour willing to be trained; several mineral deposits, especially the copper at Kilembe, and a good export outlet along the railway to Mombasa which had been extended to Kilembe in 1931. Moreover, good roads linked most parts with Kampala, and lakes and rivers provided cheap water transport. All that was lacking was the power and this was solved by the construction of the Owen Falls Dam across the Victoria Nile.

The Dam

The dam was built across a narrow channel about half a mile wide, 300 yards north of Owen Falls which, with the Ripon Falls, disappeared below the Nile waters which have since risen. The dam is a low (85 feet) curving structure 2,725 feet long containing six control sluices. By agreement with the Egyptian Government the dam was built three feet higher than was necessary for Uganda's needs. This raised the level of Lake Victoria's water nearly a foot higher and substantially increased the amount available for irrigation in the Sudan and Egypt. British, Danish and Dutch firms co-operated on the dam's construction.

TABLE 21
Some other Irrigation Projects in Africa

COUNTRY	PROJECT	COST	REMARKS
Algeria	25 small dams and 3 large ones	Unknown: U.S.S.R. financed	To irrigate 21,000 acres
Tunisia	One large dam	U.S.S.R. financed	Located on Ghazalah River
Morocco	One large dam	Unknown	At Zawihat Mirbaz—35,000 acres to present 45,000 acres
U.A.R.	Dams and drainage	£10·5 million	At Kom Ombo: 108,000 acres
Upper Volta	Planned barrages for agriculture	Not decided. Eur. Dev. Fund	At Kouougou
Ghana	Accra Plains Project	£26 million	440,000 acres for rice, cotton, sugar cane, grazing
	Dams and water reticulation	£0·6 million F.A.O. assistance	80,000 acres in various places in Northern Region for cotton and tobacco
Nigeria	Water supply scheme	£5 million	Ibadan area
Burundi	Water supply	£0·4 million I.D.A.	At Bujumbura
Kenya	Dams and water reticulation	Possible finance by West Germany	Kano Plains near Lake Victoria. Kenya plans to raise £170 million for other projects
Botswana	Dams and water reticulation	£1·4 million U.N. to finance	Sashi River Project
Senegal, Guinea, Mali and Mauritania	Gounia Dam	Partly U.N. financed	Essential part of Senegal River Basin Scheme. Interstate co-operation. Study to last 2½ years
S.W. Africa	Cunene River Scheme. Power and irrigation for Ovamboland	£25 million	First stage in a £60 million development plan for S.W. Africa

Republic: The Aswan High Dam; Mali: The Interior Delta region of the Niger; South Africa: The Orange River Scheme; Rhodesia-Zambia: The Kariba Dam; Nigeria: The Kainji Dam Project.

Practical Work

Typical practical questions on irrigation and hydro-electric power might be:

1 Describe the importance of rivers and water supply in the human geography of any small area which you have studied in the field.
2 Describe the ways in which any river in your country or home area is being harnessed to increase the economic potential of a region or district.

The following topics are suggested as vacation work which the student may find interesting and profitable:

1 The keeping of records of observations made on the flow of local rivers. These records should include a map of the river's full course, the variations in level throughout the year according to rainfall amount, the occurrence of floods, photographs taken at high and low levels for comparison.
2 A visit to a local irrigation project or power site if possible. A map could then be drawn showing the location and a description including acreage, number of people, types of crops, use to the country's economy, export of crops and so on could be written.

CHAPTER EIGHT

INDUSTRIAL DEVELOPMENT IN AFRICA (1)—THE EXTRACTIVE INDUSTRIES

Africa is a late arrival in the field of industrial development. African landscapes are predominantly rural and there are no smoke-blackened regions as in Europe or North America. The continent has learned from the experiences of older nations and industrial areas are spacious, well-planned and usually located outside the major towns.

The Basis for Industry in Africa— Fuel and Raw Materials

The growth and location of modern industry depends on several factors—large supplies of suitable coal, oil and hydro-electric power, a labour force with developed skills, large easily accessible markets with a high buying power, and an efficient transport network to serve markets and carry raw materials at economic rates. Few areas in Africa can claim these advantages. Except in the Transvaal there is no fortunate combination of coal, iron ore and useful minerals to form the basis of heavy iron and steel industries; Nigerian coal lies 1,300 miles from Liberian iron ore, Moroccan ores are used in Europe, Tanzania's coal remains in the ground for want of rail transport.

Africa has thus played the rôle of a mineral supplier to the more industrialised nations. Mineral ore processing is still in its infancy, the continent producing only 1 per cent of the pig iron, 1 per cent of the crude steel, and only 3 per cent of the lead and zinc of the world. Africa is however, the world's third largest producer of processed copper (25 per cent) after the U.S.A. and Chile and possesses some rich deposits of minerals vital to the world's eco-

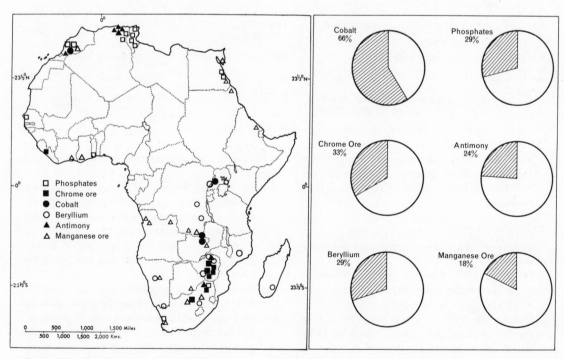

FIG. 1: Africa—location of some important minerals

Africa—percentage of world production of some important minerals

156

nomy—diamonds (96 per cent world production), cobalt (66 per cent), gold (70 per cent), manganese (18 per cent) and chromite (33 per cent); her output of bauxite has increased from 2 per cent in 1950 to 7 per cent today.

Africa is short on coal, her economy as yet too under-developed to make full use of the tremendous volume of oil her rocks are yielding, and her hydro-electric power potential has scarcely been touched. Coal lies in widely scattered deposits not all easy to get at. The chief producers are South Africa (annual production 49 million tons—compare Britain's 200 million), Rhodesia (3·6 million), Nigeria (0·8 million), Morocco (0·5 million) and the Congo (0·45 million). While southern Africa has a mono-poly of the known coal deposits, northern Africa possesses almost all the oil, with Libya the foremost producer (1967, 83·5 million tons) followed by Algeria (nearly 30 million tons) and Nigeria (now producing 1·5 million tons a month).[1] While produc-tion of hydro-electric power has taken great strides since 1945 Africa still produces only 1 per cent of the world's output although her power potential is 23 per cent of the world's.

It should be remembered, however, that Africa is one of the last continents to be fully explored geo-logically and that the discovery of economically important minerals has been hampered in many places by the thick mask of sedimentary deposits which cover many parts of Africa's surface. New mineral deposits are coming to light with increasing frequency. The most dramatic example is that of Libya, where the discovery of oil transformed a country whose economy formerly rested almost en-tirely on the export of groundnuts into the world's eighth largest oil producer (output 1,200,000 bar-rels a day); the country's per capita income has risen from £12 to £155 a year. Thus the economic position of any single country in Africa may change overnight with the discovery of a vital mineral and the picture presented by today's statistics may be changed radically tomorrow. The map (Fig. 8:**1**) illustrates the more important mineral deposits in Africa.

The Fuels: Coal

Despite its size as the second largest continent Africa is one of the poorest in coal reserves. Coal

[1] Prior to internal hostilities.

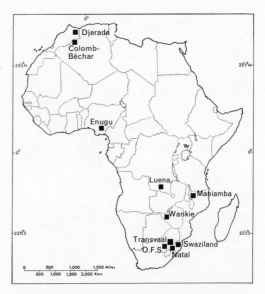

FIG. 2: Africa—location of important coal producing regions

deposits are limited to isolated pockets, mainly in the southern half of the continent where luxuriant forest and fern growth flourished during the Permo-Carboniferous age—in South Africa, Rhodesia and Tanzania. Lower grade coal is mined in Nigeria, Mozambique and the Congo and there are other deposits in Madagascar, Malawi and Zambia.

These deposits form only a fraction of the world's total coal reserves (4,700 billion tons); of these the United States and Canada own 38 per cent, the Soviet Union 24 per cent, Communist China 20 per cent and Europe 13 per cent. Africa's share is a meagre 1·5 per cent.

Coal as the Basis for Heavy Industry— the Importance of South African Deposits

The first coal mined at Molteno, Cape Province, in 1864 began the extraction of a mineral which was to form the basis of South Africa's industrial expan-sion over the following 100 years. In 1879 the Vereeniging field was discovered and large-scale exploitation began. Helped by the discovery of gold, the general development of mining and secondary industry, and the needs of the railway and bunker-ing trade, South Africa soon became Africa's foremost coal producer. Increasing amounts were used for thermal electric power after 1900 and by the

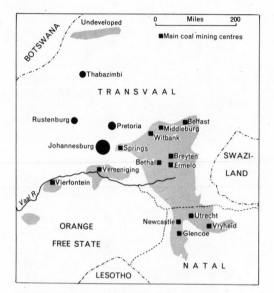

FIG. 3: South Africa—main coal producing areas

southern continents during the First World War.

The main producing fields are shown on the map (Fig. 8:3). Of the three producing states the Transvaal is the largest (approx. 62 per cent), followed by the Orange Free State (23 per cent) and Natal (15 per cent). The Transvaal Witbank collieries are the heaviest producers and the coal is good steam coal but rather unsuitable for coking. Its rapid exploitation is due to its closeness to the Rand (80 miles) and to the ease of extraction. Seams average 60 feet thick and lie close to the surface, while mining is safe for the seams are stable and there is little gas. These factors and the low labour costs make the coal the cheapest in the world (15 shillings per ton at pit head). Other major mining centres in the Transvaal include Vereeniging, Bethal, Ermelo, Belfast and Boksburg. The Witbank field produces about 13 million tons a year, the Springs field 2 million and the Vereeniging 4 million tons.

In the Orange Free State coal mining is confined to the northern fringe centred around Vierfontein with a small mining zone 17 miles south-east of Vereeniging where the lower quality coal goes to the power station near Klerksdorp on the Vaal and to the Sasolburg oil-from-coal plant (page 161).

In Natal the chief centres are Vryheid (half the field's output), Utrecht, Dundee and Newcastle. Seams are thinner here and more faulted but there is much high-grade coking and steam coal.

South Africa's coal is vital to the nation's economy. Ten per cent of annual output is used on the railways and by the secondary industries. Urban centres take over a third, while the iron and steel industry uses 2·5 million tons annually of the higher grade coking coals. The monthly internal consumption of coal in South Africa is greater than the annual production of Rhodesia, Africa's second largest producer—4·25 million tons of bituminous (worth £3·2 million) and 50,000 tons of anthracite each month. A large proportion of Natal's output goes to Durban for bunkering, while 685,000 tons of bituminous and 425,000 tons of anthracite are exported annually.

What of the future? South Africa's coal reserves are estimated at a staggering 75,000 million tons with 90 per cent in the Transvaal, and at the present rate of consumption this will last South Africa for 1,500 years. Coal output is increasing rapidly—1964 production was 48,621,370 tons worth £60 million, an increase of 2,481,720 tons over the 1963 total. In 1966 South Africa produced 51·7 million tons of bituminous and 1·2 million tons of anthracite. Even if we discount South Africa's growing industrial needs for coal, production is likely to be expanded within the next fifteen years for Europe is beginning to feel an energy shortage and South Africa plans to expand production to 70 million tons by the 1970s.

The Strategic Value of Coal

Rhodesia also possesses coal reserves of considerable size. In the Wankie area of the south-west there are 5,000 million tons of bituminous coal, much of high coking quality. At West Sabi there are 4,250 million tons of poorer grade non-coking coal with a rather high ash content in beds some 50 feet thick.

The Wankie field is the only one to be exploited commercially and, although production is but a tenth of South Africa's, the coal plays a vital rôle in the industrial economy of central Africa. The deposit lies close to the surface in seams 5 to 25 feet thick and inclined shafts are used; the coal is amongst the world's cheapest (22 shillings at the pit head and £3 delivered price). Some 250,000 tons of coke are produced annually for use in the iron and steel plants of Rhodesia and in the copper belt. A special type of coke—char—is now being produced at Gwelo at the rate of 700 tons a month for use in smelting ferro-chrome.

Coal imports via Lobito route

Joint owned Zambia-Tanzania refined oil pipeline completed end August 1968.

CONGO

Ndola

Possible site for new £6 m. oil refinery

Kafue

Lusemfwa

Mulungushi

Kafue

LUSAKA

Zambesi

MOZAMBIQUE

Construction work to begin 1967 on Kafue H.E.P. scheme

Msambansovu

KARIBA

Marowa

Livingstone

Kaonga

SALISBURY

Sengwe

Modern refinery uses crude oil piped from Beira

Wankie

Lubimbi

Gatooma

Hartley

Que Que

Umtali

Gwelo

Bulawayo

■ Coal mines
● Urban centres
□ H.E.P. stations
◌ Coalfields
▦ Copper Belt
╼╾ Main Railways

Gwanda

W. Nicholson

Mongula

MOZAMBIQUE

Singwesi

TRANSVAAL

Fig. 4: Rhodesia and Zambia—fuel and power resources

Coal production from Wankie began in 1903 and grew with the development of the Copper Belt and the railways. By 1927 over a million tons a year were being mined and with the post-war boom the three collieries at Wankie were able to produce 5 million tons. Although this amount was never needed by Rhodesia Wankie could, like South Africa, be geared to feed coal-hungry Europe over the next decade.

The railways, on which depend the movement of Rhodesia's many minerals, take over a quarter of production, the Wankie mines and associated industries take 10 per cent and the rest goes to the Copper Belt and iron and steel plants. With the greater use of Kariba power there has been a lessening of demand from these consumers (page 143).

The coal is probably more vital to Zambia's industrial structure than Rhodesia's for Wankie coal

is one of the few imports Zambia cannot replace from other sources. No less than 70 per cent of Zambia's fuel needs for her locomotives, thermal power stations and copper smelters come from Wankie.[1] The Katanga-Zambia Copper Belt takes 760,000 tons of coal annually. Zambia is striving to break this economic dependence by searching for coal deposits within her own boundaries. Work began at the end of 1965 in removing the overburden at Zambia's first coal mine, an opencast mine at Nkandabwe, and by June 1966 300,000 tons had been mined at less than £3 per ton. The mine is now producing at the rate of 60,000 tons a month and, although the coal is considered inferior to that at Wankie, it has been found suitable for copper smelting. A new deposit of higher grade coal has also been discovered in the Gwembe Valley and there is a possibility of the Sinkadoba deposit being opened up.

Due to the recent ban on trade with Rhodesia the Societé Général Congolais des Minerais (see page 164) plans to import U.S. or other foreign coal, probably along the Benguela railway from Lobito. The Katanga copper mines and refinery plants take about 100,000 tons of coal and coke annually from the Wankie Colliery Company.

Tanzania's Untapped Coal Reserves

Some 200 million tons of good quality coking coal also lie in the Ruhuhu River basin on the eastern side of Lake Nyasa (Malawi) and in the Kivira-Songwe field near the north-western end of the lake in the Southern Province of Tanzania. But these are at present unworked for no railway has yet reached them, nor has the economy of Tanzania really required the expense of opening them up. While only a small reserve, the deposit could be important in any future industrial expansion in Tanzania.

The Fuels: Oil

While her coal output is negligible when compared with total world output, Africa is fast becoming one of the world's leaders in the production of mineral oil. In 1950 only Egypt was a significant producer (2·3 million tons out of world's 539 million); by 1960 Africa's output had leaped to 13 million tons (world—1,091 million) and in 1964 to 80 million

[1] Malawi also purchases Rhodesian coal in large quantities for her thermal power station at Blantyre.

tons (world—1,456 million). While this is small compared with the Middle East (385 million tons) and the United States (425 million tons), the rate of expansion ensures Africa of a prominent position among oil producing continents.

The Oil-Deficient South

While states south of the Equator monopolise Africa's coal, north African countries control the continent's oil. Except for Gabon and Angola there are no important fields in the south. The following table shows the production by country:

TABLE 22
Oil Production in Africa

| COUNTRY | PRODUCTION IN TONS (ROUND FIGURES) | | |
| | 1960 | 1964 | 1967 |
	PERCENTAGE OF AFRICA'S TOTAL PRODUCTION IN BRACKETS		
Algeria	8,800,000 (67·8 %)	26,200,000 (33·2 %)	48,000,000
Egypt	3,350,000 (25·0 %)	6,700,000 (8·5 %)	3,400,000
Nigeria	870,000 (6·5 %)	5,000,000 (6·3 %)	18,500,000
Angola	67,000 (0·4 %)	1,000,000 (0·1 %)	N.A.
Gabon	60,000 (0·3 %)	1,000,000 (0·13 %)	N.A.
Libya	negligible	40,000,000 (50·6 %)	83,500,000
Total	13,047,000	79,000,000	153,400,000

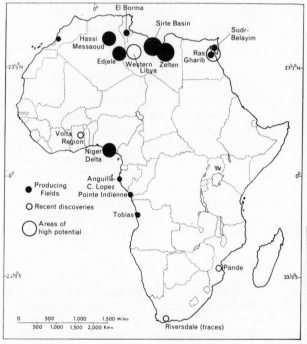

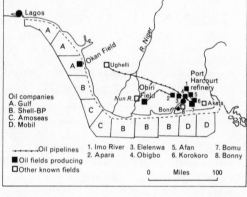

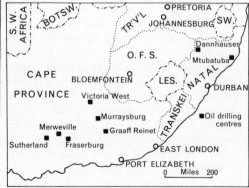

FIG. 5: On the left is a map of Africa showing main oil producing regions. FIG. 6: Nigeria: oil fields and concessions in the Niger Delta; FIG. 7: South Africa: location of oil drilling rigs; the Southern Oil Exploration Corporation (SOEKOR) is operating at six places in Cape Province while the Geological Survey is operating at two places in northern Natal

Africa south of the Sahara produces only 9 per cent of the continent's oil with none from coal-rich South Africa and Rhodesia. *East Africa* is also poor, no known commercially important deposits as yet discovered. In Kenya alone some £10 million has been spent in the seemingly fruitless search for oil. Countries in East Africa are forced to import vast quantities of oil. *South Africa* imported £51·6 million worth of crude petroleum, motor spirit and other oils in 1966, nearly 12·5 per cent of all her imports.[1] To break the dependence on outside supplies the South African Government embarked on the Sasol oil-from-coal Project in 1952, some 17 miles from Vereeniging, at a cost of £50 million. The plant lies near 300 million tons of O.F.S. coal and produces 55 million gallons of petrol annually as well as gases, tars and 21 million gallons of oils. The plant consumes each day some 5,500 tons of coal and employs 2,500 workers housed in the near-by town of Sasolburg. The annual production meets about one-seventh of South Africa's needs so that the Republic still relies heavily on imports. There are plans to set up similar plants and to construct a £17·5 million oil refinery near Sasolburg which will receive crude oil from the recently constructed pipeline from Durban to Johannesburg.

The recent political and economic disturbances in Central Africa have underlined the great dependence the central African States have on imported oil. *Rhodesia* consumes 400,000 tons of crude oil annually, mostly brought from the Middle East and then fed through a 180-mile long pipeline which starts at Beira and ends at the Feruka Valley refinery near Umtali just within Rhodesia's border with Mozambique. Oil accounts for 27 per cent of Rhodesia's energy requirements; some is used in diesel locomotives and 43 per cent is used by motor vehicles. This dependence on imported oil prompted Rhodesia to develop her coalfields and was a contributory factor to the construction of the Kariba Dam.

Zambia also relied on the Mozambique pipeline, 92 per cent of its oil imports coming through Umtali and thence by lorry and rail; half of these imports are used as petrol. However, Zambia is less dependent on oil than Rhodesia and it supplies only 14 per cent of Zambia's needs. Zambia uses about 315,000 tons of oil a year. Nevertheless the pipeline is vital to land-locked Zambia since other methods of importing oil have proved extremely expensive.[1]

The recent oil embargo on Rhodesia has affected the economy of another country—Mozambique. Mozambique usually has a trade deficit but this is normally offset by 'invisible earnings' on the heavy transit trade between Beira and Rhodesia, Malawi and Zambia, and between Lourenço Marques and the Transvaal. The oil pipeline from Beira to Umtali yielded almost £1·7 million to Mozambique in 1965, but the oil embargo has completely cut off this income. But Mozambique herself may have considerable oil reserves, for an oil geyser discovered at Pande 160 miles south of Beira has been flowing since November 1965 and it is believed it may stand on a large basin of oil and natural gas.

The Oil-Rich North

While southern and central Africa import vast quantities of oil the northern territories are among the world's largest exporters of crude petroleum, since their own industrial economies (except for Egypt) are insufficiently developed to absorb their huge production. Prior to 1957 only Egypt produced any oil of note but since then several countries have leaped into prominence.

Egypt has small oilfields west of the Suez Gulf and in the south-west of the Sinai Peninsula. Pre-war production was an annual 250,000 tons, but with the development of secondary industries great efforts were made to increase oil production and cut imports. The late 1950s saw production rise to over 3 million tons but Egypt still relies heavily on imports. Intensive prospecting is going on in the Western Desert, and U.S. experts claim that the Suez Gulf area could become one of the major producing fields in the Middle East; an earlier estimate of the El Morgan field's potential output of 2·5 million tons has now been raised to 10 million tons a year. New finds have also been made in the Western

---

[1] The search for oil in South Africa has been stepped up since the U.N. voted in November 1963 to cut off oil supplies to South Africa. The search has been concentrated in northern Natal where traces of oil have been noticed, and in the arid Karroo region of the northern Cape Province.

[1] The air lifting of oil to Zambia from Tanzania in the 1965/66 troubles cost the British Government over £4 million in a three-month period. Because of this, a pipeline has been constructed from Dar es Salaam by an Italian company at a cost of £16 million. It is 1,100 miles long and took two years to build.

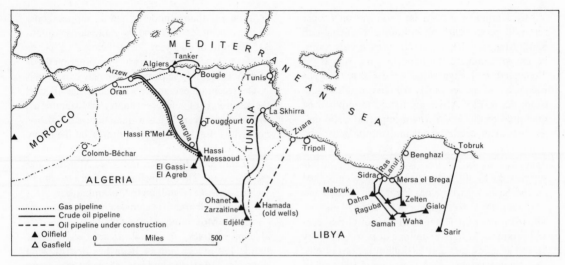

FIG. 8: North Africa—location of major oil fields

Desert but Egypt has suffered a setback in production due to the Israeli-Arab War (see page 198).

Algeria's oil production began only in 1958. Oil was first discovered at Edjele in 1956 followed by several other finds, of which the most important was the Hassi Messaoud field. Algeria is now a major world producer—in 1959 she produced 1·3 million tons, 1960—8·6 million, 1963—23·3 million, in 1964—26·2 million tons, of which half came from Hassi Messaoud; the 1967 production is estimated at 48 million tons. The world's largest natural gas field lies at Hassi R'Mel. France takes 65 per cent of Algeria's oil and Britain, Belgium, West Germany, Italy and the Netherlands the remainder. Pipelines lead to coastal fuelling points—from Hassi Messaoud to Bougie (length 460 miles, completed 1959) and from Edjele to La Skirra (500 miles, opened June 1960), with a combined capacity of 25 million tons annually. A third pipeline (annual capacity 22 million tons) has been built from Haoud el Hamra to Arzew. Oil and natural gas together provide 60 per cent of Algeria's total exports and oil revenues for 1966 were approximately £38 million.

Libya's rise as a world oil producer has been even more meteoric than Algeria's. Oil had been known to exist in 1900 and traces of oil and gas discovered before 1914. The Italians made extensive reconnaissances but the Second World War delayed efficient exploration, first concessions being granted to oil companies in 1959 and production beginning

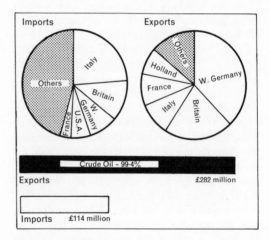

FIG. 9: Libya's trade in 1965

in 1961. By 1963 Libya was producing 22 million tons, by 1964, 40 million tons and production reached 50 million tons by mid-1965. Her crude oil exports for 1965 amounted to nearly 443 million barrels, an increase of 130 million barrels over 1964, and those rose to 547 million barrels, worth £351 million in 1966. British, United States, Italian, West German, Dutch and Spanish firms are investing staggering sums of money. Today oil pours along two pipelines (Zelten and Raguba to Mersa el Brega and Dahra and Marbruk to Es Sider) and two more are under construction.

162

Nigeria, while short of high-grade coal (she produces about 50,000 tons annually, mainly for the railways) is one of the fastest developing oil regions in the world and the Niger delta may become the richest oilfield in Africa. Oil mining began in 1937 but it was not until 1956 that commercial deposits were discovered and 1958 when production began at the Oloibiri Field. Important deposits have been discovered off-shore in the Okan Field, and gas and oil located 60 miles south-west and 40 miles north-west of Port Harcourt.

Nigeria produced less than one million tons in 1960 but her 1966 production reached 18·9 million tons and already oil has taken over from groundnuts as the first export. The country's first refinery (opened at Port Harcourt in November 1965) processes over one million barrels a month. By 1970 Nigeria hopes to be exporting 50 million tons of oil a year and 100 million cubic feet of natural gas—equal to Britain's present imports from Algeria. A pipeline carries the crude oil to a tanker terminal at Bonny. In 1965 crude oil accounted for almost one-quarter of all Nigeria's overseas sales; nearly 420,000 barrels were produced daily in 1966—a 54 per cent increase over 1965 daily output.[1] At the time of writing, however, the Federal Government's military action against the Eastern States (Biafra) has severely curtailed oil production and exports; figures for February, 1968 show a 90 per cent decrease on February, 1967 totals.

The Significance of Oil Discoveries in Africa

The sudden discovery and exploitation of oil deposits in Africa has brought great advantages to several African states:

a There has been a tremendous increase in revenue. Libya for example receives over 50 per cent of oil royalties and these vast sums are used for many purposes—in 1965/66 £150 million were spent on public services, defence and agriculture and a five-year plan to build 100,000 houses costing £400 million is under way.

[1] By June 1967, oil production had reached a peak of 578,264 barrels a day but fell to only 51,940 barrels as a result of the blockade of Biafra by Federal Nigeria.

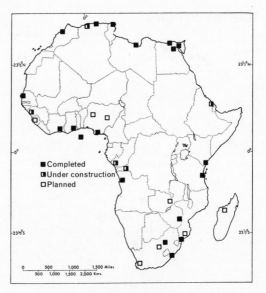

Fig. 10: Africa—location of oil refineries

b The oil companies train workers as welders, geologists' assistants, and oil plant operatives. These represent a skilled body of workers and are a future asset to the country.

c The oil companies often assist where possible with other undertakings, such as the oil spraying and fixing of dunes in the Libyan Desert where the Libyan Forestry Department is planting vegetation.

d The exports of oil broaden the country's economy. Libya's chief export prior to oil discoveries were groundnuts, while in Nigeria oil has replaced groundnuts as the chief export.

e The development of secondary industries, once hampered by lack of fuel, can now proceed in the knowledge of almost unlimited oil supplies.

f The oil producing nations are assured of a market in fuel-hungry Europe. They are more conveniently located than the Middle East countries and their oil is often of a higher and lighter quality free from sulphur. Nigeria will probably send the bulk of its exports to the United Kingdom, since the United States will curtail imports to protect U.S. production. European oilfields produce only one-tenth of the continent's annual consumption of 200 million tons of oil. Africa, in the traditional rôle of a raw materials supplier is well situated to tend her needs.

The Mineral Ores

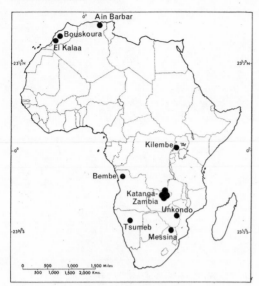

FIG. 11: Africa—major copper producing areas

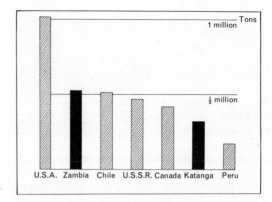

FIG. 12: World production of copper in 1965

Copper—The Zambian-Katangan Monopoly

Copper is one of the most sought after metals of the modern technical age. With its alloys, bronze and brass, it is used extensively in the manufacture of household utensils, food processing equipment, brewery vats and stills, machinery bearings, rust-resisting tubes, the wire of dynamo armatures and giant alternators, electronic equipment, coins, television screens, military weapons and the world's network of submarine cables and high tension wires all need copper.

Copper is thus in great demand by the industrial nations and production has been increased to satisfy the demand. In 1865 world production was 100,000 tons, in 1913, 1·0 million, in 1939, 2·0 million, in 1955, 3·0 million, in 1960, 4·0 million and in 1966, 4·7 million. Of this 87 per cent is taken by North America, Japan and Western Europe. By 1970 the world will need 5·5 million tons of copper each year.

Fig. 8:12 shows the important position which Africa holds in the production of this vital mineral. Zambia ranks second after the United States and Katanga lies sixth. Combined, the two form the Copper Belt of central Africa, a mining zone 280

miles long by 160 miles wide which produces 25 per cent of the world's copper and 66 per cent of its cobalt, a valuable heat-resisting alloy.

In 1867 Livingstone described the smelting of copper ore by the Katangan natives into large ingots weighing 50 to 100 lb. which were later used to make anklets and rings. At the end of the nineteenth century several British and Belgian prospectors discovered large copper ore deposits near the native diggings. A short-lived commercial partnership was struck between Belgian and British companies but with the establishment of the Union Minière du Haut Katanga[1] in 1906 the Copper Belt was worked as two separate entities.

Zambia

Copper production in Northern Rhodesia (Zambia) did not begin until the southern railway reached Broken Hill in 1909. Development was retarded by disease, inaccessibility and technical ignorance. The First World War caused further delay but by the 1920s large-scale development had begun, followed by the opening of several mines—Roan Antelope and Nkana (1931), Mufulira (1933) and Nchanga (1939). The Second World War stimulated production and the post-war years saw the opening of the Chibaluma (1955) and Bancroft (1957) Mines. The

[1] The Union Minière du Haut Katanga which has its headquarters in Brussels, Belgium, was taken over by the Congo (Kinshasa) Government in January 1967; all the Company's assets and concessions to mine copper and cobalt in the Congo were transferred to a newly formed state-controlled Company called the Societé General Congolais des Minerais (GECOMIN). Under a new mining code all further exploitation of minerals in the Congo by foreign companies must be carried out in association with Congolese companies.

new Chambishi Mine became fully operational at the end of 1965 with the commissioning of the new concentrating plant there. The Anglo-American Corporation also intends to operate another entirely new mine near Nchanga in three years' time—the Mimbula Fitula Mine where ore reserves estimated at 11·6 million tons with a 3·9 per cent copper content lie at a depth of only 500 feet. This new mine will cost about £6 million and will be of the open cast type. Old mines such as the Allies Mine near Lusaka are to be opened up; this mine was abandoned in 1920 but it still contains some 165,000 tons of ore worth about £3·5 million.

Today the Zambian Copper Belt covers a zone 70 miles long by 30 miles wide and accounts for 15 per cent of world production (excluding the Soviet Union). The belt contains 25 per cent of the world's proved copper reserves and copper accounts for 60 per cent of Zambia's exports. In 1968 Zambia received £232·6 million from copper out of a total mineral production valued at £278·0 million. The mineral completely dominates the country's economy, the copper industry being the largest customer of the railways and the greatest consumer of power. The belt is a complex of mining towns with a total population exceeding a quarter of a million. Near each of the six major mines townships have developed with African and European residential areas, shopping centres and commercial zones. The largest is Kitwe (95,000) near Nkana Mine, a commercial and industrial centre with electrolytic copper refineries. Ndola (93,000) lies north of the Bwana Mkubwa Mine (closed in 1931)[1] and is the main junction for the Copper Belt and Katanga. It has copper, cobalt and sugar refineries and its regional airport serves Zambia.

Various other minerals are mined in the Zambian belt—cobalt (Chibaluma and Nkana) and gold and silver are extracted during copper processing, while zinc, manganese and lead are mined in the Broken

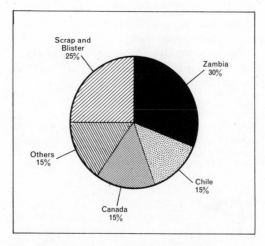

FIG. 14: The importance of Zambia's copper to Britain

Hill district. But copper is dominant and accounts for more than 90 per cent of Zambia's mineral output by value.

Katanga, Congo (Kinshasa)
The Katanga Copper Belt was linked to the outside world when the Broken Hill line reached Lubumbashi, then Elizabethville, in September 1910, and the first copper exports reached Antwerp, Belgium in 1912 via the southern rail routes. The completion of other outlet routes (see below) resulted in the Union Minière becoming the world's largest producer of copper and cobalt in the early 1930s, a place later yielded to Rhodesia.

The Katanga Belt extends 200 miles from Lubumbashi north-westwards to Kolwezi and is a concentration of deep and open-cast mines, refineries, concentration plants and hydro-electric

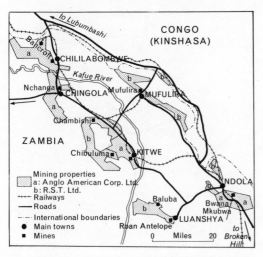

FIG. 13: Zambia—the Copper Belt towns and concession zones

[1] This mine may be re-opened; it has been recently investigated to ascertain whether further copper extraction would be economically worthwhile.

165

power stations. The main deposits lie close to the surface and are open-cast at Kolwezi, Ruwe and Musonoi-Kamato. The ore, which contains 6 to 8 per cent copper, is sent to the Shituri plant near Jadotville and to the Luili refinery at Kolwezi. Poorer ores (4 per cent copper) are mined at Kipushi, where shafts go down to 1,600 feet. The belt produces over 250,000 tons of copper annually.

Besides copper, there are 150 various other mineral deposits including cobalt (10 per cent of the Congo's exports), radium and uranium (at Chinolobwe), lime, manganese, tin, zinc, coal and iron ore. Copper represents about 30 per cent of all the Congo's exports. The chief city of Katanga is Lubumbashi (page 136) with Jadotville (76,000) as a secondary regional centre.

The Problems

Two major problems have faced the Copper Belt throughout its development—the great fuel needs for copper refining processes and the need for commercial outlets for the refined copper.

The Katanga Belt used rather poor coal from Luena but when this was exhausted expensive imports had to be railed from Rhodesia's Wankie field. Several hydro-electric stations were built, e.g. at Le Marinel on the Lualaba and at Mwadingusha on the Lufira, and before Kariba these supplied power to the Rhodesian Belt. The Rhodesian section was able to supply power by importing H.E.P., coal and oil, and by using local coal and wood (nearly a quarter of a million acres were cut). Today the Kariba Dam will be able to fulfil the Copper Belt's major power requirements for many years to come.

The construction of outlets for the refined copper from the land-locked Copper Belt illustrates how political considerations override economic ones. The routes which have been or are used for exporting are:

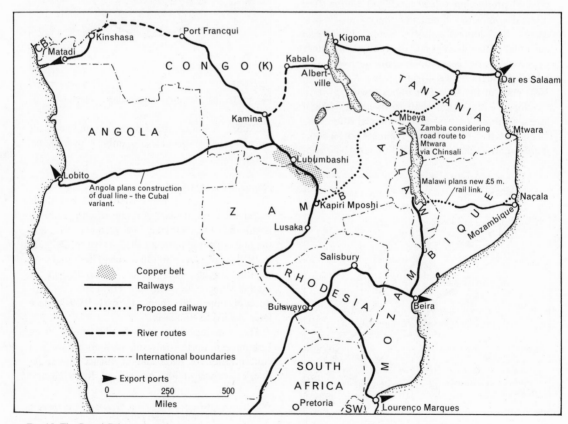

Fig. 15: The Copper Belt—main outlet routes

166

a The Cape route, briefly used during the early twentieth century.

b The Benguela route (918 miles) begun by the British with Belgian and Portuguese consent in 1900 and completed 1933; the line was extended to Lobito since Benguela became unsuitable for large ore vessels. At present, approximately 15,000 tons of Zambian copper ore are sent by this route.

c The Voie National, conceived by King Leopold to break Katanga's dependence on foreign export routes. The railway runs north from Lubumbashi to Port Francqui where the ore is unloaded onto river barges which take it down the Kasai River to Kinshasa; it then travels by rail to Matadi to be loaded onto sea-going ore vessels.

d The Kamina-Albertville-Kigoma-Dar-es-Salaam route which is now little used but is being considered as an alternative route by Zambia.

e The more direct railway route via Umtali, Rhodesia and Beira, Mozambique. This was much used but Beira suffered congestion during the post-war boom period in the Rhodesias.

f A subsidiary rail route to Lourenço Marques via Bulawayo. This round-about route was replaced in 1957 by the Limpopo line via Bannockburn and this route took increasing amounts of copper concentrate until recent disturbances.

The spotlight has recently been thrown on the question of outlet routes. Zambia would like to loosen her ties with Africa's southern states (all her outlets run through minority-ruled territories). An alternative route involves the construction of a line from Kapiri Mposhi south of Broken Hill, through Mbeya in Southern Tanzania to the Central Tanzanian Line at Kilosa. The proposed line will pass through some of Africa's most rugged country and will cost at least £70 million. Experts believe that it will have certain economic advantages:

a It will orientate Zambia towards Tanzania rather than to southern Africa and will aid Tanzania's economy.

b Dar es Salaam will increase in importance as an export port for copper ore and concentrate and for the expected agricultural products which the line would encourage.

c The remote southern region of Tanzania with its coal deposits and agricultural potential will be open to development, as will the northern regions of Zambia.

The 1,042-mile long railway will take ten years to complete, however, by which time political conditions may have changed.[1]

Other suggestions are a new Dar road route which is now handling some 25,000 tons of ore a month to be supplemented by two air freighters and the greater use of the Lobito route. Zambia attempted to conclude an agreement with the Congo (K) for the latter to ship all her ore along the Port Francqui route while Zambia increased her exports along the Lobito route to 38,000 tons of copper a month, but the latter route is vital to Katanga shipments. However, in view of the situation, the Portuguese intend to double the capacity westwards of the Lobito route from 1·5 to 3 million tons a year, the traffic to include her own ores as well as those of Zambia and Katanga. It will run from Cubal to Lobito (the Cubal variant), will take two years to build and will cost up to £5 million. Other important copper deposits known to exist in southern Africa but not yet exploited commercially are the 33 million tons proven by the Roan Selection Trust in Botswana, and the rich reserves discovered in 1968 in Vendaland, in the northern Transvaal, South Africa; the latter, located near Sabasa, are believed to be twice as rich as the deposits in South West Africa and may have enough copper to support five or six mines.

Iron Ore—Its Effects on the Economy of African States

Iron ore is one of the basic minerals for heavy industrial development. While Africa produces only 4 per cent of the world's iron ore several important recent finds indicate that the continent could be a major producer (Fig. 8:**16**). The deposits so far exploited for large-scale steel production lie in South Africa and Rhodesia near to limestone and coal. Elsewhere iron ore is mined by large foreign companies for export. Like oil, the discovery of iron ore has broadened the economy of several nations, e.g. Liberia, Swaziland and Mauritania, and has attracted tremendous international interest and investment.

Swaziland

In Swaziland, where the population is traditionally engaged in cultivation, minerals are helping to

[1] Communist Chinese technicians began surveying the route in April 1968.

167

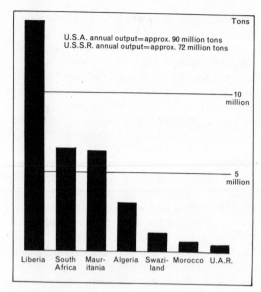

USA. annual output=approx. 90 million tons
U.S.S.R. annual output=approx. 72 million tons

Tons

10 million

5 million

Liberia | South Africa | Maur-itania | Algeria | Swazi-land | Morocco | U.A.R.

FIG. 16: Africa—iron ore production in 1965

broaden the economy and already form 25 per cent of export earnings. The territory is rich in mineral deposits particularly asbestos and iron ore, the latter being by far the most important discovery in recent years. There are 47 million tons of high-grade haematite discovered at Bomvu Ridge (Ngwenya) in 1954 and now being mined by the Anglo-American Corporation and a British firm. The mine has an assured market in Japan for the next ten years. The exploitation of the deposit depended on the railway built from Ngwenya through Sipofabeni to the Mozambique border near Goba (completed September 1964) to link with the line to Lourenço Marques. This will make further exploitation of other Swazi minerals feasible, particularly her coal deposits.

In 1964 Swaziland produced £2,808,918 worth of iron ore which was increased to £5,171,151 in 1965, of which £2,213,367 worth was produced at the Ngwenya Mine (1,124,310 tons). Swaziland Collieries Mine at Mpaka produced 33,000 tons of coal in 1965 (worth £33,000) and the Havelock asbestos mine produced 20,441 tons of asbestos (worth £2,896,750). The value of Swaziland's total export trade has risen from £6·1 million in 1960 to £19·2 million in 1966; iron ore worth £4·3 million and asbestos worth £2·5 million formed 35·4 per cent of 1966 exports. Mineral production figures for 1967

reached a record of £10·2 million (iron ore £6·6 million, asbestos £3·4 million).

Liberia

Liberia's economy has been broadened by the exploitation of her iron ore deposits. In an effort to diversify exports and break the dependence on rubber the government granted concessions to Liberian, Swedish, United States and German firms to mine iron ore. A special railway was completed in 1951 to link Monrovia with the Bomi Hills deposits 45 miles away. The ore here is very rich haematite (68 per cent iron content) and there are 20 million tons of reserves as well as 100 million tons of poorer grade (35—40 per cent Fe.). Iron ore accounted for three-quarters (£40 million out of £56 million) of exports in 1965. All four concessionary companies have now begun production in Liberia and it is estimated that output, which increased to 14·5 million tons in 1965, and 17 million tons in 1966, will reach 20 million tons by the end of 1968. Plans are being carried out to improve handling equipment and the possibility of constructing a steel plant at Buchanan is being investigated. Such a project would produce 700,000 tons of steel a year, sufficient to meet the requirements of most of West Africa; the main problem is that of obtaining assurances from other West African states that they would support such a scheme and would not build competitive plant. Liberia is now the third largest exporter of iron ore in the world (11·25 million tons were exported in 1964).[1]

The Bong iron ore mining area, situated about 50 miles north-east of the Liberian capital of Monrovia, is representative of many of the large, self-contained mining settlements in Africa. Here, at a height of about 1,300 feet, lies a 22-mile long range of ore with a 38 per cent Fe. content and estimated to contain 300 million tons of iron ore. First discovered in 1935, the field was prospected in 1958 by a German company working under an agreement with the Liberian Government which now takes five per cent of all profits. Construction of the mine began in 1962 and it now has a potential production of 3 million tons of concentrated ore a year which the company hopes to increase to 5 million tons a year in the future. Some 1,500 Liberians and 300

[1] U.S. steel companies are also interested in the possible exploitation of another iron ore deposit, located in the Wologisi Hills in north-west Liberia.

168

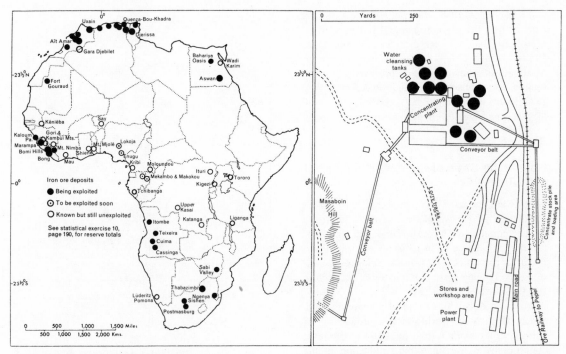

FIG. 17: Africa—location of iron ore deposits

FIG. 18: Sierra Leone—layout of Delco Mines, Masaboin Hill, Marampa Concessions

Europeans, mostly Germans, are engaged on the project.

The mining of the ore is done by open-cast methods, benches about 40 to 45 feet high being cut into the mountain face; then the ore is drilled out and loaded by a huge grab crane into massive dumper trucks which transfer it to the crushing mill where it is mixed with water and the waste separated from the concentrate. From this mill the concentrate is sent along a 50-mile long railway to the Bong Mining Company's pier loading terminal in Monrovia port. Here it is stockpiled until it can be loaded into ore vessels by a special grab.

The mining site itself is now a self-contained settlement with its own workshops, warehouses, vehicle service station, schools, 60-bed hospital, shops, police station, club, laundry, stores and houses.

Mauritania

Perhaps the most spectacular effect that the discovery of iron ore has had on a country's economy is seen in Mauritania. Prior to 1960 Mauritania, a country larger than Nigeria but with under 2 per cent of Nigeria's population, was a poor nation with large stretches of waste desert and an economy based on livestock and the cultivation of poor grains. France supported the country with massive injections of aid. With the discovery of 250 million tons of high-grade ore (63 per cent Fe.) in the Kedia d'Idjil Hills of the north-west and the completion of the railway from Fort Gouraud to Port Etienne the economy has been transformed. The gross domestic product of Mauritania has increased by 10 per cent per annum since 1962 (1962—£35 million; 1966—£50 million). The balance of trade also moved into a surplus in 1963 and was £10·8 million in 1964 compared with a deficit of £11·7 million in 1962. This sharp improvement in the trade position was almost entirely due to the export of iron ore, which only started in 1963. Exports of iron ore in 1964 were worth £15·4 million (about 94 per cent of total export income), and £18·8 million in 1965.

Prospects for the future of iron production in Mauritania are good. The Miferma Company produced 6·3 million tons of iron ore during 1965 compared with 4·6 million tons in 1964 and estimated figures of 6·4 million in 1966, 6·8 million in 1967, and 7·5 million in 1968. This company has a backing from British, French, German and Italian sources; Mauritania has a 5 per cent interest and takes 50 per cent of profits, which provide 40 per cent of Mauritania's revenue. Some of this revenue is being used to create the new capital of Nouakchott and by 1970 Mauritania should be receiving some £3·0 million from royalties, enough to break her financial dependence on France.

Gold—The Basis of International Finance and Commerce

Gold is not the most valuable metal but it is the foundation of the world's monetary system and modern commerce. The ore is found in quartz veins, metamorphic rocks or in redistributed sediments; usually it cannot be seen with the naked eye and it often takes the processing of one ton of rock to obtain 0·1 ounce of gold.

Africa produces 70 per cent of the world's gold. South Africa is the world's largest producer (71·1 per cent of the world output excluding Communist countries) with five times the production of the Soviet Union. In 1967 the Republic produced over 30·5 million fine ounces worth £384 million (Ghana, sixth world producer—0·8 million fine ounces; Rhodesia—0·6 million fine ounces). Moreover, gold output, although becoming more costly, is maintaining its present output and should reach a peak about 1970.

The Goldfields of South Africa
Gold was first discovered near the Olifants River, Transvaal in 1868 but it was only in September 1886

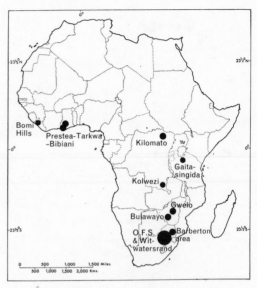

FIG. 19: Africa—location of major gold producing areas

when the Witwatersrand Goldfields were proclaimed public diggings that true expansion began. Since then over £5,000 million worth of gold has been mined and expansion is still continuing—in 1962 the world's largest gold mine was opened in the Kinross region, the Kloof mine opened in 1968, and the first shaft of the Vaal Reefs South mine expected to be in full production in 1975, was sunk in 1967. Old fields are being re-opened and mined with new techniques. Several old mines in the Randfontein District, closed in the 1920s, may be producing again in the near future.

TABLE 23
Production of Gold in South African Goldfields, 1965–66

FIELD	OUTPUT IN OUNCES (MILLIONS)		PERCENTAGE OF OVERALL OUTPUT (IN ROUND FIGURES)	
	1965	1966	1965	1966
Evander	1·61	1·62	5·5	5·5
West Rand	0·59	0·51	2·0	1·7
Far West Rand	6·94	7·40	23·0	24·3
East Rand	4·00	3·70	13·5	12·2
Central Rand	1·24	1·10	4·0	3·6
Klerksdorp	4·86	5·05	16·0	16·6
Orange Free State	10·77	11·00	36·0	36·1
Total	30·01	30·38	100·0	100·0

However, about a third of the gold output is from old mines and costs are increasing as seams become thinner and old machinery has to be replaced. The relative importance of the Rand's five major goldfields is shown in Table 23.

Gold is not only an important earner of currency for South Africa but forms a broad base for other industrial operations (page 180). An important mineral mined with gold is uranium and latest estimates put South Africa's reserves at between 205,000 and 270,000 tons, second only to Canada. Uranium, the source of atomic energy, has lead to the rapid development of the chemical industry in South Africa. Although a uranium processing plant costs between £3 and £4 million it was felt that this expense was justified because of the support to the chemical industry and the great earning power in foreign exchange. In 1965 South Africa produced 5·9 million lb. of uranium worth £15·9 million, and in 1966, 6·6 million lb. worth £10·5 million.

Gold and uranium are found together in the mines. The ores are ground to fine pieces and mixed with water to produce slimes which is passed through a cyanide solution. The cyanide dissolves the gold but not the uranium; the gold-bearing solution is drawn off to leave filter cake which contains uranium. The filter cake is fed into sulphuric acid tanks which dissolve the uranium and this liquid is filtered and purified with chemicals.

South Africa's Largest Goldfield—The Orange Free State

The Orange Free State Goldfield is the youngest of all the fields; today it stretches 30 miles from north to south from Allanridge to Virginia and is about 7 miles wide (Fig. 8:**20**). At present twelve mines are in full operation.

Gold reefs were known to exist here in 1904 but it was not until 1946 that the Basal Reef was discovered by the Anglo-American Corporation. The first shaft was sunk on 1 January 1947 in the St Helena section and then leases were granted to several other companies. These companies mainly work the Basal Reef, a $7\frac{1}{2}$-inch thick stratum of

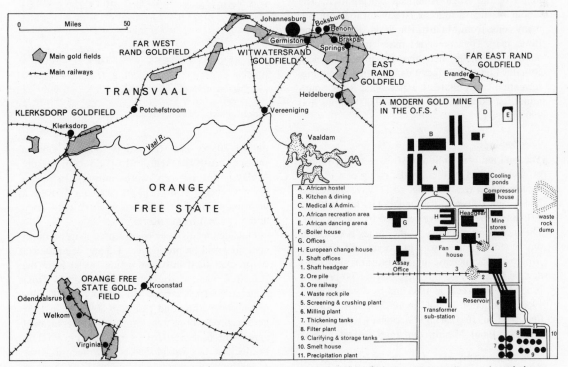

FIG. 20: South Africa—distribution of main gold mining areas in the Transvaal and Orange Free State. The inset diagram shows the layout of one of the Anglo-American Corporation's goldmines in the O.F.S. goldfield

steeply dipping gold-bearing ore found at an average depth of 4,000 feet.

The opening of a new goldfield requires tremendous capital investment for the construction of towns, communications and mines. A huge power station was built at Vierfontein at a cost of £20 million, more power is brought from the Taibos and Highveld stations and water from Balkfontein 44 miles away. Railway connecting lines were constructed and air services financed by the mining companies.

Welkom, a small hamlet with 100 Europeans in 1947, was selected and designed as the chief centre. In 1958 its population had risen to 38,000 Africans, 24,000 non-Europeans, and 26,000 Europeans. In September 1966, its population was 97,614. The town has benefited from modern planning and has well-laid out shopping, entertainment, industrial and residential zones with pleasant parks and gardens. Many secondary industries have been attracted—flour milling, concrete pipe manufacture, panel beating, soft drinks and food processing.

Fig. 8:**20** shows the layout of one of the O.F.S. mines of the Anglo-American Corporation. The labour of such a mine is largely local Bantu but many come from Malawi, Rhodesia, Tanzania and Botswana.[1] The unmarried mens' hostels can accommodate 4,500 men and the mines are self-contained units with facilities for eating, shopping, recreation and welfare. The new Vaal Reefs South mine, for example, will employ 9,000 Bantu and 900 whites.

The Problems

The gold industry in South Africa is facing several problems. Chief of these is the rising cost of production; average working costs have increased 21 per cent between 1930 and 1945 while between 1945 and 1964 costs have rocketed by 130 per cent. The increasing efficiency in the mines is cancelled out by these rising costs of goods and services. Moreover, the increase in gold output is showing a decline. Net gold output increased by 7·0 per cent in 1964, 5·3 per cent in 1965 and by 3·9 per cent in 1966; production of gold in 1967 declined for the first time in 16 years (30·5 ounces against 30·9 ounces in 1966). Mining companies are seeking new

[1] There are 130,000 Basutos working in South Africa (14 per cent of the total Basuto population), and 2 out of every 10 workers in Botswana have moved to employment in the Republic.

ideas and methods and speedier administrative techniques. One result is the speedier sinking of shafts by private companies on contract.

Tin mining in Nigeria

Over half the world's tin output is used for coating steel, used in the manufacture of 'tin' cans, while the remainder is used in type metal, bearing alloys, bronze manufacture and solder. The brownish-black tin ore—cassiterite or tin oxide—contains

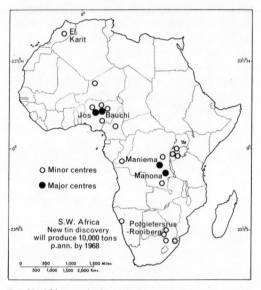

FIG. 21: Africa—main tin producing areas

almost 80 per cent tin and is found in fibrous masses, crusts or veins. Most tin comes from Malaysia (35 per cent world output), Indonesia (19 per cent) or Bolivia (17 per cent) but Africa is a growing producer with 9 per cent from the Congo and 5 per cent from Nigeria.

Outside the Soviet bloc and China, Nigeria ranks sixth in world tin production. Tin and columbite (a by-product used in heat-resisting steels) form the principal metalliferous minerals exported from Nigeria; in 1950 exports amounted to 8,400 tons of tin concentrate and rose to 9,800 tons in 1957 before production was limited by international agreement. Since restrictions were lifted in 1960 tin production has established a new record—over 12,000 tons of cassiterite annually: 12,885 tons in 1965 and 12,566 tons in 1966.

Tin has been mined from alluvial deposits on the Jos Plateau since 1903 and until 1961 tin ore was exported for smelting. Now most tin is exported as ingots from two smelting plants recently opened at Jos. The United Kingdom takes the bulk of exports.

Practically all the tin produced in Nigeria is obtained by opencast methods from alluvial deposits associated with younger granites found on the Nigerian plateau of the Bauchi, Benue, Kano and Zaria provinces. The various methods used are:

a Hand Paddocking where labourers cut steps with spades in the overburden down to the cassiterite.

b Ground Sluicing where the area is covered by a network of drainage channels and water fed into the highest point of the network. Cassiterite is shovelled into the running water and the heavier tin ore sinks to the channel bed. Methods *a* and *b* are mainly used by private operators.

c Gravel Pumping involves the breaking up of the ground by water jets and the sludge trapped in sluice boxes. This method is termed *hydraulicing* when the sludge is lifted into sluice boxes by hydraulic elevators.

d Mechanical Mining by dragline and excavator is used for deep deposits. The spoil is dumped onto the surface from the pit and washed down with a monitor.

e Lotoing is used where the alluvial deposits lie more than 20 feet below the surface; pits are dug into the overburden and tunnels connect each pit.

These methods produce a rough concentrate containing a mixture of cassiterite, columbite, quartz sand, zircon (a gem stone) and a variety of iron minerals. These are separated in the dressing mills. Table 24 shows Nigeria's production of cassiterite and the number of workers involved.

Diamonds—Africa's Monopoly of World Production

Diamonds are pure carbon crystals formed by intense heat and are the hardest known substance. Imperfectly shaped and coloured stones are used in industry in lathe and dressing tools for the hardest steels, in high speed drills and glass cutters. Diamonds are associated with volcanic pipes and are found in a matrix called kimberlite or Blue Ground. Erosion of these pipes has caused the resistant diamonds to be washed into rivers and later deposited on river banks lower downstream. There are thus two methods of recovering the stones—by sifting the silts of rivers or by crushing the matrix rock from the pipe.

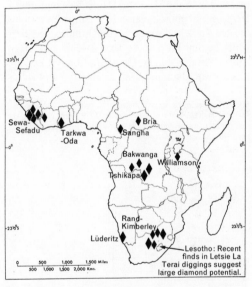

FIG. 22: Africa—main diamond producing areas

TABLE 24
Nigeria: Production of Cassiterite, Columbite and Tantalite[1] in tons, 1960–65

	1960	1961	1962	1963	1964	1965
Cassiterite	8,310	10,596	10,634	11,275	11,845	12,885
Columbite	1,701	2,201	2,416	2,185	1,941	2,548
Tantalite	11·4	10·1	11·6	17·3	15·9	9·0
Labour Employed	31,710	37,468	40,994	44,359	45,695	49,823

[1] Used as an alloy in surgical instruments.

Africa produces 96 per cent of the world's diamonds, the Congo (Kinshasa) producing 52 per cent and Ghana and South Africa about 12·5 per cent each. Sierra Leone is fourth with just under 9 per cent although this figure does not take into account the large number of illicit diamonds produced.[1] Two countries illustrate the two different mining methods—Tanzania where the rock is crushed by modern machinery, and Sierra Leone where river panning by Africans and foreign companies is more important.

Mining a Kimberlite Pipe in Tanzania—The Williamson Diamond Mine at Mwadui

At Mwadui (4,000 feet) in the Shinyanga District of Tanzania lies the Williamson Diamond Mine. It is close to the Mwanza-Tabora road and is linked by private rail to the Mwanza-Dar es Salaam railway. Here, several million years ago, a volcanic explosion created a mile wide crater several hundred feet deep which became filled with volcanic debris of kimberlite and granite breccia. Later eruptions infused this breccia with diamond bearing material and subse-

[1] Other important producers include the Ivory Coast which exported 204,000 carats in 1965 worth £1·95 million, and the Central African Republic—1964 production, 442,300 carats; 1965, 500,000 carats.

quent erosion reduced the crater to a level gravel surface rich in diamonds, mostly clear, colourless gem stones.

The diamond-rich plug was discovered by Dr J. T. Williamson in 1940 and a company was formed which now operates one of the most modern diamond plants in Africa. Since 1942 nearly one ton of diamonds has been recovered from over 15,000,000 tons of treated rock. Mechanical shovels and draglines load the kimberlite into dump trucks or onto a conveyor belt at the opencast site. The material then goes into the treatment plant where it is crushed and washed, passed through filtering screens, then through a special solution which separates the diamonds and heavier material from the lighter waste. For every 400 tons entering the plant only one ton remains as diamond-bearing concentrate. This concentrate is fed onto greased belts where the diamonds with their water repellent surfaces stick to the belt and the wet waste rolls off the grease. An electrostatic separator removes the finer waste from the stones. Finally the diamonds are hand sorted. Fig. 8:23 shows the layout of the plant and the Mwadui Township which is virtually self contained.

The Williamson Diamond Mine earns valuable capital for Tanzania by its exports and pays

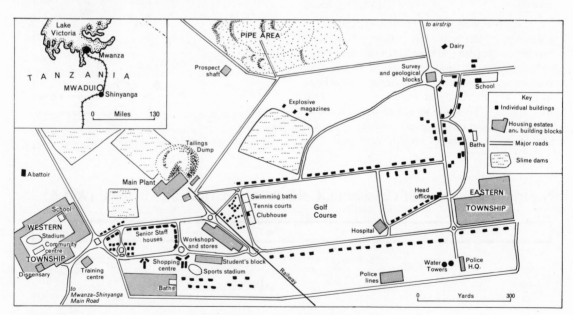

FIG. 23: Tanzania—the layout of Mwadui township (Williamson Diamond Mine), Shinyanga

174

approximately £1·7 million a year to the government in taxes, royalties and dividends. Diamond production by the mine represents nearly 75 per cent of Tanzania's mineral production by value and is worth £5 million a year. Diamond exports equal one-thirteenth of all exports by value.

Gravel Diamond Production in Sierra Leone

Diamonds form a very large proportion of the exports of Sierra Leone. In 1966 some £15·8 million worth were exported (90 per cent of them gem stones), representing 53·4 per cent of total export value, while the production of alluvial diamonds alone amounted to £11,360,000 in 1965 and £9,541,000 in 1966.

Diamonds were first discovered in 1930 in the Kono District and the Sierra Leone Selection Trust was formed to prospect, produce and market the stones. But so great was the traffic in illicit mining that the Trust's territory was limited to 500 developed square miles and licences granted to private individuals. These private operators, working in partnership or employing workmen, obtain the diamonds by two main methods—river mining and swamp and terrace mining.

River mining involves several simple methods. In early days divers crawled down underwater sticks to scoop the gravel from the river bed onto an anchored raft, but the divers now use aqualungs. Dams may be constructed to seal off and drain an arm of the river and the bed is then sifted. A more efficient method is to extract the gravel from the bed by suction through a tube and to dump it for sorting on the river bank.

In swamp and terrace mining the overburden is removed by pick and shovel, the gravel washed, sieved and sorted. Most of this activity is by private individuals or groups and takes place mainly along the Sewa River and its tributaries.

The Sierra Leone Selection Trust operates on more large-scale lines in its 500-square mile tract around Yengema and Panguma. The overburden is stripped by dragline and the waste dumped into railway trucks or dumper trucks to be taken to the pan plant. Here the material is sluiced and fed onto a greased belt where the diamonds separate. There are several pan plants operating in various sections of the concession; each employs an average of 45 workers at the mine and 33 at the plant.

The diamonds are then sent to the Government Office at Kengema for sorting and grading and are checked again at Freetown before export. The Government Diamond Office buys about £1 million worth of diamonds a month while the diamond polishing factory at Freetown takes £56,000 worth. The Sierra Leone Selection Trust's and private diggers' production is shown in the Table 25.

1. Marampa Concessions (Iron ore)
2. S.L. Ore & Metal Co.
3. Sherbro Minerals
4. S.L. Selection Trust (Diamonds)
5. Government Closed Area

FIG. 24: Sierra Leone—iron ore and diamond mining concessions

TABLE 25
Sierra Leone: Production of Diamonds, 1960–65 ('000s of carats[1])

YEAR	1960	1961	1962	1963	1964	1965
S.L. Selection Trust	670·5	901·5	621·6	771·9	718·5	809·5
Alluvial Diamond Mining Scheme (Private Diggers)	1,215·6	1,406·3	1,033·9	639·5	n.a.	n.a.

[1] A carat equals 0·2 grammes and there are 452 grammes to the pound.

175

The figures for production would be much higher but for the activities of illicit diamond smugglers which the Sierra Leone authorities find extremely difficult to check. This is a problem which faces most diamond producing countries in Africa. In the *Congo Kinshasa*, for example, over 12 million carats of diamonds were exported last year through legitimate channels but according to mining officials, more than half of this amount again was smuggled out of the Congo by illicit traders. In 1966 the Congo exported 12,417,566 carats of industrial diamonds worth approximately £9·93 million but the government lost a revenue of about £6·43 million because of illegal trading. The Congo's diamond mining areas lie around the towns of Mbuji Mayi, Luluabourg and Tshikapa in the provinces of Western and Eastern Kasai.

Another Extractive Industry—Forestry

The Equatorial Forests represent a great natural asset in Africa. The exploitation of this asset has however been greatly retarded by several factors— the absence of pure stands of trees of one type, which means that particular types must be searched for; once found the tree must be hauled through the forest to waterways; the local market for wood is often very small and to be economical the wood must be exported; the wood is bulky and difficult to transport without special facilities. Thus the timber industry in Africa has become a specialised operation involving the selection of only expensive woods which can command high prices in overseas markets. The export of expensive timbers is an important aspect of the trade of Ghana (1964 export value £14·7 million, 1965, £12·2 million, and 1966 £10·4 million), Nigeria (see Fig. 8:25) and Congo (Brazzaville) where wood represents nearly 80 per cent of exports by tonnage and 55 per cent by value. But in no other African country does the exploitation and export of timber assist the economy as in Gabon.

Gabon—An Economy Based on the Forests

Gabon is a land of dense tropical rain forests which cover practically all the country except in the southeast and south. These forests contain the valuable okoumé (used for plywood) and are traversed by a convenient river system focusing on the Ogowe River (Fig. 8:26). Besides having a virtual monopoly of the world's supplies of okoumé Gabon also

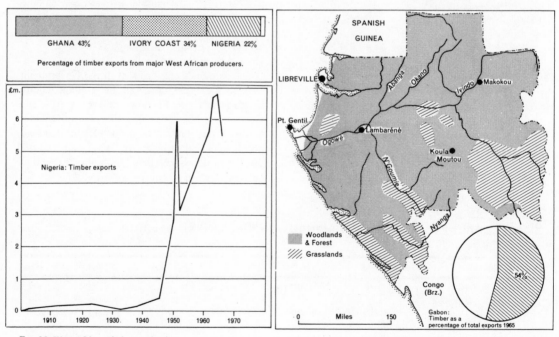

FIG. 25: West Africa—timber production

FIG. 26: Gabon—timber areas and exports

has valuable reserves of ebony and mahogany. About 750,000 tons of wood are exported annually worth nearly £10 million.

Production is mainly by large timber companies although family production now represents about 15 per cent of total output. The companies are granted concessions in the forest and work these systematically. The forest concession is divided into rectangles and each of these rectangles is subdivided; teams of men under a supervisor move through these sections marking trees for cutting. The selected trees are then cut, trimmed and hauled by tractor and by hand through the forest to a base collecting point usually situated near a river. Here the logs are rolled into the water and lashed together in huge rafts which are either rowed or pulled by tugboats downstream to one of the 17 plywood and timber dressing mills along the lower Ogowe. The largest mill and one of the biggest exporters of plywood in the world lies at Port Gentil. Here the African Co-operative Agency of Equatorial Woods handles all exports, which go largely to countries of the European Economic Community of which Gabon is an associate member. The remainder is purchased by the United States, the United Kingdom and other West European countries.

Gabon's forests provide sufficient revenue to give the country a very favourable balance of trade but there have been several problems. The coastal areas, worked since 1902, have become exhausted of their timber through mismanagement and conservation measures have had to be undertaken which will result in the saving of 1·8 million tons of okoumé over the next 30 years. Moreover, the economy was precariously dependent on timber, and agriculture had been largely undeveloped. The government has introduced cash crops—cocoa, coffee, groundnuts and rice. Recent valuable mineral finds will also help to diversify the economy —oil near Port Gentil, manganese, iron ore (250 million tons), uranium and potassium. However, timber and timber products still represent 54·2 per cent of Gabon's exports.

The chief problem facing the exploiters of these mineral deposits is the rugged and forested relief of the country. Over 200 miles of railway are being built by large foreign companies to link the manganese deposit to the Point Noire line. Gabon is fortunate in her geographical location for the exploitation of these minerals, for all parts are less than 500 miles from the major port.[1]

Summary

The most striking factor regarding mineral exploitation in Africa is the massive investment by overseas countries from both Western and Communist nations. A striking example of this is Guinea, where the discovery of iron ore at Mt Nimba and Mt Simandou and of large bauxite reserves at Fria (200 million tons), Boké (700 million tons) and on Los Is. at Kassa have attracted huge capital investments from U.S., British, French, Swiss, Canadian and German firms (at Fria and Boké) and Soviet, Polish and other eastern European firms at Kassa.

Again one notices that African economies cannot absorb their tremendous mineral production at their present stage of development. Africa must export in exchange for money for development programmes; the continent is still in the initial stage of supplying raw materials to industrialised nations but this will gradually change as secondary industries based on mineral deposits within the countries are developed.

For questions, practical work and discussion topics see end of Chapter Nine, page 188.

[1] Mineral production in Gabon reached new records in 1965, compared with 1964, petroleum production rose by 20 per cent to 1·3 million tons, manganese extraction by 36 per cent to 1·3 million tons, and that of uranium concentrate by 24 per cent to 1,591 tons.

CHAPTER NINE

INDUSTRIAL DEVELOPMENT IN AFRICA (2)—SECONDARY INDUSTRIES

The comparatively recent knowledge of the full extent of Africa's minerals and their export to industrial nations reduced the pace of the continent's secondary industrial growth. Many colonial powers preferred to ship the raw materials to processing factories in their own countries rather than invest money in factories in the colonies. The world economic depression of the early 1930s followed by the Second World War also reduced the effectiveness of industrialisation policies for the colonies.

Secondary industrial development is therefore, except for South Africa, Rhodesia and Egypt, largely the outcome of several influences which developed mainly in the post-war years:

a The war of 1939–45 caused import restrictions and stimulated home industry in South Africa and Rhodesia with their large European markets.

b The occupation of Europe caused many firms to move to colonies and set up their factories there.

c War demands for tough fibres (sisal), lubricating oils (palm and seed oils), copper ore and bauxite encouraged processing industries.

d The purchasing power of an emerging money-earning African labour force created a steadily increasing market for manufactured articles.

e European firms found it cheaper to process raw materials in Africa than to transport them to Europe for processing. Firms, attracted by the spacious building sites and cheaper labour, set up subsidiary factories in many African countries.

f The post-war years saw the granting of independence to many African nations. The new governments, anxious to broaden their countries' economies, encourage economic experts to evaluate the possibilities of industrial development and often act on this advice. With growing populations and many landless people, African governments are seeing the need to provide alternative employment in industry.

g While colonial powers ran their territories on limited budgets and discouraged investment by other nations, countries such as West Germany, the United States, Japan, the Soviet Union and China

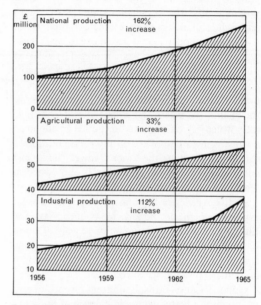

FIG. 1: Tunisia—the increasing importance of secondary industry to the national economy

are now free to invest capital in the newly independent nations. Financial aid, greater foreign investment and the advice of skilled technicians have boosted industrial development in recent years.

Stages in the Growth of Industry

Industrial enterprises are not new to Africa. The processing of dyes, the manufacture of gold, silver and ivory ornaments, the treating of hides and skins flourished along the coast of East Africa as long ago as the tenth century; West Africa was famed for its iron smelting, weaving and dyeing, basket making and wood carving; the Maghreb was noted for its blue pottery, carpets, leather goods and brassware. These specialised industries have survived through the centuries (see Chapter Two).

Today the modern African states have reached various stages of industrial development. South Africa is the most industrially advanced; Rhodesia, the United Arab Republic, Morocco and Katanga Province have attained industrial maturity; Kenya, Tanzania, Ghana and Mozambique have yet to see great industrial expansion. The various levels of industrial attainment have generally been reached through certain recognisable stages:

a African countries were at first mainly suppliers of raw materials to external nations, usually the colonising power—Algeria produced grains, fruit, vegetables, hides and meat for France; West Africa and the Congo exported palm oil, cocoa beans, rubber, timber and tropical fruit to France, Belgium and Britain; East Africa exported cotton, coffee, sisal and tea; South Africa shipped wool, gold and diamonds.

b Processing plants were then set up—cotton ginneries in the Sudan, Nigeria and Uganda; coffee mills in Kenya; oil mills in the palm belt, and groundnut-oil crushing mills in Guinea.

c The new factories needed labour, spare parts, improved transport facilities; ancillary services developed—vehicle maintenance, the manufacture of containers for the export produce, electrical and mechanical engineering, coach building, machine tool maintenance and tyre retreading.

d The growing urban labour force needed housing, offices and administrative buildings which led to the development of the construction industry—the manufacture of bricks, corrugated iron sheets, pipes, wire, paints and constructional timber.

e The growing wage-earning workforce needed consumer goods and factories were set up to supply canned foods, beer, cigarettes, household utensils, light clothing, soap and polishes.

Most African countries have reached these last stages of industrial development. But there is one limiting factor—low purchasing power. In East Africa the annual monthly wage of a manual worker lies between £8 and £10—not a great deal with which to support a family and buy a suit of clothes or a modern radio.[1] Many people still rely on food grown on their small plots of land while money is spent on basic necessities such as razor blades, soap and household utensils. But purchasing power is growing as many Africans enter jobs formerly held by Europeans and many are obtaining good cash

returns from agriculture. The growth of this huge middle-class market is a great attraction for industry.

In the following samples South Africa represents a nation that is the most heavily industrialised in Africa, Egypt a country where industrialisation has progressed steadily despite several natural disadvantages, Kenya a developing nation with few natural resources, and Ghana a country where there has been massive industrial development and foreign investment.

The Republic of South Africa—Africa's Most Industrialised Nation

Before the 1930s South Africa played the traditional rôle of a raw materials supplier and a market for manufactured articles. As late as 1938 South Africa was importing far more than she was exporting by value, since a large proportion of the imports were manufactured articles. But the postwar period saw a rapid expansion of secondary industries, and of the Republic's total exports in 1966 (excluding gold) of £595·8 million, £217·7 million or 36·5 per cent consisted of manufactured articles; this is the measure of secondary industrial expansion in South Africa (Fig. 9:2).

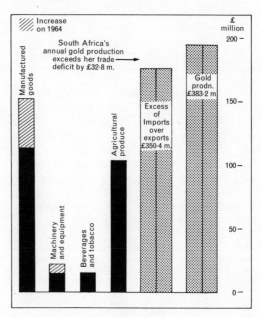

FIG. 2: South Africa—the increasing importance of mining and secondary industry to export trade (1964 figures)

---

[1] For comparison a bus driver in Cairo receives £15 a month, and a secondary school teacher £33 a month; a servant receives £8–12 a month. A small European private car costs approximately £2,500 in the U.A.R.

The Reasons for Industrial Expansion

The rapid expansion of the Republic's secondary industries is due to:

a The solid base provided by coal and gold. Lacking fuel oil South Africa's secondary industries would hardly have developed but for the colossal reserves of coal. The gold mining industry provided a tremendous market for secondary industries and in 1964 alone purchased £165·9 million worth of stores from local industries, particularly benefiting engineering (£22·7 million worth purchased).

b The Range of minerals Besides those minerals listed in Table 26 South Africa also produces substantial quantities of tin,[1] lead, magnesite, silver, tungsten, vanadium, vermiculite, salt, fluorspar, limestone, phosphates, clay and antimony.

d Foreign Investors find South Africa attractive with its low-wage labour, large European market, unrestricted sites and cheap coal and raw materials. The Government actively encourages foreign investment to reduce exports of raw materials and to process them within the Republic. Examples of foreign investment appear in the motor industry (Ford, British Motor Corporation, General Motors), rubber (Dunlop), and electrical goods (Hoechst of Germany and English Electric).

e Government Policy encourages home production by restricting certain imports and financing large basic industries—iron and steel, electricity supply, the Sasol oil-from-coal plant, phosphate, and cellulose production. Individual projects are also sponsored—the phosphate and copper plants

TABLE 26
South Africa: Production of Industrial Minerals

MINERAL	APPROX. ANN. PRODUCTION	% AFRICA'S PRODUCTION	POSITION IN AFRICA	REMARKS
Iron Ore	6·5 million tons	11	2nd after Liberia	High grade (60–66% Fe)
Asbestos	240,000 tons	51	1st	World's 3rd producer
Chromite	1·0 million tons	55	1st	2nd after U.S.S.R.
Platinum			1st	1st in world
Manganese	1·8 million tons	37	1st	2nd after U.S.S.R.
Copper	65,000 tons[2]	5	3rd	14th in world

c Agricultural Raw Materials have given rise to many secondary industries—wool for scouring mills and knitting plants; fruits for jam, canning and bottling factories; sugar for confectionery, syrups and refineries; fish for canning, freezing, fish meal and fertiliser plants; grapes for wine producers; tobacco for pipe and cigarette factories, and hides and skins for the production of 20 million boots and shoes a year. South Africa's industries use 65 per cent of raw materials from home sources.

[1] The new tin deposits discovered in south-west Africa should be producing 10,000 to 17,000 tons of tin a year by 1968 and will supply all South Africa's needs. Tin will earn £10 million a year in exports for South-West Africa. A modern £2 million tin refinery is to be built.
[2] The new copper plant at Phalaborwa in the north-east Transvaal will have a capacity of 33,000 tons of copper a day. The recently discovered Vendaland deposit in northern Transvaal (see page 167) may be of great economic significance.

at Phalaborwa, the paper plant at Tugela River in Natal, a wood and rayon factory at Umkomaas, a textile factory at Kingwilliamstown. The Government is also spending £25 million a year on improving and extending the communications system.

The Rate of Industrial Expansion in South Africa

These powerful influences have caused a rapid development in the field of secondary industry. Manufacturing industries are now the biggest single contributor to South Africa's national income. Between 1961 and 1965 the growth rates for agriculture were 7·6 per cent, for mining 14·7 per cent, for the distributing industry 29·6 per cent and for manufacturing industries 48·4 per cent. Despite this growth, however, the Republic still relies on overseas sources for more complicated machinery and electrical goods, and in 1964 over 72 per cent of her imports were classed as manufactured articles (Fig. 9:**4**).

TABLE 27
South Africa: Increase in Industrial Establishments and Production Values, 1945–60

YEAR	NO. OF INDUSTRIAL ESTABLISHMENTS	VALUE OF PRODUCTION
1945	10,887	£385·3 million
1956	12,610	£1,230·0 million
1960	14,308	£1,480·0 million

The Range of South Africa's Industries

The food and processing industry is the biggest industrial sector and has doubled its production since 1939. It exports 90 per cent of its output chiefly to the United Kingdom. *Metal working and engineering* are second in importance and have progressed rapidly with the demands of the mining and iron and steel industries. There are over 700 *electrical machinery and equipment* factories in the Republic, 226 *clothing and textile* plants and 100 *leather goods and shoe* factories. *The chemical industry* has been encouraged by the gold and uranium mine demands;

SASOL and FOSKOR, the oil refinery at Wentworth, Natal and the Moddersfontein explosives plant near Johannesburg produce a wide range of chemical by-products. *Pulp and Paper manufacturing* is very dependent on imports; the Umkomaas plant in Natal uses over 180,000 tons of eucalyptus trees a year and produces 45,000 tons of rayon pulp. Other important industries in South Africa include motor car assembly, tyres and rubber goods manufacture, the making of glass, pottery, cement, aluminium and hollow ware, brushware, plastic goods, beer, soft drinks and confectionery. The heavier iron and steel and metallurgical industries are concentrated in the Rand.

The Distribution of South Africa's Industries

Two-thirds of South Africa's gross national output is derived from four major industrial concentrations—the Rand, the Western Cape centred on Cape Town, the Eastern Cape centred on Port Elizabeth and East London, and the Durban-Pinestown region of Natal. Secondary industries have tended to concentrate at markets and in the major ports and in each of these centres there is a duplicated range of industries catering for the local market. Some industries such as dairying, leather working, fruit and vegetable canning are more widely distributed and lie nearer their raw materials.

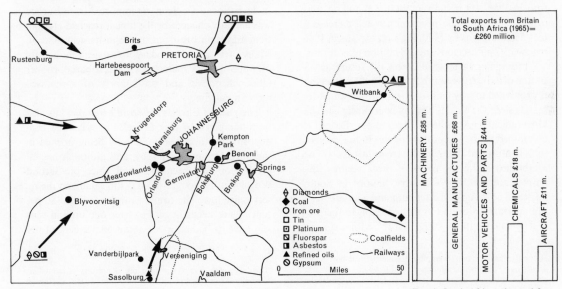

FIG. 3: South Africa—the Rand

FIG. 4: South Africa—the need for manufactured goods

The Rand is the only true industrial conurbation in Africa. Extending sixty miles from Randfontein to Springs on the level veld its location and growth is due to the gold fields, the local coal and iron ore, the Vaal's water, the ease of communication construction on the veld, the cheap labour supplies, and numerous local minerals—fluorspar, fireclay, dolomite, chromite and magnesite (Fig. 9:**3**).

The Rand has 35 per cent of all industrial establishments in South Africa and employs 43 per cent of all industrial workers. *Johannesburg* (1,225,000) is a gold mining, banking and commercial centre with numerous secondary industries—metal working, engineering, textiles manufacture, diamond cutting, paper and printing, chemicals, tobacco and food processing, canning, electrical equipment, jewelry manufacture, saw milling and furniture making. *Springs* (141,000) is a coal and gold mining centre with factories manufacturing mining machinery, electrical goods, printing machinery, sheet glass, paper, alloy steels, cycles and canned foods. *Germiston* (215,000) has gold refineries and explosive plants, *Krugersdorp* (90,000) has gold and manganese mines. *Pretoria* (423,000), the capital, has railway workshops and plants making glass, sheet metal, cement and matches. The nearby ISCOR steel works and the Vanderbijl Park plants near Vereeniging produce 76 per cent of South Africa's steel; steel ingot production was 1·5 million tons in 1956, 1·8 million in 1960, 3·9 million tons in 1967 and extension programmes will increase it to 4·5 million tons by 1970. Pig iron exports in 1966 reached 3·7 million tons and 3·8 million tons in 1968.

Three major factors will affect the future distribution of industry in South Africa. The Rand region is prohibited to new industries with heavy water demands since the Vaal is already overburdened. The Government's Apartheid (Apartness) Policy is committed to the segregation of the Bantu peoples into 'bantustans' and many future industries will be established along the edges of these regions; examples are the largest hosiery factory in South Africa to be set up at Rustenburg and a large cotton mill at Harrismith (O.F.S.) in addition to the present woollen mill (see Fig. 6:**14**).[1] Moreover, although secondary industrial development will be greatest in the populous south and east, the Orange River Scheme will certainly exert an attraction for industry in certain eastern areas of the Republic.

The Development of Secondary Industry in the United Arab Republic (Egypt)

Egypt, like South Africa, has experienced a rapid growth in her secondary industries since 1938 (her industrial output is increasing by about 10 per cent per annum). But the country's basis for industry—raw materials, markets both internal and external, fuel supplies and communications network—have never become fully integrated like those of South Africa and this has been a limiting factor for industrial expansion.

Thus, although Egypt possesses several industrially useful minerals they do not occur in sufficiently large quantities. *The most important minerals* produced include mineral oil, manganese, feldspar, and iron ore which is sent to the large Helwan iron and steel plant near Cairo (annual output half a million tons).[1] There is also a small range of other minerals—lead, zinc, gypsum, copper, gold, phosphates and chrome ore. Several new mineral deposits have been found in recent years, e.g. the iron ore deposit at Bahariya Oasis, but exploitation has been restricted up to now by the inadequacy of the transport network and the lack of water facilities in desert locations. Iron ore imported from Europe was actually cheaper by the time it reached Helwan than Egyptian ore from the deposits near Aswan. Many of Egypt's secondary industries rely heavily on imported raw materials such as tobacco, rubber latex, chemicals and on imports of specialised modern machinery.

The pace of Egypt's *industrial expansion* has also been hampered by lack of fuel. Egypt has few coal deposits, her first coal mine only being opened in the Sinai Peninsula in 1964, and although her oil production has been increased since pre-Second World War (see page 161) it is still small and the reserves are low. The country produces about 80 per cent of her needs in oil but over one million tons still have to be imported; about 60 per cent of her

---

[1] In 1960, 55,000 Bantu were employed in industries in border and Bantu areas; by 1967 the figure had risen to 94,000. In the same period industrialists invested about £148 million in the border areas and the Government £65 million, particularly in the Rosslyn and Hammardale zones.

[1] The large Bahariya Oasis iron ore deposit is estimated at 250 million tons, and production of iron and steel at Helwan should rise from 0·5 million tons to 2·5 million tons by the end of the second industrial development plan.

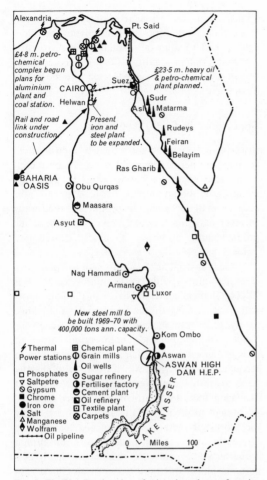

Alexandria
Pt. Said
£4·8 m. petro-
chemical
complex begun
plans for
aluminium
plant and
coal station.
CAIRO
Suez
£23·5 m. heavy oil
& petro-chemical
plant planned.
Helwan
Sudr
Asl
Matarma
Rail and road
link under
construction
Present
iron and
steel plant
to be expanded.
Rudeys
Feiran
Belayim
Ras Gharib
●BAHARIA
▲OASIS
Obu Qurqas
Maasara
Asyut
Nag Hammadi
Armant
Luxor
New steel mill to
be built 1969-70 with
400,000 tons ann. capacity.
Kom Ombo
Aswan
ASWAN HIGH
DAM H.E.P.
L A K E   N A S S E R

⚡ Thermal
Power stations
⊞ Chemical plant
◐ Grain mills
▮ Oil wells
□ Phosphates
▽ Saltpetre
⊙ Gypsum
■ Chrome
● Iron ore
▲ Salt
△ Manganese
◆ Wolfram
—— Oil pipeline
◔ Sugar refinery
◑ Fertiliser factory
◒ Cement plant
◨ Oil refinery
▣ Textile plant
⊗ Carpets

0   Miles   100

FIG. 5: The U.A.R.—location of minerals and manufacturing
centres

output comes from the Belayim field in western
Sinai. But Israeli occupation of Sinai (1967–68) has
deprived the U.A.R. of half its total oil output. The
Aswan High Dam (page 144) will do much to relieve Egypt's fuel problem and it is always possible
that commercial deposits of oil will be discovered:
important strikes have already been made in the
Western Desert, notably at Qattara and El Alamein,
which have a potential annual output of 2·5 million
tons. In the Nile delta large reserves of natural gas
have been discovered which are estimated to be
sufficient for 25 years supply.

Egypt also lacks the large highly sophisticated
market which South Africa possesses. Although
many richer Egyptians demand more manufactured goods of a high quality the general mass of

the people buys little—only about one-fifth of all
purchases made in the U.A.R. consists of manufactured articles. This means that there is only a
limited opportunity for a few firms to sell their
manufactured goods and there is not the industrial
competition that one finds in western industrialised
states. Moreover, most of the production of processed articles is in the hands of a few cartels who
exclude competitors by dominating the market. The
average Egyptian is a farmer at heart and his profits from the small plots are usually so low that he
never acquires enough capital to invest in industrial
enterprises. Most of the big concerns are in government hands.

As a result there are a few large firms and many
small concerns running on *limited capital*; about
80 per cent of all industrial units in the U.A.R.
employ less than 50 workers and about one-fifth
have between 50 and 500. The smaller concerns are
mainly handicraft establishments making carpets,
shoes, textiles, leather goods and ceramic ware. The
government is actively encouraging this type of
industry and the development of cottage and village
industries—the weaving of rugs and carpets, the
home spinning of cotton and fruit bottling. The
bigger firms are concerned with petroleum refining,
paper making and textile manufacture. Typical of
the bigger concern is the Aswan fertiliser factory
constructed with the help of German and French
engineers. The plant uses power from the old
Aswan dam but will make use of that from the new
dam further upstream and has a capacity of 500,000
tons of calcium nitrate per annum; the plant employs 2,000 Egyptian staff and workers. Another
large nitrogen fertiliser plant is located at Suez.

The greatest growth since the pre-war years has
been in the textile industries (today five times the
1938 output), seed oil production (twice 1938) and
cement production (six times 1938). New factories
erected since the war include iron and steel, oil refining and motor car assembly plants. About half
of the industrial concerns are located in Cairo and
Alexandria (Fig. 9:**5**) although the Aswan region is
becoming a focal point for new industry, and more
industries will be established along the Nile Valley
as electric power becomes more readily available.
Egypt suffers somewhat from the rather elongated
shape of the country, accentuated by the narrow-
ness of the fertile strip flanking the Nile. Transport
lines are thus stretched out and this makes the

183

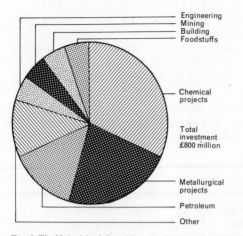

Engineering
Mining
Building
Foodstuffs

Chemical
projects

Total
investment
£800 million

Metallurgical
projects

Petroleum

Other

FIG. 6: The United Arab Republic—distribution of investment in the second development plan which was begun in 1965 and which has been extended from five to seven years; heavy industry receives the bulk of investment

hauling of raw materials more expensive. For this reason industry has been attracted mainly to the delta region with its easy access to European markets, its convenience for imports, its well-developed transport network, and its dense local market and skilled workforce. Most of the foreign capital invested in Egyptian industry tends to gravitate here.

Egypt's industrialisation programme is thus hampered by over-concentration of industry in certain locations, by an expensive transport network and raw materials, and lack of capital for greater internal investment by Egyptians themselves. Too great a proportion of the country's rapidly growing population is devoted to producing enough to eat to be spared for industrial work. Moreover, hostilities with Israel and the loss of Canal royalties have placed a great strain on the economy; the destruction of the refinery installations at Suez in October 1967 removed the source of 80 per cent of the U.A.R.'s domestic fuel supply.

Despite these drawbacks, the U.A.R. government has embarked on plans to increase power supplies and foreign investment. Among the most notable industrial undertakings planned or under construction are a petro-chemical plant to produce insecticide, chemicals, drugs, plastic, rubber, nylon, animal fodder and chemical cleaning fluids to cost £4·8 million and to be built at Alexandria in 1968; a heavy oil, coking and petro-chemical plant at Suez using local oil (cost £23·5 million); a £13 million factory at Mex near Alexandria to extract

70,000 tons of rutile and 70,000 tons of iron oxides from black sand deposits; four plants for atmospheric and vacuum oil distillation in Alexandria and Suez, and an aluminium factory and coal station in Alexandria to be constructed with the help of Soviet finances.

Secondary Industry in Ghana

In contrast, Ghana is not a heavily industrialised country and her economy relies heavily on the returns from exports of agricultural produce and minerals. As we have seen (Chapter 4, page 77) the cultivation of cocoa and the products of the forests together make up half of Ghana's gross domestic product and dominate Ghana's exports (see Table 8, page 77).

In the industrial field development has been concentrated until recently on the mining sector. Over 22,000 Ghanaians are employed in the gold mines and a further 6,000 on the diamond diggings, while nearly 40,000 are classed as miners of some sort. While gold and diamonds are important earners of foreign currency for Ghana, minerals useful to secondary industry and which occur in sufficiently large quantities are few. Manganese is mined at Nsuta and there are several other scattered deposits. At present most of this is exported, Ghana being the world's largest exporter of manganese; the United States takes just under two-thirds, Britain a quarter and Norway the remainder. Nearly £4·1 millions' worth was exported in 1964. Ghana possesses some large reserves of bauxite, the mineral ore of aluminium, an estimated 205 million tons. The chief deposits worked are at Kanayerebo near Awaso in the Western Region and some 45 miles north-west of Dunkwa. Other deposits are at Yenahin, 35 miles west of Kumasi and, although these are the largest, they are untapped since no transport facilities are available at present. Other minerals include beryllium (a strengthener of alloyed metals) and small deposits of copper. An iron ore deposit (270 million tons) lying near Shiene in the Northern Region now lies close enough to Lake Volta to be exploited (Fig. 9:7), while a second deposit of £150 million tons (45–50 per cent Fe) was discovered in 1968 in the Opon-Mansi Forest about 70 miles north of Takoradi.

But minerals vital to secondary industries are missing. Ghana lacks fuel; all coal is imported for

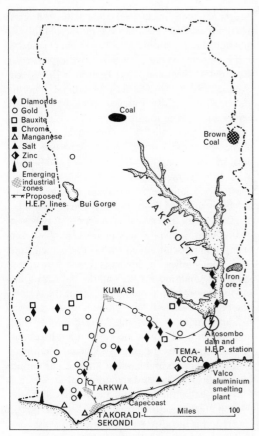

Diamonds
Gold
Bauxite
Chrome
Manganese
Salt
Zinc
Oil
Emerging industrial zones
Proposed H.E.P. lines

Coal

Brown Coal

LAKE VOLTA

Bui Gorge

KUMASI

Iron ore

Akosombo dam and H.E.P. station

TEMA-ACCRA

Valco aluminium smelting plant

TARKWA

Capecoast

Miles   0   100

TAKORADI-SEKONDI

FIG. 7: Ghana—location of minerals and industrial zones

use on the railways (about 40,000 tons a year) and timber is the major source of fuel outside the larger towns (annual consumption 180 million cubic feet, mainly from the natural forests). A large oil refinery at Tema supplies Ghana's present needs but all the crude oil is imported. The lack of fuel was one of the major reasons for embarking on the Volta River Scheme (page 147). Another hindrance which has retarded the development of secondary industries has been the lack of capital due to the diversion of much of it into the large schemes, while most of the foreign capital invested in the past has gone to the mining and agricultural sectors of the economy. Again, Ghana has lacked the skilled manpower necessary for running highly specialised industries, since where there is little secondary industry there can be little scope for training.

The successive governments of Ghana, both colonial and independent, have realised the need to broaden the country's economy by encouraging secondary industrialisation. In 1947 the Industrial Development Corporation, now a government body, was set up with the purpose of investigating and promoting industrial undertakings. A Seven Year Plan was begun which aimed at increasing the pace of industrialisation by certain measures—the replacing of imported goods with those which could be manufactured locally, the processing within the country wherever possible of those minerals and agricultural products which were being exported in their raw form, the expansion of the building and construction industry, and the development of fields of industry hitherto neglected and which would be necessary to larger-scale industries—machine tools and electrical and electronic industries.[1]

Although secondary industries still make only a small contribution to Ghana's total domestic output it is a rapidly growing sector. The true growth however has mainly taken place within the last twenty-five years, as shown in Table 28.

TABLE 28
Ghana: Growth in the Establishment of Major Manufacturing Concerns

YEAR	NUMBER OF CONCERNS IN OPERATION	YEAR	NUMBER OF CONCERNS IN OPERATION
1909	31	1939	79
1919	34	1949	159
1929	55	1959	378

A survey of secondary industry in Ghana made in 1962 showed that while in 1948 only 16 per cent of people living in urban centres were employed in industry the figure had increased to 23 per cent by 1960. But the survey also revealed that really large-scale industries were very few in number. Thus of 92,095 manufacturing establishments of all kinds only 14 employed more than 500 workers and only 1 per cent employed more than six paid employees. Many of the 'factories' employed relatives who were unpaid.

Many of these small concerns tend to concentrate

[1] In an effort to stabilise Ghana's economy this plan has been abandoned by the National Liberation Council (the N.L.C.); a new plan is to be formulated by 1968 when it is hoped most of Ghana's present short-term difficulties should have been solved.

in the urban centres and are largely 'consumer' industries catering for the needs of the local market, their range of goods including cloth, woven articles, soap, silver and gold ornaments, simple metal instruments and tools, furniture, coconut oil, lime juice, bricks, tiles, pottery, bread, confectionery, baskets and so on. These local industries continue to multiply, however, and over the last ten years or so there has been an increasing proportion of comparatively large establishments. There has certainly been an emergence of secondary industrial complexes on a small scale in the Accra and Tema industrial areas and at Takoradi-Sekondi, Cape Coast, Kumasi, Nsawam, Tarkwa and Tamale.

The greatest possibilities for development lie in the aluminium industry. Aluminium is in increasingly great demand by all industrial nations for it is a strong, rustless, and lightweight metal extensively used in the aircraft and motor car industries. The processing of bauxite to produce aluminium requires vast quantities of electric power which Ghana now possesses in the Volta Scheme. Since it requires ten tons of bauxite to produce one ton of aluminium and aluminium is worth about seven times as much as the same weight of bauxite, the development of this industry will greatly benefit Ghana and earn her considerable foreign exchange. Most of the present output of 300,000 tons (which is far below Ghana's producing potential) goes to the United Kingdom. However, the Valco smelting plant at Tema was completed in November 1966 and production of aluminium commenced in March 1967, when the first 250 ingots were exported to the United Kingdom. The expected production of 3,000 to 3,500 tons a year will cause a decrease in unrefined ore exports; potential production will exceed 100,000 tons a year.

Ghana is at present going through a difficult economic period. The expenditure of money in the past on large 'prestige' projects has left a considerable foreign debt which the present government is seeking to reduce by stringent measures. The support given to Ghana by the International Monetary Fund in her present difficulties shows, however, that there is every confidence in the future of the country's economy.

Industrial Development in Kenya

Kenya's economy is largely based on the production of agricultural raw materials for export—coffee, tea, pyrethrum, sisal, canned fruits, hides and skins. There are no fuels except wood, no useful minerals in commercial quantities except sodium carbonate, and at present the rather small hydro-electric power potential of the country has been little developed. Coal, oil and hydro-electricity have to be imported and despite intensive searches no major oil or ore deposits have been found.

Kenya is therefore heavily dependent on imports of manufactured articles; of the total value of imports in 1967 of nearly £121 million, over 90 per cent were manufactured or processed articles, especially machinery, motor vehicles, rubber products, metal goods, fertilisers, fabrics and paper products.

The country thus displays an economy typical of *a developing nation*—a high percentage of workers engaged in agriculture, a high unemployment rate, few opportunities for jobs outside the agricultural sphere, a small income per capita, and thus a low buying power in internal markets. But the country has certain assets—a large volume of agricultural raw materials, an emerging African middle class, and stability of government. Of the three East African territories the rate of secondary industrial expansion has been greatest in Kenya. The pattern of growth and the present industrial structure is fairly typical of the developing territories of Africa. This pattern has been reached through certain stages and is largely a post-war development.

Before the Second World War Kenya possessed few industries except those processing local raw materials—coffee, wheat, sugar and tea. There was a small increase during the war in industrial production due to shortages but it was only at the beginning of the 1950s that industrial expansion really began. Table 29 illustrates *the industrial structure* of Kenya.

There is thus no heavy industry although there is a large oil refinery at Mombasa and a small steel mill using scrap metal at Nairobi. The map (Fig. 9:**8**) shows the location of Kenya's major centres and natural resources.

Most of the factories are small in size. Just over 70 per cent have workforces of less than 20. Most are located in urban areas in specially designed estates with railway and road access; these factories are thus close to markets and to export routes. A few factories lie outside the major urban areas close to labour supplies and to raw materials and these are usually self-contained units with accommoda-

TABLE 29
Kenya: The Present Structure of Industry

INDUSTRIAL SECTOR	RANGE OF GOODS PRODUCED	MAJOR LOCATIONS
Food Processing	Flour, beer, canned fruits, jams and vegetables, dairy products, coffee, tea, sugar, canned and fresh meat, tobacco and cigarettes, edible oils, soft drinks	Nairobi, Mombasa, Nakuru, Thika, Limuru, Nyeri, Miwani, Machakos
Material Manufacture	Matting, rope, sacks, coarse fabric, cordage, soap, tannin, wooden products, knitted goods, paper, shoes, tyres, polishes	Nairobi, Mombasa, Limuru, Thika
Ancillary Services	Motor vehicle repair, motor engineering, rolling stock and locomotive engineering, ship construction and repair	Nairobi, Mombasa, Kisumu

tion, eating and entertainment facilities for their employees. The Bata Shoe factory at Limuru is typical of this enterprise, employing over 800 workers and producing footwear, cycle tyres, and inner tubes. Local materials are used—chalk, salt, soda, wattle extract, hides and skins—but chemicals and fuels are imported.

In 1940 there were 40 companies with factories in Kenya, most of them subsidiaries of British firms.

Today there are nearly 4,000 representing a wide range of foreign investors—Japan, West Germany, the United States, India, France and Italy. These companies can afford to construct factories and market the products efficiently. Up to the present the lack of capital on a large scale has prevented the African from entering this section of the economy. Any expansion in the secondary industrial field in Kenya will depend on the local market in East Africa. Recent economic moves suggest that the idea of an East African Federation or, at least, customs union, is becoming more attractive to the three territories. A common market would enlarge the number of consumers to 28 million, whereas the individual markets are limited to between 8 and 10 million (see page 207). But as the economy progresses to a more modern one and education and training programmes increase, there will be a speeding up of the growth of commercial and industrial enterprises in Kenya and in East Africa generally.

Kenya, however, possesses one source of wealth which she is now developing to the full—her national parks, game reserves, magnificent scenery and sunny climate. Nairobi is the centre for *tourism* in East Africa and serves as the base for visits to Tanzanian and Kenya parks. Nearly four times as many tourists came to Kenya in 1964 as to Tanzania (77,290 as against 20,260). The fantastic amount of revenue spent by tourists who come from almost every part of the globe can be seen in Table 30; from this it is clear that Kenya takes the lion's share.

Because of its unfavourable trade balances Kenya

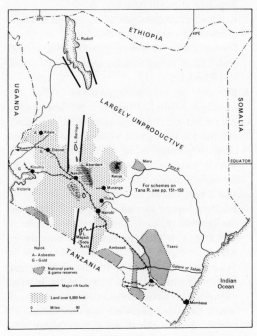

FIG. 8: Kenya—the Highlands, game areas and communications

187

TABLE 30
East Africa: Foreign Exchange Obtained from the Tourist Industry (in millions of £s)

COUNTRY	1960	1961	1962	1963	1964
Kenya	4·4	4·7	5·6	7·3	7·0
Tanzania	1·2	1·6	2·1	2·4	2·3
Uganda	0·5	0·6	0·9	1·2	1·3

is making every effort to use this asset to the full. The parks and reserves are being made more accessible by the provision of tarmac roads, new game lodges are being set up, and increased hotel facilities are being provided in Nairobi. Kenya expects to receive nearly 150,000 visitors by 1970.

Conclusions

Secondary industrialisation in Africa depends on a variety of factors—the appropriate infrastructure, the availability of skilled labour, qualified technicians and engineers, wide markets, and increasing investment. Outside South Africa, Rhodesia, and, to a lesser extent the U.A.R., most manufacturing is concerned with the processing of primary produce such as coffee milling, palm oil extraction, timber preparation, fish canning and so on. In most tropical African countries there has been a big increase in food processing factories—Dahomey, the Ivory Coast, Senegal and the Cameroons are steadily increasing their output of palm oil, the Congo and Malagasy Republic their refined sugar production, while flour mills are increasing in number in many countries as the market demands more white flour products.

By granting concessions to home and overseas investors African countries are encouraging the establishment of textile and clothing industries, constructional concerns, metal and rubber industries. But most of these establishments tend to be small or medium sized; exceptions are ore smelting plants, wood processing and veneer mills, and some large textile concerns.

The most important industrial activity takes place in the extractive sector—ore and timber mining. Even this is unevenly distributed, there being large mining complexes in Rhodesia, South Africa, the Congo and South West Africa. There is here, however, more scope for expansion in tropical African countries—Liberia, Sierra Leone, Nigeria, Ghana and Tanzania probably have the most mineral potential.

Questions

1 Comment on the prospects for the further development of mining and manufacturing industries in *one* of the following countries: Ghana, Nigeria, Guinea, Tanzania, the U.A.R.
2 Locate by sketch-map *a* the Rand, *b* the Katanga mining areas, and describe the exploitation of minerals and the industrial activity associated with each.
3 Locate and assess the importance of deposits of coal, diamonds and copper in Africa south of the Sahara.
4 Illustrate from specific examples the contribution made by Africa to the industrial needs of Western Europe.
5 Give a reasoned account of the distribution and character of manufacturing industry in the Republic of South Africa.
6 Examine the importance of mining to the economy of any one country in Africa.
7 Outline and comment on the distribution and problems of manufacturing industry in Zambia and Rhodesia.
8 Discuss the relative distribution of fuel resources in Africa and comment on their relative use for industrial purposes *within* the continent.
9 *a* What are the factors which are indicative of developing countries in Africa? *b* Discuss the ways in which secondary industry can aid development. Confine your answer to one country with which you are familiar.
10 Briefly compare the industrial development of the Republic of South Africa or the United Arab Republic with one less developed country in Africa.
11 Trace the factors which lead to the establishment of secondary industries in African states. In what ways does this secondary industrial development benefit the country in which it is established?
12 Discuss Africa's rôle as a raw mineral ore supplier to industrialised nations.

Practical Work

Typical practical questions on industry might be:
1 Select any mining centre of which you have first-hand knowledge and discuss the effects of mining upon the growth of settlements and communications within its immediate area.
2 Discuss the reasons for the establishment of secondary industries in any region familiar to you.
3 In what ways could secondary industrial development be stimulated in *either* your home district *or* in a region in your country with which you are familiar.

The following topics are suggested as vacation work which the student may find interesting and profitable:
1 A visit to a local mine and the writing of an account of the mine using the following headings: *a* Location (with map); *b* General facts—labour force and, if possible, their origins; annual and monthly production figures; *c* Processing and mining techniques; *d* Markets; *e* Importance of the mine's products to the general economy of the country.
2 The mapping of the location of secondary industries in the country, especially large concerns, in relation to the raw materials they use. Local newspaper cuttings giving news of new plants should be collected and the information in note form inserted on the map.
3 A visit to a local factory and the writing of an account. Particularly important in the account should be the marketing, the use of local or imported raw materials, and the importance to the economy of the country as a whole. The student should not dwell too much on processing, welfare schemes and similar topics.

Discussion Topics

1 Africa as a market and raw materials supplier.
2 In what ways can African states make a fuller use of their raw materials?
3 What are the chief methods of promoting industrial expansion in African states?

Statistical Exercises

Either in your notebooks or on large sheets of paper to act as wall charts draw pie, bar or simple curve graphs to illustrate the following statistics:
1 South Africa. Sales of Rough and Uncut diamonds 1963–1966.
1963—£231,956,882; 1964—£266,372,098; 1965—£296,633,882; 1966—£355,691,648.
2 Uganda. Total Mineral Exports by Quantity and Value for 1965 and 1966.

MINERAL	1965 QUANTITY (TONS)	VALUE (£)	1966 (PROVISIONAL) QUANTITY (TONS)	VALUE (£)
Beryl	268·9	21,174	221·8	21,646
Columbite Ore	11·46	4,868	10·6	6,137
Tin Ore	293·6	260,101	180·3	171,982
Wolfram	64·2	68,796	100·4	65,060
Blister Copper	16,734	8,738,591	16,041	6,995,500

3 Morocco. Mineral Production, 1965:
Phosphates: 10,082,000 tons; Lead: 58,300 tons; Zinc: 45,800 tons; Iron ore: 63,000 tons.
4 Sierra Leone. Iron ore production at Marampa:
1964 production—1,936,000 tons.
1965 production—2,097,500 tons exported to the Netherlands (638,000 tons); West Germany (620,500 tons); United Kingdom (547,000 tons); Italy (292,000 tons).
1966 production—2,310,000 tons.
5 The Congo (Brazzaville). Crude Oil Production:
1962—123,400 tons; 1963—109,000 tons; 1964—82,500 tons; 1965—71,000 tons.
6 Tanzania. Mineral Production (figures for 1965):
Total production value—£9·8 million (7·3 per cent over 1964).
Exports: diamonds (£7·25 million), gold (£1,014,000), tin concentrates (£336,000), salt (£389,000), mica (£105,000).
7 Algeria. Mineral Production 1964/65:

MINERAL	1964 TONS	1965 TONS
Iron Ore	2,693,180	3,131,550 (exports 3,119,000)
Zinc	64,264	62,990
Copper	3,900	3,660
Lead	13,600	14,920

8 Kenya. Sodium Carbonate Exports:

Value (£'000)

1958	1959	1960	1961	1962	1963	1964	1965
1,205	1,713	1,317	1,587	1,241	1,234	708	805

Volume ('000 *tons*)

1958	1959	1960	1961	1962	1963	1964	1965
104·0	148·2	115·2	142·7	111·2	106·9	64·0	73·5

(est)

9 Libya: Annual Exports of Crude Oil, 1961–1967:

YEAR	THOUSANDS OF TONS	PERCENTAGE INCREASE
1961	696	0
1962	7,848	1,027
1963	22,044	180
1964	41,472	88
1965	58,476	41
1966	12,240	22
1967	83,500	15

10 Africa: Iron Ore Reserves. (This exercise may be done on a political base map of Africa using pie- or bar graphs and different colours for the differing grades of ores; Fig. 17, page 169 should be used to locate the deposits.)

COUNTRY	GRADE (PER CENT IRON CONTENT)	RESERVES (IN MILLIONS OF TONS)
Morocco	43–45 56	40 50
Algeria	52–53	100
Tunisia	55	50
United Arab Republic	43	140
Mauritania	63 40+	100 1,000
Upper Volta	55	1,000
Ghana	40	100
Guinea	51	2,000
Liberia	64 57	300 300
Sierra Leone	57	100
Cameroun	40	100
Gabon	43–45 60	200 500
Angola	35–53 62	2,000 100
Swaziland	63	40
South Africa	60–65	700

CHAPTER TEN

TRANSPORT AND COMMUNICATIONS

Although work on the first railway in Africa was begun at Cape Town in 1859 it was not until the late nineteenth century that the spate of railway building began to open up the continent. Until then the chief form of transport, in tropical regions at least, was by human porterage, an exceedingly slow and laborious method. Here, except in the tsetse-free highlands, transport animals were virtually unknown. In the Maghreb the donkey and the horse were the chief methods of transport; in the Sahara the camel was superbly adapted to its environment, and on the high level veld the ox-wagon was the chief wheeled vehicle.

The Rivers

From what has been said on Africa's rivers in Chapter Seven it will be obvious that they are severely limited in their usefulness for transporting passengers and goods. The tremendous seasonal variation in volume, the dangerous shoals and sandbanks, the numerous falls and rapids and the floating masses of vegetation are all physical obstacles to smooth transport. But despite these handicaps the rivers are used for carrying passengers and goods along parts of their courses at least. The Congo is navigable up to 85 miles inland, then its course is broken by a series of rapids and falls up to Stanley Pool; from here to Stanley Falls is a navigable stretch of 1,000 miles. The upper Niger and its tributary the Benue are also navigable, the Benue as far as Garoua in the Cameroons (730 miles to its confluence with the Niger) during the rains; the Niger, 2,600 miles long, is navigable in its upper course between Kouroussa and Bamako, but between Bamako and Koulikoro is interrupted by rapids and again between Ansongo and Jebba. From Jebba to the oil rivers of the delta the river is again navigable. Other rivers in West Africa which can be used for navigation mainly during the wet season include the Senegal (as far as Kayes, 550 miles) and the Gambia (as far as Georgetown, 175 miles, for light vessels). Mention should also be made of the lagoons along the coast which provide safe water courses for small vessels.

The River Nile is navigable from Lake Albert to Nimule on the Sudan border with Uganda but the steamer service has now been discontinued. At Nimule the papyrus reeds close in and navigation is impossible until Juba is reached. The river is then navigable for all seasons to Khartoum (about 800 miles) but is interrupted by a series of cataracts until Wadi Halfa. The steamer service was then continued between Wadi Halfa and Aswan-Shellal and the Nile is then navigable to its mouth. Some idea of the amount of goods that are carried on these river stretches can be gathered from the fact that, before the drowning of the Shellal-Wadi Halfa stretch by Lake Nasser, the Sudanese ran a twice-weekly steamer service which in recent years carried 100,000 passengers, 7,000 head of cattle and 12,000 tons of cargo annually; between Dongola and Karima (between the third and fourth cataracts) the annual totals were 65,000 passengers and 33,000 tons of cargo.

Most of the other rivers of Africa—the Orange, the Vaal, the Limpopo, the Zambezi—are virtually useless for navigation over long stretches because of seasonal variations in level.

The lakes of Africa are extremely useful for commercial shipping. Lake Victoria provides an

TABLE 31
East Africa: Lake and River Traffic 1963–64[1]

	PUBLIC GOODS (TONS)		PASSENGERS	
	1963	1964	1963	1964
Lake Victoria	218,600	194,800	394,500	422,000
Lake Tanganyika	8,100	7,200	26,700	28,000
L. Albert–R. Nile	5,600	200	—	—
Totals	232,300	202,200	421,200	450,000

[1]Source: East African Railways and Harbours Annual Report, 1965. The Lake Albert-River Nile stretch is now closed.

important inter-territorial communications network for Tanzania, Kenya and Uganda. A new train ferry service has come into operation with terminals at Kisumu, Jinja, Mwanza and Musoma. Large cargoes of coffee, cotton, oil seeds, sugar cane and many passengers are transported annually.

Considerable amounts of tung oil, groundnuts and rice are transported on Lake Malawi between Kota Kota, Karonga and Nkata Bay and Chipoka. The new man-made lakes—Kariba, Nasser, Volta—will also provide new communications networks.

The Railways

The arrival of the colonial powers and the final agreement on their political spheres of control led to the rapid development of railways, the fastest means of gaining access to the interior and estab--lishing strategic control. No attempt was made to co-ordinate the various lines, which were often on different gauges. Railways often ran directly inland for strategic rather than economic reasons although economic development usually followed the line—Mombasa to Lake Victoria (1896–1900), Lourenço Marques and Cape Town to Pretoria (1895), from Tanga inland (from 1891), from Djibouti to Addis Ababa (in 1894), and from Matadi to Leopoldville (1898) to by-pass the Stanley Pool.

The pioneer railway builders faced innumerable difficulties. Although Africa consists of broad, flat plateaux it must not be thought that the construction of communications has been easy because of this. The plateaux often lie at between 3,000 and 5,000 feet and may only be reached by traversing several steep escarpments and deep river valleys. The grain of the land often runs parallel to the coasts, erosion bevels form steep steps into the interior, and steep banked dongas and rivers present continuous obstacles. The tremendous variations in relief along railway routes is shown in Fig. 10:**1**.

Physical features are not the only problems which railway builders and maintenance teams have to contend with—disease, dense vegetation and the problem of fuel supplies have to be overcome. Frequent tropical thunderstorms may wash away vital sections of line, sandstorms cover the railway to great depths, and rolling boulders destroy bridges. Such storms can be quite serious; in 1961 most of Kenya and Uganda was completely cut off from the coast because rains had washed away two vital bridges and the roads were impassable. Railway lines in the Congo were only completed after the removal of dense masses of tropical forest.

Once the railway has been built it has to be supplied with fuel, easy in coal-rich Rhodesia and South Africa but a great problem in East Africa and several West African states. East African Railways rely on the import of over 5 million gallons of fuel oil each year, which cost £1·84 million in 1964. Another great difficulty is the vast unproductive distances over which track must be maintained.

The Railway Network

The legacy of colonial separatism in railway construction is reflected in today's map of railway

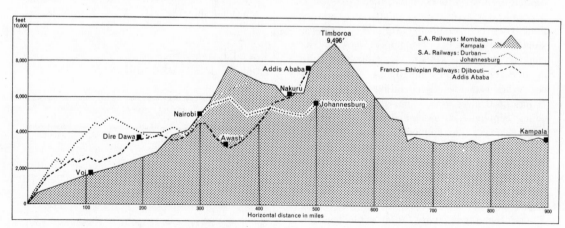

FIG. 1: Variations of relief along three railway routes

communications in Africa. Only in South Africa is there a true network directly comparable with those in Europe or North America; northwards, railways become long straggling lines running to the interior with vast areas where railways do not exist at all. The virtual geographic heart of Africa, the Chad Basin (covering almost half a million square miles—enough to cover an eighth of Europe) has never seen a railway line although one is now being constructed through Cameroon. Even today political factions prevent the economic and sensible planning of railway networks. The excessive demands of the Spanish Saharan authorities in return for passage through their territory forced the Mauritanian Government to construct a £3 million tunnel for their Kedia d'Idjil line; the railway running between Mali and Senegal was severed when these two territories broke politically and alternative routes had to be constructed through the Ivory Coast. In earlier days the denial of the Gambia River as an outlet for the French in Senegal resulted in their constructing the 153-mile long railway between St Louis and Dakar in 1885. Again, the Sierra Leone and French Guinea lines were deliberately built on different gauges to prevent joining, the Guinean line being built across the Futa Djalon Plateau to forestall British penetration in that area. This line is now being rebuilt with Soviet aid.

But there are signs of more rational planning of railway routes within the framework of Africa's economic communities—the Trans-Cameroon Railway within the framework of the UDEAC (Fig. 10:2) is a good example, as is the construction of the connecting line between the Uganda-Kenya railways and the Tanzanian lines (the Mruazi-Ruvu connection). The latter with the southerly extension of the Central Tanzanian line from Kilosa to Kidatu and beyond are the first signs of the beginnings of a true railway network for East Africa designed to tap new potentially productive areas and to permit the free movement of railway rolling stock to regions which need it most. The proposed line from Kilosa via Mbeya to Kapiri Mposhi will, if completed, completely reorient the trade of Zambia towards eastern rather than southern Africa. In West Africa the OCDN—the Dahomey-Niger Common Organisation—recommends the planning of a rail extension to Niger; the line will run from Cotonou to Parakou, Dahomey, and will be extended to Dosso in Niger.

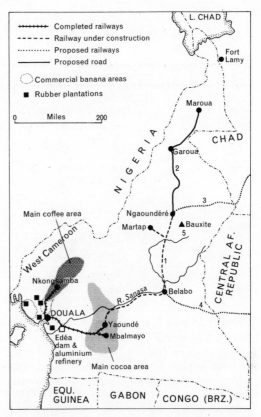

FIG. 2: The Trans-Cameroon Railway. If agreement is reached on all parts of the plan this will be one of the first planned integrated railway networks in Africa. Work is now proceeding on the 440-mile long line from Yaoundé to Ngaoundéré (1). This will connect with a modern tarmac road to Maroua and will thus unite the economically different north to the south. When the railway is finished in March 1968 it is planned to construct a 350-mile branch line (3) which will run to the important cotton growing region around Fort Archamboult in southern Chad. Another branch line of 350 miles (4) may then be built from Belabo to Bangui, the C.A.R. capital, to promote the external trade of that country. The Trans-Cameroon Railway will undoubtedly stimulate economic growth of the Cameroon Republic, particularly the port of Douala and the development of the bauxite site south-east of Ngaoundéré (5)

The Inadequacy of the Railways

The railways of Africa are, however, beginning to feel the strain of the tremendous economic developments taking place on the continent. African countries now produce 60 per cent more cultivated crops than they did in the 1930s, exports of groundnuts doubled between 1950 and 1960, coffee production is five times higher than in the 1930s, cocoa production has increased 30 per cent since 1946 and the

TABLE 32
Transported Commodities and Rail Routes in Selected African States

COUNTRY	MAJOR COMMODITIES	RAIL ROUTE
Senegal, Mali	Cotton, groundnuts	Koulikoro–Dakar
Sierra Leone	Coffee, oil palm produce	Pendembu–Freetown
Ivory Coast	Cocoa, oil palm produce, coffee, timber	Bouake–Abidjan
Ghana	Cocoa	Kumasi–Accra–Sekondi–Takoradi
Nigeria	Cotton, groundnuts, oil palm produce	Kaura–Zaria–Lagos, Kano–Lagos
Sudan	Cotton, oil seeds	Gezira–El Obeid–Port Sudan
Ethiopia	Oil seeds, pulses, coffee	Addis Ababa–Asmara–Djibouti, Massawa
Kenya	Coffee, sisal, tea	Nairobi–Mombasa
Uganda	Coffee, cotton	Kampala–Jinja–Mbale–Mombasa
Tanzania	Sisal, cotton, coffee	Mwanza–Morogoro–Arusha–Korogwe–Dar and Tanga
Congo (Kinshasa)	Tea, palm oil	Kivu Province–Kasese–Mombasa
Zambia	Copper	Kitwe–Ndola–Beira

output of cotton is 30 per cent higher than the 1930s average annual total. Mineral production too has increased at a colossal rate—Africa produces twice as much copper, iron ore and manganese, four times as much cobalt, six times as much asbestos and a third as much again of tin concentrates as she produced in 1938. Imports of heavy machinery and transport equipment now form between 20 and 35 per cent of the imports of most countries and bulky imports of fuel oils represent between 6 and 12 per cent of imports. The rapid post-war development of secondary industries has accentuated this growth.

The increasing volume of imports and exports has not been accompanied by a similar increase in the rate of development of the transport system of Africa. While the volume of freight carried on Africa's railways is now three and a quarter times what it was in 1938 the length of railways has remained virtually stable and in some parts of Africa has even decreased.[1] In 1950 Africa had just over 42,100 miles of railway track or 5 per cent of the world total. The congestion of shipping in Mombasa, Beira, Lourenço Marques and other major ports testifies to the inability of the railways to cope with the increasing flow of goods.

[1] The Southern Tanzanian line, for example, has been removed from between Mtwara and Nachingwea because it failed to attract sufficient trade.

Roads

The present slow rate of railway expansion can be explained partly by the vast increase in the number of roads being built on the continent. This is the fastest growing medium of transport in Africa. Within the last twenty years Algeria and Rhodesia have doubled their existing road network, Ghana has increased hers by $2\frac{1}{2}$ times and Kenya by a half. Thus some of the extra burden created by developing economies has been taken away from the railways, but not all, for the railway is especially adapted to the cheaper transport of bulky goods—ores, mineral oils, and coal. Moreover roads vary tremendously in Africa; they may be simply bulldozed tracks of murram or red earth, hard and flinty during the dry season, slippery and impassable during the rains and kept reasonably level from time to time by a grading machine. From this there are many intermediate stages—the Rhodesian roads have in many places single tarmac strips the width of one car, while the 1,300-mile long Cape Town–Beit Bridge road is one of the finest super highways in the world. Many African nations are devoting large amounts of capital to the construction of all-weather roads, realising that an efficient transport system means economic growth in all spheres. Algeria and Kenya now have four times as many miles of hard-surface road as they did in 1948 and

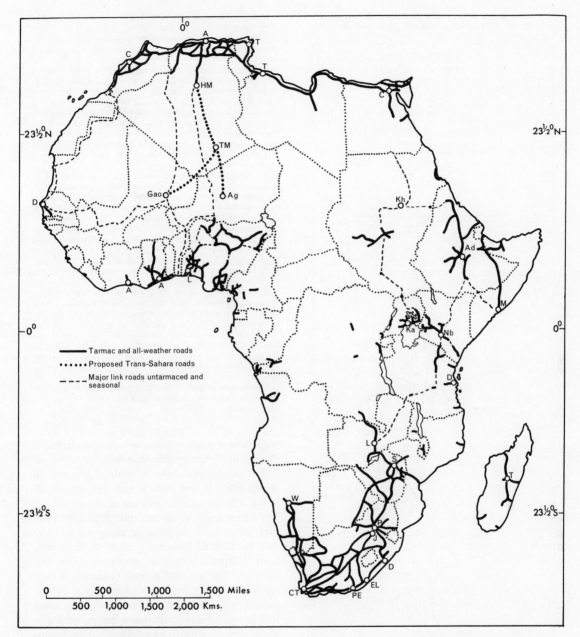

FIG. 3: Africa—the developing road network

the U.A.R., Ghana, Nigeria and Zambia two and a half times as much.

But it is only recently that true road networks have begun to evolve. Before the 1950s the road transport system of most African countries was based on the railways which linked the main commercial zones with the major ports and these were often several hundreds of miles apart, especially in eastern and southern Africa. The post-war expansion of agricultural production has led to the development of feeder roads in the main agricultural areas which lead directly to the railheads. Thus the

195

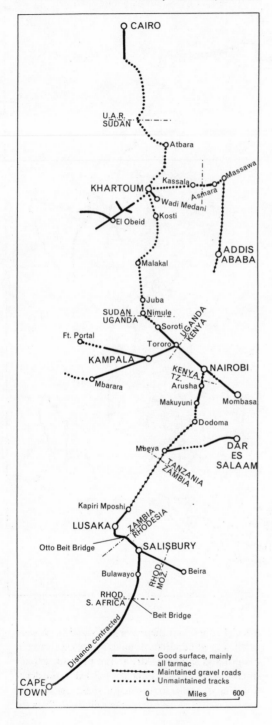

diagrammatic illustration here shows it will need much improvement before it becomes a true highway of trade. In the Sudan all-weather roads exist only in the southern part, while the northern parts have mere desert tracks which are several miles wide in parts and cross numerous rocky outcrops. With the longer rains further south these roads become impassable for long periods. The Khartoum-Nimule stretch is a poorly maintained gravel track but a longer, better maintained alternative route goes from El Obeid to Wau and from Wau to Nimule.

In Ethiopia it is only around Addis Ababa and Asmara that there is a true road network; the Kassala-Asmara road is better maintained on the Ethiopian side, where it has a tarmac surface over a quarter of its length. Road connections with Kenya are virtually non-existent, but a road is to be improved to allow a coach service.

Uganda has one of the best road systems to be found in East Africa with large stretches of tarmac connecting to Kenya and the border regions with the Congo (K). Together with the roads in Kenya this forms the main east-west highway leading into the Congo and West Africa. In the Congo it links with an alternative route to the north (Cape Town-Lubumbashi-Uvira). In Kenya the main trunk road is nearly all tarmac and there is a good network of tarmac roads in the highlands and well-maintained roads to game parks and outlying regions. A gravel road links with Tanzania whose government has tarmacked the stretch from the border at Namanga to just beyond Makuyuni in the Lake Manyara region (about 80 miles). But from there to Mbeya the roads are very bad and there are plans to bituminise large stretches in view of possibilities of increasing trade with Zambia. In Zambia the stretch to Kapiri Mposhi is a well-maintained gravel road which is now taking considerable traffic, particularly loads of oil and copper ore. From there to Otto Beit Bridge on the southern border the road is tarmacked, and throughout Rhodesia and South Africa the Great North Road has mainly tarmac surfaces all the way to Cape Town.

Malawi is completely by-passed by the road, but in 1965 a £3 million loan from the World Bank was granted to improve road connections with Zambia

main flow of traffic remains in most cases from the interior to the coast rather than between individual countries. For example, in eastern and central Africa international trade is negligible except between Kenya, Uganda and Tanzania and outside this region most goods are transported by other means than roads. The Sudan, except for its trade with the U.A.R., has very restricted trade connections with its southern neighbours— coffee, tea, dairy produce and fresh vegetables come either via the Nile or on sea routes, while her grain exports go entirely by sea. Ethiopia uses her own rail routes and then sea to import metal boxes, butter, soda and aluminium sheeting from East Africa. Malawi sends only tea to the Nairobi auctions and imports butter in exchange, while Zambia exports mainly zinc and metal products to East Africa. The principal commodities moving between Kenya and Uganda and the Congo (K)—petroleum, machinery, vehicles, fish, tea and palm oil—move largely by rail via Kigoma, Albertville and Bujumbura.

Thus cross-frontier transport by road in these regions is confined to specific areas—between Kenya, Uganda and Tanzania; between Zambia, Malawi and Tanzania, and between Rwanda, Congo (K) and Uganda. Of these only the Tanzania-Zambia-Malawi routes can be classed as long-distance traffic; commodities, mainly petroleum and some copper ore, at present move between Kapiri Mposhi and Mikumi, the present terminus of the branch railway from Tanzania's Central Line. Malawi's trade with Kenya travels along the Iringa-Dodoma-Arusha route, while a considerable amount of Tanzania's exports from her southern regions uses this road northwards to Kenya. Many of the roads in East Africa carry a growing amount of tourist traffic, especially in Kenya there are good road links to all the major game parks, an important aspect in promoting the tourist industry.

It is clear that there is a great need to improve the linking roads between countries to promote international trade within Africa. The main basis for such a road is the so-called Great North Road which, if fully developed, could form a major trans-Africa highway running from Cairo through to Cape Town. This road is shown in diagrammatic form in Fig. 10:4. The main sections which greatly need improvement are between Iringa (Tanzania) and Kapiri Mposhi (Zambia) since the political trend in Zambia will result in greater trade orientation towards the Dar es Salaam outlet. This improvement would entail the expenditure of approximately £8 million in addition to the present road development programmes in Tanzania. The proposed Kapiri Mposhi-Mikumi railway will not pass through the Iringa region which Tanzania wishes to develop. A development programme for a Zambia-Tanzania-Nairobi trunk road has been advocated since 1957 but it has been hindered by lack of capital. The two other weak links are those between the Sudan and Ethiopia and between Ethiopia and Kenya.

The Great North Road is crossed at three points by east-west highways—the Mombasa, Uganda, Kivu Province route to Kisangani and Matadi; the Port Sudan-Geneina route; and the Beira-Lobito route. Of these three the Mombasa to Matadi route has the most potential from the point of view of international trade and the road from Mombasa to the western Uganda border is tarmac over long

stretches, while the road to Kisangani has been well maintained in recent years. This east-west route is joined by the second major north-south route (Cape Town-Lubumbashi-Jadotville-Albertville-Uvura) at Bukavu.

In the western region of Africa one of the greatest needs is for the improvement of the trans-Sahara routes. The Sahara is already being crossed by specially designed vehicles but it is still a hazardous journey and methods are too uneconomic for the large-scale movement of goods. Already tarmac roads run 500 miles from Algiers to Hassi Messaoud, but there are then 1,200 miles of rough tracks. Eight West African states (the U.A.R., Mali, Chad, Niger, Tunisia, Mauritania, Algeria and Morocco) together with assistance from oil companies, have planned a route from Fort Flatters near Hassi Messaoud to Tamanrasset in the Ahaggar and then branch routes to Gao and Agades. Such a proposal, if put into practice, would cut freight costs by 50 per cent.

Roads therefore are receiving great attention in Africa and most of this attention has been concentrated into the last fifteen years. But roads are costly to build and their maintenance is often more expensive than that of railways. Many governments are therefore content to realign and tarmac the existing roads while new road building is undertaken on a 'feeder' basis from important economic regions. Other improvements are also being carried out—road widening, bridge strengthening and route diversion to avoid notoriously dangerous areas. The railway is still the most economical means of carrying large, cheap, bulky loads over great distances, but the road has the advantage in flexibility.

Air Transport

Air transport has undergone an even more rapid expansion than roadways in Africa since the Second World War. In the 1930s British Imperial Airways made only one flight each week through Cairo, Entebbe, Nairobi, and Salisbury to Cape Town and return. Today there are several flights daily to all these places, not only by British airlines but by the national airlines of East Africa, Ethiopia and the U.A.R., and regular flights to London from Johannesburg and Cape Town via the Portuguese territories by South African Airways. Less frequent services are provided by other international airlines

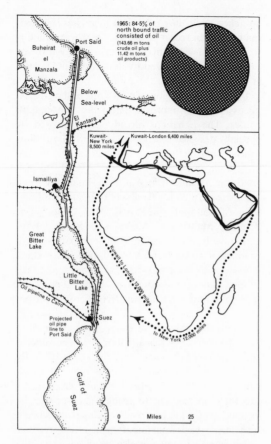

FIG. 5: The U.A.R.—the Suez Canal. The canal was completed in 1869, is 103 miles long and after many improvements could, before Arab-Israeli hostilities, accommodate vessels of 60,000 tons and 35·5 foot draught. It was aimed to increase this for vessels of 37 foot draught. This will entail making the canal 48 feet deep and 76 feet wider in parts. But the Suez Canal will still be too small for the 42 tankers of more than 90,000 tons on order. Plans have therefore been made to construct an oil pipeline from Suez to Port Said to transfer oil from one tanker to another. In 1965, 20,289 vessels passed through the canal of which 9,663 were tankers. Of the 183·44 million tons of cargo which passed northwards through Suez 84·5 per cent was oil (155·08 million tons). The other 15·5 per cent included soya beans, minerals, textiles, fibres, rubber and oil seeds. Southward bound cargoes include machinery, metal goods, cement, cereals, pulp, timber and paper.

In 1961 the U.A.R. received £47 million in tolls; this had increased to £70 million by 1965 and to £78 million in 1966. The proposal to make Port Said a free trade zone is likely to attract much foreign exchange currency.

Outbreaks of hostilities between the U.A.R. and Israel constantly threaten the use of the Canal; it was closed for six months in 1956 and is closed again at the time of writing following hostilities in June, 1967. The economic effects of the political friction are the increased costs of transport round the Cape and the loss to the U.A.R., which spends £100 million annually on food imports, of £80 million in Canal dues and £40 million annually from Western tourists as well as an oil production loss of £12 million a year from fields now under Israeli control. Tankers operating from the Persian Gulf to Europe now take 63 days on the journey instead of 39, the round trip being some 9,500 miles longer.

The closure has given renewed impetus to alternative methods: giant tankers of up to 250,000 tons are now being built and Cape Town and Durban harbours are being improved (in the 1956 crisis, 2,700 ships were diverted to South African ports, a shipping tonnage of 25 million). The Israelis plan to build a 42-inch diameter pipeline from Eilat on the Gulf of Aqaba across the Negev Desert to the Mediterranean coast near Ashlekon; tankers of 150,000 tons can berth at Eilat.

to Europe, to the Far East and India, and to North America. The Second World War hostilities in the Mediterranean and North Africa meant that alternative routes had to be found and West Africa in particular benefited by the great improvement programmes to many of its local airstrips and by the construction of new airfields. Today Africa is but a day's journey to any one of the major continents of the world and this has greatly assisted in bringing Africa more into the centre of the world's stage.

The growing use of air transport for shipping exports abroad (especially those of a perishable nature) and of moving food supplies from one region to another is also an important feature in recent years. Fresh fruits are flown from Nairobi to London and dairy produce to Aden, fresh vegetables are flown from Mozambique to the mining districts of Rhodesia, meat supplies are transported from northern Nigeria to the southern cities and also from the stock regions of the Congo to Katanga and the towns in the more humid and tsetse-infested areas. Aircraft are being increasingly used in geological and cartographical surveying, especially in relation to the planning of land resettlement schemes and new cultivation zones. The aeroplane is invaluable for the policing and administration of remote districts in Ethiopia, northern Kenya and South-West Africa. The ease with which security forces can be moved from one trouble spot to another is an important factor in maintaining political stability.

Questions

1 Discuss the relative merits and demerits of rail and road transport in fostering the economy of African states.
2 In what ways have political considerations overridden economic ones in the construction of railways in Africa?

3 Compare the part played by rivers, railways and roads in the internal communications of *either* East Africa or West Africa.

4 Which factors have hampered and which stimulated railway construction in Africa?

5 You are to plan two new railways to supplement those existing between Zambia, Rhodesia and Malawi and the coasts of Africa. With the aid of a sketch-map justify your proposals.

6 Where and why is inland water transport important in Africa south of the Sahara?

7 With the aid of a sketch-map illustrate the main proposals you would make to improve the communications system in your own country in relation to the available resources.

8 Describe the communications system of any one country in Africa and show how it is related to the economic resources of the country.

CHAPTER ELEVEN

TRADE, AID AND DEVELOPMENT PROGRAMMES

Trade

The newly independent territories of Africa rely heavily on the export of primary produce and partially processed minerals for their foreign earnings. All are making great efforts to diversify the range, to increase the exports of their produce and to find new markets. The revenue obtained in this way is preferable to that obtained by loans from abroad since no interest has to be paid on a nation's own efforts. The main difficulties facing the newly emerging states are the lack of capital and trained labour. Some countries are passing through a stage of economic transition and are at present unable to increase or effectively check the decrease in the output of various products.

The Dominance of Traditional Markets

The independent states of Africa are still oriented in their trade to traditional markets, usually those of the former colonial powers who developed the economy to supply their home industries with raw materials. Trade was restricted with other countries and, although many African countries are attempting to widen the range of markets, this dominance still persists. Such organisations as the French Community (see page 210) tend to accentuate the reliance on traditional markets. The former French states of central Africa and the Maghreb are strongly tied to France commercially. Algeria (regarded as part of France from 1870 until 1962) sends 80 per cent of her exports to France and 50 per cent of her

TABLE 33
Britain's Trade with African Members of the Commonwealth

COUNTRY	IMPORTS FROM BRITAIN (AS A PERCENTAGE OF TOTAL)			EXPORTS TO BRITAIN (AS A PERCENTAGE OF TOTAL)			OTHER TRADING PARTNERS IN ORDER OF IMPORTANCE
	1964	1965	1966	1964	1965	1966	
WEST AFRICA Nigeria	28·0	30·9	30·0	41·3	37·0	37·0	U.S.A., Japan, Netherlands
Ghana	27·4	25·8	28·9	23·1	20·9	24·8	W. Germany, U.S.A., E.E.C., Eastern Bloc
Sierra Leone	38·0	34·2	28·3	78·3	65·0	58·0	W. Germany, Netherlands, Japan, France
EAST AFRICA Kenya	33·4	28·3	33·6	22·3	21·3	21·7	W. Germany, Kuwait, U.S.A.
Uganda	35·8	38·4	36·0	29·0	16·8	18·3	U.S.A., W. Germany, India, Japan
Tanzania	36·8	n.a.	n.a.	36·7	n.a.	n.a.	U.S.A., W. Germany, Japan
CENTRAL AFRICA Rhodesia	30·3	30·4	n.a.	23·1	19·9	n.a.[1]	S. Africa, W. Germany, U.S.A.
Zambia	17·7	20·0	22·1	47·0	37·6	32·4	W. Germany, Japan, S. Africa
Malawi	23·4	25·4	35·0 est.	45·4	45·9	n.a.	Rhodesia, S. Africa

[1] Rhodesia's officially recorded total trade with Britain dropped from £29·2 million in 1965 to £4·57 million in 1966.

imports are French; Morocco (French from 1912 to 1956) obtains 55 per cent of its imports from France and sends 45 per cent of its exports there.

Similarly, the Commonwealth countries have strong trading relations with Britain, membership of the Commonwealth ensuring them certain trade preferences over non-members (see Table 33).

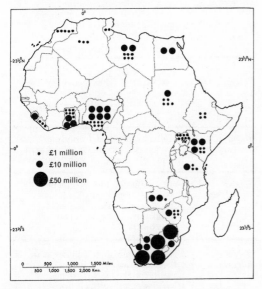

FIG. 1: United Kingdom trade with Africa—exports to Africa July 1965 to July 1966

South Africa, a former Commonwealth member, has always had traditional markets in Britain especially for her fruits and wines. Since her departure from the Commonwealth she has experienced a considerable drop in her sales of these commodities due to the loss of her Commonwealth preference. South Africa still relied heavily on Britain for heavy machinery and electrical goods in 1966; 27·3 per

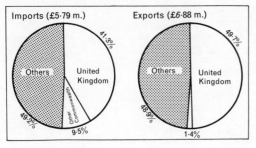

FIG. 2: Gambia—the U.K. as a traditional trading partner, 1965

cent of her imports are U.K. goods and Britain was a market for 33·1 per cent of her exports. The United States is South Africa's second biggest market and supplier, supplying in 1966 17·7 per cent of South Africa's imports and taking 11·2 per cent of her exports; the Republic is thirteenth on the list of suppliers to the U.S. Uranium oxide, diamonds, wool, copper metal and sugar molasses were the main exports while machinery, motor vehicles and agricultural equipment were the main imports.

New Trading Partners

Since the granting of independence to many African states the United States, West Germany and Japan have become increasingly important suppliers and markets. *West Germany* takes more oil than any other nation from Libya (page 202), takes 10 per cent of South Africa's exports, supplies Kenya with 15 per cent of its imports, while her exports to Nigeria increased from £12·5 million in 1963 to £18·0 million in 1964 to £27·4 in 1966 and her imports from Nigeria increased from £21·5 million to

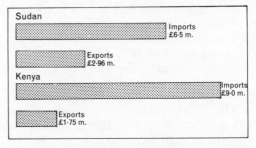

FIG. 3: Sudan and Kenya—trade imbalances with Japan, 1965

£29·0 million in the same period. *Japan* has been actively seeking markets in Africa for her manufactured products but has been rather reluctant to take the equivalent in agricultural produce in return. For example, in 1966 Japan supplied Sierra Leone with 10 per cent of her imports (£3·8 million out of £35·8 million) but took less than £50,000 worth of Sierra Leone's products. Similarly Japan supplied Uganda and Tanzania with over 14 per cent of their imports in 1965 and supplied Kenya with a tremendous volume of expensive high precision articles—cameras, transistor radios, cars, binoculars and other optical instruments—while taking only nominal quantities of agricultural produce in exchange.

Many of Japan's other articles are also in direct competition with African industries—textiles for instance. To check this unfavourable trade the East African territories were forced temporarily to ban all Japanese goods except spare parts. Japanese exports to Uganda, for example, fell from 10·2 per cent in 1965 to 5·4 per cent in 1966 and imports from Uganda adjusted from 2·6 per cent to 4·9 per cent of the total.

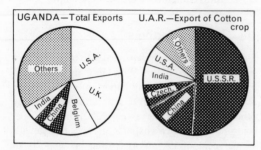

Fig. 4: Uganda and the U.A.R.—relative significance of Communist markets in trade, 1965

Another significant feature of the trend to find new markets is the beginning of trade with *Communist bloc* territories although the volume in most countries is as yet small. Thus the first exports of soda ash left Kenya for the Soviet Union in 1966; Tanzania now supplies East Germany with coffee

TABLE 35
Trade of Selected African States with Communist Bloc Countries

COUNTRIES	COMMODITIES
U.A.R.— Soviet Union	Cotton, rice, vegetables and fruit in exchange for machinery, equipment, oil and coal under trade agreement plan for 1966–70 to increase trade volume from £65 million to £100 million
Ghana— East Germany	Cocoa beans, precious woods, tropical fruit in exchange for machinery and equipment, vehicles, pharmaceuticals and consumer goods
Ghana— Hungary	Cocoa and tropical woods in exchange for construction of brick and lime works and consumer goods
Guinea— Yugoslavia	£2·1 million trade agreement; bananas, pineapples, coffee for textiles, pharmaceutical goods, foodstuffs, spare parts and machinery
Morocco— Bulgaria	100,000 tons of phosphates as well as iron and zinc ore, cotton and citrus fruits for chemical products, fertilisers, tobacco, electrical appliances and radio equipment

TABLE 34
West Germany: The Increase in Trade with Selected African States, 1964 (in millions of £s)

COUNTRY	IMPORTS	% INCREASE/DECREASE ON 1963 IMPORTS	EXPORTS	% INCREASE/DECREASE ON 1963 EXPORTS
United Arab Republic	11·2	−3·0	36·3	+9·0
Libya	82·5	+101·0[1]	8·2	−21·5
Morocco	19·6	+21·1	10·6	+20·9
Algeria	22·1	+9·5	4·8	+26·3
Ghana	13·6	no change	8·9	−9·4
Nigeria	29·7	+27·4[1]	18·1	+43·8
Sudan	10·5	−5·2	5·5	+8·4
Kenya/Uganda	11·4	−6·4	8·7	+22·6
Total Africa Trade and Overall Balance	200·6	+26·3	101·1	+13·0

[1] Due to West Germany's increasing imports of Libyan and Nigerian oil.

and has signed trade agreements with Hungary and Poland; Nigeria exported £2·14 million of goods to Czechoslovakia in 1964 and took £1·35 million worth of Czech goods; Sierra Leone is exchanging agricultural produce for Soviet agricultural machinery; Morocco has concluded trade and technical agreements with the Soviet Union and the People's Republic of China; Ghana's trade with the Eastern bloc has increased from 8·2 per cent to 21 per cent of her exports and from 7·5 to 14·7 per cent of her imports between 1962 and 1966. These new trading partners are, to a certain extent, replacing South Africa as a supplier and market.

Most African governed nations refuse to trade with South Africa on account of its apartheid policy. Kenya's exports to the Republic fell from nearly £1·9 million in 1963 to £671 in 1964, while Uganda and Tanzania exported nothing at all to South Africa in 1964 whereas in 1963 they exported goods to the value of £1·15 million and £0·55 million respectively. Since Rhodesia's unilateral declaration of independence many African states have severed diplomatic and trade relations. Such is the influence of politics in the economic sphere.

The Composition of Exports

Since the development of secondary industry is only in its infant stages in most countries in Africa it is not surprising that their exports consist largely of raw of semi-processed agricultural and mineral products. In many cases exports are dangerously dominated by one product, as shown in Table 36.

There are several other countries whose exports rely heavily on one crop— Kenya (coffee, 28·8 per cent of exports), Tanzania (sisal, 36·2 per cent), Uganda (coffee, 30·4 per cent), Liberia (iron ore,

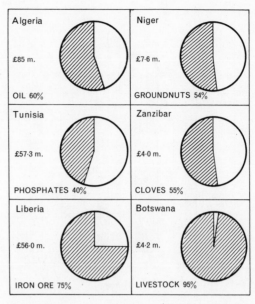

FIG. 5: The dominance of single products in exports of selected African states

75·0 per cent), Gabon (timber, 54·2 per cent), Dahomey (oil seeds, 80 per cent), Senegal (groundnuts, 85 per cent), the U.A.R. (cotton, 70 per cent) (1965 figures). Such one-product-dominance is a weakness in a country's economy. Restrictions by world agreement have caused a cutting back of production of coffee in Kenya, the decline in cocoa prices has caused considerable unease in Ghana, the manufacture of man-made fibres is always a danger to sisal in Tanzania. Moreover, minerals such as oil and iron ore are a wasting asset; although recent mineral finds are tremendous the rate of exploitation by giant companies may soon exhaust them.

TABLE 36
Africa: Domination of Products in Exports

COUNTRY	MAJOR EXPORT	EXPORT VALUE (£million)			% OF TOTAL EXPORTS BY VAL.		
		1964	1965	1966	1964	1965	1966
Libya	Oil	248·0	280·3	351·0	99·1	98·5	98·8
Zambia	Copper	135·0	171·6	230·0	88·5	90·2	90·3
Mauritania	Iron ore	15·4	18·8	n.a.	94·0	n.a.	n.a.
Ghana	Cocoa	72·5	68·2	51·5	64·9	66·1	52·0
Sierra Leone	Diamonds	19·9	18·4	15·8	58·6	58·4	53·4
Sudan	Cotton	32·3	31·2	34·8	46·8	45·9	49·2

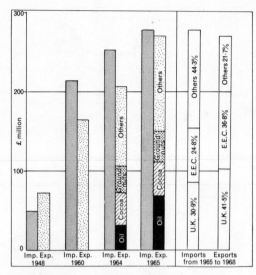

FIG. 6: Nigeria—trade analysis

It is for these reasons that African nations are attempting to make a fuller use of their raw materials by developing secondary industry and exporting manufactured and processed articles. The percentage of manufactured articles in exports is slowly increasing but high imports of manufactured goods, particularly machinery and vehicles, reflect the underdeveloped nature of secondary industry.

These figures in Table 37 are typical of the developing nations and show a marked contrast to heavily industrialised countries, e.g. Britain's manufactured imports represent 32 per cent of the total, but her imports of raw unfinished materials equal 67 per cent.

TABLE 37
Africa: Approximate Percentage of Manufactured Articles in Imports of Selected African States

COUNTRY	% MANUFAC-TURED ARTICLES IN IMPORTS	COUNTRY	% MANUFAC-TURED ARTICLES IN IMPORTS
U.A.R.	45·0	Cameroon	70·1
Ethiopia	68·9	Ivory Coast	69·3
Kenya	60·5	Liberia	71·6
Tanzania	69·4	Nigeria	72·8
Uganda	64·5	Rhodesia	66·2

The Balance of Trade

Among the most important factors affecting a country's balance of trade are the amount of productive land within the territory's boundaries, the degree of industrialisation, the variation in the amount of perishable articles produced (dairy products and fresh fruit for example) as opposed to non-perishable articles (such as mineral ores), and the degree of expensive manufactured articles needed by the population.

In 1966 the East African territories (Kenya, Tanzania and Uganda) imported £219·6 million worth of goods and exported £214·0 million—a slightly unfavourable balance of £5·6 million. On closer inspection the territories are not all in the same fortunate position. Kenya, with its comparatively large number of Europeans (41,000) and Asians (177,000) with their high demands for luxury goods and expensive commodities, its large areas of unproductive land, its high degree of specialisation on cultivation of perishable goods (vegetables, dairy products), and its high imports of machinery, has a very unfavourable balance or trade deficit of £50·1 million (1966—imports, £112·4 million; exports, £62·3 million). Uganda (imports, £42·9; exports, £67·1) and Tanzania (imports, £64·2 million;

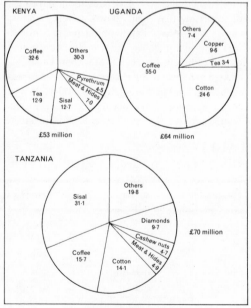

Exports 1964 (excld. interterritorial total)

FIG. 7: East Africa—export percentages, 1964

TABLE 38
Analysis of the Trade of Selected African States

COUNTRY	TRADE WITH ALL COUNTRIES (£ MILLION)				MAJOR EXPORTS	MAJOR IMPORTS
		1963	1964	1965		
Algeria	Exports	237	254	n.a.	Oil and natural gas (60% of exports), citrus fruits, wines, cereals	Cars, constructional machinery, refinery equipment, consumer articles
	Imports	275	264	n.a.		
	Balance	−38	−10	n.a.		
Angola	Exports	58·2	72·9	71·4	Iron ore, crude petroleum, sugar, maize, sisal, coffee	Machinery, refinery and drilling equipment, iron and steel
	Imports	52·1	58·6	69·6		
	Balance	+6·1	+14·3	+1·8		
Botswana	Exports	4·0	4·2	5·1	Livestock products (95% of exports), gold, manganese, asbestos, citrus, groundnuts, cotton	n.a.
	No import figures are available					
Dahomey	Exports	4·6	4·7	4·8	Palm cabbage products (35%), palm oil (27%), groundnuts, cotton, fish, coconuts, coffee, copra, castor oil, tobacco	Foodstuffs, vehicles, machinery, clothes, petroleum products
	Imports	11·9	11·2	12·3		
	Balance	−7·3	−6·5	−7·5		
Gabon	Exports	26·2	33·5	n.a.	Okoumé (a tropical hardwood), manganese, crude oil, uranium concentrate	Heavy equipment and consumer goods (55%), factory plant, vehicles
	Imports	17·2	19·9	n.a.		
	Balance	+9·0	+13·6	n.a.		
Ivory Coast	Exports	82·0	106·0	94·0	Timber, coffee, cocoa	Factory equipment
	Imports	61·0	84·0	81·0		
	Balance	+21·0	+22·0	+13·0		
Kenya	Exports	70·8	79·4	81·5	Coffee (18%), tea (7·5%), sisal, pyrethrum, meat products	Vehicles, consumer goods, fuel oils, canned goods, clothes
	Imports	82·9	87·9	100·7		
	Balance	−12·1	−8·5	−19·2		
Liberia	Exports	28·9	47·1	56·4	Iron ore (75%), rubber (16%), diamonds, coffee	Iron ore mining equipment, transport vehicles
	Imports	40·0	39·6	42·1		
	Balance	−11·1	+7·5	+14·3		
Malawi	Exports	10·8	12·4	n.a.	Tea, cotton, tobacco and groundnuts account for 85% of exports	Coal and consumer articles from Rhodesia account for 40% of imports, factory equipment and plant
	Imports	15·0	16·2	n.a.		
	Balance	−4·2	−3·8	n.a.		
Morocco	Exports	137·2	154·3	153·7	Phosphates, citrus, meat, cotton, manganese, cobalt	Factory machinery, consumer goods, vehicles, cereals, fodder for livestock
	Imports	159·8	163·9	162·0		
	Balance	−22·6	−9·6	−8·3		

COUNTRY	TRADE WITH ALL COUNTRIES (£ million)				MAJOR EXPORTS	MAJOR IMPORTS
		1963	1964	1965		
Mozambique	Exports	36·1	37·9	n.a.	Cotton, cashew nuts, tobacco, sugar, tea, sisal, copra	Oil and petroleum products (largely for transit), vehicles, constructional equipment
	Imports	50·7	55·7	n.a.		
	Balance	−14·6	−17·8	n.a.		
Niger	Exports	7·7	7·6	n.a.	Groundnuts (over half)	Textiles, plant and equipment
	Imports	8·6	11·7	n.a.		
	Balance	−0·9	−4·1	n.a.		
Nigeria	Exports	186·7	214·6	267·0	Oil (over 25%), palm nuts and oil, groundnuts and oil, and cocoa	Consumer goods, vehicles, factory plant and equipment
	Imports	207·5	253·9	274·4		
	Balance	−20·8	−39·3	−7·4		
Senegal	Exports	39·5	43·8	n.a.	Groundnuts (over 75% of exports) cotton, sugar, fish, tropical fruits	Rice, manufactured goods, factory equipment and machinery
	Imports	59·9	61·3	n.a.		
	Balance	−20·4	−17·5	n.a.		
Somali Republic	Exports	11·4	12·9	11·9	Livestock and bananas	Animal feedstuffs, food processing equipment, textile plant machinery, constructional equipment
	Imports	16·0	19·5	17·7		
	Balance	−4·6	−6·6	−5·8		
Tanzania (mainland)	Exports	63·9	70·2	62·9	Sisal (23%), cotton (19%), coffee (14%), gold, diamonds	Vehicles, constructional equipment, factory plant, fuel oils
	Imports	40·4	44·0	50·0		
	Balance	+23·5	+26·2	+12·9		
Tunisia	Exports	52·9	57·3	62·9	Phosphates and other minerals (40%), oil, wine, olive oil	Processing machinery, cereals, animal feedstuffs, mining equipment, steel plant
	Imports	93·7	110·8	129·1		
	Balance	−40·8	−53·5	−66·2		

exports, £84·6 million) with their less demanding populations, greater productive areas, and greater mineral wealth—diamonds, gold, copper—are in a more favourable position.

In general, therefore, countries which rely on large exports of agricultural produce in return for heavy imports of expensive manufactured articles show an adverse trade balance. Countries in this category include the Sudan and Ghana (Table 39).

The sudden discovery of an economically important mineral could, however, change the position drastically. Nigeria's oil exports, for example, have produced a £26·9 million favourable trade balance in 1966. Compare this with an adverse balance of £7·4 million for the whole of 1965.

TABLE 39
Adverse Trade Balances
(millions of £s)

	1960	1961	1962	1963	1964	1965	1966
Ghana	−33·5	−52·6	−28·2	−21·6	−7·0	−58·3	−38·5
Sudan	−0·3	−20·6	−11·3	−20·4	−26·8	−4·3	−6·7

Mauritania's balance of trade moved into surplus in 1963 and was £10·8 million in 1964 compared with a deficit of £11.7 million in 1962, a sharp improvement which is due almost entirely to the export of iron ore; Libya's oil discoveries have had the following effect shown in Table 40.

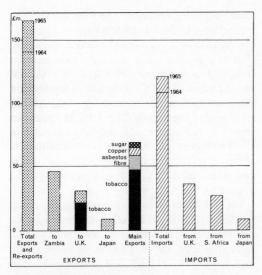

FIG. 8: Rhodesia—trade analysis, 1965

TABLE 40
Libya: The effect of Mineral Production on Trade Balances (millions of £s)

YEAR	1960	1961	1962	1963
Surplus or Deficiency	−56·3	−45·4	−22·9	−49·5

1964	1965	1966
176·8	+191·9	+224·9

The concept of the common market, that is, the removal of trade barriers and customs duties between the former territories of neighbouring states to promote trade and widen markets, has met with varying degrees of success in Africa. The *Central African Federation* (between Northern Rhodesia, Nyasaland and Southern Rhodesia) was formed in 1953 but from the start it was doomed to failure. The Federal Government took over responsibility for external affairs, posts and telegraphs, communications, agriculture and trade. At first there were visible economic benefits from the free movement of goods between the territories. But the countries are vastly different politically and racially, Southern Rhodesia—now Rhodesia— being a zone of European settlement (population—3·7 million Africans, 240,000 Europeans), Northern Rhodesia—now Zambia (Africans 2·7 million, Europeans 80,000), while Nyasaland—now Malawi (4 million Africans,

9,000 Europeans) is almost completely African. Moreover, Zambia produces little that is needed in Rhodesia except copper and her former partners in the Federation were and are small markets; Rhodesia's imports were £6·9 million and Malawi's £0·5 in 1964. With imports of £30·9 million out of a total of £78·2 million from Rhodesia, Zambia had a very unfavourable trade balance with that country. For these and political reasons the Federation was dissolved in 1963. It would now appear that Zambia and Rhodesia at least will drift even further apart and that economic trade barriers will be increased rather than eased.

Until quite recently the idea of a *common market in East Africa* (Kenya, Uganda and Tanzania) was strong. It has everything to recommend it. The three had been governed by Britain who had imposed similar systems of local government and education and had run essential services such as railways and harbours, posts and telegraphs, defence, currency distribution and trade through the East African High Commission which was formed in 1948. Except for certain goods there were no customs duties between the territories. Kenya found valuable markets for her manufactured articles and high quality produce; Uganda found a large demand for her sugar, cottonseed oil and raw tobacco and exported electricity to Kenya; Tanzania's chief interterritorial exports were raw tobacco, coconut oil and pulses.

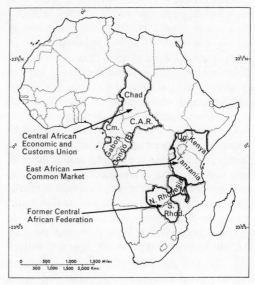

FIG. 9: Africa—common markets referred to in text

207

The trend seemed to be leading to the break-up of the common market in East Africa. Protective trade tariffs were placed on certain interterritorial imports by all three territories to foster their own industries, and each territory now has its own banking and monetary system based on the pound.

The fundamental cause underlying the beginnings of the trend to break up the E.A. Common Market is the feeling (as in the Central African Federation) that the profits of the market may not be equally shared. In the past Kenya has attracted most of the secondary industrial development, especially at Nairobi and Mombasa, and the value of her exports (mainly processed or manufactured articles) to the other two territories has steadily increased without a corresponding increase in imports. Two solutions have been put forward—the sharing of profits and costs fairly among the three territories and the establishment of industries in underdeveloped regions by giving incentives to investors.

The break-up of the E.A. Common Market may be detrimental to the economy. Industrialists are attracted by large markets and, as a customs-free market, East Africa has a population of 29 million potential buyers. Divided, it becomes three separate smaller markets of 10 million (Tanzania), 9·8 million (Kenya) and 8 million (Uganda). Again, with agreement among the three territories, industries could be located in the most favourable spots; with each territory pursuing its own industrialisation programme there is bound to be duplication of certain industries.[1] Planned industrialisation is being successfully carried out in the Central African Economic and Customs Union (see below). The cost of administering railways and harbours, post and telegraphs and other services on a separate basis would be much greater than at present.

The signing of the treaty on East African Co-operation on 1 December 1967, will do much to further common market principles among the three territories. Under it, the countries will have a common external tariff, will abolish quantitative restrictions on manufactured goods, and abolish tariffs among the three countries themselves.

The Central African Federation and the East African Common Markets are concepts formed

under colonial governments and have since proved unacceptable to the independent African states. *The Central African Economic and Customs Union* (the UDEAC) formed on 1 January 1966 between Gabon, Congo-Brazzaville, Chad, the Central African Republic and Cameroon is an organisation which has stemmed from the desire of the African governments themselves. The UDEAC countries cover 1 million square miles and have a population of 9·5 million people. The main economic products of the region include cocoa, coffee, cotton, manganese, uranium, diamonds, petroleum, bauxite and tropical timber.

The five states as separate entities have several problems. Gabon and Congo are amongst the smallest nations in Africa with less than 1 million population each, the resources of all territories are underdeveloped and the C.A.R. and Chad have no access to the sea. But the states, all former French possessions, have a common language and similar institutions and had been integrated from 1910 to 1959 in the Federation of French Equatorial Africa. The most significant measure of co-operation is the system of duties and taxes aimed at encouraging trade and industry. The more populous markets of the interior states, who are seriously handicapped by their position in setting up industries and exporting materials, are compensated for loss of customs duty if they purchase goods from within the union from the new industries in countries near the coast. A single tax replaces a whole series of taxes and dues levied on imports and exports and manufactured items, the tax divisible between the territories annually.

Within the Union trade and industrial growth have been logically planned. Chad, for example, foregoes establishing a cement plant but buys from a new factory in North Cameroon; in exchange Chad obtains certain advantages in textile industry and trade. Again, the five states reached agreement on the setting up of the oil refinery at Port Gentil, feeling that this was the best geographical location (construction began in June 1966); when the market demand justifies it a second refinery is to be built in Cameroon. The Trans-Cameroon Railway was begun in late 1964 to link the C.A.R. and Chad with Cameroon (see Fig. 10:**2**, page 193).

In southern Africa also there appears to be the emergence of a common market; the smaller countries here—Lesotho, Swaziland and Botswana—

---

[1] As, for example, the oil refineries at Mombasa and Dar es Salaam.

have very close economic ties with South Africa and are entirely dependent on South Africa's infrastructure. They have a common currency and a large proportion of their working population finds employment in the Republic. Despite political differences, Zambia's trade with South Africa has lost none of its importance. There are many examples of economic co-operation as, for example, between South Africa and Mozambique on the construction of the new Cabora Bassa dam project. South Africa would naturally dominate this emerging common market for, of the national product of the ten territories estimated at £4,500 million in 1965, 67 per cent of it is in South Africa. Moreover, of the 45 million population of the region two out of every five people live in the Republic, 75 per cent of the interregional trade of approximately £270 million is accounted for by trade with South Africa, and South Africa possesses over 65 per cent of the railway mileage of the common market.

The significance and success of logical planning of economic resources on a regional basis which goes beyond political boundaries has been demonstrated by the UDEAC. The Union has gained a large measure of its success because it stemmed from a genuine desire of its member states to improve their common economic status and was not a system superimposed by foreign governments. The economic success of a union between politically separate states could be one of the first stages in the growth of such ideas on the continent of Africa; it is an essential prerequisite for the sound economic development of the continent's resources.

Aid and Development Programmes

The new African nations are in the first stages of independent economic development after sixty years of colonial rule. It is clear that the African states will not be in a position to develop their economies and their administrative and social systems entirely on their own. These systems of social government, welfare and administration, introduced during the colonial era, are beneficial but entirely non-productive and African nations at their present stage of development cannot be expected find the funds to support these systems and at the same time to expand their economies.

Economic expansion in the new African nations depends on several factors. Most important is the encouragement of the efforts of the African peoples themselves by introducing programmes of development, self-help, new secondary industries and agricultural projects. But these programmes cost money and, at present, some of this must be obtained from external sources. This overseas aid must be regulated so that it is not so high that it tends to discourage greater efforts within the recipient country, and the amount must be related to the ability of the country to meet the recurrent costs of the projects financed. Moreover, most recently independent countries in Africa desire to be independent of foreign aid as soon as possible and they will not wish to have their development programmes too heavily dependent on money from overseas sources.

Aid may come from two main sources apart from that generated in the country itself. It may be private aid in which a company makes a direct investment

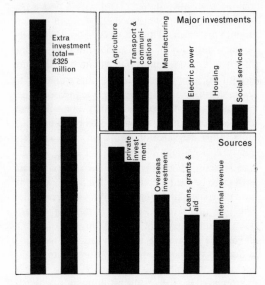

FIG. 10: Kenya's Development Programme, 1965-70

and sets up a subsidiary organisation in the country concerned. This is very advantageous because the country gets the benefit of technical experts, direct financial investment, a continuing flow of capital from the re-investment of profits, and the employment of local staff. A less useful form of investment is where a loan is raised in an overseas money market for investment in some enterprise in an African country. This is termed an 'indirect loan' but it means that money flows out of the country concerned in the form of dividends to shareholders abroad.

The second type of loan is that provided by government bodies overseas, termed Public Aid. Such money can be obtained from various organisations:

a Large international organisations such as the International Bank for Reconstruction and Development (the I.B.R.D.), the World Bank and the United Nations Fund.

b Economic Communities such as the European Economic Community (the E.E.C.) or the Special Commonwealth African Assistance Plan.

c From single governments, e.g. a direct loan from West Germany to Togo. This is termed bilateral aid.

This aid may be in the form of straight loans, 'soft' loans, or direct grants. A straight or ordinary loan may have an interest rate of between 6 and 8 per cent and be repayable immediately over a term of from 15 to 20 years. This is not very useful to a developing country for it finds it has to start repaying the money with interest immediately, and over the long term of the loan, interest charges alone amount to 25 per cent and more. Moreover, such loans take a very high proportion of the country's income from its sales of exports just when it needs ready cash the most. Thus the value of such loans is greatly reduced. A 'soft' loan however has a lower interest rate—usually about 3 per cent, the first payments need only be made after about ten years, and the term of repayment is stretched over a longer period. This gives the recipient chance to develop its economy before repayment begins.

There is always the tendency among receiving nations to view aid from single countries or continental associations with some reserve and to fear interference in the recipient country's internal affairs. Yet it is not unnatural for the donor countries to expect evidence of the wise use of the money which they loan or grant. *The European Economic Community* (France, West Germany, Italy, Holland and Belgium) has trade relations with several African states who provide markets and raw materials, while customs duties are so arranged as to give them trade preferences over non-members. Some African nations see such a community as a genuine attempt at closer co-operation, others regard it as merely another form of exploitation which

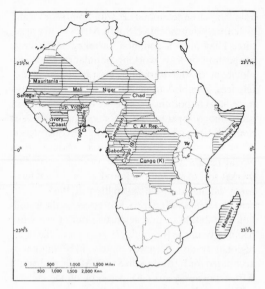

FIG. 11: Africa—associate members of the E.E.C.

will benefit Europe more than Africa. Britain also provides trade preferences, technical, economic and educational aid to African *Commonwealth* members. The *Franco-African Community* (La Communauté) formed in 1958 is also an association of states, all formerly French administered. The original French conception of internal self-governing members

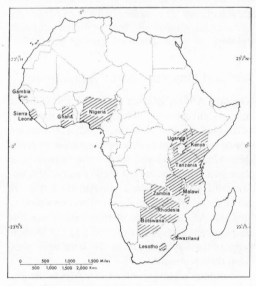

FIG. 12: Africa—members of the Commonwealth

within an economic framework was unacceptable to African governments; Guinea refused to join and the others obtained full independence but retained the framework of the Community for their own economic plans. Customs unions have been formed (see page 208) and the aims of the Community are to foster agricultural production, improve public health, education, transport, mining and energy production.

The development of such organisations, while a step in the right direction, has not resulted in the fostering of really strong and trusting bonds of trade and economic association between Africa and the western European nations. The hard-won independence of the African states is still new and the new

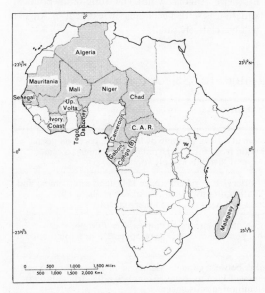

FIG. 13: Africa—members of the Community

nations are slightly suspicious of any aid originating from former colonial rulers. They prefer instead the aid and assistance provided by non-political bodies such as the *United Nations Economic Commission for Africa* (the UNECA). It is appropriate here to note the aims of this body which was founded on 29 April 1958 and which meets regularly in Addis Ababa. These are:

'To promote and facilitate concerted action for the economic development of Africa, including its social aspects, with a view to raising the level of economic activity and the level of living in Africa,

and for maintaining and strengthening the economic relations of countries and territories of Africa, both among themselves and with other countries of the world.'[1]

The Commission sponsors research, studies problems of economic and technological development, formulates development policies and provides advisory services for its member states in Africa.

The Use of Development Aid

How do development programmes work and how is the foreign aid used? One can only answer these questions by examining their application in selected countries (see Table 41) which have varying stages of development. It must be remembered that such aid is supplementary to that generated in the country itself. Let us consider one of the poorest countries in Africa first—*Dahomey*.

With a population of 2·5 million and a comparatively high density of 52 per square mile, a persistent trade deficit (Table 38, page 205) and a lack of important raw materials, Dahomey's economy is one of the poorest in West Africa. Her overall trading position deteriorated in 1965 and the value of her main export, palm cabbage, fell by 70 per cent; groundnut sales fell by 35 per cent, but there was an increase in the sales of palm oil and cotton. Dahomey depends very largely on France to buy her produce although she also exports to neighbouring West African countries. Her high level of imports (£12·3 million in 1965) comprises vehicles, foodstuffs, machinery, clothes and petroleum products.

Dahomey is thus a poor country and has to rely almost entirely on outside aid to cover her budget deficit and to finance the development of industry and social services. Between 1961 and 1966 French technical assistance and financial aid amounted to £27·8 million while considerable assistance has been received from the E.E.C. and the United States (which is helping to construct a new harbour at Cotonou). Various schemes are under way to improve cotton, palm oil, coffee and tobacco industries. Dahomey has few mineral resources of any kind but a Canadian firm has built an aluminium rolling mill which came into production in 1967. A

[1] Page 51, 'Co-operation for Economic Progress', U.N. Office of Public Information, New York.

Five-Year Plan has been inaugurated by the government which will concentrate on rural and agricultural development; about 75 per cent of the money for this plan will have to come from overseas sources and Dahomey will obviously have to rely on foreign aid for many years to come.

Political disturbances can have a severe effect on the economy of countries in Africa. We have already seen how Mozambique has lost considerable revenue because of the oil embargo on Rhodesia (page 161). Portugal's other African territory, *Angola*, is also suffering because of political uncertainties. Angola's economic prospects are potentially good. She had a trade surplus of £14 million in 1964, her sugar exports in 1965 increased more than 50 per cent over the 1964 total and her maize exports by over 60 per cent. Krupps of Germany and a

Danish-British consortium are developing the Cassinga iron ore field and Japan has agreed to import 4 million tons of ore between 1968 and 1973. The Portuguese oil company, Petrangol, is to invest almost £20 million over a five-year period in developing oil reserves in the Cuanza and Congo Districts and oil production is to be increased by 2 million tons annually to help meet a growing demand in South Africa. Belgium's Petrofina Company has interests in the oilfields and Britain has a stake in the Benguela Railway. But apart from these activities there has been little really large-scale investment despite extensive government measures to attract foreign investors. This is a direct result of political uncertainty in Portugal itself and disturbances in northern Angola. Until the long-term political situation is settled economic investment in Angola will be relatively small.

TABLE 41
Summary of Aid and Development Programmes for Selected African States

COUNTRY	SOURCES OF AID (OTHER THAN INTERNAL)	NEW DEVELOPMENTS
Ivory Coast	E.E.C., I.B.R.D., France	New Dam at Kossu, planting of 100,000 acres of oil palms (£12 million from E.E.C.), £6 million oil refinery, a cement plant, several sawmills and plywood factories
Kenya	U.K., U.S.A., W. Germany, I.B.R.D., Israel, Sweden	Seven Forks H.E.P. scheme (page 151), land resettlement and consolidation, improvement of harbour facilities at Mombasa and Kisumu, road improvement
Morocco	I.B.R.D., A.I.D., Kuwait Development Bank	Extension of Safi chemical complex, Renault motor car assembly plant, agricultural development, a new international airport
Niger	U.S.A., France, W. Germany, U.N. Special Fund, I.D.A., E.E.C., I.M.F.	Road link between capital, Niamey, with Zinder. Four Year Development Plan to spend £62 million (70% from abroad) on agricultural improvements
Somali Republic	Italy, U.S.A., E.E.C., U.N., I.M.F., Saudi Arabia, U.S.S.R., W. Germany	Banana fibre and textile plants, extension of port of Berbera, fish canning factory, oil prospecting
Tanzania	U.N. Special Fund, I.D.A., U.S. Agency for International Development, China, U.S.S.R., Finland, Denmark, Sweden, Norway, Italy, Canada and W. Germany	Secondary industrial development, extension of existing H.E.P. supplies, extension of agricultural schemes, research on irrigation possibilities in Central Province, new cotton ginneries, experimental farms
Tunisia	World Bank, W. Germany, U.S.A., Italy, Consultative Group for Aid	Opening of El Borma oilfield (June 1966), natural gas discoveries, opening of Menzel Bourguiba steelworks, expansion of existing phosphate workings, Four-Year Plan for agricultural improvement
Uganda	W. Germany, U.K., U.S.A., I.B.R.D.	Expansion of secondary industry (textile, steel, milk processing, distilling, clothing, glass, bicycles, polyethylene), diversification in agriculture

Senegal is a good example of a country which has realised the need to diversify its economy since it relies almost entirely on the production of groundnuts (75 per cent of exports). To embark on a programme of diversification Senegal will need plenty of capital. Under her present Four-Year Plan (1965–1969) Senegal is expanding production of rice to reduce imports, developing sugar and cotton plantations and giving attention to increasing production of bananas, tomatoes, pineapples, fishing and cattle raising. Foreign aid to finance these programmes and to establish processing plant is being provided largely by France and the E.E.C. (the latter provided £7.6 million between 1963 and 1966).

Some countries depend on one foreign power to supply them with the necessary finance for their development. *Liberia* has long looked to the United States for assistance but there are signs that this monopoly is decreasing. Nevertheless, Liberia still relies for the bulk of her foreign capital inflow from U.S. sources. U.S. suppliers have instigated plans for a £9·6 million hydro-electric plant at Mount Coffee and a £2·5 million water supply programme, and American companies have also made investigations to find opportunities in the pharmaceutical, soluble coffee, and distilling industries. An agricultural programme has been planned with aid from the Food and Agricultural Organisation (the F.A.O.) and a £1·5 million loan is to be provided by the I.B.R.D. for two roads to farming and rubber producing areas. A Five-Year Plan is now being prepared to co-ordinate these projects.

Gabon and Mauritania are two African countries whose economy is being transformed by overseas investment. In the case of *Mauritania* we have seen the tremendous significance of foreign investment in the iron ore mining industry (page 169). But Mauritania possesses several other minerals vital to modern industry and these have attracted aid and finance from all over the world. One of the larger of recent mineral discoveries is a 30-million ton deposit of copper at Akjoujt, initially developed by a French consortium which constructed installations at Akjoujt. They were replaced by an international group consisting of U.S., Canadian and French concerns; several leading Japanese firms are also interested in the project while numerous other foreign firms are engaged in prospecting for oil, gypsum, manganese, and titanium. As is usually the case, once the spotlight has been thrown on a country it attracts attention from other organisations. The E.E.C. for example is partly financing the present Four-Year Plan which entails the improvement of transport and communications and urban development. Further funds are being made available for the development of Port Etienne.

Gabon, encouraged by the discovery of large deposits of important minerals, has embarked on a new Five-Year Plan (1966–1970) which gives priority to the expansion of mineral production, the further development of timber processing and the encouragement of secondary industrial undertakings. Industrial projects under the Plan include the building of an oil refinery, a brewery, a battery plant, a cement factory, and a glass works. It is hoped that foreign private investment will provide 60 per cent of the total finance. Investment in other ventures include the exploitation of Gabon's high-grade iron ore deposits by the construction of a 350-mile long railway to a new deep-water port by a consortium including the World Bank, the expansion by Shell-Gabon of oil production from newly discovered fields, and the financing of geological research, mineral prospecting and rural development by the French Government.

Other countries in Africa are not as fortunate as Gabon and Mauritania, for they do not possess large deposits of minerals and their economies are precariously based on one product. The newly independent state of *Botswana* (formerly Bechuanaland) obtains 95 per cent of its export revenue from the sales of livestock and livestock products. During the last few years, a severe drought badly damaged the country's economy and 400,000 cattle, about 25 per cent of the total, were lost. It is hoped that copper deposits will be found in workable quantities in the Matsitamma area and that production of sodium carbonate from the Makarikari salt pans will provide additional revenue. There are also some deposits of low- and medium-grade coal which could be used to provide future power. These may ease Botswana's economic situation, but at present famine relief has to be provided for 60 per cent of her population and the country is relying on overseas aid from Britain to cover the three years from 1967 to 1970. *Lesotho* (Basutoland) is in much the same position as Botswana. It would seem that, in view of their land-locked geographical position and the fact that a high proportion of their male workers are dependent on the Rand mines for their incomes, that these two countries will eventually become completely dependent on South Africa unless aid is available to maintain their economies.

Conclusion—The Need for Co-operation

Africa is the continent of the future, for in no other continent is there such a huge potential for development. But the overriding problem which faces Africa as it emerges from colonial rule is the hindrance to economic growth of individual countries caused by the artificial division of the continent into 49 separate states, a division stemming from the political ambitions of European states of some 75 years ago. That these political divisions bear little relation to the distribution of population and the economic needs of Africa can be gathered from the facts that nearly one-third of Africa's total population is contained in three countries (the U.A.R., Ethiopia and Nigeria), a further third in eight other countries, and the rest among some 38 states which, although several times larger than many European countries, have populations no greater than some European cities.

Are the smaller African states doomed to only gradual economic growth, their revenues too small to provide for ambitious programmes of development, or must they continue to supplement their finances with overseas loans for development when it is their desire to be economically independent from outside help at the earliest possible opportunity? The real answer to economic viability is economic integration with other African nations on a regional basis. On their own, such countries are economically unbalanced, but seen within a regional framework within Africa they would be able to plan their economies and avoid unnecessary waste and duplication of effort and investment.

The world today displays a general pattern of co-operation which is evolving in many regions. While the idea of a global union among all nations is still remote there is the definite emergence of regional groupings among nations. Throughout history people have grouped together for defence or for economic advancement—the Greek City States, the Hanseatic League, the Customs Union of nineteenth-century German states. The most successful alliances have not been those formed for political

reasons but those which have been based on economic activities, e.g. the European Common Market has stimulated the economy of Western Europe and formed a strong balancing power between Russia and the United States; in Asia, regional groupings have been formed to remove trade barriers and promote economic growth; in the Americas the Central American Common Market has increased commercial activity within its sphere from some £11 million in 1961 to £53 million in 1966.

Thus, while political co-operation is often vague and based on 'a gentlemen's agreement', economic co-operation with its abolition of customs duties and high degree of legislative agreement results in a large measure of practical action and integration between participating countries. But religious and political ideals and differences often form barriers or at least strong obstacles to economic integration as, for example, between the Maghreb Arab states and the U.A.R., or between the strongly Islam-orientated north African states and the African states south of the Sahara. The Commonwealth membership of English-speaking African countries and the membership of French-speaking African countries in the E.E.C. are outward-looking tendencies, whereas the national pride of newly emergent countries is yet another factor reacting against regional economic integration.

Yet it is remarkable how the former British- and French-governed territories have found a common basis amongst themselves on which to establish narrower or wider group organisations, and in addition have found sufficient common interests on which to found supra-regional groupings to include nations from both former French and British territories.

What is the record of integration on a regional basis among independent African states?

The first common market can be said to have originated in the Customs agreement between Kenya and Uganda in 1917 with Tanganyika becoming a third member in 1927. We have seen that the three East African territories have recently realised the value of such co-operation (page 207) and at the same time there are signs of a new community developing, consisting initially of seven states (Ethiopia, Burundi, Kenya, Malawi, Mauritius, Tanzania and Zambia) and interest has been shown by Uganda and Malagasy. The 'East African Seven' met in Lusaka in October 1965 and agreed on the possible

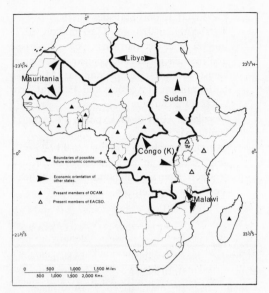

FIG. 14: Africa—possible future economic unions

formation of an East African Common Market in 1970, within which there would be the gradual removal of customs formalities.

The *Union of African States* was formed between Guinea, Ghana and Mali in November 1958 with the hope that Liberia would join, its main objective being a political, economic and defensive union, but it was dissolved in 1963 since it failed to attract other members. The *Mali Federation* had similar aims but disintegrated, largely owing to political differences. The *African Entente* was begun in 1959 and achieved more success since it was largely an economic union designed to remove all restrictions on trade between Upper Volta, Ivory Coast, Dahomey and Niger. The *West African Customs Union* founded in July 1959 between all the states of former French West Africa except Guinea has been less successful due to the imposition of protective tariffs by some members. In 1962 the *West African Monetary Union* was formed to establish a single monetary system among members, with a central issuing bank.

In 1960 twelve former French territories founded the *Brazzaville Group* to foster mutual trade and political interests; the group has achieved a relatively high degree of co-operation and has fostered co-ordination of development programmes. This same group founded the *Organisation Commune Africaine et Malagache* (the OCAM) with political and economic objectives, but several states have

withdrawn due to political differences. In some regions a common geographical feature has helped to bring states together for mutual benefits as, for example, the agreement between Mali, Senegal, Guinea and Mauritania for the greater control of the Senegal's waters, especially its damming for irrigation purposes; a similar agreement has been made between states through which the Niger flows. Again we have already seen the economic advantages which have benefited the states belonging to the *Central African Economic and Customs Union* (page 208).

In the Maghreb, however, economic co-ordination between states is proceeding only slowly. Morocco, Libya, Algeria and Tunisia find a great difficulty in the similarity of their products, the long road distances between marketing centres, and the lack of adequate sea-lane communications in the Mediterranean. An interesting bridge between African and Arab states, although largely political, was the formation of the *Casablanca Group* (the U.A.R., Morocco, Ghana, Guinea and Mali), but this association was dissolved when the OAU was formed.

The *Organisation of African Unity* formed in Addis Ababa in May 1963 has been the most successful so far in attracting the attention of all African states although its aims are largely political. All independent states in Africa (except South Africa) have joined this organisation. It could be a possible framework on which to build a wide economic organisation designed to include all African-governed states.

Questions

1 What economic advantages are to be gained by the co-operation of African states within the framework of common markets? Discuss this question with reference to specific examples.
2 With reference to specific examples discuss the trade problems which face the newly independent states of Africa.
3 Discuss the reasons which lead to an unfavourable balance of trade and suggest ways in which African nations can reverse these tendencies.
4 With reference to particular examples discuss the causes which lead to the breakdown and growth of common market concepts in Africa.
5 In what ways are African nations attempting to diversify their exports and their range of markets?

215

6 Illustrate the relative importance of the United Kingdom, the United States, West Germany, Japan and the Communist Bloc nations in the external trade of the African continent.

7 Select any country in Africa with whose trade figures you are familiar. With reference to these figures show to what degree that country's trade is representative of African states as a whole.

8 'Foreign aid is essential for the assured growth of African economies at their present stage of development.' Discuss this statement with reference to particular nations in Africa, and show how foreign aid is being used in your country.

Statistical Exercises

Either in your notebooks or on large sheets of paper to act as wall charts draw pie, bar or simple curve graphs to illustrate the following statistics:

1 The Maghreb and Libya's Trade with the United Kingdom. Figures for 1965 in £millions.

COUNTRY	EXPORTS TO U.K.	IMPORTS FROM U.K.
Algeria	17·97	6·84
Morocco	11·38	4·49
Tunisia	3·50	3·86
Libya	73·80	21·56

2 a South Africa. Origin of Imports 1965:
United Kingdom—28·1 per cent; European Common Market Countries—21·2 per cent; U.S.A.—18·8 per cent; Japan—5·7 per cent; Others—26·2 per cent.
b South Africa: Direction of Trade, 1966/67:

	1966 (£ MILLION)	1967 (£ MILLION)
EXPORTS TO		
Africa	98·1	112·7
America	81·5	66·9
Asia	53·4	102·0
Europe	351·7	363·8
Oceania	5·9	7·2
IMPORTS FROM		
Africa	64·1	71·0
America	181·0	198·2
Asia	111·2	134·2
Europe	438·3	528·2
Oceania	15·3	17·0

3 a Swaziland. Export Statistics for 1965:
Total Value of Exports, £15·1 million (£3·75 million or 25 per cent over 1964); Processed and manufactured goods (sugar, wood pulp, forest products), £8·72 million; Minerals, £5·14 million; Livestock and Pastoral Products, £1·24 million.
b Swaziland. Growth of Exports, 1960–66 (in £millions):
Overall Growth, £6·1 million to £19·25 million; Increase in agricultural and forestry products, from £3·2 million to £12·45 million; Individual commodities,

ITEM	VALUE EXPORTS, 1960	VALUE EXPORTS, 1966
Minerals	£2·95 million	£6·80 million
Cattle	£0·50 million	£1·20 million
Cotton	£0·27 million	£0·70 million
Citrus	£0·09 million	£0·65 million

4 Malawi. Imports from Rhodesia and the United Kingdom:

	1964	1965	1966
Rhodesia	39%	36%	26%
U.K.	23%	25%	35%
Value of total imports (£ million)	14·9	20·0	27·0

5 Zambia. Development Plan 1966–70:
Total Investment, £429 million; Constructional Industry, £250 million; Secondary Industries, £55 million; Education, £48 million; Electric Power, £26 million; Iron and Steel, £12 million; Civil Aviation, £7 million.

6 Trade of the Chad Republic (figures for 1965):
Total Exports Value, 6,720 million fr. C.F.A.; Total Imports Value, 7,700 million fr. C.F.A.; Cotton Exports valued at 520·7 million fr. C.F.A.; Live Cattle Exports valued at 516·7 million fr. C.F.A.; Meat Exports valued at 210·7 million fr. C.F.A.
There are 691 fr. C.F.A. to £1.

7 Rhodesia. Distribution of Trade, 1964/65:

	1964 (£ MILLION)	1965 (£ MILLION)	PERCENTAGE OF TOTAL 1964	1965
IMPORTS FROM				
United Kingdom	32·80	36·35	30·3	30·4
South Africa	26·36	27·46	24·4	22·9
United States	7·35	8·19	6·8	6·8
Others	41·71	44·77	38·5	39·9
Total	108·24	119·79	100·0	100·0
EXPORTS TO				
United Kingdom	30·87	31·44	23·1	19·9
South Africa	10·05	14·44	7·6	9·1
West Germany	7·95	12·91	5·9	8·2
Others	84·59	99·11	63·4	62·8
Total	133·47	157·89	100·0	100·0

N.B. £ totals may vary due to rounding in columns.

8 Zambia. Distribution of Trade, 1964/65:

IMPORTS FROM	£ MILLION 1964	1965	1966	PERCENTAGE OF TOTAL 1964	1965	1966
Rhodesia	30·87	35·54	23·18	39·5	33·7	18·8
United Kingdom	13·41	21·04	27·20	17·2	20·0	22·1
South Africa	16·20	20·69	29·23	20·7	19·6	23·8
Others	17·73	28·10	43·40	22·6	26·7	35·3
Total	78·23	105·37	123·01	100·0	100·0	100·0
EXPORTS TO	1964	1965	1966	1964	1965	1966
United Kingdom	54·48	71·57	80·08	33·1	37·6	32·4
West Germany	21·82	25·17	34·70	13·3	13·2	14·1
Japan	18·55	23·09	34·73	11·3	12·2	14·1
Others	72·90	70·30	97·20	42·3	37·0	39·4
Total	167·76	190·15	246·71	100·0	100·0	100·0

N.B. £ totals may vary due to rounding in columns.

9 Ethiopia. Composition of Trade, 1964:

Commodity	Approx. percentage of exports by value
Coffee	65%
Skins	6%
Hides	1%
Oil Seeds	9·5%
Pulses	5·0%
Miscellaneous	13·5%

Commodity	Approx. percentage of imports by value
Textiles	19%
Machinery and tools	13·5%
Building materials	9·5%
Raw materials	9·5%
Vehicles	15%
Fuels	6%
Medical supplies	2%
Raw cotton	1·5%
Miscellaneous	22%

10 Ghana. Direction of Trade (percentage of total trade):

	1962	1963	1964	1965	1966
IMPORTS FROM					
United Kingdom	33	28	24	21	25
European Economic Community	27	28	29	27	22
U.S.A.	17	15	21	15	14
Eastern Bloc	9	14	12	21	21
Others	14	15	14	16	18
EXPORTS TO					
United Kingdom	35	34	28	26	29
European Economic Community	23	25	24	22	21
U.S.A.	8	7	9	9	16
Eastern Bloc	8	11	15	26	15
Others	26	11	24	17	19

11 The World. 'Invisible Trade' in Tourism, 1964/65:

AREA	TOURIST ARRIVALS		RECEIPTS (£ MILLION)	
	1964	1965	1964	1965
Europe	79,097,082	84,000,000	2,323·7	2,630·0
Middle East	2,459,500	2,850,000	70·0	71·5
Africa	2,185,000	2,336,750	103·6	111·1
Latin America and Caribbean	3,301,000	2,710,000	415·5	470·0
Asia and Australia	2,041,800	2,300,000	164·2	190·5
North America	18,075,000	19,280,000	610·0	670·0
Totals	107,159,382	114,476,750	3,687·0	4,143·1

Table based on U.N. statistics.

APPENDIX 1
THE MODERN STATES OF AFRICA: A FACTUAL SUMMARY

A. North Africa

STATE	AREA (sq. mls.)	POPULATION	RELIGIONS	ECONOMY	TRADE	POLITICAL	CAPITAL
Morocco	171,000	13,700,000	Muslim	*Agriculture*: Cereals, citrus fruits, olives, sheep, goats, cattle, fish *Minerals and Power*: Small coalfields, plentiful hydro-electric power, phosphates, silver, lead, manganese, gold, zinc *Manufactures*: Cement, superphosphates	France, U.S.A., U.K., Western Europe	Partitioned between France and Spain; independent 1956	Rabat (230,000)
Algeria	952,000	11,600,000 (160,000 Europeans)	Muslim	*Agriculture*: Cereals, vines, tobacco, citrus fruits, olives, goats, sheep, poultry *Minerals and Power*: Some coal, hydro-electric power, oil, natural gas, iron ore, phosphates, zinc *Manufactures*: Textiles, footwear, handicrafts	Mainly France	Ex-French department; independent 4 July 1962	Algiers (885,000)
Tunisia	48,000	4,550,000 (160,000 French and Italians)	Muslim	*Agriculture*: Olives, vines, cereals, dates, poultry, goats, sheep, fish *Minerals and Power*: Phosphates, silver, lead, mercury *Manufactures*: Processed agricultural products, carpets, leather, pottery	Mainly France also U.S.A., U.K., Italy	Ex-French protectorate; independent 20 March 1956	Tunis (700,000)
Ifni	740	55,000	Muslim	*Agriculture*: Dates, cereals, cereals (irrigated), fish *Minerals and Power*: None *Manufactures*: None	Spain	Spanish province	Sidi Ifni (not available)

STATE	AREA (sq. mls.)	POPULATION	RELIGIONS	ECONOMY	TRADE	POLITICAL	CAPITAL
Spanish Sahara	103,000	24,000	Muslim	*Agriculture*: Largely desert, nomadic tribes keep a few cattle, goats and camels *Minerals and Power*: Prospecting for oil *Manufactures*: None		Spanish province administered from Canary Is.	Chief Town—Villa Cisneros
Libya	679,000	1,700,000	Muslim	*Agriculture*: Small area of dates, vines, olives, tobacco, sheep, goats, cattle, camels *Minerals and Power*: Oil and natural gas *Manufactures*: Handicrafts—textiles, leather, metalware	U.K., Italy W. Germany, Egypt	Ex-Italian colony; independent 24 December 1951	Tripoli (185,000)
United Arab Republic (Egypt)	386,200	30,100,000	Muslim	*Agriculture*: Cotton, cereals, rice, sugar cane and beet, oil seeds, groundnuts, dates, vines, poultry, cattle, sheep, goats, camels *Minerals and Power*: Coal, petroleum, phosphates, manganese, gold *Manufactures*: Cement, textiles, footwear, sugar refining, oil refining	U.S.A., U.K., W. Germany, Italy, France, U.S.S.R., India, Czechoslovakia, Japan	Occupied by Turkey, France, Britain. British occupation ended 1936, united with Syria in 1958 as U.A.R.	Cairo (3,350,000)

B. Southern Sahara

STATE	AREA (sq. mls.)	POPULATION	RELIGIONS	ECONOMY	TRADE	POLITICAL	CAPITAL
Mauritania	419,000	770,000 (1,000 Europeans) (470,000 white nomadic Moors)	Muslim, traditional	*Agriculture*: Livestock, fishing, poor cereals *Minerals and Power*: Iron ore *Manufactures*: None	France	Ex-French colony; independent 28 November 1960	Nouakchott (6,000)
Mali	465,000	4,400,000 (7,000 Europeans)	Muslim, traditional	*Agriculture*: Nomadic pastoralism, irrigated rice, cotton, groundnuts, river fish *Minerals and Power*: Prospecting for oil, coal, diamonds, gold *Manufactures*: None	Mainly France	Ex-French colony; independent 20 June 1960	Bamako (135,000)
Niger	459,000	3,120,000 (3,000 Europeans, 1 million Hausas)	Muslim	*Agriculture*: Millet, rice, groundnuts, nomadic pastoralism *Minerals and Power*: None *Manufactures*: None	Mainly France	Separate territory within French West Africa; independent 3 August 1960	Niamey (42,000)

Country	Area	Population	Religion	Products	Trade	Political Status	Capital (population)
Chad	496,000	2,800,000 (4,000 non-African)	Muslim	*Agriculture*: Cattle, sheep, goats, horses, camels, millet, sorghum, cotton, groundnuts. *Minerals and Power*: None. *Manufactures*: None	Little outside trade	Ex-German and French colony; independent 11 August 1960	Fort Lamy (92,000)

C. West Africa

Country	Area	Population	Religion	Products	Trade	Political Status	Capital (population)
Senegal	76,000	3,365,000 (62,000 non-African)	Muslim	*Agriculture*: Groundnuts, millet, fishing. *Minerals and Power*: Bauxite, phosphates. *Manufactures*: Fish canning, groundnut oil, textiles. Plans for fertilisers, oil refining, chemicals	Mainly France	Ex-French colony; independent 4 April 1960	Dakar (385,000)
Gambia	4,000	378,000 (about 300 French and British)	Christian, traditional	*Agriculture*: Groundnuts, palm kernels, beeswax, hides and skins production, livestock. *Minerals and Power*: Ilmenite. *Manufactures*: Shelling of nuts	Mainly the U.K.	Ex-British colony and protectorate; independent February 1965	Bathurst (30,000)
Portuguese Guinea	14,000	550,000 (2,500 Europeans)	Traditional	*Agriculture*: Groundnuts, palm oil and kernels, copra. *Minerals and Power*: None. *Manufactures*: None	Portugal	Portuguese province	Bissau (20,000)
Guinea	95,000	3,360,000	Muslim, traditional	*Agriculture*: Rice, oil palm, tropical fruits, cereals, coffee, livestock. *Minerals and Power*: Bauxite, diamonds, iron ore. Aluminium manufacture. *Manufactures*: None	U.K., Australia, U.S.A., Canada, India, New	Ex-French colony; independent 2 October 1958	Conakry (115,000)
Sierra Leone	28,000	2,455,000	Muslim, Christian, traditional	*Agriculture*: Palm, kernels, palm oil, piassava, rice, cocoa, coffee, groundnuts, cassava, bananas, ginger, timber. *Minerals and Power*: Iron ore, chromium, diamonds. *Manufactures*: Oil milling, rice milling, furniture	U.K. mainly	Ex-British colony; independent 27 April 1961	Freetown (130,000)
Liberia	43,000	1,310,000	Traditional, Christian	*Agriculture*: Rubber, much subsistence agriculture, rice, cocoa, coffee, sugar cane, tobacco, palm kernels. *Minerals and Power*: Some hydro-electric power, iron ore, industrial diamonds. *Manufactures*: Handicrafts, soft drinks, rubber processing	U.S.A., U.K., W. Europe	Independent Negro Republic, 1847	Monrovia (81,000)

STATE	AREA (sq. mls.)	POPULATION	RELIGIONS	ECONOMY	TRADE	POLITICAL	CAPITAL
Ivory Coast	124,000	3,670,000 (15,000 Europeans)	Traditional, Christian	*Agriculture*: Coffee, cocoa, bananas, rice, yams, cassava, maize, other grains, cattle rearing, palm kernels, forestry products. *Minerals and Power*: Gold, manganese, copper. *Manufactures*: Fruit canning, coffee and cocoa processing, timber working	France mainly	French annexation from 1893; independent 7 August 1960	Abidjan (215,000)
Voltaic Republic (Upper Volta)	106,000	4,655,000 (5,000 Europeans)	Traditional, Muslim	*Agriculture*: Guinea corn, millet, groundnuts, sisal, cotton, cattle. *Minerals and Power*: None. *Manufactures*: None	Mainly with neighbouring territories	Ex-French colony; independent 5 August 1960	Ouagoudougou (100,000)
Ghana	92,000	8,000,000 (7,500 non-African)	Traditional, Christian, Muslim	*Agriculture*: Cocoa, grains, livestock, plantains, cassava, cocoyams, shea butter, groundnuts. *Minerals and Power*: Hydro-electric power in Volta scheme, bauxite, gold, manganese, diamonds. *Manufactures*: Aluminium smelting, steel (from scrap), chocolate, agricultural processing, canning	U.K., U.S.A., Japan, W. Germany, Netherlands	Ex-British colony; independent 6 March 1957	Accra (340,000)
Togo	20,000	1,565,000	Traditional, Christian	*Agriculture*: Coffee, cocoa, palm oil, palm kernels, groundnuts, maize, cassava, sweet potatoes, copra. *Minerals and Power*: Phosphates. *Manufactures*: None	Mainly France	Formerly German, then divided between British and French; independent 27 April 1960	Lomé (80,000)
Dahomey	45,000	2,500,000 (3,000 Europeans)	Traditional, Christian	*Agriculture*: Oil palm, fish. *Minerals and Power*: Phosphates. *Manufactures*: None	Mainly France	Ex-French colony; independent 1 August, 1960	Porto-Novo (65,000)
Nigeria	357,000	55,660,000 (25,000 Europeans)	Muslim, Christian, Traditional	*Agriculture*: Oil seeds, cocoa, palm oil, timber, cattle, goats, cotton, root crops, rubber, shea butter. *Minerals and Power*: Oil, tin ores and concentrates, coal, columbite, natural gas. *Manufactures*: Timber, oil seed crushing, textiles, handicrafts (metal working, leather, dyeing, mats), meat canning, sugar refining, furniture	U.K., Japan, Netherlands, U.S.A., W. Germany, Italy	Ex-British colony; independent 1 October 1960	Lagos (675,000)

D. North-East Africa

	Area (sq. miles)	Population	Religion	Products	Trade	Political Status	Capital
Sudan	967,000	13,200,000 (part Negro, part Arab)	Muslim, Traditional	*Agriculture:* Cotton, sorghum, dates, sesame, gum arabic, pulses. *Minerals and Power:* Some gold. *Manufactures:* Cotton ginning, textiles, hides and skins preparation	U.K., India, France, Egypt, W. Germany	Ex-British and French colony, independent 1 January 1956	Khartoum (135,000)
Ethiopia	395,000	21,800,000	Eastern Orthodox, Christian	*Agriculture:* Coffee, cotton, sugar cane, citrus fruits, grapes, wheat, barley, sheep, cattle, beeswax. *Minerals and Power:* Hydro-electric power (Koko Dam). *Manufactures:* Handicrafts—weaving, pottery; some agricultural processing	India, Italy, U.S.A., U.K.	Independent kingdom since 11th century B.C., under Italian occupation 1936–1941	Addis Ababa (450,000)
States of Affar and Issas	8,900	81,000 (7,000 Europeans)	Muslim	*Agriculture:* Little economic importance. *Minerals and Power:* Salt chief mineral. *Manufactures:* None	Of little importance	French since 1883; colony since 1901; autonomous since 1957	Djibouti (41,000)
Somalia	246,000	2,300,000	Muslim	*Agriculture:* Sheep, goats, camels, cattle, gum arabic, sesame, maize, cotton, groundnuts, sugar cane. *Minerals and Power:* Salt, prospecting for oil. *Manufactures:* Handicrafts	Mainly Italy	Ex-British and Italian colony; independent 1 July 1960	

E. Equatorial Africa (West)

	Area (sq. miles)	Population	Religion	Products	Trade	Political Status	Capital
Cameroon	182,000	4,600,000	Traditional, Christian	*Agriculture:* Cocoa, coffee, bananas, rice, yams, tobacco, groundnuts, cattle, cotton, rubber, palm oil and kernels. *Minerals and Power:* Bauxite. *Manufactures:* Aluminium smelting, soap, timber, cigarettes	France	Ex-German colony; under French and British mandate since 1922; independent 1st January 1960	Yaoundé (93,000)

STATE	AREA (sq. mls.)	POPULATION	RELIGIONS	ECONOMY	TRADE	POLITICAL	CAPITAL
Central African Republic	238,000	2,800,000 (5,000 non-Africans)	Traditional	*Agriculture*: Millet, maize, cotton, tobacco, cattle *Minerals and Power*: Little *Manufactures*: None	Local countries	Annexed by France 1888; independent 17 August 1960	Bangui (82,000)
Rio Muni (now part of Equatorial Guinea)	10,850	245,000	Christian, Traditional	*Agriculture*: Timber, palm oil, cocoa, coffee *Minerals and Power*: None *Manufactures*: None	Spain	Two Spanish provinces (mainland area of Rio Muni and islands of Fernando Po and Annobon)	Santa Isabel (not available)
Gabon	103,000	460,000 (4,000 non-Africans)	Traditional, Christian	*Agriculture*: Subsistence crops, coffee, rubber, palm oil, palm kernels, valuable hardwood, ivory *Minerals and Power*: Petroleum, manganese deposits, iron ore *Manufactures*: Plywood	France	Annexed by France 1888; independent 17 August 1960	Libreville (31,000)
Congo (Brazzaville)	132,000	870,000 (10,000 non-African)	Traditional, Christian	*Agriculture*: Forestry, bananas, citrus, fruits, rice, groundnuts, coffee, cocoa, tobacco *Minerals and Power*: Small deposits of copper, lead, gold, zinc, diamonds *Manufactures*: Small output of footwear, soap, cigarettes, textiles	France	Ex-French colony; independent 17 August 1960	Brazzaville (137,000)
Congo (Kinshasa)	905,000	15,010,000	Traditional, Christian	*Agriculture*: Oil palm, cotton, gold, rubber, sugar cane, cocoa, fish, livestock, tobacco *Minerals and Power*: Copper, gold, tin, lead, zinc, manganese, coal, hydro-electric power *Manufactures*: Mineral refining, soap, textiles, soft drinks, cigarettes, bricks, cement, car and bicycle assembly, barge construction	Belgium, U.K., U.S.A.	Ex-Belgian colony; independent 14 July 1960	Kinshasa (405,000)

F. Equatorial Africa (East)

STATE	AREA (sq. mls.)	POPULATION	RELIGIONS	ECONOMY	TRADE	POLITICAL	CAPITAL
Rwanda	10,000	2,855,000	Traditional	*Agriculture*: Largely subsistence vegetables and fruits, cattle, coffee, rice, lake fish *Minerals and Power*: None of economic value *Manufactures*: None	With neighbouring territories	Formerly part of German East Africa, Belgian mandate 1916, under U.N. Trusteeship; independent 1 July 1962	Kigali (4,500)

	Area	Population	Religion	Economy, Trade and Political as for Rwanda	Trade	History	Capital
Burundi	11,000	2,650,000	Traditional		With neighbouring territories	Formerly part of German East Africa, Belgian mandate 1916, under U.N. Trusteeship; independent 1 July 1962	Bujumbura (70,000)
Uganda	94,000	8,150,000 (72,000 Asians, 10,000 Europeans)	Christian with some Traditional	*Agriculture:* Coffee, cotton, cattle, tea, sugar cane, maize, oil seeds, tobacco *Minerals and Power:* Hydro-electric power, limestone, copper, tin, small deposits of iron, nickel, chromite, mica, oil, gold, galena *Manufactures:* Tobacco processing, textiles, copper refining, fish freezing, tea and coffee processing, steel from scrap, saw milling, cement and fertilisers	With neighbouring territories, U.K., U.S.A., W. Germany	Ex-British colony, independent 9 October 1962	Kampala (51,000)
Kenya	225,000	10,258,000 (188,000 Asians, 41,000 Europeans)	Traditional, Christian, Muslim	*Agriculture:* Coffee, tea, sisal, pyrethrum, maize, wheat, dairy and beef cattle, sugar cane, subsistence crops *Minerals and Power:* Hydro-electric power development, soda ash, small amounts of copper, diatomite, columbite, gypsum *Manufactures:* Processing of agricultural produce, tanning, footwear, metal containers, soft and alcoholic drinks, vehicle repair, textiles, ship repair, cement	U.K., U.S.A., Japan, Italy, W. Germany, India, neighbouring territories	Ex-British colony and protectorate; independent 12 December 1963	Nairobi (275,000)
Tanzania (mainland)	363,000	12,125,000 (23,000 Europeans)	Traditional, Muslim	*Agriculture:* Sisal, coffee, sugar cane, cotton, groundnuts, rice, oil seeds, tobacco, cattle *Minerals and Power:* Small hydro-electric power schemes, diamonds, gold, lead, coal (untapped) *Manufactures:* Cigarettes, processing of agricultural products, meat canning, footwear, soap, ship repair, hides and skins preparation, cement, paints and dyes	U.K., Japan, India, W. Germany, China, Belgium, Netherlands	Formerly part of German East Africa, then British Trust territory; independent 9 December 1961	Dar es Salaam (135,000)

G. Southern Africa

STATE	AREA (sq. mls.)	POPULATION	RELIGIONS	ECONOMY	TRADE	POLITICAL	CAPITAL
Tanzania (islands)	Zanzibar: 640 Pemba: 380	180,000 140,000 (African and Arab; 500 Europeans)	Muslim, Traditional	*Agriculture:* Cloves, fishing, copra, cattle *Minerals and Power:* Limestone *Manufactures:* Clove oil extraction, lime juice	With Middle East, Mainland China, East Germany	Formerly British, protectorate, independent sultanate in African republic, 1964, now part of Republic of Tanzania	Largest Town— Zanzibar (60,000)
Angola	481,000	5,015,000 (175,000 Europeans)	Traditional, Christian	*Agriculture:* Coffee, cotton, groundnuts, maize, palm oil, sisal, sugar cane, cattle, fish *Minerals and Power:* Hydro-electric power, copper, phosphates, salt, zinc, manganese, oil, diamonds, iron ore *Manufactures:* Processing agricultural produce, canning, fish processing, railway repair	Mainly with Portugal	Portuguese colony	Luanda (230,000)
Zambia (formerly Northern Rhodesia)	290,000	3,890,000 (75,000 Europeans)	Traditional, Christian	*Agriculture:* Maize, tobacco, soy-beans, sugar cane, wheat, vegetables, cattle *Minerals and Power:* Kariba hydro-electric power, copper, zinc, lead, cobalt *Manufactures:* Sugar refining, chemicals	U.K., U.S.A., Canada, India, Australia, W. Germany	Ex-British colony; independent 24 October 1964	Lusaka (88,000)
Rhodesia	150,000	4,020,000 (225,000 Europeans)	Traditional, Christian	*Agriculture:* Tobacco, maize, tea, groundnuts, cotton, citrus fruits, sugar cane, barley, rice, wheat, potatoes, cattle *Minerals and Power:* Asbestos, gold, chromite, coal, lead, zinc, lithium, tin, limestone *Manufactures:* Canned meats, dairying, sugar milling, grain milling, soft drinks, textiles, footwear, cigarettes, cement, chemicals	U.K., S. Africa, U.S.A., Canada	Formerly self-governing colony under British Crown declared unilateral independence on 11 November 1965	Salisbury (315,000)

Country	Area	Population	Religion	Economy	Trade	Status	Capital
Malawi (formerly Nyasaland)	37,000	4,142,000 (7,050 Europeans)	Traditional, Christian	*Agriculture*: Subsistence—millets, maize, rice, groundnuts, cassava, tobacco, tea, cotton, fishing, coffee, tung oil, forestry. *Minerals and Power*: Small hydro-electric power development, small amounts of gold, galena, mica limestone, coal, large bauxite deposits. *Manufactures*: Mainly processing of agricultural products	Mainly with local territories	Ex-British protectorate; independent 6 July 1964	Lilongwe, formerly Zomba (22,000); new capital under construction
Mozambique	298,000	6,790,000 (165,000 non-African)	Christian, Traditional, Muslim	*Agriculture*: Cotton, groundnuts, copra, rice, sisal, sugar cane, cashew nuts, tea, tobacco, timber, cattle, maize. *Minerals and Power*: Coal, bauxite, beryl, mica, gold, silver. *Manufactures*: Cement, sawmilling, fish canning, cigarettes, beer, footwear, railway repair, oil refining, rubber processing, textiles, sisal products	Portugal, S. Africa, Rhodesia, Zambia	Portuguese colony	Lourenço Marques (185,000)
Botswana (formerly Bechuanaland)	275,000	565,000 (3,000 Europeans)	Traditional	*Agriculture*: Sheep, cattle, dairy farming, maize. *Minerals and Power*: Gold, silver, asbestos. *Manufactures*: Meat chilling, dairy products	With neighbouring territories	Ex-British protectorate, then High Commission Territory; independent 30 September 1966	Gaberones (12,000)
Lesotho	12,000	730,000 (2,000 Europeans)	Traditional, Christian	*Agriculture*: Subsistence—maize, sorghum, beans, peas, wheat, cattle, sheep, goats. *Minerals and Power*: None. *Manufactures*: None	With neighbouring countries	British High Commission Territory; independent 4 October 1966	Maseru (12,500)
Swaziland	6,700	290,000 (8,000 Europeans)	Traditional, Christian	*Agriculture*: Cotton, cattle, tobacco, maize, sugar cane, pineapples, citrus, rice, forestry. *Minerals and Power*: Asbestos, iron ore, gold, coal. *Manufactures*: Processing of agricultural produce, timber	With neighbouring countries and U.K.	British High Commission Territory; independent 6 September 1968	Mbabane (9,000)

STATE	AREA (sq. mls.)	POPULATION	RELIGIONS	ECONOMY	TRADE	POLITICAL	CAPITAL
South West Africa	318,000	555,000 (75,000 Europeans)	Traditional	*Agriculture:* Subsistence—maize, potatoes, groundnuts, beans; cattle, sheep, goats, fish *Minerals and Power:* Diamonds, some copper, lead and zinc *Manufactures:* Preparation of skins and karakul pelts, fish canning, fish-meal, fertilizer	With S. Africa and U.K.	Ex-German colony now administered by S. Africa under League mandate[1]	Windhoek (36,000)
Republic of South Africa	472,000	18,500,000 (African 69%, Europeans 19% Coloured 9%, Asian 3%)	Christian, Traditional, Muslim	*Agriculture:* Cattle, sheep, goats, dairying, wheat, maize, citrus, vines, deciduous fruits, sugar cane, tobacco, vegetables, fish *Minerals and Power:* Gold, coal, iron ore, diamonds, uranium, chromite, platinum, copper, manganese, asbestos *Manufactures:* Steel, refining of ores, coal processing for oil, very wide range of secondary industries, ship repair	With U.K., U.S.A., W. Germany, Canada, Rhodesia	British and Dutch colonies became the Union in 1910, independent in 1931, and Republic in 1961	Pretoria (425,000)
Malagasy Republic (Madagascar)	230,000	5,950,000	Muslim, Traditional, Christian	*Agriculture:* Rice, coffee, sugar cane, sisal, cassava, tobacco, maize, cattle, vanilla *Minerals and Power:* Graphite, mica, some coal *Manufactures:* Processing of rice, sisal, sugar, cassava; canning	France mainly	Ex-French colony; independent 4 April 1960	Tananarive (260,000)

[1] On 27 October 1966, the United Nations General Assembly proclaimed the end of South Africa's 50-year old mandate and declared that the territory now becomes a direct responsibility of U.N.O.

APPENDIX 2
THE MAJOR CASH AND SUBSISTENCE CROPS OF AFRICA

A. Cash Crops

NOTE: Those crops marked * are also used substantially as subsistence crops.

CROP	CLIMATIC NEEDS	SOILS	MAJOR PRODUCERS
Banana*	Hot, moist tropical climate: average temperature 68°F (20°C); minimum temperature is 59°F (15°C); total annual water requirement, 55 to 98 inches (1,397 to 2,489mm) with at least 8 inches (203mm) a month; high humidity, warm moist nights, heavy dews are beneficial; dislikes strong winds	Heavy, deep, well-drained soils, organically rich; heavy clays or very sandy soils unsuitable; alluvial river deposits best	Cameroon, Guinea, most tropical African countries produce bananas for subsistence
Cocoa	75 to 82°F (24 to 28°C); found only in lowlands and at moderate elevations, upper limit 2,500 ft; annual average rainfall, 70 inches (1778mm) uniformly distributed; likes shade and high humidity but too high humidity encourages fungus growth;	Loams developed on granite with low quartz content are best; sandy soils rich in quartz unsuitable; soils must retain water, be deep and permeable; best areas are those previously under primary or secondary forest; humus content must be high	Ghana, South-Western Nigeria, Ivory Coast, Cameroon, Fernando Po, Rio Muni
Coffee	Average annual temperature, 68°F (20°C); optimum for Arabica, 63 to 71°F (17 to 22°C); for Robusta, 68 to 77°F (20 to 25°C); altitude ranges from 1,500 to 5,500 feet; likes alternate wet and dry seasons; Arabica lowest annual rainfall, between 40 and 59 inches 1,016 and 1,499mm); Robusta, 79 inches (2,007mm); shading and shelter trees needed	Deep, freshly cleared virgin forest soils with high organic content best; permeable and moisture retaining although not subject to waterlogging	Ivory Coast, Angola, Ethiopia, Kenya, Uganda, Rwanda and Burundi Tanzania, Madagascar
Copra (Coconut Palm)	Uniform warmth; minimum temperature, 68°F (20°C); average annual temperature, 77 to 86°F (25 to 30°C); rainfall, 59 to 79 inches (1,499 to 2,007mm) uniformly distributed; smaller rainfalls tolerated where water-table is high	Deep, sandy loams, rich in humus derived from coral, limestone and volcanic rocks; withstands brackish or salty water	Coasts of central Mozambique, Zanzibar
Cotton	Minimum temperature, lies between 59 and 61°F (15 and 16°C); optimum, 65 and 86°F (18 and 30°C); temperatures should lie between 60 and 77°F (15·5°C) during growing period; regions with 60% cloudiness are unsuitable; water needs are low, often less and 20 inches (508mm); distribution of rain very important; dislikes high humidities	Except for extreme sandy or clayey soils all soils are suitable; well drained with low water-table	U.A.R., the Sudan, Northern Nigeria, Uganda, Tanzania, Congo (K), Rhodesia, Mozambique

CROP	CLIMATIC NEEDS	SOILS	MAJOR PRODUCERS
Groundnut*	Between 57 and 68°F (14 and 19°C) needed during growing season (3½ to 4 months); sensitive to night frost; higher temperatures produce higher oil content; needs plenty of sunshine; rainfall between 20 and 23½ inches (508 and 597mm); dry weather during harvesting	Light, permeable, sandy soils best with no special humus requirements	Senegal, Gambia, Northern Nigeria
Oil Palm	Average annual temperature, 75 to 82°F (24 to 28°C); will not grown at high altitudes (up to 2,300 feet in the Cameroons); temperatures must be fairly constant throughout the year; rainfall, 79 to 118 inches (2,007 to 2,997mm) per annum, minimum 59 inches (150mm) with high soil moisture content; optimum humidity conditions, 50 to 70% at mid-day	Best yields on deep, permeable soils rich in humus; deep roots may tap better sub-surface soils	Throughout tropical rain forest belt at low altitudes about 8° north and south of the Equator, heaviest producers: Nigeria and Congo Basin
Olive	Average annual temperature, 53 to 78°F (12 to 15·5°C); 10 to 30 inches (254 to 762mm) of winter rainfall; in areas with low rainfall trees may be grown but must be more widely spaced	Well-drained calcareous, clayey, sandy or gravelly soils will suffice; can grow in thin soils if well spaced	Tunisia, Libya, Algeria, Morocco
Pineapple	Average annual temperature, 60 to 90°F (15 to 32°C); optimum, 75 to 85°F (24 to 29°C); about 30 inches (762mm) of rain should be available in hot season for growth but can exist on much less than this; over 100 inches (2,540mm) a year is detrimental	Dislikes waterlogged ground; drainage must be good; medium to heavy loams best with slightly acid reaction; soils must be well aerated, rich in nutrients; some heavy black cotton soils found very suitable	In most tropical coastal regions especially Mozambique, Tanzania and Kenya; Kenya Highlands produce large amounts
Rubber	Average annual temperature, 75 to 86°F (24 to 30°C) with a mean of 80°F (27°C); minimum rainfall, 60 inches (1,524mm) with even distribution; will grow up to nearly 2,000 feet in equatorial regions	Deep, not too heavy soil at least 5 feet deep because of tap roots; shallow soils may result in wind damage; high water table injurious to growth	Hot, wet tropical rain forest regions; Liberia, Southern Nigeria, Central Congo
Sisal	Average annual temperature, 68 to 82°F (20 to 28°C), plenty of sunshine; minimum rainfall, about 16 inches (406mm); maximum about 47 inches (1,194mm) per annum; can withstand dry season of up to 3 months duration	Deep sandy soils and loams are most suitable although sisal will flourish on poorer types; Red Earths and Coral derived soils best; heavy, moist soils generally unsuitable although Black Cottons are used	Tanzania, Kenya, Mozambique
Sugar Cane*	Lowest temperature, 68°F (20°C); optimum, between 77 and 82°F (25 to 28°C); found in tropical lowlands mainly but can be grown at up to 3,500 feet; can be grown at much higher altitudes but is less profitable and requires longer growing season (up to two years); cannot stand frost or very long dry periods; needs 70 to 100 inches (1,778 to 2,540mm) of rain per annum or irrigation (in Egypt the cane is watered up to twenty-six times during the growing period); long sunny days are best	Deep and well-drained soil needed; volcanic, sandy, weathered limestone, alluvial, and laterite soils can be used. Must be well aerated and moist heavy sticky soils unsuitable due to bad aeration	In practically all lowland areas of tropical Africa and along Natal coast, South Africa and Nile Valley of Egypt under irrigation

Crop	Climate and temperature requirements	Soil requirements	Regions
Tea	Optimum temperature, 65 to 77°F (18 to 25°C); some varieties can grow at low temperature of 55°F (13°C) and withstand short frost periods; but warm, moist climate is best with high air humidity; evenly distributed rainfall of about 75 to 130 inches (1,905 to 3,302mm); protection from drying winds necessary; shade trees are grown on estates but is now believed that their value is not important to growth	Deep, well-aerated, permeable soil is best; good humus content with good drainage needed; moist soils suitable; former forested land often best	Kenya Highlands, Malawi, Rhodesia, Mozambique, Rwanda, Burundi, Cameroon
Tobacco	Optimum temperature for germination of 88°F (31°C); minimum temperature for growth is 50°F (10°C); optimum, 95°F (35°C); needs 100 to 120 frost-free days; about 16 to 24 inches (406 to 610mm) of rain needed with humid air during harvesting; plenty of sunshine needed	Deep, well-drained, aerated soil best; sandy or loamy types suitable with permeable sub-soils which retain some moisture	Rhodesia, Malawi, Zambia, Natal coast, Lower Nile Valley on commercial scale and in many smaller areas throughout tropics
Vines	Temperature limits, between 48 and 70°F (9 to 21°C) annual average temperature; sensitive to frost and high temperatures; growing period, 180 to 250 days; withstands long dry period due to deep root penetration: about 20 to 26 inches (508 to 660mm) of rain needed annually without irrigation; heavy showers during ripening unfavourable; dislikes high humidity which causes fungoid diseases	Best grown in medium fertile, loamy types which are well-drained and easy to cultivate	Cape, Algeria, Tunisia

B. Subsistence Crops

Crop	Climate and temperature requirements	Soil requirements	Regions
Barley	Minimum temperature for germination, 37 to 39°F (3 to 4°C); optimum growth at 68°F (20°C); can grow at high altitudes and needs little water, 18 to 22 inches (457 to 559mm)	Friable loams best, loess and black earths also suitable; some types adapted to heavier soils	Throughout North Africa and desert oases and Ethiopia
Cassava or Manioc	Nine-month frost-free period; mean annual temperature, 68°F (10°C) during growing season; heavy and well-distributed rainfall, but will grow in dry regions if sub-soiled soaked; high humidity, sunshine and wind protection are beneficial	Deep, well-drained soils most suitable, sandy, loose permeable soils best; waterlogging very bad	Very important in Congo Basin and fringe regions, East African Coast, Southern Tanzania and Madagascar
Maize	Demands much warmth and no frost; below 34°F (1°C) not tolerated. Minimum germination temperature, 48°F (8°C); optimum temperatures, 86 to 90°F (30 to 32°C); tolerates wide rainfall range from 10 to 200 inches (254 to 5,080mm); short showers with sunny intervals most suitable for growth	Deep, well-drained, humus-rich loams best; sandy or peaty soils in better-watered warm regions	Coastal belts of North-West Africa, Lower Nile, in most lowland and areas up to 6,000 feet in Africa south of latitude 10°
Millet	Fairly high temperatures during day with high diurnal range; can grow in most regions requiring under 28 inches (711mm) but generally in regions with 11 to 16 inches (279 to 406mm) annually; dislikes humidity and needs sunny weather	Light loamy or sandy soils with little humus	Main cereal in all drier areas of tropical Africa

CROP	CLIMATIC NEEDS	SOILS	MAJOR PRODUCERS
Rice	Minimum temperature, 68°F (20°C) during main growing period; upland rice requires minimum temperature of 65°F (18°C); temperature for optimum growth, 83 to 90°F (28 to 32°C); growing period, 50 to 100 days; very high water requirement (in Egypt 1·0 to 1·8 million gallons are used per acre; with no irrigation rice requires 14 to 30 inches (356 to 762mm) a month during growing season	Alluvial swamp soils, loess are best; topsoil should have high water capacity and clays and loams are very suitable; in Africa, Black Cotton soils have proved successful	Very important in Madagascar, river basins and coastal lowlands of Tanzania, Sierra Leone, Liberia, Northern Congo Basin
Wheat	Minimum temperature for germination, 37 to 39°F (3 to 4°C); optimum, 77°F (25°C); winter wheat withstands temperatures well below freezing point; minimum annual rainfall for most varieties is 19 inches (483mm) with 10 inches (254mm) distributed over four growing months	Sandy or peaty soils generally unsuitable, black earths and loess soils are best and clays suitable; low permeability is unsuitable but can be offset by good drainage	Throughout North Africa and in desert oases, Ethiopia, Kenya Highlands, the South-West Cape
Yams	A tropical plant needing high temperatures although some varieties will grow in cooler highland areas; yams are grown in rainfalls varying between 20 and over 400 inches per annum in Africa; can withstand dry periods well if soil is fairly moist	Permeable loams and sandy soils give good yields with high humus content required; grown on hills to avoid waterlogged soils if irrigation is used; makes large demands on soil nutrients	Equatorial areas of Africa, especially lowland area and in Madagascar

APPENDIX 3

SUGGESTIONS FOR FURTHER READING

General Textbooks on Africa

The most exhaustive textbook on the whole of Africa, up-to-date and full of excellent maps, diagrams and photographs is 'The Geography of Modern Africa' by William A. Hance, published by Columbia University Press, 1964. It is rather expensive but every good geography library should have a copy. A useful text for advanced study is 'Africa and the Islands' written by four geographers with experience in different regions in Africa, Longmans, 2nd edition 1967. A useful book which deals with special aspects of Africa's geography is 'A Geography of SubSaharan Africa' by H. J. de Blij, Rand McNally, Chicago, 1964. 'Africa' by H. R. Jarrett, Macdonald and Evans, 1962, and 'Africa: A Geographical Study' by A. B. Mountjoy and Clifford Embleton, Hutchinson Educational, 1965, are also recommended for the more advanced student.

Regional Textbooks
Regional books which provide a more detailed approach are 'West Africa' by R. J. Harrison Church, Longmans, reprinted 1966: a very exhaustive study. Should the student want something lighter H. R. Jarret's 'A Geography of West Africa', Dent, revised 1966, and 'A Certificate Geography of West Africa' by F. G. Higson, Longmans, 1961, are recommended.

There is no equivalent of Church's 'West Africa' for East Africa but 'Lands and Peoples of East Africa' by Hickman and Dickens, Longmans, provides an excellent range of sample studies. 'The Natural Resources of East Africa' edited by E. W. Russel, Hawkins, E.A. Literature Bureau, 1962, although not written exclusively by geographers, contains a wealth of information and many excellent maps. A recent work, 'An Economic Geography of East Africa' by A. M. O'Connor provides all the economic material a student needs. For lighter reading my 'A Geography of East Africa', Dent, 1962, fourth edition, would form an introductory work.

No textbook really covers Central Africa exhaustively. 'A Secondary Geography of Rhodesia and Nyasaland' by Michie and Hawkridge, Longmans, 1961, provides a good introductory background. For the very advanced student 'A Social Geography of Zambia' by George Kay, University of London Press, 1967, has a wealth of information with many excellent photographs and maps. The 'Handbook to the Federation of Rhodesia and Nyasaland, 1960', edited by W. V. Brelsford, provides much useful material but is now a little out of date.

Monica Cole's 'South Africa', Methuen, revised 1966, contains everything that the advanced student requires and is full of excellent material.

For North-West Africa, J. M. Houston's 'Western Mediterranean World', Longmans, 1964, and 'A Survey of North-West Africa', edited by N. Barbour, Oxford University Press, 1959, are recommended. Georg Gerster's 'Sahara', Barrie and Rockcliffe, 1960, while not a textbook, has excellent descriptions of the physical and economic aspects of the Sahara region, and to this should be added 'Trade Routes of Algeria and the Sahara' by B. E. Thomas,

University of California Publications in Geography, 1957. The best general work on Libya is 'The Economic Development of Libya', an IBRD publication, Baltimore, 1960. For Egypt, C. Issawi's 'Egypt in Revolution: an Economic Analysis', Oxford University Press, 1963, is the most modern work available in English.

History Textbooks
'A Short History of Africa', by R. Oliver and J. D. Fage, Penguin, 19 ; 'Atlas of African History', by J. D. Fage, Edward Arnold, 1958; 'West Africa 1000–1800', by B. Davidson with F. K. Buah and J. F. A. Ajayi, Longmans, 1966; 'East and Central Africa to the late Nineteenth Century', by B. Davidson with J. E. F. Mhina and B. A. Ogot, Longmans, 1967; 'Southern Africa', by B. Fagan, Thames and Hudson, 1966.

ATLASES

Survey

Very useful and detailed atlases for specific countries are now being produced by survey departments in Africa and they are not particularly expensive, considering the wealth of beautifully produced maps they contain.

Most central libraries will have copies of their own country's atlas.

Ghana, Sierra Leone, Kenya, Uganda, Tanzania, the Congo, South Africa and Rhodesia have produced atlases of this nature.

General

Philips' 'Modern College Atlas for Africa' is very good for general use, while for specific geographical regions, Philips' also provide regional atlases, e.g. Philips' 'East African Modern School Atlas', 1966.

Collins-Longmans Atlases: These are a number of very recent Atlases, designed for Junior schools but containing the best and most up to date maps on a variety of topics.

Books in the series so far are: 'School Atlas for Sierra Leone', 1967; 'Atlas for Malawi', 1967; 'The New Kenya Primary Atlas', 1967; 'New Junior Atlas for Rhodesia', 1967.

MAGAZINE ARTICLES

G.J.—Geographical Journal

G.R.—Geographical Review

T.I.B.G.—Transactions of the Institute of British Geographers

E.G.—Economic Geography

S.G.M.—Scottish Geographical Magazine

G.M.—Geographical Magazine

G.—Geography

A.A.A.G.—Annals of the Association of American Geographers

Physical Geography

1. Slope Development in Uganda, J. W. Pallister, G.J., 1956, 80–87.
2. The Ancient Erg of the Hausaland, and similar formations on the south side of the Sahara, A. T. Grove, G.J., 1958, 528–33.
3. The Glaciers of Mount Baker, Ruwenzori, J. B. Whittow, G.J., 1959, 370–79.
4. Geomorphology of the Tibesti Region with special reference to western Tibesti, A. T. Grove, G.J., 1960, 18–31.
5. Sand Formations in the Niger Valley between Naimey and Bourem, J. R. V. Prescott a d H. P. White, G.J., 1960, 200–203.
6. The Jebel Marra, Darfur, and its Region, J. H. G. Lebon and V. C. Robertson, G.J., 1961, 30–49.
7. Notes on the Geomorphology of the Northern Region, Somali Republic, J. W. Pallister, G.J., 1963, 184–87.
8. Vegetation and Geomorphology in Northern Rhodesia: an aspect of the distribution of the savannah of Central Africa, Monica M. Cole, G.J., 1963, 290–310.
9. Recent Expeditions to Libya by the Royal Military Academy, Sandhurst, M. A. J. Williams and D. N. Hall, G.J., 1965, 482–501.
10. The Landforms of the Central Ruwenzori, East Africa, J. B. Whittow, G.J., 1966, 32–42.
11. Surface, Drainage and Tectonic Instability in part of Southern Uganda, J. C. Doornkamp and P. H. Temple, G.J., 1966, 238–52.
12. Some Residual Hillslopes in the Great Fish River Basin, South Africa, G. Robinson, G.J., 1966, 386–90.
13. The Lake Albert Basin, W. W. Bishop, G.J., 1967, 469–80.
14. The Nile at Murchison Falls, A. B. Ware, G.J., 1967, 481–82.
15. Five Naturalists in the Eastern Congo, D. Happold, G.M., 1960, 360.
16. Mountains of the Moon, R. A. Redfern, G.M., 1962, 395.
17. Some Problems of Agricultural Climatology in Tropical Africa, A. H., Bunting, G., 283–94.

Land Use

1. Cattle in Africa, W. Deshler, G.R., 1963, 52–58.
2. Staple Subsistence Crops of Africa, G. P. Murdock, G.R., 1960, 523–40.
3. The Dairying Industry of South Africa, H. J. R. Henderson, T.I.B.G., 1960, 237–52.

4. The Changing Patterns of Agriculture in East Africa: the Bemba of Northern Rhodesia, A. I. Richards, G.J., 1958, 302–14.
5. The Influence of European Contacts on the Landscape of Southern Nigeria, G.J., 1959, 48–64.
6. Overpopulation and Overstocking in the Native Areas of Matabeleland, J. R. V. Prescott, G.J., 1961, 212–15.
7. The 'White Highlands' of Kenya, W. T. W. Morgan, G.J., 1963, 140–55.
8. A study of Tribal Readjustment in the Nile Valley: the Experience of the Ingessana, H. R. J. Davies, G.J., 1964, 380–89.
9. The Decolonisation of the 'White Highlands' of Kenya, N. S. Carey Jones, G.J., 1965, 186–201.
10. Berbers of the High Atlas, H. Becket, G.M., 1956, 221.
11. The Fellahin of Egypt, T. Hindley, G.M., 1956, 327.
12. Bedouin Wedding Feast, T. H. Work, G.M., 1957, 219.
13. The Dancing Dervishes, Sir H. Luke, G.M., 1960, 309.
14. The Gidicho Islanders of Ethiopia, R. N. D. Read, G.M., 1962, 507.
15. The Northern Frontier District of Kenya, Sir G. Reece, G.M., 1964, 698.
16. The Tuaregs, J. Welland, G.M., 1964, 386.
17. Lake Rudolf, C. C. Trench, G.M., 1966, 729.
18. The Bamenda Highlands, M. F. Thomas, G.M., 1966, 283.
19. Kenya's White Highlands: The End of an Experiment, Elspeth Huxley, G.M., 1962, 414.
20. Some Government Measures to Improve African Agriculture in Swaziland, J. B. McI. Daniel, G.J., 1966, 506–15.
21. Land Planning and Resettlement in Northern Ghana, T. E. Hilton, G., 1959, 227–40.
22. On the Human Geography of the Nile Basin, J. H. G. Lebon, G., 1960, 16–26.
23. Yafele's Kraal. A Sample Study of African Agriculture in Southern Rhodesia, J. H. Beck, G., 1960, 68–78.
24. Plantation Agriculture in Victoria Diversion, West Cameroon, S. H. Bederman, G., 1966, 349–60.
25. Resettlement in the Meru District of Kenya, N. D. McGlashan, G., 1958, 209–10.
26. Mechanised Cultivation of Peasant Holdings in West Africa, H. P. White, G., 1958, 269–70.
27. The Co-operative Movement in the Southern Cameroons, J. H. Jennings, G., 1958, 208.
28. Consolidating Land Holdings in Kenya, McGlashan, G., 1960, 105–106.
29. Changes in the South African Pineapple Industry, I. L. Griffiths, G., 1961, 360–63.
30. New Tea-Growing Areas in Kenya, D. R. F. Taylor, G., 1965, 373–75.
31. The Botswana Livestock Industry, A. Storey, G., 1968, 87–89.

Towns, Ports and Settlements

1. The Growth and Functional Structure of Khartoum, G. Hamdan, G.M., 1960, 21–40.
2. Lourenço Marques in Delgoa Bay, W. A. Hance and I. Van Dongen, E.G., 1957, 238–56.
3. Dar es Salaam, The Port and its Tributary Area, W. A. Hance and I. Van Dongen, A.A.A.G., 1958, 419–35.

4. Gabon and its Main Gateways: Libreville and Port Gentil, W. A. Hance and I. Van Dongen, Tijdschrift voor Economiche en Sociale Geografie, 1961, 286–95.
5. Matadi, Focus of Belgian African Transport, W. A. Hance and I. Van Dongen, A.A.A.G., 1958, 41–72.
6. The Port of Lobito and the Benguela Railway, W. A. Hance and I. Van Dongen, G.R., 1956, 460–487.
7. Bathurst—Port of the Gambia River, H. R. Jarratt, G., 1951, 98–107.
8. The Economic Expansion of Jinja, Uganda. B. S. Hoyle, G.R., 1963, 377–388.
9. Population and Settlement in the Gambia, H. R. Jarratt, G.R., 1948, 633–36.
10. The Rural Village in the Ethiopian Highlands, C. Brooke, G.R., 1959, 58–75.
11. New Railroad and Port Developments in East and Central Africa, H. C. Brookfield, E.G., 1955, 60–70.
12. Port Etienne: a Mauritanian Pioneer Town, R. J. Harrison Church, G.J., 1962, 498–504.
13. Morocco's Expanding Towns, Hassan Awad, G.J., 1964, 49–64.
14. Tangier: International City, M. Crowder, G.M., 1957, 596.
15. Lost Cities of the Libyan Sahara, J. Weelard, G.M., 1964, 602.
16. The Lost City of the Kalahari, A. J. Clement, G.M., 1965, 818.
17. Travellers Tales: Imperial Meknes, J. Woodyatt, G.M., 1966, 722.
18. Kano—Ancient and Modern, N. H. Doutré, G.M., 1964, 594.
19. Geographical Planning in Urban Areas for the 1960 Census of Ghana, J. M. Hunter, G., 1961, 1–8.
20. Tema: The Geography of a New Port, D. Hilling, G., 1966, 111–25.
21. New Ports in Dahomey and Togo, H. P. White, G., 1961, 160–63.
22. The Drift to the Towns of the European Population in Rhodesia and Nyasaland, G. T. Rimmington, G., 1963, 320–22.
23. Lusaka, a City of Tropical Africa, E. Wilson, G., 1963, 411–14.

Water

1. Progress and Geographical Significance of the Kariba Dam, W. H. Reeve, G.J., 1960, 140–46.
2. Problems and Development of the Dry Zone of West Africa, R. J. Harrison Church, G.J., 1961, 187–204.
3. Waters of the Nile, A. Smith, G.M., 1956, 289 and 337.
4. African Water Engineers, Elspeth Huxley, G.M., 1959, 170.
5. Kariba: Dam of Superlatives, D. Howarth, G.M., 1960, 1.
6. And the Waters Prevailed, E. Balneaves, G.M., 1960, 13.
7. Africa's Strangled Waterways, Professor A. S. Boughey, G.M., 1963, 407.
8. The Limpopo Scheme, R. J. Harrison Church, G.M., 1964, 212.
9. The Volta River Project, D. Hilling, G.M., 1965, 830.
10. The High Dam, B. St Claire McBride, G.M., 1965, 169.
11. Irrigation in the Sudan, K. M. Barbour, T.I.B.G., 1959, 243–63.
12. The Kariba Project, M. M. Cole, G., 1960, 98–105.
13. The Rhodesian Economy in Transition and the Role of Kariba, M. M. Cole, G., 1962, 15–40.

14. Irrigation Developments in Sudan, H. R. J. Davies, G., 1958, 271–73.
15. The Aswan High Dam and the Resettlement of the Nubian People, R. A. Beddis, G., 1963, 77–80.
16. The Guma Valley Scheme, Sierra Leone, G. J. Williams, G., 1965, 163–68.
17. Akosombo Dam and the Volta River Project, T. E. Hilton, G., 1966, 291–95.
18. The Expansion of Electricity Production and Distribution in Uganda, B. S. Hoyle, G., 1967, 196–99.

Secondary Industry and Mining

1. Industrial Development in E.A., N. C. Pollock, E.G., 1960, 344–54.
2. Oil in Libya: Some Implications, J. I. Clarke, E. G., 1963, 40–59.
3. The Copper Belt in Northern Rhodesia, R. W. Steel, G., 1957, 83–92.
4. The Wind of Change in the Western Sahara, H. T. Norris, G.J., 1964, 1–14.
5. Conversations on the Copper Belt, J. Jeffers, G.M., 1956, 231.
6. The Sahara and Its Oil, J. Benois, G.M., 1960, 399.
7. Diamonds, J. Burly, G.M., 1965, 141.
8. The Wealth of Katanga, G. Martelli, G.M., 1961, 294.
9. Morphology of a bauxite summit in Ghana, J. M. Hunter, G.J., 1961, 469–76.
10. Saharan Oil, J. I. Clarke, G., 1960, 106–108.
11. The South African Fertiliser Industry, G. Whittington, G., 1961, 363–64.
12. New Oil Refinery Construction in Africa, B. S. Hoyle, G., 1963, 194–96.
13. Developments in Southern African Diamond Production, G. Whittington, G., 1963, 194–96.
14. Iron Mining in Angola, G. Whittington, G., 1964, 418–19.
15. Iron-Ore Mining in Liberia, K. Swindell, G., 1965, 75–78.
16. The Establishment of a Sugar Industry in Nigeria, H. A. Moisley, G., 1966, 142–47.
17. Industrial Developments at Jinja, Uganda, B. S. Hoyle, G., 1967, 64–67.
18. Industrial Development in Malawi, N. C. Pollock, G., 1966, 316–19.

Problems

1. Soil Erosion and Population Problems in S.E. Nigeria, A. T. Grove, G.J., 1951, 291–306.
2. The Ranching of Wild Game in Africa, H. C. Pereira, G.M., 1964, 642.
3. The Threat of Bilharzia, V. de V. Clarke, G.M., 1966, 864.
4. A Geographer with the World Health Organisation, G.J., 1962, 489–93.

Transport

1. Aviation in Africa and South America, W. H. Melbourne, G.M., 1961, 103.
2. British East African Transport Complex, I. Van Dongen, Pamphlet, University of Chicago Press, 1954.
3. The Trade of Lake Victoria, V. C. R. Ford, E.A. Inst. of Social Research booklet, 1955.
4. Trans-Cameroon Railway, J. I. Clarke, G., 1966, 55-58.
5. Triumph of the Benguela Railway, D. Botting, G.M., 1967, 255-69.
6. Internal Transport Developments in East Africa, A. Long, G., 1965, 78-82.

General Articles on Specific Countries

1. Revolution in Senegal, M. Crowder, G.M., 1957, 478.
2. Portuguese Guinea: An African Arcadia, M. Teague, G.M., 1957, 530.
3. Ethiopia: An Island in Africa, T. Pakenham, G.M., 1957, 209.
4. Nigeria's Cultural Heritage, I. Brinkworth, G.M., 1959, 425.
5. Mysterious Madagascar, G.M., 1959, 549.
6. Sudan's Hopes and Needs, P. F. Holmes, G.M., 1959, 27.
7. Somalia and its Neighbours, L. Silberman, G.M., 1959, 85.
8. Two Cameroons or One, M. Crowder, G.M., 1959, 303.
9. Ethiopian Journey, Barbara Mons, G.M., 1960, 426.
10. Morocco: Land of the Setting Sun, M. Pope, G.M., 1961, 486.
11. Around Tunisia, F. Stark, G.M., 1961, 706.
12. The Gambia, M. Teague, G.M., 1961, 380.
13. Liberia Faces the Future, Dr E. N. Gladden, G.M., 1962, 61.
14. Tanganyika: The Path to Independence, R. Gorbold, G.M., 1962, 371.
15. Fernando Po: Spain in Africa, G.M., 1964, 540.
16. Fortunes of Libya, P. Fenwick, G.M., 1964, 547.
17. Congo and Angola, R. Hallett, G.M., 1964, 264.
18. Mauritania, T. Brierly, G.M., 1965, 754.
19. North and South in Sudan, a Study in Human Contrasts, K. M. Barbour, A.A.A.G., 1964, 209-26.
20. Ethiopia, L. T. C. Kuo, Focus, June 1955.
21. Major Natural Regions of the Gambia, H. R. Jarrett, S.G.M., 1949, 140-44.
22. Geographical Regions of the Gambia, H. R. Jarrett, S.G.M., 1950, 63-169.
23. Liberia, P. W. Porter, Focus, September 1961.
24. The Changing Economy of Gabon—Developments in a new African Republic, D. Hilling, G., 1963, 155-65.
25. Recent Developments in the Portuguese Congo, R. J. Houk, G.R., 1958, 201-21.
26. The Economic Geography of Madagascar, W. A. Hance, T.E.S.G., 1957, 161-72.
27. Economic and Political Changes in the Sahara, J. I. Clarke, G., 1961, 102-19.
28. The Non-African Population of the Federation of Rhodesia and Nyasaland, C. Baker, G., 1958, 132-34.

General Articles

1. Political Africa: A Summary of Information, G.M., 1964, 169.
2. Education in East Africa, Prof. Fergus Wilson, G.M., 1962, 385.
3. A Voyage Round Africa, H. W. Tilman, G.M., 1958, 415.
4. Contemporary Africa: Trends and Issues, W. O. Brown (Ed.), Annals of the American Academy of Political and Social Science, 1955, 1–179.
5. Social Change in Africa, L. P. Mair, International Affairs, 1960, 447–56.
6. National Parks of Africa, R. and L. Harrington, G.M., 1960, 318.
7. The West African in the Economic Geography of the Sudan, H. R. J. Davies, G., 1963, 222–235.
8. Maps for the Study of Uganda, B. Waites, G., 1965, 65–68.
9. The Changing Face of Africa, Hodgkiss and Steel, G., 1961, 156–160.
10. Japanese Cars in Southern Africa, I. L. Griffiths, G., 1968, 90–92.

INDEX

Words are listed in this index which have a significant reference in the text. Figures in bold refer to diagrams or maps and are preceded by the number of the chapter in which the diagram appears.

DATE DUE

APR 7 '86			
APR 22 '86			
GAYLORD			PRINTED IN U.S.A.